# WELCOME TO MY WORLD

## by

## C G WALKER

Pen Press Publishers Ltd
London

# WELCOME TO MY WORLD

## C G WALKER

ISBN 1 900796 42 2

Published by Pen Press Publishers Ltd
39-41, North Road
London N7 9DP

# Contents

# Acknowledgements

I would like to thank my wonderful mam. After 50 years this is the very first time that she has ever been given the recognition she deserves. If only for that reason, then this has all been worthwhile. She gave me everything I have and made me all I am today.

Thank God we are all blessed with having had a mother. That woman pushed and shoved and made her offspring strong, like it or not. She was strong-willed and still booking removals and pushing my dad out to work when she was lying in bed in the front room, dying of cancer.

My dad was still out there humping furniture at 67 years of age. I am proud of my mam and dad and proud to have been a part of them. They were great characters, and there are very few like them left. We have been very lucky, my wife and I. We both had great parents, stable homes, and we were a part of a wonderful world - the real one.

What with three wonderful kids of our own and five grandchildren that anyone would be proud of, well, who could ask for anything more? I certainly couldn't.

I must not forget the many people who have made the writing of this book possible, who have made my life so very, very special.

In particular, my wonderful wife Jean. Without her, I would not have had a life of any consequence.

My three lovely daughters, especially Anne, who gave me a new purpose in life by forcing me into writing this rubbish. (Well, at least I tried).

All the people I have known and who have made all this possible.

All those friends who worked for me.

All the people who have helped and given me the opportunities to do what I had to do. I thank them all. Many are a part of this book, because they were also a part of my life. It is they who have made this story possible.

But there are also so many more who are not included, and my thanks are due to them too. It has been a privilege to have known them all.

# Foreword

### The Future Doesn't Belong To The Brightest Amongst Us,
### But To The More Determined!

So if you out there have the time to take note and if you are ready to join me and step out of that comfortable little protected existence that you think is a life.

If you are prepared to walk with me and to share with me, the challenges, the satisfactions and the achievements

Along with the disappointments, the hardships, the blood, the sweat and tears;

Then come with me, as I welcome you into my world.

I have deliberately tried, not to be too serious and have introduced a joking, light-hearted approach, but nevertheless, this is a true story, stranger than fiction, but true nonetheless.

It is about real hopes, real fears.

It is about a real life and it is dedicated to my family and the real people who lived in my world, the real one!

Come on, I dare you, come with me as I introduce you to the truth and to my skeletons, which (unlike yours), I have released from my cupboard, to beguile, to entertain and to amuse you.

Come as I take you into my world. The real one!

Welcome to My World

I would like to extend a special thanks to Heppy my old mate Frank Hepworth, who was one of the very few who took the trouble to offer encouragement when I needed it the most.

Frank may I thank you, for giving me a ring
Ringing me last night was quite a special thing.
And I must thank you again, for your special thought,
Now it just came at the right time, when encouragement I sought.
Keep those praises coming, you know your very good.
And I knew that when you had read my book, you clearly understood.

So thanks again for giving, giving, me new heart.
I shall start to write again tomorrow, tomorrow I start.
It was only for a stimulant, that I had a basic need.
And it had to come from you, a friend, a friend indeed.

So when my story is finished, and it will, with a bit of luck.
You will be the one, to get the first published book.
And I shall dedicate it to you, where it will be clearly seen.
As a record of our shared moments
and what life was once meant to mean.


BUT HERE IS WHAT I REALLY WANTED TO SAY

Forever you will remain a truly special friend
Remembering our shared moments I will to the end.
And I will always remember, the day that we met
Now as old as I am, I won't ever forget
Keeping those moments special, I want you to know
It is like a Golden wedding, we met just 50 years ago.

# Part 1

## Welcome To My World, The Real One

Writing this, the story of my life has made me realise that I have had a heavy penalty to pay. For by opening my heart and revealing my soul, I have opened the door, taken down the barriers and invited whoever may choose to read this story into my life.

Yes, you have been allowed into my life to delve, to dissect, to analyse and then you are allowed to judge. I am in fact on trial, so be sure to judge me well.

For I have just lost my privacy, my self respect, my dignity and probably I have earned your contempt too, but this story needed to be written, if only for the benefit of my grandchildren, the next generation and maybe their children too.

I was born in 1931 in Pinderoaks Maternity Hospital in Barnsley and at birth I weighed in at 3lbs 4ozs. My cot for the first few weeks of my birth was a sideboard drawer in the kitchen.

I was a sickly child. I had mumps, Brights disease (whatever that was), and I had been poisoned with deadly nightshade berries. I also contracted rheumatic fever, which left me with a weak heart, or so the doctors said. I was told many times later in life that I didn't have one at all, so it wasn't to become a problem really.

At school (or at the many, many, oh so many different schools I attended) I had to lie down every afternoon because of my so-called weakness. I soon grew out of that, except when Mam couldn't get me out of bed to go to work years later. I always put the blame for this problem on my early school life and I am sticking to it.

I attended many schools because my family had to move around quite a lot and the reason for this was probably because my mam couldn't pay the bills and my dad was often unemployed.

Dad was an ex-miner whose brothers had also been, or were still, miners. My dad had moved up in the world, hadn't he? He had become a lorry driver-come-sometime labourer.

1

I have heard many stories about my dad's fruitless searches for work in the good old days before the war; about the means tests that were carried out before one could sign on the dole; about the times that Dad had to get on his bike, and cycle from Barnsley to places as far away as Selby and even to Scunthorpe in Lincolnshire, looking in vain for work, all to no avail.

So on reflection the MP Norman Tebbit wasn't far off target when in the 1980's he suggested that people 'get on their bikes', because our generation did; they had to. Thousands and thousands of them were uprooted from their homes and families in their desperate and often futile attempts to find work.

The ones who were lucky and did manage to find work sometimes had to leave their friends and families behind as they settled into the areas where work was available.

Yes, those indeed were the so-called 'good old, bad old days'. But for all that, we were happy with our lot; we had to be, because we just didn't know any different.

It is often said (and I believe it,) that "it takes a war or poverty to bring people together" and it most certainly did. In those days of yore, we had great neighbours who were also good friends and we all looked after each other.

We didn't need to lock our front doors in those days, the communities looked after their own. Social workers and probation officers were not even invented in the days before the war.

The people of today's generation in Britain ought to be ashamed when they use the word "poverty", as they think that it applies today. For today's generation cannot ever really know the true meaning of that word, or what real poverty means. They ought instead to take a short step back in time, or have a quiet word with some of their forebears.

For if my generation did not know the true meaning of the word poverty, then how can they, sheltered as they are within the arms of our ever-protective Welfare State?

Could it perhaps be that today, shame is now a lost and long forgotten virtue?

I can well remember feeling shame as a child at having to hide under the kitchen table when the greengrocer came around to collect his money and my ma had none to pay him.

I well remember having to wear second hand clothes or having to borrow my dad's "best suit" right up till I went into the army. There I obtained my first new suit - army uniform and it was free.

Yes, those were the days all right. We had very few toys at Christmas and if it had not been for my dear old Gran, my dear old Auntie Phil and Uncle Harry, we kids would have had very little indeed, other than maybe an apple or an orange, and a few worthless charms placed in our Christmas stockings - but only if we were lucky.

We were kept alive on cod-liver oil and malt and lashings of brimstone and treacle.

I can well remember as a child spending hours playing in front of a coal fire on my grandma's rug with an empty cocoa tin, because there were no other toys to play with.

But for all that, those were happy, memorable days to grow up in. We were safe, we were loved, we were cared for and we were protected within the arms of our families.

My parents just couldn't afford to buy for us, (my sister and me) all the things we take for granted today.

I learned to appreciate the little that we had and never to take things for granted. I was taught never to expect "ow't for now't" and throughout the rest of my life, I was always afraid of getting into debt. If we as a family wanted things then we just had to work and save for them and we were to learn those lessons oh so well at our mother's knee, and from the struggles our parents had to endure, in their sometime failed attempts to make ends meet.

We were taught never to live beyond our means and those lessons I learned I was never to forget for the rest of my life.

I left school at 14 years of age, I worked as a butcher's apprentice for 25 shillings a week. Today that would be called cheap labour, but it helped ma to provide for us.

There was no dole in those days, or national assistance - well, not until one became an adult at twenty-one years of age. Our parents accepted responsibility for their children, until we became adults and we were not allowed to leave home until we went into the forces or got married - and rightly so. Not for us a life lived alone in a flat provided and furnished by the state. No, our pride would not have allowed that to happen, we were looked after by our own and looked after our own in turn.

There was plenty of work in those days, partly because people like me, who were not very bright academically, were allowed to leave school at fourteen and not allowed to stagnate within the education system. It was just to make employment figures look better for some silly government minister. We were employed on very low wages whilst we learned our trades, then on reaching the age of twenty-one, when we were experienced and able to make a proper contribution, we were then paid the adult wage. We left school at fourteen and became men seven years later at twenty-one . Unlike today, where my grandson has to stay at school until he is nearly seventeen, then   twelve months later he suddenly becomes a man!

I was to become a butcher, then a baker. I worked in brickyards, I dug trenches, I drove lorries. I served my time in the forces.

I saved my hard-earned cash until I had enough to get married. I struggled to survive without getting into debt. I even turned to theft; I stole cigarette ends from ashtrays, to make my hand-rolled cigarettes, as I - couldn't afford to buy them.

I had twenty-three jobs before starting my own business. Things were somewhat simpler then. I left some of my jobs for better prospects, and from some I got the sack. If I didn't like the job or my employer, I left (though only after I had found another job) and if my employer wasn't happy with me or my performance, he sacked me!  Now't wrong with that, surely.

This simple philosophy certainly helped to raise standards, until the Trade Unions decided we were all equal and all entitled to become men at eighteen, and that we were all entitled to the same pay for doing the same job - irrespective of the fact that some of us were more capable than others.

I became a socialist. I believed in the theory and principles of communism; I was an idealist. I became a Trade Union official, trusting and believing in people.

I was however, to become sadly disillusioned and when I did eventually wake up to reality, I began to realise that we humans are all hypocrites with selfish motives; that human nature will always prevail and that basically we are all out there trying to impress each other and trying to get something for nothing.

I began to grow up. I was to become a realist and, in turn, a cynic. I had, in fact, been corrupted by life. I started my own business in 1958 with £25 holiday pay that I had received from my last employer. I became a millionaire. I only mention this to give some point to this story and to try and impress you readers a bit!

I have lived in old terrace houses like millions before me. I have used outside toilets, I have had to wipe my bum on old newspaper (fish and chip wrappers). We couldn't even afford to buy proper newspapers and even fish and chips for tea was a luxury we could ill afford in those days.

I have had to use a potty to pee in and I have slopped out like our unfortunate prison inmates have to do, but I wasn't even a criminal.

What's more, I had to go out to work and work every hour that God sent to support my wife and kids. Today extra part-time work on community service is called punishment. My generation called it a necessity and we were proud to do it.

We were independent and I thank the Almighty that I never spent one day of my life on the dole. Yes, I was out of work many times, but I was lucky enough never to be on the dole.

But the most important thing of all was that most of my generation, the people who were brought up like me, never felt deprived. We were I suppose poor, but we weren't really aware of our poverty and because we didn't know better, it was never a real problem.

In those days, if you got your girlfriend pregnant, oh the shame of it, yes, but the families did rally round and looked after their own. Today the Nanny State won't allow them.

My generation saved our hard-earned money to get married and sometimes to buy our homes. We stood on our own two feet and sorted our own problems, without the need for an army of immature social workers and stress counsellors waiting on every street corner to administer to our needs.

Stress? We had never even heard of the bloody word. We were too busy sorting out our problems and we just did not have the time to look up the word in a dictionary.

We were born with stiff upper lips. It was a sign of weakness to cry; we were just not allowed to show our true feelings. It was not always easy, but that is how we were brought up.

The man of the house, well, he was God. If he was a member of the so-called lower working class and if he was also a tradesman, then he was amongst the aristocracy in the pecking order of the labour market.

But if he should just happen to aspire to become an engine driver, then he would be a prince among men. All the lads I knew as a child wanted to become engine drivers.

If a man hadn't learned a trade, he would usually be employed doing hard physical labour. But he was a man for all that! He had pride as a skilled craftsman; pride in his strength as a humble labourer and pride because he was brought up to be a man, the man of the house! The man of the house got respect; he was often feared. "You just wait until your dad comes home, lad!" was a mother's usual cry. The man of the house was also the paymaster. He would take what he thought he needed from his weekly pay packet and if there was anything left, he would give it to his wife.

The man of the house was the one to get the ham (if there was any); his wife and kids got the jam. The man of the house was the one to get the new clothes and he was the one who could go down to the pub.

Well, he was the man of the house!

But what was also true was that we were brought up to respect ourselves, the old, the infirm and women! As a boy I was taught manners; the words we were taught were 'excuse me', 'please', 'beg your pardon' and 'thank you'.

Even today, as an old man, I just could not walk into an house (even my daughter's homes) without knocking. I could not walk through a door without letting a woman go through first and I would still feel obliged to offer my seat on a bus to a young woman if she was standing, even though she would probably tell me to bugger off, or words to that effect.

Yes, we had respect. In the immediate years between the wars and just after the last war, romance and respectability went hand in hand almost as firmly as they had in Victorian times. For decades young couples were pushed into shotgun weddings to avoid the stigma of having an illegitimate child. Most of the blame and responsibility for the consequences were generally shouldered by the woman, who had consented to sex before marriage.

The women who got pregnant before marriage in my day had four choices - or so we thought at the time. She was advised by her elders to try and force a miscarriage by taking regular hot baths whilst disposing of a bottle of gin at the same time.

It didn't work, but they sure as hell enjoyed the gin. The second possibility was to take a bottle of what was known as Penny Royal, or thirdly to try and find a backstreet abortionist. If all these failed, then another method was for the boyfriend to lift the girl on to a sideboard and keep pushing her off until a desirable result was achieved. (I'm joking of course).

But if every method failed, then there was little choice but for the young man to pay his dues and do the decent thing. It was simply expected that he would accept his responsibilities and marry the girl.

It was also expected in those days that there would be a lengthy period of engagement whilst they saved to buy a home or furnishings.

There was strong disapproval of sex before marriage. The courtship rituals were acted out on the dance floors, where the man would request the pleasure of a dance with the young lady.

But what was expected was the romantic climax to the courtship, the white wedding of the virgin bride, after which the couple supposedly had sex for the first time.

When a young man's sexual advances were rejected, his frustration was as a rule tempered by the satisfaction of knowing that he had at least found and married a woman who was still a virgin. It does seem to be a great pity that as a result of the lowering of moral standards and the flippant, easy-going attitudes to sex today, women have in fact become the losers. They have fallen from grace in the eyes of men. They have allowed themselves to be toppled from their pedestals by losing the self-respect that most of my generation's women held so dear. In turn, they have lost the respect of today's generation of men. In fact they have lost the power that their own sexuality embodied by selling that sexuality too cheaply.

Such a pity really that women have had to trade their souls for a small slice of so-called equality, when in reality women have always been superior to men, and men have always known that to be true. Women have always, from the very beginning of time, by virtue of their sex, held ultimate power over men. Providing she chooses to use that power in moderation, and when it is to her advantage, then and only then can she hope to retain her power. Today she is losing it.

In the 1930s, 50s people at my level in society still worked just as hard and lived in the same conditions as our fathers and grandfathers had done years before.

But for all that, members of my generation have been lucky. We have been there, we have seen it all and we have done it all. We have experienced the good and also the poor quality of life.

We have lived in primitive conditions and known so-called poverty, and we grew stronger because of, or inspite of, it. But we have also had a taste of today's good life.

We have enjoyed our holidays to faraway places in the sun.

We have appreciated and shared in the benefits that new technology has brought. Yet one question remains unanswered and I still feel the need to ask it:

7

Has the world become a better place to live in as a result of today's extra benefits? 
And the answer must be no! Life has certainly become easier, but the quality of life has certainly not got any better.

How I now hunger, for those days gone by
Where did they go to, I now wonder why
To my misspent years, I now sadly bow
Just but a memory, is what's left now.

# How It All Started

A life that was special and lived to the full,
Often with heartache, but a life that was never dull.
There were plenty of the hard times passed along the way,
And the sharing of many pleasures, for which I would have liked
to stay.
A life that was to sweat blood and often a few tears,
But a life filled with happiness and many glorious years.
But through it all, and having done it all, I have nothing left to give,
Except to tell my story of how I used to live.

My father's name was Westby Walker. He was born in a little old terraced house at Staincross Station near Barnsley in 1897. That little old house stands to this day. Dad, as was normal in those days, came from a large family. I believe he had five brothers and two sisters. It must have been very hard for his mother and father, with ten mouths to feed and only one breadwinner while the kids were growing up.

Yes, it must have been very hard to practise the art of survival in those halcyon days between the wars, when due to a mixture of pride and tradition, it was usually the man of the house who went out to work to support his wife and family.

The woman of the house in her turn was expected to carry out her wifely duties: bear the children, cook, bake, clean, do the laundry, knit, make most of the clothes and provide all the normal home comforts for her family. That was the way of life for most women at that time.

My Grandfather Walker, Dad's father, whom I never knew, was a tradesman. He was a first-class boilersmith, no less, so in effect he must have been well up in the labour pecking order, quite a little Bantam cock in fact, or so I was led to believe.

Dad's family originally came from Sheffield, the steel town, and what with Mam's family coming from Scunthorpe and Witherensea and my own family coming from Barnsley - well this supports what I said earlier, that families were uprooted in their struggle to find work in those good, bad old days before the Second World War!

I never knew my Grandad Walker, as he died before I was born. In fact both my grandfathers died in tragic, violent circumstances.

My dad had, as a young man supposedly fathered a child (or so Mam said) out of wedlock. Some people say he took the blame for his own father's indiscretion. Whatever happened, Grandad subsequently committed suicide.

He hanged himself with a clothes line and my dad found him dead, hanging from the kitchen ceiling when he returned home from work.

So it would seem that I am either the brother or the nephew of a girl who was born in the late twenties at Staincross station, near Barnsley.

The girl's mother's maiden name was Rosie McFall.

But much as I would love to have met and known my erstwhile stepsister, or my unknown auntie (whichever was the real case), I was deprived of that dubious pleasure and I suppose I shall never know the real truth. And does it really matter anyway?

Here is a little ditty I wrote in memory of my little sister, or auntie, and my dear old Grandad, bless them. Our little Rosie had a McFall from grace, so my grandad just had to take a fall from the kitchen ceiling.

No pun intended, well, not really!

So there hangs the tale of Grandad number one,
Who chose to take his life and from the ceiling hung,
So it all ended and Grandad took a fall,
All because of young Rosie, young Rosie McFall.

My mother's name was Hetty Marris before she was married. She was born in 1900 at Mapplewell near Barnsley. I think, and if she was, then she would have been born at a house called Two Ashes, at 39 Pye Ave, better known as Happy Valley. My mother had a sister, my dear old Auntie Phil, and a brother (the champion of the world), Uncle Clarence.

I believe my mother's dad, as I mentioned earlier, originated from Scunthorpe in Lincolnshire and my Grandma Marris came from Witherensea in East Yorkshire. Her maiden name was Fanny Birkett. Grandad Marris had several brothers one of whom died in tragic circumstances - he fell down a mine shaft whilst another brother was fighting in the Boer war. I do remember clearly as a little boy rummaging through Grandma's wardrobe drawers and coming across a tobacco and a biscuit tin that were sent by Queen Victoria to her troops serving in South Africa during the Boer war. There were also some campaign medals which, as a small boy, I thought were simply marvellous. My mam was a nurse during her early years and later in life, she became a nursing sister. She was for many years a nurse at Kendrey Fever Hospital near

Barnsley, where she met and became friendly with a young lady, whom she introduced to her brother Clarence. The lady in question was to marry my uncle and she became my Auntie Maud, bless her.

My earliest memory of my grandad (number two) was as a little boy of six, standing at the bottom of Grandma's garden, waving to my grandad as he shot past like a bat out of hell in his Thomas the Tank Engine. Yes, my dear old Grandad was a real live engine driver, *par excellence*, a prince among men, no less. He used to transport coal from North Gawber colliery in Staincross to The Pummer pit at Darton, near Barnsley, on a regular daily basis. But what I didn't know at the time was that old Thomas (the engine) was beginning to get just a little fed up with Grandad and his wild aspirations. Grandad must have thought he was Sir Malcolm Campbell, a Spitfire pilot, or Roy Rogers, the cowboy in disguise. But Thomas was getting on a bit and was no longer able to cope with Grandad's antics.

One day, in 1938, when Grandad, as usual, was belting down the track, Thomas skidded to a stop. My grandad fell off and Thomas fell on top of Grandad, trapping his legs underneath the engine. A rescue team was soon organised and when they arrived on the scene, they found Grandad still conscious. I am told it was Grandad who then organised his own rescue. The rescue team had to cut him from the wreckage with burning gear and he was rushed to Barnsley Beckett Hospital, where he had to have both legs amputated.

He died a few days later. He was a wonderful man who was well liked and respected in Mapplewell and it was a sad loss to his family and indeed, to the whole community, a terrible tragedy that I have never forgotten. I do remember my uncles, Clarence and Harry, discussing this accident later and they said that at times Grandad did come down that old track far too fast and that Thomas had been derailed in the past. I was named after my grandad, Charles George Marris Walker. Sixty years on, I still have his gold ring with his initials engraved on it. I am proud to bear his name but I would have been prouder still to have borne Dad's name, Westby no less! Oh well mother's do know best, bless them.

Old Thomas came steaming down the track,
With my poor, old grandad on his back,
He thought he was a cowboy and a derring-do,
But Old Thomas threw him off and killed him too.

Moral

Never dice with death with a tank engine,
You know you never can win,
Treat them with respect and be gentle,
Smile, look happy and grin.

After my Grandad Walker died, Auntie Gertie, my dad's sister, decided to take Dad under her wing and he went to live with her in Barnsley.
Dad had vowed not to leave home while his parents were still alive, but
now that his dad was dead, he needed someone to take care of him and his
elder sister Auntie Gertie became his second mother. Now there was a
wonderful woman! I can well remember the occasions that I stayed at her
little old terraced house just off Market Hill in Barnsley, with my cousin
Trevor (he was to go to Canada later in life). We had some great times at
Auntie Gert's. I still remember how we had to say our prayers before she
tucked us into bed at night and how she taught us to put our hot water
bottles onto our pillow while we undressed, so the pillow would be warm
by the time we were ready to jump into bed.

I still warm my pillow with my hot water bottle today, more than sixty
years later.

It is because of all these little things that are passed down to us from
the older generations that I now realise all our dreams, our hopes, our
fears were once shared by them. I now know on reflection that the dead
can never be truly forgotten, because our world today once belonged to
them, and it was they who made our todays possible.

Our lives are only on loan from previous generations and, when we
have finished with them, they must be passed down to the next!

Auntie Gertie's married name was Dancer. One of her relations was
to become a funeral director for the Barnsley Co-op and another became
Mayor of Barnsley. By coincidence, so did a chap who applied to Walkers of Wakefield Ltd. for a job years later as General Manager. Funnily
enough, if he had got the job, he may have finished up as the Mayor of
Wakefield too, who knows? As for the previous two Mayors of Wakefield,
well, one had been a Cocker Spaniel, and the one before him was an
Alsation.

Still, I suppose owt does when ye're stuck eh? This same chap later
became the General Manager for Walker Trowbridge, a large haulage
company based in Barnsley. I met him over twenty years later when I was
with a great friend of mine, Keb Evans, and we were all in Keb's pub

together, the Keel Inn, which is situated on a Barnsley canal bank, near the spot where I once lived as a small boy. Keb's pub was right opposite the old Barnsley Paper Mill site, where my dad took his first faltering steps into the world of commerce in 1928. Yes, a small world indeed!

To continue: With the money that Dad got from the sale of his pride and joy, a Scott Squirrel motorbike, and some money that he had borrowed from his sister, Auntie Gertie, he started up in business and got a contract working for the Barnsley Paper Mill, where he provided a transport service. He eventually operated a small fleet of chain-driven trucks. Those were the days, when one had to jack the back wheels of the truck off the floor, put it in gear, then spin the rear wheel to start the engine. So at last Dad had a job. He was up to his eyes in debt, but at least he had a job, even if it had meant starting up in business to create one. But if that was the only way he could find work, then so be it and he did quite well for a short time. Everything was going wonderfully, until a dark cloud appeared over the horizon and Dad contracted pneumonia and nearly died. His nephew took over and managed the business, which subsequently went into bankruptcy and so my dad's little venture failed before it ever really got started. There he was, at 32 years of age, having just lost his father, out of work, destitute and about to knock on Death's door.

At this time he was courting my mother and they had been contemplating marriage.

Dad in his youth was quite a Dapper Dandy, with his Homburg hat, his spats, his Meerschaum pipe and fancy waistcoat. He was in fact a very eligible bachelor and quite a catch, and there was just no way that my ma was going to allow him to pass through that door into the Kingdom of Heaven. Well, at least not without a fight, that is, and St. Peter had no bloody chance, not against my redoubtable ma, he hadn't. So it was decided that Dad should be brought to Mam's home at 39 Pye Ave, Mapplewell, Barnsley (like it or not) and St. Peter would just have to wait his turn until my mam had done with my dad. It was to take nine months of tender loving care from both my ma and my grandma before Dad eventually recovered from his illness (I too, developed pneumonia 33 years later.) As I dig deeper into this story, there do seem to be an awful lot of similarities between my life and my dad's. For instance I'd never realised until now that he had started in business with now't, as I did; he struggled to survive, as I did; he was thirty-three or thirty-four years old when he lost his dad, as I was; we both started in business at about the same age and he was thirty-four when I was born.

Yes, indeed, it is a very, very small world and there is nothing new under the sun. Everything that I may do today has been done before - and was probably done better.

After Dad had recovered from his illness and shortly after one of his bike rides to find work, he did manage to obtain some casual work at the sugar beet factory in Selby. He would, however, have to be up at the crack of dawn to stand outside the factory gates along with two dozen or so other hopefuls, waiting for the gates to open and for the factory foreman to come along with a job offer.

After a while, Dad did get some permanent employment at the factory in Selby, and he and Mam got married before moving to Selby.

This was only the first of many moves that we made over the next few years. We were in fact just like bloody gypsies.

My sister, Lenore, was born in 1934. Our staple diet for many of those early years was fat and bread, with sugar and bread for dessert. Sometimes as an alternative, we would have condensed milk on our bread, but as for jam, well, what was that? We very rarely saw any jam in our house in those early days, but we didn't ail ow't. The bread that we had was marvellous, not like the rubbish sold today, and we could eat it with now't on it.

Oh, and I must not forget the treacle, when we could afford it, oh dear no, because Ma used to make the best oven bottom cakes in the whole of Yorkshire and as kids we would wait for them coming out of the oven to be put in the hearth to cool. Then my sister and I would pounce and devour a lump of Mam's delicious oven cake. Anybody who had not had an oven bottom cake straight out of the oven, lathered with best butter and treacle, simply hasn't lived. It was absolutely wonderful.

Over the years we kids had some great concoctions, meals that cost next to now't to make, such as neck of mutton stew. What we didn't eat got bunged back into the earthenware pot and warmed up for the next day, now't was wasted at our house. We couldn't afford to waste ow't. I remember Dad eating cheese and onion done in milk on a tin plate in the oven. That was his favourite Sunday night supper after a night out at the pub. Another favourite of his was slices of bread lathered with mucky fat (dripping), a bloody great lump of cheese, a stick of celery, a pickled onion and the salt pot (the open ones) to dip the celery in. I also remember my grandma's special meals, her chicken giblet pies. We were never allowed as kids to sit down for a meal at Gran's without all the trimmings. The plates were always warmed on the fireplace hob and vegetables and gravy were always, but always, served from tureens and a gravy bowl.

These meals were wonderful and so cheap. There would be bread and

14

butter puddings, made out of old bread crusts, milk and a few currents if we could afford them; if not, then this concoction was called milk sops There would be corned beef fritters, pieces of corned beef dipped in a flour and water batter mix and then fried. Then we would have our cow-heel pies. (Ask a modern butcher for a cow-heel or a sheep's head and he'll ask, "What's them, then?")

Maybe cows don't have heels today, and sheep are all running around without heads! We couldn't afford to go down to the chip shop in those days; fish and chips was a luxury saved for very special occasions, like if your dad happened to get a double up on t'hosses! (horses).

I could write a separate book about my mam's and gran's recipes. These so-called chefs of today, with their gourmet delights and half-cooked imitation bloody vegetables, served on separate plates and without any proper gravy to dip your bread in, are not even fit to be in the same kitchen as my ma. She wouldn't have even allowed them to wash up for her, let alone help to cook a meal! We had to have gravy at our house in those days because our staple diet was bread and bread and more bread, but it was proper bread and the gravy was to dip your bread in. Oh, that lovely gravy, we could stand our spoons up in Mam's gravy! I often think of Mam's meals if and when (by mistake) I go into a so-called up-market bloody restaurant today and see that side plate with the bit of cauliflower, the two pieces of poxy carrot (as hard as a bloody rock), those four pea pods (that Mam used to throw away when I was a lad) and the rubbish that they call 'mixed vegetables'. This excuse for proper food today is not designed to be eaten, oh no.

That chef just wants you to look at it, talk about it, take a photo of it and, if you don't like it, you may even be allowed to stuff it.

But under no circumstances are these up-market meals ever designed to be eaten!

And apart from that, why on earth use a side plate when the contents have to be tipped on to your proper dinner plate anyway? As for cabbage, well some of these up-market chefs have never even heard of that delight-ful vegetable known as cabbage. Why?

Well, cabbage tastes nice and it can be eaten, but it just doesn't look right on one of their bloody side plates, does it, and that is why it is never seen in up-market restaurants today. I suppose on reflection to-day's modern palates have become conditioned to (or corrupted by) these fancy creamed sauces that are used to give food a semblance of taste. Why, my ma would turn in her grave if she knew about the bloody rubbish they call food today. We were as poor as church crows in those day, but we knew what to eat and how to eat it. These young, part-time imitation housewives of today would be lost without their tin openers, fish shops and takeaways; still, who can blame them really, they were not as lucky as us. We knew how to rough it and how to adapt to our circumstances. Today's generation has never had the opportunity to taste reality, which is a pity, because while they remain forever cushioned and protected by that Welfare State, they can never know the real world, my world, and as a result their definition of hardship is a million miles away from mine. This is a pity, really, because one should never have to do for another what the other should, and can, do for themselves. (Here I go again, getting carried away).

During my early childhood, I would go across to Grandma's nearly every weekend and stay with her. She was, of course, on her own after Grandad died. I would catch the bus to Barnsley at the bottom of Kirkgate, near Woolworths, in Wakefield. In those days it was 7d. return on the bus, and I would travel to Mapplewell on a Yorkshire Traction bus from Barnsley or a Burrows bus from Wombell. I loved my gran, what a wonderful character she was and her Sunday teas were something really special. We enjoyed special brown bread, white bread, buttered current tea cakes and she sometimes opened a tin of salmon. Well, everybody always saved up for a little tin of salmon in those days. They very rarely ever opened it except for special occasions, like, for instance, if the Queen Mother should just happen to drop by for tea, or Princess Mary or some other such dignitary. There had to be at least one tin of salmon in the pantry. Why? Well, just in case, anybody special happened to call, like me, for instance, her favourite little grandson.

Oh, those three-tier cake dishes, oh those home made tarts, oh those cream buns, ground rice tarts and jelly and custard! But you only got any if you were good or lucky.

Never, ever was I allowed to speak at the table (little boys were seen and not heard), and I was never allowed to leave the table before everyone else had finished, or allowed to start a meal before anyone else. I reckon Gran and me were good for each other. Well, she spoilt me rotten, I suppose - aren't all grans supposed to do that? After all, I was her only grandson and that made all the difference.

She also helped to develop my education and she taught me manners too.

I do remember that Grandma was old and bad on her legs, and on a cold winter's night she would stand in front of the coal fire and lift her clothes up to warm her bum.

Just outside the back door of her house she had a veranda. Now, one of the toilets was an outside one and it was a former old midden (an ash toilet) down the yard. Granny, being bad on her legs, had decided that if she wanted a pee she could just walk onto the veranda where she had, very conveniently, placed an old metal bucket.

She would stand over this bloody bucket whilst looking up into the sky (ever so innocently) and she would start humming to herself, thinking that nobody knew what she was doing.

Then, tinkle, tinkle, well, the whole bloody street knew, didn't they, and all the neighbours would be out. "Aye up, Fanny's at it again!" She used to embarrass us something rotten and my mates would say: "Aye up Charlie, I saw thee Gran at it yesterday," and Gran never knew that we all knew what she was up to. It never dawned on me until years later that she couldn't have been wearing any bloody bloomers either.

She was Fanny Birkett - she came from Witherensea,
And she would sneak on the veranda for a crafty pee,
She would do it over a bucket, as calm as could be,
But my dear old Gran used to embarrass me. (Bless her)

My dear old Gran backed horses every day. She would bet sixpence each way on a horse and then listen to the race on the wireless (radio).

She also listened to the news during the war on her little old radio and, more often than not, she would get it all wrong. For instance, she would say: "Go round next door and tell thee Uncle Clarence that them there Japanese have just been and bombed London!" or "A Zeppelin had just crashed in Leeds!" or some such rubbish. But, best of all, she would often say to me "Here siree, take this round next door, for the Uncle Clarence's tea (bless him, the little love)." So off I would pop around to me Auntie Maud's with one of Grandma's specialities - a chicken giblet pie or a nice Lancashire hotpot, or whatever she had made especially for my uncle's tea.

Well Auntie Maud, bless her, used to go spare, but I often used to wonder why. I thought that all mams were trained to spoil their wonderful sons. Mam used to do exactly the same when I got married and my wife Jean would go bloody crackers, just the same.

For the life of me, I cannot to this day understand why!

I mean, after all Mam was a better cook than our lass and Ma was

17

only making sure I was getting fed properly. Now't wrong wi' that, is there, and after all, as men we were only being given our dues, surely. My ma and grandma between them helped me to cultivate a rather different perspective on life in general, on women in particular and the role they were born to play in society.

I began to realise that the female of the species had been designed to fulfil just one purpose in life and that was to satisfy the needs of the male. Things, of course did start to get out of control a little when women began to assert their so-called rights and all that sort of rubbish. Women just don't know how lucky they are today, because it isn't too long ago that every third girl child in China was strangled at birth. Why? Because there just wouldn't have been enough food to feed the men. Economic sense, I calls it.

The basic problem and the root cause of marital stress (for men, that is) is the fact that Parliament hasn't had the bloody sense to compel us men to lock our women away in bird cages and fetch them out only as and when they are required to satisfy our needs. The greatest benefit of all (to mankind, that is!) would be if and when, they just happened to open their gobs, a cover could be thrown over the cage, which could then be hidden away in the pantry out of the way. Now't wrong wi' that surely, is there, eh?

But back to my dear old grandma, who would give me a tanner (sixpence) to go to the pictures, for weeding the garden. For her, remember, we didn't get ow't for now't in those days.

Saturday night was picture night for me. I'd meet up with a lad called Clifford Broadhead who lived opposite Gran's and off we would go to Staincross Picture House.

I remember once when Auntie Maud (my cousin Pauline's mother) took us to the flicks. Now, if my auntie just happened to get into a conversation with a stranger, which she did on this particular night, then she would try her best to speak proper like. We were waiting in the queue for the pictures and she was talking to this woman about the coal man, sounding her 'h's' pretty proper like, when she said: '...and he put it in the coil hoil!' Well, Clifford and me nearly peed our pants with laughter.

Auntie Maud was a nurse too, like my mother; she was great. I used to spend a lot of time with my cousin Pauline, playing games indoors and out: Hop-Scotch, Kick-Out-Can, Hide and Seek, lots of word games in the house. I was always borrowing comics from our Pauline: *The Dandy* and *The Beano*, and at Christmas there would be the Boys-Own Annual. I don't think the girls had a Girl's Annual, well, they weren't as special as us lads, were they? Ow't did for them, really, like a little rag doll, or maybe a second-hand pram off the tip.

We were just like brother and sister, our Pauline and me; well, she lent me her comics, didn't she? Yes, those were happy, memorable days, great days to grow up in.

There was (and still is) a Methodist Chapel on Pye Avenue where Gran lived. Only God knows how old it is. It was there when I was born and will probably still be there when I die.

It was the focal point for the whole street. People would worship there; they would congregate; they would have their wedding receptions and their birthday parties there too.

Every Whit-Monday there would be a Whitsuntide walk from the chapel, when all the young children would set out from this Chapel-in-the-valley in their Sunday best to walk around the village of Mapplewell. This little tin hut, because that is all it was, helped to bond the people in that street together into a close-knit, happy community.

It was in fact the most important building in the street, and it belonged to and was supported and looked after by the whole street. Yes, my heart will always remain in Happy Valley where my roots were laid so many years ago. I am proud to have had the privilege of living there and to have been a part of a wonderful community. I may have settled elsewhere, I may even travel to the far corners of the universe. But my heart will always remain in that great little village of Mapplewell and I do know that if I should return there tomorrow to live, I would be known and accepted, because my roots are buried and will always remain in Happy Valley where I spent my boyhood. Who knows, perhaps, if there had been a little tin chapel built down every street today, there would be a little less crime and a few more Happy Valleys!

My Uncle Clarence, my cousin Pauline's Dad, was Chief Engineer at Barugh Green Chemical Works near Barnsley, and I used to spend hours at Grandma's listening to Uncle Harry (Mam's brother-in-law) and Clarence talking about railways and engineering with Grandad. Uncle Harry (Auntie Phil's husband) was a railway engineer and a bloody good one too. My poor old dad didn't stand a look-in. He was a very quiet man of few words and he would sit and suck his thumbs while these intelligent conversations were taking place. Dad didn't have an awful lot to say and he would never use two words when one would do, but for all that, he was a very shrewd man who kept his thoughts to himself.

Christmas at Grandma's was great, we would stay up until midnight, just me and her, and as soon as the clock struck twelve I was off like a shot out of a gun with my mates. Shouting, we called it. We would go round the street, to each door and shout, "We wish you a Merry Christmas and a Happy New Year, a big fat pig to last you all the year, please can we let your lucky bird in!" Then we would knock on the door and shout our names. "Charlie Marris!" was my name over in Barnsley in those day. Every householder stayed up at Christmas and New year, waiting for us kids, and we would go inside their homes and sing carols. We were, all of us, in those days, as safe as houses.

Every street had its own knocker-upper, a retired miner who would use a clothes prop to knock on bedroom windows and get miners off to work at 4 and 5 am. The miners walked to work then, there were no paddy buses in those days. I can remember ever so clearly, as a very small child, lying awake in Grandma's front bedroom, afraid of the dark, and hearing those old colliers walking down Happy Valley on their way to work at North Gawber Colliery, in Staincross, near Barnsley. In those days most of the miners wore clogs (they were cheaper and lasted longer than boots) and the sound of their clogs could be heard long before they came into sight. I will never forget the sound of those clogs as they marched away into the distance, like soldiers going to do battle. They are now lost forever; as they marched as a generation to be lost in time. However, as a small boy afraid of the dark, I derived some comfort from the sound of those clogs. I came to realise that I wasn't alone and there was a world out there that I was a part of; suddenly I ceased to be afraid. Oh, if only I could hear the sound of those clogs today and once again wake to find myself a part of something very special.

There were no pithead baths or changes of clothes for the miners in those day before the war; oh dear no, just an old tin bath slung outside the back kitchen door at home, which the miners managed to use, but only if they were lucky. On the other hand, if there just happened to be a large family of miners, like my dad's, then it was survival of the fittest, who dares wins, and they would fight over who would be first. That tin bath was placed in front of the fire and it would be filled with hot water from the set pot in the scullery or from the hot water tank at the side of the fire. The last man in would finish up bathing in cold water which, by this time, was blacker than ink. So the last man into the bath would finish up dirtier than when he had started!

My Uncles Bill and Cos (Oswald was his proper name) were miners all their lives. Uncle Bill was always drunk and fighting, his favourite sparring partners being the local coppers. He was in and out of jail like a bloody yo-yo, but he was a great bloke.

Later in life, as Uncle Bill got older, I would go across and take him out to his local for a pint. Now Uncle Bill was a great character, one of the old school, a real male chauvinist pig, wasn't he just; a real man, unlike the bloody wimps of today, who are even afraid to get married because they're frightened to death of a woman. But not my Uncle Bill, oh no, not him. He was a proper man who knew how to handle a woman, didn't he just! Uncle Bill used to give my Auntie Lizzie a few bob on a Friday when he got paid for a bit of grub. Then, on the Monday, when he was skint (after backing horses and boozing), he used to try and borrow it back. That was, of course, if she should just happen to have ow't left; if she didn't he would knock hell out of her. Yes, Uncle Bill was a great guy all right (the old bat). Of course he lived in an age where women were made to know their place, and their places was in the home. She had to be there as and when He-of-Little-Virtue, the breadwinner, the evil one, the man-about-the-house, the man that she was trained to see to, the man that she was taught to truly love, needed her.

Those, of course, were the good old days before Women's Lib and all that rubbish, when men were men and women knew it. I do jest, of course! Well you had better believe it!

In those days I couldn't ever, ever go into any of my aunties' or uncles' houses and come away without something, even if they were skint (and old Bill usually was).

I once named one of my recovery vehicles after him: Owd Bill (as well as Her Majesty), named after my ma. My fire engine is now called Our Hetty. They were all of them the salt of the earth and I am proud to have been one of them: rough and ready, hard as nails and all with hearts of gold.

Who could have asked for more? I certainly couldn't. I had it all: love, companionship and I was part of a great family. My Auntie Phyllis - now if anyone had ever deserved the highest possible recognition for her selfless dedication to helping others, well, she most certainly did. She did, however, get invited twice to the Queen's Garden parties and before she died, she received the British Empire Medal after over 50 years service with the WRVS. Big deal - so did the lady who worked for Sheffield Council making tea, and who got paid for her services too, along with a handsome retirement package, and who got the usual public sector perk of early retirement. Of course, that didn't matter because Sheffield Council were, as my dad used to say, spending some bugger else's brass (and that's easy, ain't it?) Our Phyllis, bless her, gave her all; she put everything in and took now't out.

From spending all her spare time knitting socks for soldiers during the war or making camouflage netting, to serving tea, visiting the sick in hospitals and collecting and making things at home for God knows how many charities - give, give, give (and boy did she give), Auntie Phyllis gave her all. One of her best friends, Mrs. (now Lady) Mason of Barnsley (Roy Mason's wife) used to visit her regularly and she thought the world of her. I remember an incident one day, just after Roy Mason became one of his Lordships, when Mrs Mason came to see Auntie. She said to me, "Hello, Charlie, how are you?" I replied." Allright, love, and how are you?" My Auntie, in disgust, said to me later, "Charlie, that was Lady Mason you were talking to!" I said. "You know, Auntie Phyllis, Lady Mason, like you, will always be a lady to me and she doesn't need a bloody title to make her one." There they were, together that day two of the greatest women that Barnsley has ever had the privilege of calling its own.

Auntie Phyllis was like a second mother to me, she was the one who provided the things, or some of the things, that my parents couldn't. At Christmas, there was always a little something to make it special. The first day's holiday that I had ever had was when she and Uncle Harry took me to Blackpool.

Oh, those donkey rides on the sands! I still remember, them sixty years later. When I got married, she was there to take my wife Jean and me out for a day to Scarborough and she bought our lunch. We couldn't have even afforded a cup of tea in those days, let alone lunch. If we ever managed a day out, we would take a flask and sandwiches. Auntie Phil looked after my kids and my grandkids, and she looked after me. She took over from my mother when Mam died, who also had a heart of gold.

How could I ever forget them? They threw the moulds away after they made my grandma, my mam and my Auntie Phyllis; they were real, very special people.

## My Fond Memories

Could I ever forget them and the love they gave to me,
And the help they gave to others, there for the world to see?
Remembering their kindness, I know I always will -
Everlasting, they remain Grandma, my mam
and dear old Auntie Phil.

I used to spend a lot of time visiting my Uncle Harry and Auntie Phyllis at their home in 28 Summer Lane, Barnsley. There was no central heating, no washing machine or television. In those days, at Auntie's, hot water came from a geyser over the sink. There was an outside toilet down the yard with newspapers to wipe your bum and a paraffin heater to stop it from freezing during the winter. The fridge was a slab of concrete down in the cellar where the coal was kept. The 'coil-hoil', eh?! The front room was the best room in the house and so it ought to have been - it was never used.

The piano was for looking at and not for playing. The three-piece suite had only perhaps been sat on three times in forty years of marriage, and then probably twice by accident (after not thinking, like); the other time would have been in the shop when Auntie Phyllis tried it out to see if it was comfortable before my grandad bought it for her as a wedding present. Well, we all had to have a nice three-piece suite. But the biggest laugh of all was that in all the fifty-odd years I visited Auntie Phyllis, or anyone else for that matter, no-one, but no-one, ever got to sit in those bloody front parlours on those three-piece suites! Auntie even had covers on the arms and the back, just in case someone just happened to trip and fall onto it by accident. There is just no other way anyone would have ever got near those three-piece suites in those trophy rooms! At my Auntie Phil's, you were allowed to glance at it (the three-piece suite) out of the corner of your eye as you were passing through to the front door. You could even have a quick furtive touch when you thought Auntie wasn't looking (or you may have even given it a little kick as you passed it by). But one thing is for sure, you never, but never, sat on it. It was for looking at, not for sitting on, and that bloody suite, well, I am sure it would look at me as I was just passing through, as if to say, "Go on then. What's tha waiting for? Go on, I dare thee!"

That's how it was everywhere one went in those days. The front parlours were like sanctuaries for the protection and safekeeping of three-piece suites. There were certain exceptions, of course. On very rare occasions we (as kids) were allowed into the trophy room if someone had died.

Then, of course, these sanctuaries were opened up for public display and after we had taken our shoes off, we were allowed into the mausoleum. It was a bit of a bugger, really, when one considers that the only way we managed to ever get to sit on those three-piece suites or enjoy a little bit of tinned salmon was when someone had died. It didn't seem quite right really, that we as kids had to wait for a relative to die just to have the privilege of sitting on a three-piece suite and having a bit of salmon for tea.

My dad's brother, Alf, was an ex-miner turned butcher who lived at Barugh Green near Barnsley and he must have been at that time the only true blue bloody Conservative in the whole of Barnsley!

He was a real radical and it's a wonder he was never lynched or hanged, drawn and quartered.

He would say to the miners in his local pub: 'There will come a day when they won't want your bloody coal!' Oh boy, was he proved right! And he would say:

"How can we compete with them Japanese when they are working seven day a week for a handful of bleeding rice, and you, yer lazy bastards, are only working five days a week, and you want paying for six!"

Uncle Alf was a big fellow, and he needed to be to match the size of his gob and the trouble it got him into. Alf's lad, our Reg, well, we grew up together. Like brothers we were, we worked and played together into our teens. After Uncle Alf had packed in the butchering business, Reg finished up delivering collier coal for a local pit and that is how I came to know Keb Evans and his brothers, who were among some of the nicest guys I have ever met. When they were young, they were wrestlers and keep-fit fanatics. Keb now has a gym, sports centre and motel at the side of his pub in Barnsley.

We had some great nights out together as lads. I have some unforgettable memories of those days of yore. Incidentally, before I forget, I think Uncle Alf must have packed the meat job in because, after the rationing of food came to an end and the black market dried up after the war, he and our Reg suddenly had to work for a bloody living, because all the fiddles had dried up and butchering was no longer profitable. So Uncle Alf decided it was a good idea to retire to his yacht, which he had conveniently parked in the Mediterranean (sorry, Barnsley Canal) and let our Reg do all the work. He did just that and never worked again for the next 20 years, up until he died.

He didn't even work two days a week; so much for his abuse of the Barnsley miners, eh? At least all those 'lazy' miners (or some of them) did manage to work four days a week. They never worked Mondays, mind, oh no, they would give themselves an extra unofficial rest day on a Monday, which was known as collier Monday.

As much as they tried to work only four days and get paid for six shifts, they never quite succeeded. This was either because of, or in spite of, Arthur Scargil, their would-be bloody saviour.

But it was to all turn out right in the end, of course, in the 1980s, when the silly bloody government paid out enormous sums to the miners in redundancy payments, which were partly funded from the taxes of other working people. Some of these were employed in the private sector and were earning much less than the miners. Yes, as they say, the sun always shines on the righteous!

This could be just about the right time to say a few words about Auntie Phyllis's husband, my Uncle Harry. As I mentioned earlier, he was a brilliant railway engineer in the days of steam engines. He worked long hours at his job, he worked shifts and most public holidays too.

He was called out many times in the middle of the night and week-ends to attend to derailments. The tales he used to tell used to fascinate me as a small boy. He bought me books on railways and railway engines. He lived and breathed his job, it was in fact his life. I also remember (how could I forget?) the wooden train he made for me out of wood!

I also remember the very special moments when, as a little boy, I would travel on the bus from my grandma's at Mapplewell to Barnsley, to stay at Auntie Phil's on those occasional Saturday nights that I would spend with her and Uncle Harry. I used to treasure those moments on the Sunday morning, when Uncle Harry would take me to his workplace at the engine sheds, behind Barnsley Bus Station, to see all the steam engines. I thought it was absolutely wonderful!

Over forty years later I was able to return the compliment when I took Uncle Harry to the Railway Museum at York. We were well fortified that day with some lovely sandwiches and rum and coffee, provided by my dear old auntie. What a wonderful day that was! While we were there, we met another old chap, an engine driver who was down from the North-East. It was a real pleasure for me to listen to the reminisces of these two old men who had served their time in life oh so well.

We saw the biggest British railway engine ever built in its day, the Beyer Garrett, and to hear these two old men talk about it, you would have thought it was they who had built it!

Uncle Harry said "I worked on that" and the other chap said. "I once drove it."

Yes, that was the culmination and the end of a never-to-be forgotten, perfect day.

Uncle Harry also took me several times to the house where he was born, at Kier St Barnsley. He would tell me stories about his brother Ernest who was an engine driver, about the times in their youth when his mam would say to the lads, "go down the cellar and fetch some coal for the fire." They would then look at each other to see whose turn it was. It was then that their father Charlie Cutts, who was a dray man at Barnsley

# Pictures tell a sad story

The boys' father, Charles Cutts, when horses were used at the Co-op's traffic department where he worked.  (S)

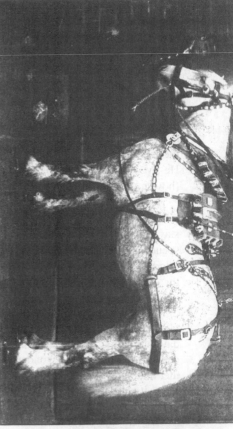

IT WAS just a pair of old photographs found at a local charity shop.

But for Glen Fearons, who discovered them while browsing at the Hospice Shop on Eldon Street, they told a story of extreme sadness and bravery of a Barnsley family.

The photographs reveal the sacrifice made by the Cutts' family during the First World War when they lost two sons — only ten months apart.

Private Frank Cutts (York and Lancs) was the fourth son of Mr

and Mrs Charles Cutts, of Keir Terrace, Keir Street, Barnsley.

He was 21 and had enlisted in January 1916 and went out to Salonika in October of that year.

After serving abroad some 16 months he contracted malaria fever and was invalided home. After a month's leave he reported back at Sunderland.

When he was later allowed home on leave he was in excellent health and spirits.

But tragedy struck afer he returned to duty when he fell victim to influenza followed by pneu-

monia.

His parents were immediately sent for and they were present when he died the following day.

He was brought back to Barnsley for burial in Barnsley cemetery following a service at St Mary's Church where he had attended for many years.

Prior to joining the army, Frank had been a woodturner at Barnsley Co-operative Society's Dearne works and was a very popular young man.

Mr and Mrs Cutts' elder son, Private John William Cutts, had

died the previous September in a London hospital following wounds received in action four months previously.

One can understand Mr and Mrs Cutts' great concern for their 19-year-old twin sons, Arthur and Walter, who were, at the time, serving in France with the West Yorkshire Regiment.

Mr Cutts (senior) also worked at the Co-op in traffic department.

Mr Fearons said: "It must have been a terrible time for the family, losing two sons in such a short space of time."

Private Frank Cutts who died in July 1918.  (S)

Private John William Cutts, who died in September 1917.  (S)

Excerpt from the Barnsley Chronicle

Coop, would look up from his paper and say just one word, "Now" and that was all that was required to start a stampede. Those lads fought and fell over each other to see who got down that cellar first!

Yes, dear reader, the man of the house was indeed the man of the house in those days. He was sometimes poor, he was sometimes illiterate, but he had respect for and he was respected by his family. He was the man of the house. I must say again my mother's often repeated phrase: "Just you wait until your Dad comes home, lad!"

And Dad never laid a finger on me. He didn't have to, for in my world he was a God and he had my respect.

I enclose a copy of an article that was published in The Barnsley Chronicle about my Uncle Harry's family and his two brothers who were killed in the Great War.

What a tragic waste of life that was. My father and his brother Bill travelled to Manchester when Dad was just seventeen, in answer to the call to fight and die for their country. Fortunately they were not allowed to enlist, because at that time miners were needed to provide the raw materials to fuel the engine of that out-of-control war machine.

It was a meat grinder of a machine that was simply allowed to go on devouring more and more human life simply to pacify the egos of the war lords who had started the Great War, but could not finish it.

Writing this has made me realise just how unimportant life really is. It is just an accident of a birth and then the follow-on to the sheer futility of life itself and the inevitability of impending death.

This story has in fact been written by accident. I was an accident waiting to happen and I only happened perhaps because my dad survived the Great War!

And my grandchildren, too, are only here today because their great grandad survived the war.

So much for the value of and the true meaning of life itself!

What an absolute, complete worthless charade we are allowed to play!

How meaningless, how obscure! Shakespeare, the immortal bard, got it about right when he penned those few words:
*"All the world's a stage,*
*And all the men and women merely players."*

Yes, life is but a futile sham.
A what am I, or a who I am.
A moving on, a forgotten name.
A charade, a nothing, but a game.

# And So, Goodbye To Barnsley

In 1938, Mr Ziegler the butcher, who was a major partner in Craven Dairies (later known as Associated Dairies and now known as Asda, the supermarket group), was travelling home from Barnsley to Wakefield when his car broke down in Staincross (where we were living at the time).

Mother happened to be passing by and as usual, she was there to help a lame dog over a stile. She asked Mr Ziegler if he needed any help and then invited him into her home where she sat him down, introduced him to her teapot and made him a nice cup of tea and something to eat (well, that's what they did in those days). Dad later helped to repair Mr Ziegler's car. At that time, my father was out of work (unknown to my mother). He had been a brickie's labourer and had just lost his job on a local building site. Mr Ziegler asked Dad if he could drive and Dad said yes, so Mr Ziegler found him a job at a bacon factory called *The Farm Stores* in Outwood near Wakefield. As they say: "One good turn deserves another" and my mother's help, freely given to someone in need had paid off, for which she had been repaid handsomely. Dad had always said to me years ago, "If tha ever does anybody a bad turn, tha will allus get paid back in kind", and he was proved so right. I have seen this philosophy in practice many times throughout my life. But what he didn't say was that the same principle also applies in reverse: Give and it shall be returned tenfold - as it was that day in Staincross in 1938.

The sun was designed, as always, to shine on the righteous and Mam and Dad, having just met an angel in disguise, were on the move again. They packed their bags and had to leave their friends and family behind in order to settle they-knew-not where. They left their roots in Barnsley, but this time they were never to return. Rather sad, really!

As I write this, I begin to realise that neither my father nor me ever had the benefit of secure employment. Like him I had dozens of different jobs. Again, I must say it - like father, like son. Dad was forty-two when we moved to Wakefield and *The Farm Stores* had just been opened by a chap called Sir Lomas Walker, whoever he was, and my dad's nickname became Lomas. He was to become the goalkeeper for the firm's football team and, as a result of this, he ended up with two broken ribs. *The Farm Stores*, was owned by Craven Dairies, which was like a co-operative that had been set up by a group of farmers and butchers. In a bid to market and sell their products, they had opened several shops in the North of England called *Farm Shops* (to which my dad delivered). I would go with him on his deliveries during school holidays from Ledger Lane school. Dad's van was a very large vehicle which could hold sixty dead pigs, hung from hooks.

*The Farm Stores* was the most modern meat processing plant in the whole of Europe. It was developed and expanded over the years and it was the beginning of a business that was started by a small band of men who had the vision and sense to realise that mountains can be moved and empires built by the pooling of resources and ideas (I was to learn these truths later). This was the beginning of Asda. *The Farm Stores* has now closed down thanks to Archie Norman, the sometime-chairman brought in from Kingfisher (Woolworth's Comet Group) to improve the Co's performance. This he did all right, but how could he justify closing a factory and knocking it down when it had a captive market for its products, a loyal dedicated work-force (who had never been on strike), as well as being the most modern meat processing plant in Europe? He must have been crackers. Dare I say it? Small world. My kids today are shareholders in Asda and Kingfisher. Archie Norman, bless him, has moved into politics, where his talents are being used to attempt to restore the Conservative Party to its former glory.

We lived at Grandstand Road, off Lingwell Gate Lane in Outwood (a road named after a racecourse which had a grandstand), and we then moved to 25 Ledger Lane, Outwood. It was at Ledger Lane when my father floored my mother. He was normally a nice, quiet gentleman who weighed in at eleven stone. My mother weighed approximately eighteen stone and she would nag and nag at him, usually with some justification, because my dad used to fancy himself as a bit of a ladies' man. On this occasion he was sniffing around Old Abe, *the Farm Stores* boilerman's daughter. Well, Ma got to know about this and she opened her gob, didn't she? Well, he-of-few-words promptly closed it and he flattened her with one punch, bang on the chin. Me mam was laid spark out for over an hour, in a heap up against the back kitchen door. He-of-few-words had lost control that day and it was the first and only time I saw my dad lose his temper. I am pleased that I never saw that again. I was about ten years old at the time. He would normally let her ramble on while he read the paper. One day, however, when the radio was playing and Ma was in full throng about something or other that he had or hadn't done, he

29

just stood up, calmly picked up the radio and chucked it out of the closed window, saying: "I can't listen to thee and to that an all." Then he-of-few-words sat his sen (self) down again and carried on reading his paper.

The basic problem with Mam and Dad's relationship was one of communication. There just wasn't any full stop. He-of-few-words would just ignore her-with-the-big-gob and, of course, this would frustrate Mam, causing her to grow madder and madder. He-with-now't-to-say would just go on reading his bloody paper. How he managed to do that I will never know. I remember the times when we would be in company and Ma would be talking and she would say to Dad someing like: "Didn't he, Wes?" and he would look up and say: "Aye, if tha says so." I used to idolise my dad, but he must have been a right bastard to have been married to. He would take the dog for a walk just to get a bit of peace and quiet. Or at least that's what he told me mam. That was until the night he forget to bring the dog back from the pub and the landlord brought it home. Those were the days. A pint of beer for just 10d. and never a dull moment. It was at Ledger Lane that I got my first taste of Wimsol, thinking it was pop (lovely!), and where me mam used to chase me up the street with a rolled-up clothes line. If she had caught me I would have been dead!

We moved to 7 Johns Avenue in Lofthouse around 1941, to a house that we had rented from Sharphouses, the Wakefield provision merchants. Dad had moved jobs again and this time he had gone to work for the Busy Bee who had shops in Leeds and in the Springs in Wakefield. The Busy Bee were butchers who'd had a contract to deliver rationed meat from the Wakefield slaughterhouse to all the butchers in the Wakefield district areas during the war. Dad got to drive a snub-nosed Commer meat delivery wagon, which was a flat-back with curtain sides - no such thing as a specialised-fridge vehicle in those days. How on earth did we manage to survive without fridges and all those hygiene police that the powers-that-be insist are essential today to keep us in good health? Well, we survived all right and were probably much fitter than today's generation. What a ridiculous, absolute load of nonsense. Dad's wagon used to be kept at Coopers garage and filling station at the top of Warrengate in Wakefield. When she heard we were to move into our new home in Lofthouse, Mam thought it was wonderful! We were now in the real world. In the land of the living. At last we had arrived. We had all the modcons: a big semi-detached house with a built-in dishwasher where you had to put all your mucky pots into a bowl and pull a string. But this was too much trouble for me mam. She would put all the mucky pots into the sink, which was conveniently situated inside a cupboard behind closed doors in the corner, all nicely set out in a bloody great pile. The only trouble was that when you wanted a cup or a pint pot, it was usually at the bottom of the muckheap. What a bloody mess! I used to get my own back on my mother and revenge was sweet. I'd wait until a neighbour came round, then I would go and get a drink of water and deliberately leave the door open.

She used to go bloody crackers. It was around this time that I started reading and writing poetry. I think I was between ten and eleven years of age. I used to write about anything and everything. Quite a young and budding Rudyard Kipling wasn't I just! I would spend hours as a kid indoors, writing poetry. Mind, it was probably a good thing really because if I hadn't been inside, I would have been outside trying to knock hell out of me best mate Ken Newton. I must have been a right little prat really; and here I am at sixty-seven and still a prat.

# Chuck Walker's Schooldays

But for now I am nobbut a schoolboy and in 1941, the war was on and all the people in our street had a Nissen hut in our gardens. Well, it were wartime, weren't it? There were also air-raid shelters built on every corner of our street, although what good they would have been in a proper German bomber raid, I just do not know, because they were useless, built of brick. The shelters in our gardens were made of tin, yes tin, they were called Anderson shelters. I believe the inventor's name was probably Rin Tin Bloody Tin, or whatever. He ought to have been buried alive in one! Nobody in our street ever used those monstrosities. We were all safer sheltering from Adolph's Doodlebugs under the kitchen table than we could ever have been in those bloody air-raid shelters. However, they were not a total loss; us young lads were able to pursue our sex education with the little girls inside those shelters. Perhaps it would be more cost-effective if today's young generation were given the same opportunities as we were, with a Nissen hut provided by the state erected in everybody's back garden. I doubt if the provision of shelters would cost more than the employment of an index-linked sex educational therapist in every school!

I remember my first nearly real sexual experience (well, it was an experience!) I decided to move in and set up home in our shelter with Shirley Berry, the girl next door, and her mother caught us together. There was all hell to pay, yet I hadn't done anything, I didn't get the chance!

Yes, dear reader, in those days we didn't need sex therapists and free condoms, oh no: You could have placed Shirley bloody Temple herself, bound, gagged and stark naked in bed with any of my mates, and not one of us would have dared to touch her with a bargepole, oh no! Our mothers would have skinned us alive, dread the thought. Shirley Berry was the girl next door and my first love. God knows what may have happened had I soiled her pretty little lips with a kiss - probably a shotgun wedding. Yes, those were the days. I used to dream about Shirley and I would lust after and fantasise about her mam, whom I used to fancy something rotten. I was growing up all right and Mrs Berry knew all about that. She would tease me something shocking. On Valentine's Day, she sent me a card along with a tiny, sexy pair of knickers that she had made.

The card said:

'Only a pair of panties, you can see at a glance they're mine,
And I would show them to no other, but, you my Valentine'.
Was I embarrassed?  Not 'arf.  My face was scarlet.

I will never forget Mr or Mrs Berry, they were wonderful people.
Mrs Berry used to take me with them to local Saturday night dances at
Outwood Institute and the village hall at Lofthouse.  I had some wonderful times with Mrs Berry and my first love, her daughter Shirley, until a
prat of a mate of mine called Alan Proctor, from Lofthouse, stole her
from me.

Speaking of growing up, I remember some of the boys (and I mean
only some) at our school used to play cheekies with the girls in the school
toilets.  I still thought my 'bits' were just to pee through!  Ah well, we
live and learn.  I attended Lofthouse Primary School until the age of eleven.
It was there that I used to play inside-left at football.  Wonderful position,
that I couldn't see out of my right eye, could I?  Boxing was my favourite
sport in those days and I finished my days at Lofthouse being the cock-
of-the-school (it was a girls-only school, weren't it).  I remember when I
started Stanley Modern School and we used to have to catch the bus at the
end of Canal Lane at Lofthouse Gate (well, some of us did).  I used to
miss it at least three times a bloody week and consequently had to spend
the first two hours waiting outside the headmaster's office for the cane.
Lovely, that.  They do say that anticipation is greater than realisation and
that bastard of a headmaster knew it, didn't he just.  While I was stood
there petrified, I had time to think about the error of my ways and he, the
bastard, the bastard with the cane, was applying psychology, wasn't he?
That kind of applied psychology could do today's kids a world of good.
It didn't do me any harm.  I don't think it did me much good either, but
that's another matter, eh!

I had a fight in the first week at school, the first of many.  I was always
teased because I had a squint in my right eye and did I get some stick
from my so-called mates.  You can bet your beautiful bottoms I did.  I
had to wear glasses too, which didn't help.  I was known as 'Squinty
Eyes' or 'Four Eyes', or worse.  If the kids today had to be bullied like we
were, they would have sued the school.  I can remember, time after time,
being chased around the school by a crowd of lads.  If they had been girls,
I am sure I would have coped nicely, but it wasn't to be.  I was always in
trouble and I always seemed to be fighting either my own or someone

else's battles. But things were a little different in those days. You sorted your own problems out, usually by punching someone in the mouth, and then the problem was resolved one way or another. As simple as that. Not like today. Now there is a social worker of about eighteen years of age on every bloody street corner just waiting for your cry for help, and stress counsellors all stood in line, waiting, just waiting, for their chance to comfort and advise.

A lad called Ken Newton was my best mate and to prove it he used to knock seven bells out of me (he flattened me more than once). My dad used to say to us when we were scrapping, "Now look, lads. There's just no point in throwing punches to see who can hit the bloody hardest. You won't learn owt like that. Yer will just have to be a bit moor gentle like. A bit moor scientific, like." (No, he couldn't spell it). But it didn't make any difference to Ken and me. We still tried to kill each other. We were growing up and boys will always be boys, I suppose. Well, some of them will. But I do sometimes wonder, today, who are the girls and who are the boys? The bloody powder puffs with their designer haircuts who use the same hairdressers as their mam's! Ah well, here I go again! They ought to start using the ladies toilets too, then they could have a sit-down for a pee, the wimps.

Here is a poem I wrote for my grandson's fifteenth birthday:

**Happy Birthday Andrew, Yer Wimp**

Grandson's are wonderful (well, so their mam's say),
Really they ought to be just locked away,
Andrew, whilst I digress, I would just like to know,
Now, for your hairdressing, to the ladies do you go?
Do you now sit down when you have a pee?
Surely you don't (well, I must just wait and see),
Oh, I know I'm a cynic and all that stuff,
Now Andrew be honest, are you really a puff?

Andrew, it's your birthday and your special day,
Now, as it's your birthday, I just wanted to say,
Dare I wish you the best, the best that I can,
Remembering you, always, as a real macho man,
Even though you use the ladies as often as can be
We don't really believe that you sit down to pee.

We wish you all the best and this is written in fun,
because you are our favourite, favourite grandson.
(Creep). Now, I can't think of ow't, ow't else to say,
except, we love you and happy birthday.

One morning at Stanley Modern school, during assembly, we were singing hymns when a bastard-of-a-so-called mate grabbed and squeezed my goolies. I let out such an almighty yell that the singing stopped and I cracked the prat on his nose. A teacher grabbed me, pulled me out of assembly and gave me a good hiding. We were then taken to the school gym to sort things out and I knocked seven bells out of him. So I suppose, in a way, it was all worthwhile.

I failed my 11-plus because I wasn't very good academically (can't you tell? I was in the Bs all through school. I never moved up and I never moved down. I was just like a bloody hermaphrodite, neither one thing or the other. I won prizes for English, though. Guess why? - read on).

We used to gamble at school breaks with cigarette cards and marbles. If one won, one would sell the cards ten for half a penny and twenty for a penny, then one could buy oneself a woodbine from the corner shop and nip into the school toilets for a crafty drag. Well, one would, wouldn't one? Wouldn't you too? One would think so, wouldn't one? How's about that for grammar, then?

(Me grammar couldn't spell either).

It was about this time that I fell in love with our history teacher at Stanley Modern School. She was a cracker, wasn't she? A real ravishing blonde, and 'ravish' was the operative word, because that was just what all of us lustful young lads wanted to do to her. Every time she bent over the blackboard, the whole class dropped and bent to pick up their pencils so we could all get a crafty look at her stocking tops. Oh yes, all proper women wore stocking in those days. We lucky lads were spoilt, we did not have to put up with unnecessary obstacles, like having to associate with a girl who wore bloody tights!

One day, as our beautiful teacher was as usual bent over the stationery cupboard, showing her bloomers, one of the lads cupped his hands around his mouth and sounded the Post Horn Gallop. She turned around and said, "Stand up, the boy with the horn" and all the bloody class stood up!

I enjoyed my history lessons and I think perhaps our teacher was the reason why. I remember another time, when she bent over the cupboard to get some books and showed her stocking tops, one of the lads gave a loud wolf whistle. She turned around and said, "The boy who made that noise - come with me." So, this lad went, didn't he. Ten minutes later, he comes back to the classroom, a little out of breath and with a smile all over his face. "Well," we all said. "What did she do to thee then?"

This lad replied, "Well, I don't know really, but it were better than peeing!"

Tom Brown and his schooldays had nothing on us. Great days - I hated every moment. One day in the class, we had a boys-versus-girls poetry lesson using the words Blue and Pistol:

Boy's Effort:

My father is a policeman, all dressed in navy blue,
And when he goes on duty, he takes his pistol too.

Girl's Effort:

Mary went to a party, all dressed in pink and blue,
She drank champagne until midnight and went, and pistol too.

Guess who won!

It was about this time that my Uncle Clarence won the small bore rifle championship of the world. Boy, was I proud! The headlines in the papers read: "Gloria beats G men of America - but Barnsley boy beats her." On the final shoot he got six consecutive bulls. I used to brag about this to all my mates. My Uncle Clarence, a real Champion of the World. My dad's brother was also a champ: he was once the Yorkshire NUR and spell champ. As for me, I was the school conker champion, so there.

In fact, once I had to go to juvenile court for stealing conkers off a tree in Stanley churchyard, so I was something of a celebrity too. We didn't have playing fields or football fields when I was a kid. We had brick air-raid shelters on every street corner where we would play at 'truth or dare, kiss or promise' with the girls. We lads called it by its proper name: Cheekies or Mammies and Daddies. It was great! We played football and cricket on the street and a lot of our time was spent playing in Lofthouse Park, now the home of WMDC Repair Department. Before the First World War, it was a proper park where there used to be tram excursions from Wakefield to Lofthouse for visitors to the park. It even had a bandstand (so they tell me) and during the First World War it was used as a prisoner-of-war camp. After the war, it became rundown and overgrown and was to become our special playground. We'd swing from the trees, play Cowboys and Indians and we would dare each other to do things. We played football and rugby using our coats, or even girls' knickers if there were any available, for goalposts. Yes, we had a great life.

The park was ours and there were gangs of us every night after school, and every weekend, over in the park. I had a great set of mates: there was Ken Newton my sparring partner and the now-famous painter, Geoff Reeve (that there David Hockney couldn't hold a candle to our Geoff). He was so laid-back, how he managed not to fall over, we never knew. Then there was Geoff Kellet, the milk bottle recovery man who would pinch bottles from doorsteps and sell them back to a firm called Milk Vessel Recovery. He was later to become one of the company's chief executives. Ah well, we all have to start somewhere. From little acorns and all that rubbish, eh?

Ray and Dennis Dobson were the formidable, terrible twins of whom Dennis was the nicer and better looking (sorry, Ray). Those two daft buggers haven't spoken for years and they have both forgotten what they fell out over in the first place, all those years ago. Ah well, it takes all sorts. Eric Sutcliffe was a lovely lad. When Eric smiled, it was like a ray of sunshine after a storm. He now lives in America, the wimp, and thinks he's Al Capone. The bloody traitor. I used to work with his dad (Little Billy, we called him) at Ropers Brickworks at Lofthouse Gate. At least his dad never allowed himself to become corrupted by them Yanks. No, Eric's dad was true to his roots, which were in a proper country with a bit of history and a bit of blue blood running through its inhabitants' veins. He didn't choose to go and live with a nation of immigrants (bloody mongrels, in fact). No, Little Billy had some pride and he stayed where his roots are. He, of course was a proper patriot and he had a bit of pride, unlike some of the bloody traitors. He believed in a bit of yer *Land of Hope and Glory* and was quite happy to stay in a proper country with his mates, unlike some. I suppose we are well rid of the ones who choose to desert the sinking ship in search of pastures new. The bloody wimps!

Billy Richardson, (sorry George), used to race (and beat) West Riding Buses from Lofthouse to Wakefield on our usual Saturday and Sunday nights out to the Playhouse (now known as Casanovas) or the Electric, or Regal cinemas in Wakefield. As a result of these escapades, his legs are now knackered. Come to think of it, those old buses finished up in knacker's yards too, so Billy is in good company. It now takes him all his time to hobble across the road to catch a bloody bus, let alone race one to Wakefield. But as a small consolation and in memory of the old days, he does have a go, on the odd occasion, in his turbo-charged, souped-up wheelchair.

Peter Green and Barry Marley: Well now, these two highly educated, up-market people (who were given bikes for passing their 11-plus), they of Rothwell Grammar School fame. 'Grammar School Gorbies' we used to call 'em), the pair of Ps, neither of them offered to give me a hand to write this nonsense, for all their higher educational qualifications. Anyway, I am sure that all the rest of us lads could have passed our 11-plus if we had really wanted to. So there. It was just that we were not promised a bike if we passed. But they were, the jammy gits. Well, we didn't want a poxy bike anyway. My good mate Ben's dad was the Warburton of the 40s. Well, Mothers Pride had nowt on Ben's dad, cos he didn't have any. If he did, he wouldn't have fathered Ben in the first place. Ben and I did our reserve training together in the army and we copped for a couple of birds in London. Ben's girlfriend says, "Does yer know owt about sex, then?" Ben says, "Aye lass. I've filled many of 'em with tatties!" (I joke of course, he has never picked up a bloody shovel in his life). There was Keith Lawson who was another good lad. None of us lads wanted to tangle with Keith. He was as hard as nails. It wasn't that he couldn't be beaten. Oh no, It was just that he was built like (and looked like) a brick toilet and if you got into a shindig with Keith, it became so frustrating, because you could hit him with everything, including the proverbial kitchen sink and Keith would still be there like that bloody great rock of Gibraltar. He wouldn't go down and you just had to give in because you were bloody worn out hitting him. Yes, quite a guy, our Keith. He built me a garden path years later, and it was just like him. You could have launched the bloody QE2 from that path. The one man that I must not forget, or ever will, is a guy called Frank Ward. He was a neighbour, a good friend and would do anything for anybody. A real caring guy. Frank served as an airman (a flight sergeant) during the war. He was quite a few years older that us lads and we thought he was marvellous. He always had time for us. I remember the time I spent in the Ida Hospital in Leeds, having the squint taken out of my eye. Who was it that gave up a part of his precious leave to come and see me in hospital? Frank did. He always brought me cigs when he came home on leave - Senior Service and Three Threes, none of your bloody Woodbine rubbish. Oh no, only the best from Frank, and I wasn't even old enough to smoke. Yes, that guy was my idol and I admired him no end.

He was the man that I always wanted to be: good-looking, admired by the ladies and a real man. It was he who first took me dancing to the Embassy Ballroom down Market street in Wakefield. I think he felt sorry for me, somehow, what with my glasses and that squint in my eye. He was like a brother to me. It was a real tragedy when, years later, after he had come out of the forces, he was involved in a motor cycle accident that resulted in him sustaining severe head injuries from which he never properly recovered. Frank never married and he died comparatively young..

When I got married and moved away from home I lost touch with Frank. I wasn't there for him the way he had been for me, but I will never forget him. My pal Ken Petty was an apprentice mechanic to Frank at the West Riding Bus Company in Wakefield and Ken used to tell me about Frank and how he would give him pocket money every week. He would always tell me about what a wonderful mechanic Frank was, which was praise indeed from a man who himself became a brilliant mechanic in his own right. Yes, Frank was full of life. He lived it to the full while he was able but, unfortunately, he was never allowed to fulfil his true potential. Yes, a tragedy indeed.

To return to my errant schoolmates, a right set of no good, useless gits, the lot of them. I could write a whole book about my mates and it is just impossible to include everyone because I just couldn't live that long. However, below is a poem I wrote for Ray Hodgson's sixty-fifth birthday which we all shared and enjoyed together recently at the Wrenthorpe Cricket Club, by courtesy of our good friend (the prat!) Gerry 'the carpet' Booth. I have personally bought enough bloody raffle tickets from Gerry on behalf of that bleeding club, that it ought by now to be big enough to support the whole of the Yorkshire cricket test series right into the next century. In fact, the money that I have ploughed into that bloody club would have taken the English cricket team on ten world tours. Instead, it was probably used to take Gerry and his delectable wife Shirley, on their last six world cruises.

PS. As I cannot afford (due to Cricket Club donations) an expensive lawsuit, I want it to be known that I am only joking.

# A Tribute To A Very Special Friend

For Ray on his 65th birthday. From all his old mates of yesterday.

R is for Raymond, that's his name,
A really great guy, his main claim to fame,
You are young at heart, with new hip joints too,
Memories of yesterday are not always true,
Oh but we love you and think you're just great,
No one could have had a much better mate,
Do you remember all those years gone by?


How, when your mummy left you, how you would cry
Oh, for those days of long, long ago,
Do you remember? You ought to, you know,
Great to be with you as your story is told,
And it is great to be still with you, now that we are old,
Our youth was shared together, as a very special treat,
And we are still here together, which makes it all complete,
It is not everybody who can live to be sixty-five,
Who has been dead thirty years but still looks alive,
Who is falling apart with senile decay,
But friends it is possible, just ask Ray!

Ray and I, on being demobbed from the forces, were going to start up in business together.

We had put a deposit on an old London taxi cab which a chap called Johnnie Littler had to sell. Now this fellow had (and still has) a Garage at Garforth and before Ray and I had a chance to pay the balance of what we owed and collect the taxi, this prat had sold it for more money. My dad had worked with this chap at Smith and Robinsons of Rothwell when he was a tanker driver there, and he went over to Garforth to see this Littler fellow. He says to him, "Tha had better give these lads that brass back that tha's taken off 'em because if tha doesn't, a shall just hev to tear thee bloody head off and stick it up thee bum!" (or words to that effect). We got our money back. He-of-few-words had spoken, had he not. I do often wonder, looking back, what would have happened had Ray and I managed to buy that old taxi.

Would we have become millionaires or finished up as paupers? I often wonder. If we hadn't got our brass back off Littler, would he have still been running around like a headless bloody chicken? Who knows, eh? There was a brickyard at the lower end of the park and a quarry filled with water which was closed during the war. This was also to become our stamping ground where we would break into the brickyard and play with the lorries.

I remember once when we were playing in the brickyard quarry, we pulled the side out of an old shed and threw it into the quarry, which at that time, during the war, was flooded and not in use. Then, using the side of this shed as a raft, we jumped onto it for a little fun. Well, it turned into a bloody nightmare. I would run to one end of the raft until the water came up to my knees and then run to the other end to do the same again. All the lads were frightened to death, including me. Ken Newton shouted something nice like, "Stop it, you daft bastards." It was so funny - but not for long. We all finished up in the water struggling to get out. I was stood on Ken's head, so he had quite a problem until he threw me off! What a bloody state we were in. We found a cave and tried to dry our clothes by lighting a fire. We dared not go home until it was dark. Needless to say, we were in trouble with our parents. I had lost my glasses and my mother bloody near killed me when I arrived home.

My dad, at this time, had an old 1936 Jowett two-cylinder fish and veg van in which I used to give all my mates a ride round our estate. We were, I suppose, really very poor. We hadn't a lot, but we were happy. We would go to Outwood Pictures and sit downstairs in the 7d. section. You had to give an adult your money and ask them to get you into the cinema because we were not allowed in on our own in those days. We lads would stand there outside the cinema with our hands held out, holding our money and begging some adult to take us inside. Just imagine doing that today!

I would sit on the front row, right-end seat with one woodbine in my pocket, well that was all I could afford, unless I could manage to nick one of me dad's capstan full-strength fag ends off the mantelpiece while he was asleep in the chair. I was only about twelve and I used to have half the cig when the first picture came on, saving the other half for the big picture. I thought it was great, even if I did have to take empty pop bottles back to the shop to get the money to go.

We loved it at Saturday dinner (sorry, lunch) times. All us mates went together to the Electric Picture House next to Argos on Westgate in

Wakefield. We would see cowboy films such as *Tom Mix* and serials like *Destry Rides Again* or *The Lone Ranger and Tonto* (and I must not forget his horse Silver too)  Bloody marvellous.  I can't remember what you do when you have sex, or what I did five minutes ago, but I still remember, after fifty-five years, what they called that bloody horse.

Sometimes we went roller-skating, but it was very rare, as we couldn't afford the entrance fee.  Besides, none of us could skate anyway, we only went to see the girls' frilly knickers!

# Life In Wartime

The roller rink used to be where Argos now stands and once a week, they would hold wrestling matches. Yes indeed, in those days Wakefield was quite the merry city.

As my sister and I grew older, Sunday dinner was always special at our house. Meat, veg, Yorkshire puddings and gravy. For sweet, we always had Yorkshire pudding with sugar on. Breakfast was cooked every Sunday morning in the oven on a tin plate by Dad (who couldn't afford the gas, perhaps), Lovely bacon and sausages, tomatoes, eggs swimming around in a sea of fat: a true gourmet's delight. The fat was to dip your bread in and boy did we mop it up! Sunday breakfasts were always special at our house. Sunday tea was usually a salad with jelly and custard for afters.

I remember the times when Mam would shop on a Saturday night at Leeds Market and she would wait until the butchers had nearly finished for the day, when the meat would be sold off cheap.

She would buy the biggest, ugliest and cheapest lump of meat on the stall and bring it home. Then she would tenderise it by knocking hell out of it with a bloody great lump hammer and, boy, was that meat tender. It had to be. If it hadn't succumbed, she would have torn it limb from limb with her bare hands. It just had to surrender, or else. We all had to! My old ma weighed in at eighteen stone and had arms like the back legs of a bloody great shire horse. When she said 'jump', we said 'how high?' Quite a woman, our Hetty, my mam. She would help any lame dog over a stile. We were poor, but both my parents would always find something that they could give to others. Mam always kept a good table. My dad always used to say: "If they don't get it (grub) when they're young, it will be no bloody good to them when they get older", and he would say, about the neighbours opposite who were buying their homes: "That lot are pining (starving) themselves to bloody death, just to have their fine homes."

We were always short of money but we were nourished, sustained and we survived. Dad survived on Carter's little liver pills and, his own favourite, blood and stomach pills. He smoked Capstan full-strength cigs, all well washed down with liberal amounts of Bentley Breweries Best Bitter (and at only 11d. a pint, too).

My ma did her little bit for the war effort. She went back to nursing in Leeds in order to help out and in her spare time, she was the local layer-outer, her own particular speciality.

When any of the neighbours died, our Hetty went along and, laid them out and prepared them for their last journey on earth. You can bet your life that no-one was better prepared for entry into the Kingdom of Heaven than the fortunate corpses laid out by my ma. She was the best and I am sure that Saint Peter, he-who-opens-the-pearly-gates, was proud of her. Even now, as she sits at God's right hand, looking down on us, she is, no doubt, guiding this hand that wields the naughty pen. Her influence has helped me write every line. I am, after all, blood of her blood, life of her life. Yes, she was a very special, assertive, caring, loving woman, was my ma. Quite a lady. I would imagine Moses himself is wilting under the power of her tongue and has become, perhaps, just a little more humble as a result of meeting Ma in all her glory.

During the war, Dad worked as a re-distributer of rationed meat. He was either a modern day Robin Hood or simply a robbing bastard - whichever you may prefer. He would distribute meat to some of the intended destinations and the rest would be delivered to his friends for a small re-muneration. He delivered rationed meat from Wakefield Slaughterhouse to all the butchers in the Wakefield area. What a fiddle that was! He used to short deliver and then deliver the surplus to a well known local butcher. What a character the butcher was. I used to go with Dad on his visits to the butcher over 50 years ago. He had a nice little earner going, what with Dad's knocked-off meat and a few illicit pigs he killed on the side. He was quids in and had more back door customers during the war than all those that used the front doors of his two shops. You did not need a ration book to shop at that butcher's in those days, all you needed, was a purse full of money and a bloody great shopping basket.

I must just mention an instance involving my Uncle Alf (Dad's brother, the butcher) who, during the war, had his own private slaughterhouse and used to kill a few beasts on the side. But the Ministry of Food Inspectors got a whiff that he was on the fiddle. However, they could not prove anything against him, even after breaking into his premises one night to check on him. They found nothing. But when Alf found out, he went to his slaughterhouse, dragged some meat outside, called the Ministry and complained that they had broken into his premises and left all the doors open, allowing the neighbourhood dogs to stroll in and steal and destroy his meat. He won and they had to make up his so-called loss. More stuff was sold on the black market than was ever bought with the ration coupons. That black market was far bigger during the war than the bloody common market is today. I can remember Dad and his mates going on the moors and buying sheep, or even goats, for meat. We didn't starve during the war. In fact, we ate better during that period than we had ever done before the war.

After the war, Dad lost his job at the Busy Bee to an ex 8th airborne paratrooper because, after the war had finished, all returning ex-servicemen were entitled to a job with their ex-employers and quite rightly so, I suppose. Dad was thrown onto the scrap heap again. I'll never forget one day, while on holiday from school, I was helping Dad to load the meat wagon and this ex-soldier had been sent over from Leeds to learn all about Dad's job. Dad was, in effect, showing him the ropes. Now, this young, fit ex-paratrooper was about twenty-five years of age, about six foot in height and about two stone heavier than Dad, and he started to take the mickey out of him in front of Dad's mates, telling Dad what he was going to do with him. But he had obviously underestimated him-of-few words, hadn't he? My old man slowly raised his head, looked at this young kid and said: "Look, lad, tha's on me easy list. Tha won't ever be big enough to do me. No, not while ever tha's got an hole in thee arse and if tha ever does grow to be big enough, tha will just be too bloody old. Now shut thee gob and pee off." (or something similar). He was fifty-one years of age. Now, that paratrooper had landed at Arnhem and he had fought the best that Hitler had to offer. But he had never met anyone before quite like my old dad. No siree. That paratrooper quickly returned to earth with a bang, and soon got his head out of the clouds. I was proud of Dad that day.

I cannot finish this chapter without mentioning some of the great characters that were around at that time: Oliver Taylor and his brothers, Benny and Cyril, were all butchers with stalls on Wakefield market. Big Cyril worked part-time at the slaughterhouse humping (he was a meat porter). He later became the Landlord at The Elephant and Castle in Lofthouse. There was Little Pitchforth the slaughterman. Kenny Gebherd had two butchers' shops, one of which was located at the bottom of little Westgate, near the Ridings entrance. He also had pig-sties just off Leeds Road in Outwood where the council estate is now and where I used to live. There was Joe Law, George Gardner, George Woodcock. I could go on and on. Simmy Stageman had four shops and used to work for my old boss. Old Kilburn, Billy Lumb, Frank Avison, Frank Jowett, Osterliens Hoffman.

On and on. All gone now, but they all left their mark. They were all loveable villains, every one, whose like will never be seen again. Just as an afterthought, it would seem that every bloody butcher in Wakefield kept a few pigs on the side during the war, just to augment their meagre rations, and, of course, to help make their bloody fortunes. That's where they all went, the bastards. They retired to go live on the French Riviera and I am proud to say they were all a part of my life. But, just as it did for my dear old Uncle Alf, the butcher, after the war it all came to an end. Well, all good things must come to an end, as they say. It was good while it lasted.

Uncle Alf retired to his fireside chair and Dad started a little business at the age of fifty-one. This was an age when most men would be thinking of retiring today, but my mam and dad were just starting out again.

# Now It All Begins

After Dad had lost his job at the Busy Bee, he was once again out of work. At that time, after the war, there was very little work to be had due to all the ex-servicemen returning home from the forces and expecting jobs. So what could he do? Where could he go? He was, at this stage in his life, rather desperate and he wasn't a young man. Mother suggested that Dad start his own business. He couldn't get a job so he had no choice. He had just fifty pounds in his pocket, which he had earned from his exploits as a meat re-distributer. He had won some of it at a game called tossing. This was a game that he used to play behind Wakefield meat market, in which they would toss coins into the air and play odds and evens. Unfortunately, my mother found out about the winnings so the plans that Dad had made for spending his ill-gotten gains didn't come to fruition. He, my mother insisted, had to go out and buy an old van. So he purchased an old pre-war 1932 Jowett van.

Now, listen to this. They both started from scratch. No business, no customers, no nothing. They went to Leeds market, bought some fish, and travelled around the Barnsley area, knocking on doors until they had sold it. They didn't come home until it was sold because it wouldn't keep 'til the next day. I used to sit outside on the front wall and wait for them to come home, scared to death of the dark. They then diversified into fruit and veg, going to the Leeds market at 4am every morning in order to bring home celery and fish etc. They would clean it in the upstairs bath before setting off on their travels. Wonderful! That was the woman who was behind the man, who was behind me. She was responsible for it all happening. For my part, I thought it marvellous that they had a van and over the next few years, I would wash the various vans and sometimes, with a little help from Mr Berry (our next door neighbour), I would help to repair them. Dad didn't bother much, just so long as they kept going. He would wait until a cylinder block cracked before he ever thought about antifreeze. Tyres would wear down to the canvas and blow out before Dad would change them. I think, on reflection, he was at an age where it didn't matter any more. Not that anything had ever mattered much to my dad anyway. He still floated through life, like a petal on the breeze, without a bloody care in the world. Come a day, go a day. God send Sunday. That was me dad. Mam did all the worrying for the both of them. She had to. As long as Dad managed to get his newspaper and his few pints down at the pub, then he was happy. I have never met a more contented man. It was Ma that had all the aggro.

I learned to drive at fourteen years of age in the old Jowett, taking my mates for a ride round the streets. Dad used to rent some pig-sties at the side of the Woodman Inn on Leeds Road in Outwood. Yes anybody with any sense had a pig in their back garden during the war. Why? Well, meat was rationed and there was a thriving black market out there. One had to bring home the bacon, hadn't one?

Dad used to go to the Woodman Inn on Leeds Road at Outwood for a pint every Sunday lunchtime while I mucked out the pigs. I was as happy as the proverbial. I think Dad rather fancied the landlady and while her husband was away in the army, doing his duty, fighting for king and country, Dad was also perhaps doing his little bit (on the side) for the war effort by looking after the pub landlady, or so me mam thought.

That was until her husband got back home from the war of course. Unfortunately, my dad never did get the medal he was entitled to for doing his bit during the war. However, when I knew it was time for the pub to close, I would start his van's engine for him. You could never use the starter motor because either that or the battery was always knackered. Dad hadn't a care in the world: brakes, starters and things like that were luxuries. You had to slur you feet on the floor to stop any of Dad's motors. Anyway, this particular Sunday, as I tried to start the van, the starting handle kept slipping out and banging against the radiator. The radiator sprung a leak at that precise moment that he-of-a-few-words came out of the pub. "Ah," says he. "I see tha's thumped it and thumped it till tha's thumped a bleeding hole int' radiator." I wanted to die! Then he says, "Well, we'd better get in it and let's see what sort of a bloody tow tha makes at driving it." That was Dad all right, man-of-few-words. But the words that he did use were clearly understood, even if I did need a French dictionary to decipher a few of his choicer phrases. On very rare occasions, we used to go to the seaside in that old van.

(Well, we often tried). It took so long to get there that by the time we got to Scarborough it would be time to set off back. But it was great. Mam and Dad in the front (our Lenore and me) in the back. We had to stop going up Garrowby Hill and all get out to look for the bloody impro-vised rubber radiator cap which used to blow off every time the radiator boiled. Yes, it was great fun and a real treat. It was quite an event in those days to be able to go to the seaside. The number of times Dad ran out of petrol was unbelievable. Some of us learn by our mistakes, but not

Dad. He just carried on, dropping his own goolies in his own sweet way. Nothing, but nothing, bothered him. I suppose after being married to my mother all those years and being lashed with her tongue every day of his married life, he had become immune, insulated, and impervious to everything and anything around him. He was, perhaps, in a permanent trance. Well, who could really blame him for switching off?

I remember an occasion when he was travelling up Kirkgate in Wakefield with Ivor Applegarth, the auctioneer, when a couple of wagon wheels passed them by. Dad said to Ivor, "Bloody hell, Ivor, some silly bugger's just lost their wheels!" Then, two seconds later, there was a bump and a squeal as the back end of Dad's van hit the floor. Dad says to Ivor, "Oh, bloody hell! I reckon they must have been mine!" He couldn't have cared less. He used to park anywhere. It just didn't matter. It is a bloody good job that he never considered going down to London to see the Queen because if he had, those guardsmen would have stood no bloody chance, not with my dear old dad. Oh no, he would have driven straight up to those Palace gates in London and parked outside until Her Majesty chose to see him, guards or no bloody guards. I remember when he would park right outside the police station in Wood Street in Wakefield, while he collected some house keys from Laidlaws, the Estate Agents. Old George, the bobby, used to come out and he would say to me, "Bloody hell. Charlie, where is he? We can't have this. I shall have to do him. He can't park here, what will the Superintendent say?" He never got done though. When he did, his mate the Superintendent used to look after him. He got reported, yes, a few times, but he was never charged. It was just like when he used to do long distance removals, when he was only supposed to travel within a fifteen mile radius of Wakefield Post Office. He would say, "If I have to pay the same bloody road tax as BRS and they can go anywhere, then so can I!"

So that's just what he did. He was reported. But I don't ever remember him being prosecuted. I think our local coppers just gave up on him. He would go the wrong way down one-way streets and then, when he was confronted by oncoming traffic, he would say, "Where the bloody hell do they think they're going, then?" He used to leave me in the van at the top of Westgate in Wakefield in the rush-hour traffic, while he popped across the road to the building society to draw some brass (as he used to call it). Everyone had to wait, including me, with a red face, while Westby got his brass. We were once parked in the middle of Huddersfield at a set of traffic lights on green, while he-of-few-words went across the road to ask directions to Beaumonts Furniture warehouse. Meanwhile, a bloody great line of frustrated motorists had to wait until Westby was ready to move on. Just imagine all that naked power! I would just love to have the guts to do that. Even Nero, who fiddled while Rome burned, couldn't have held a candle to my dear old dad, bless him. He was a law unto himself, a true non-conformist, of the old school of radicals!

Mam and Dad eventually bought a new Bradford Jowett van in 1948. At that time, just after the war, there was a waiting list of twelve months or more for all new motor vehicles. So Dad in his wisdom had ordered two, a Bradford and a Ford. They both arrived at around the same time, so Dad, not to be deterred, took them both and sold the Ford to his mate at a substantial profit.

But after a while of hawking fish, fruit and veg and trying to come to terms with the fact that, because of bad debts, they were owed more than they were taking, Mam and Dad decided to move on to pastures new. Well Mam did. Dad couldn't have cared bloody less. They sold the little van and bought a second hand 15cwt 1934 Commer and, once again, they found themselves with no customers and no work. So Mother went out and found some. She would go to Saville, Kilburns and Laidlaws salesrooms in Wakefield and she would bribe the auctioneers with cups of tea. Yes, she was a very resourceful lady, was Ma. Then, after the sale was over, she would go to all the people who had bought things and ask if she could deliver the goods for them, which, believe me, takes some guts.

So that was how Walkers of Wakefield Ltd was born in 1948. It came into being through the enterprise, persistence and determination of my old mam. In the meantime, my dad was getting part-time jobs in the salesrooms, which put him where he needed to be, right at the centre of things. This provided him with an income while he got himself established. From there he moved on to collecting furniture and bringing it to the salesrooms. He charged 25 shillings an hour and gave a bloke on the dole 30 shillings a day (as well as buying his dinner) for helping him. He moved from there on to house removals. Years later he still didn't have a proper licence to do removal work, and Pickfords removals shopped him to the Licensing Authority in Leeds. They objected to him doing removals without a licence. It was here that a chap called Mr Gilbey, who had sold his business to Pickfords, was to step in. Mr Gilbey was an influential notary in Wakefield at that time and went with Dad in front of the Traffic Commissioners in Leeds to fight Pickfords, a battle which Dad was to win. The Traffic Commissioner asked Dad how long he had been doing removals, to which he replied, "Fourteen years, Sir."

He then showed him a photo of the van, which had a draft board on the front saying:

'YOUR MOVE NEXT' and on the side it said, 'LET US DO YOUR MOONLIGHT FLIT'

The court was in stitches.

The Traffic Commissioner laughed and said to Pickford's

solicitor, "If it has taken you fourteen years to find out that this man has been operating outside the law, then you are just a little too late, because after fourteen years, he has obviously established a need and I shall grant him a licence.

"Good luck," he says to my Dad. So there he was again, not even the mighty Pickfords in all their glory, or for that matter, the law of the land, got the better of my old man.

He had most definitely been breaking the law for fourteen years and he had got away with it too.

So for the first time in fourteen years, he was able to do removals within the law and it was thanks to Mr. Gilbey and the Traffic Commissioner that he was able to remain in business.

Mind, I think he would have anyway, no matter what the verdict, eh? It was from these humble beginnings that I was to take over W. Walkers and Son and make it into a nationally known company, Walkers of Wakefield Ltd. But the tragedy was that my father and mother never lived to see the acorn that they had planted in 1948 grow to become such a mighty oak.

(And that, dear reader, is my one regret).

Dad had said to me when he became ill, "Tha will have to take it over and tha will have more work than tha knows what to do with."

When he died, I did what he had asked and he was right.

The turnover in 1964 was £1,500 a year and by 1987 we were earning up to £300,000 a month.

I eventually did, as my dad had predicted in 1964, get more work than I needed for my own fleet of vehicles. But, contrary to what Dad had thought when he said, "Tha will have more work than tha knows what to do with," I knew exactly what to do with it. I subcontracted all the surplus work to other haulage contractors from all over the country and to many who were nationally known and much larger than we were. But that is another story, for another day...

# A Butcher Boy To Be

I was to leave school at fourteen and went to work at Zieglers the Buthchers. I was a pork butcher's apprentice, but I first worked in the bakery making buns, tarts, pies and bread etc. We developed a way to give hard, stale bread a new lease of life. We soaked it for four hours in a pansion (a big bowl) of water and then put it back in the oven. It came out as fresh as ever - great! We killed pigs, made sausages, brawn, potted meat, haslet, penny duck etc. Lovely grub!

We would cure our own bacon down in the cellars beneath the shop. Yes, bacon that was properly cured, unlike the bloody rubbish sold in supermarkets today, where it is cut as thin as tissue paper and full of water. It didn't need a fridge for keeping in, either. Proper cured bacon will keep for months. Well, I suppose supermarkets and today's modern housewives deserve each other, because a young woman of today would not recognise a decent piece of meat even if it was to talk to her. She just doesn't have a clue what cuts to ask for. She is quite happy (like those up-market chefs) as long as it is lean and looks nice. It just don't matter what it tastes like. There used to be an old saying that our grandmothers, in their wisdom, would utter from time to time: "The nearer the bone, the sweeter the meat and you need the fat from the meat to cook it in." (They were right too). But today the fat is trimmed from the meat to be used by fish fryers, to give the fish and chips a decent taste.

The best cuts come from the loins (of men, too). Crop of beef is the best cut - it is near the bone and has its share of fat. Loins of pork and lamb come next, hence yer chops. Ah, well. There is nothing wasted on a pig. They even fitted its squeal onto Ford truck brakes. All the best butchers in Wakefield were Germans such as Zieglers, Hoffman and Oesterlein. The all came over between the wars.

After about a year at Zieglers, I moved to Kilburns in Wakefield. The making up department, or food processing plant as it would be called today, was down Queen Street at the back of the shop.

There used to be toilets opposite, on the other side of the road, where Argos is now situated. Those toilets were for us men to use. The ladies had their toilet upstairs, above the shop.

Well, they just would, wouldn't they?

There were coal cellars under the road in those days. I should know, I used to go down there for coal every time I saw a cracking bit of stuff waiting for a bus in a queue down on Queen Street. Oh, what a view I had through that coal grate! Much, much better than anything the butler saw and it was all for free!

Which reminds me: the two shop girls we worked with, Hilda and Mona, were much older than me. We would boil pig bag and chitlings and put them in a large container of water for Hilda and Mona to collect and sell in the shop. They always came in at 2pm and I always put the container at the top of the cellar steps. I was never there, of course, I was always busy down the cellar - especially when they were bending over to retrieve the pig bag and chitlings. Yes, I was growing up!

We had some great times at Kilburns. Jack Talbot, the best pork butcher in Wakefield, was my gaffer. Jack was as deaf as a bloody post, I knew that all right, but I didn't know he could lip read. That was until I felt his clog on my arse. A local celebrity Frank Hepworth (Heppy) was my best mate. Frank had just come out of the Navy, where he had been employed as a ship's radio operator. Well, that's what he told everybody. I personally think he was the ship's cabin boy, yer know, a proper little nancy boy, like. Those little cabin boys, whilst at sea, were employed to sleep with the Captain and all his mates, so I suppose Frank, in his small way, did his own bit for the war effort. But that is all he bloody did. For while our gallant sailors were risking life and limb, braving those Atlantic storms and dodging those German U-boats, bringing all those urgent war materials and foodstuffs from America to Britain, where was our hero, the redoubtable Frank? Well, he was in bed with his Captain, sailing somewhere off the coast of Bermuda on a bloody cruise liner.

Now, Frank's dear elder sister, Audrey, had just married Frank Kilburn Junior and I actually think she married him just to make sure that their Frank could get a job, because to my mind there was just no other way that lazy, idle little git could have got a job anywhere at that time in his life. Later in life, he became a famous entertainer - one of the original, redoubtable Kalahari Bushmen of Wakefield. Why they chose that name, Christ only knows, because the real, proper Kalahari Bushmen live in hiding in a remote part of Africa and are very small, little people. Well, that about sums up the Wakefield lot, I reckon. Maybe they should have done us all a favour and settled in Africa with their erstwhile adopted relatives. The prats.

After retiring, Frank did manage to get a little worthwhile, part-time job delivering flowers for their dear Audrey, but that is another story. I think he probably made a better job of that than he ever did of singing. Oh, the sacrifices that woman made for her brother were just unbelievable. I am of course joking.

It was around 1946 that Frank was given a job at Kilburns and he naturally copped for a bloody soft job, didn't he? He drove the meat delivery van, an old pre-war Daimler with a pre-selector box that had been converted into a van. Just as a matter of interest, Frank's van driving days didn't last too long because shortly after she got Frank a job, Audrey left Frank Kilburn and upped and married George Malcolm the florist, and as a result our hero Heppy finished up selling bacon butties from a little shop at the bottom of Warrengate. Funnily enough, now that he has retired from business, Frank does occasionally deliver flowers for their Audrey and George Malcolm from their florists, right next door to that little shop where Frank first started in business. So their lass is bailing him out again, after all these years. I think he rather liked driving vans, the lazy git.

There was an old family tradition at Kilburns: you always got your breakfast and dinner for free, but by God you worked hard for your grub and the 25 bob a week you were paid. Mind you, I got a bonus once a year at Christmas. I would walk to work on a Sunday, work all day plucking poultry, and at the end of it all, I would be given 2 shillings and sixpence for my trouble - wonderful! I must have been barmy, or perhaps I just couldn't resist those breakfasts. Oh, those breakfasts! We had an old codger called Percy who used to cook breakfasts and dinners for us upstairs. Every morning Jack, my gaffer, used to send me upstairs with a great dollop of sausages and bacon and these were, with out a doubt, the best bloody sausages in Wakefield. Why? Because the best sausage is not ready for eating until it is just on the turn (just going off). When it becomes sticky, it is ripe for eating and our sausages were kept until they were ripe. Ours were made from special, secret ingredients, handed down through the generations and as only a proper sausage can, they could, and did, burst in the frying pan.

I know I shouldn't be harping on about something as mundane as a mere sausage, but boy, what sausages they were! Those superbly succulent, sensuous sexy sausages, sizzling together in throbbing, hot fat, just dying to burst out of their skins and on to one's plate, and when they did it was like an erotic symphony of pure magic; a sight to behold, a moment to remember. Those sensational sausages, singing and dancing in that sea of steaming hot fat. Yes, what a moment, truly a moment to savour, a crescendo of sound and music, a rhapsody to hear and to cherish, yes an unforgettable moment.

Yes, indeed they were a true gourmet's delight. I will never, ever forget those bloody brilliant, wonderful sausages that Jack made. Old Percy, the cook, used to always save some potatoes from the previous

54

day's lunch which he would fry with the sausage and bacon. We had fresh bread and tomato sauce, cooked in our own kitchen upstairs. It used to be an old tradition in those days that all pork butchers shops would provide there staff with dinner and breakfast. Well, what more could a man want?

We had meals fit for a king. The only problem was, of course, that having fed us, our employers didn't feel the need to pay us a wage as well!

At sixteen, I was as fit as a buck lop and as strong as a horse. I used to carry hinds of frozen beef (hard as a rock, weighing well over 200 pounds), ten stone bags of rusks upstairs, and one hundredweight bags of salt, one under each arm, into the cellar. Boy, were we fit! Jack could lift himself up with one arm and, hand on a meat hook, he could pull his whole body off the floor and raise his chin above the hook with only one hand. This was all down to our wonderful sausages.

We wore clogs at work, they kept your feet warm and on some feet they became lethal weapons. Jack was a master with his footwork. Anybody who hasn't been kicked in the arse by a sixteen stone man wearing size ten clogs simply hasn't lived. It is most definitely an unforgettable experience. He was quite a character, our Jack. He had fiddles going everywhere. Every week I would take parcels of meat out to his barber and his bookie. He didn't pay for ow't, but he was a great guy. I will never forget those days. He came to see me as an old man when I was in business at Flanshaw some forty years later, and he came back to my home, later with a parcel of - guess what? Yes, his special, wonderful, glorious sausages! They were wonderful days to grow up in. It was hard work, but very satisfying and I shall never forget Kilburns and the great people I worked with. We would play cards at lunchtimes with the shop girls and the bakery staff. We fellas would have preferred to play at cheekies with the girls, but they just wouldn't let us. I do remember one girl, Mona Sandy was her name, and for some reason she always seemed to win at cards (probably because she cheated).

### Pontoon

When Mona played cards, she always called the tune.
Never was she known to ever lose at pontoon
Mona would always get twenty and often twenty-one.
So I decided to never play cards with a daughter,
I would only play cards with a son.

Frank Kilburn was also a great guy and he was a very, very imaginative businessman who had some brilliant ideas for producing unusual, made-up concoctions. We would make brawn and then ladle it into pansions, but this wasn't good enough for Frank. He went out and bought some metal jelly moulds into which half of the brawn would be placed and sold for twice as much as normal. We used to roll brisket and put it into brine (salt and water) for three days and then boil it and press it. He would then sell it like hot cakes in the shops by the quarter. He would also make all sorts of blancmanges and creams etc. in fact anything that would increase his already massive profitability. He once went out and bought a bloody canning machine with which we would fill empty cans with sausage meat. We would then put water in the top, put the lid on and squeeze out the air and water as the top was sealed. These cans of sausage meat would then be placed in the boiler and, once they were cooked, Frank would empty the can and sell the sausage meat in the shop by the quarter. He called it chicken and ham roll. Not bad, eh?

We used barley kernels as the binder for our pie meat. They shared wooden bins upstairs with cockroaches and God knows whatever the other insects were called. The rats had a beano, and all those obscure ingredients along with their droppings must have been all that was required to give our pies that very special flavour. It was probably these little, special extras that made them simply the best pies in Wakefield. Ah well, so much for modern hygiene improvements. What a blessing they are. Truly, you cannot buy a decent bloody pie today and there have been many deaths from salmonella, an infection we had never even heard of when I was a lad. Perhaps we should bring some of those cockroaches and rat droppings back to help us develop healthier eating habits, and to stimulate our immune system eh!

While I was at Kilburns, one of the lads in the bakehouse used to come to work on a motorbike and he used to park it outside the toilet. Now I had been dying to have a go on this motorbike for weeks, not withstanding the fact that I had never ever been on one before. I didn't know how to do it without the owner hearing me start it up, but then like a bolt out of the blue, I had a brilliant idea. I would jump on it and ride down Queen Street without the engine running and once I got to George Street at the bottom, I would put the bike into gear, let out the clutch, start the engine and away I'd go.

However, things didn't quite turn out like that. The bloody thing just wouldn't start, and I carried on past George Street onto Ings Road and the bloody thing still wouldn't start! I stopped and tried to kick-start the bike but all to no avail. I pushed it all the way back onto Ings Road, up Kirkgate, onto Westgate and back down Queen Street. Lo and behold, who should be stood there waiting for me with hands on hips and looking quite aggressive, nasty in fact? The baker who owned the bike and Jack, my boss. There they stood like two avenging angels. The first to strike was the baker, who cracked me around the ear hole, calling me a silly bastard. Then he told me that if I ever wanted to borrow his motorbike, I should ask him for the key first, because the poxy thing just wouldn't start without a key (it was fitted with coil ignition!) Boy, was I knackered! I had pushed that bleeding bike about two miles, but it hadn't ended yet. Oh no. Now it was Jack's turn. He booted me up the arse and called me a silly little prat.

Well, I suppose he was somewhat justified (but I wish he had taken his bloody clogs off first!) because it was, after all, 3pm and I was only allowed one hour for dinner, if I was lucky. But what a way to learn to ride a bloody motorbike.

# The Teenage Years

Around this time, my old mate Frank Hepworth was going around with a beautiful, ravishing blonde called Pat. A real cracker, in fact. Unfortunately for Frank, Pat was the daughter of Nash Shakespeare, who, unlike his namesake, William (of *A Midsummer Night's Dream* fame and 'To be or not to be'), was trying to make sure it was certainly not going to be. Well, not with his darling daughter, anyway.

Nash was a redoubtable character around town in those days. He was quite a villain and a bloody hard-case to boot, and there was just no way he was going to allow Frank to violate his lovely daughter. So Nash decided he would kill Frank instead. This was developing into a bloody pantomime and becoming far more exciting than anything Nash's namesake had ever written. Frank dared not go out of the house for three months since Nash would have killed him. So Frank decided he would give up the chase (by chase I mean Nash chasing Frank, not Frank chasing Nash's lovely daughter). Ah well! Instead, Frank decided to retire to his bed, perchance to dream (wet ones preferred and as many as possible).

In the end, Frank was not prepared to die for it and decided to do a far better thing than he had ever done before. So he came out of hiding with a white flag and he upped and surrendered, the bloody coward. But who could really blame him?

We had some great times together in our youth, going on pub crawls and to nightclubs. I was only a kid of around sixteen or seventeen and I hadn't a lot of money, but Frank always saw me right. In fact, on reflection, he bloody well corrupted me. I was only a minor and he was the elder brother. I was sixteen and he was in his twenties. I was nobbut a baby.

We had some right nights out in *The Ram* at the bottom of Queen Street. I used to prop myself up around the piano, with Frank and all the lads singing *When the Saints Come Marching In* before heading off to the *Embassy* Ballroom down Market Street. Then, after about ten pints of Tetleys Bitter, at 11p. a pint, Fred Astaire had nothing on us lads. We were the bees' knees. Well, at least we thought we were (and that's all that mattered!)

It was so funny because between 8pm and 11pm, The *Embassy* was deserted (apart from the girls), since us lads dared not go near the bloody place, let alone ask a girl to dance, without our few pints of Dutch courage. But, after the pubs turned out, well, that was a different story all together. Away we would dash to the dance and, on arrival, stand in the doorway and shout, "Here we are. Come and get us, girls!" and boy could we dance! If we couldn't we just stood in the middle of the dance floor and squeezed the lucky girl. More often than not, we usually got there just in time for the last waltz and just in time to walk the girl of our choice home afterwards, whoever she may have been. Yes, we were proper little gentlemen in those days and looked after our charges.

It's not like that today. The girls are bunged into a taxi after he-of-ill-repute has had his wicked way with her, and sent home to her mum like a discarded chocolate wrapper after that selfish bastard of a modern male has tasted and enjoyed the chocolate (the jammy git).

No, we were just not like today's modern youths, not at all.

We were just silly, daft prats who couldn't afford taxi fares. We sometimes had to walk the girlfriends home to their front gates, maybe three or four miles, before proceeding to our own homes, which could perhaps even be the same distance again. For our troubles, if we were lucky, we would maybe get a peck on the cheek or, if our hands happened to stray to the wrong parts of her-of-high-virtue's anatomy, we would get a smack in the gob instead!

Gee, but it was great staying out late, walking your baby back home on a Saturday night. But it wasn't so bloody great at three o'clock on a cold and frosty winter's chuffing Sunday morning, having left her with her virginity intact and a little smug smile on her face, hopping away with one leg stuck up in the air, making your own way home. On that lonely road back home, one had plenty of time to exercise one's thoughts and give vent to one's frustrations and pent-up emotions, by attempting to kick oneself in the goolies or by taking one's revenge on an unsuspecting, passing cat (preferably a female one) or someone's front door. Yes, it was wonderful (and, may I add, very satisfying) to know that one had behaved like a proper little gentleman and that one was, after all, a decent chap who had taken his mum's advice and had, once again, held out against those sins of the flesh. It was also nice to know that one's virginity was still intact too. But at odd times, and on deeper reflection, I couldn't help myself thinking that chance would have been a bloody fine thing and what a bloody idiot I had been.

Anticipation is great than realisation (as they say) and I was ever the proverbial frustrated optimist with an unfulfilled mission in life, flogging a dead horse in my unremitting search for the perfect deaf and dumb, partly paralysed nymphomaniac.

But I had to struggle on, mile after unforgiving mile, before I realised she just didn't exist. I searched, oh how I searched, but I was to search in vain.

However, I was learning my lessons in life and yes, I was growing up.

Wakefield was indeed the merry city in those days. There were six cinemas, four dance halls and dozens of pubs. Every pub had music or dancing and occasionally both.

Kirkgate and Upper Kirkgate, to the top of Westgate, was the bunny run.

This was where boys and girls paraded up and down on a Saturday night in there best bibs and tuckers, eyeing each other up and down and sniffing each other out. Yes, we were all out there on display.

The girls would probably be saying, "Oh, I fancy him with that crew cut" or "What about him in them there brothel creepers (suede shoes)?" or "Oh, he's dishy. Him with the squint eye." (me) I should have been so bloody lucky.

Of course, us young innocent boys would be saying, in our turn:

"Whoa, I'd love to give her one. I wonder if she's got her knickers in her handbag?" Oh, how we would dream. But it was rarely fulfilled. Well, that was unless, of course, one was lucky enough to fall asleep and have an erotic dream, only to wake up with rice pudding for breakfast. Ooh, aarh!

Those girls were like bloody Black Widow spiders, whose only ambition in life seemed to be to want to get some silly fellow to place an engagement ring on their finger. Then, given half a chance, they would have eaten us alive, whereas we young innocent lads, with our now't but honourable intentions, had but one objective, and that was to help the unsuspecting female to lose her virginity - and as soon as possible.

The girls probably had the same idea but they had no chance because their mas, the rotten sods, had fitted them all with chastity belts (or at least that's what we were told!) and then hung the keys around their own necks, just for safe-keeping like. In those day, just saying you loved your girlfriend wasn't quite enough to make her capitulate. You had to go the whole hog and buy her a ring and promise to marry her and all that rubbish. Then, and only then, she-of-high-virtue, might (I said only might) succumb to your blandishments. That is if she could ever steal that bloody key from around her ma's neck!

When we lads went a-courting in those days, it was a real challenge because we didn't just carry a condom in our back pockets, oh no. We had to carry a bloody tin opener, an electric drill and a pair of bloody pliers to gain access to - or through - those bloody awful chastity belts.

I must repeat again, Wakefield was indeed the place to be in the 1950s. People travelled in from miles around just to be in our town. We had music, dancing and waiter service in the pubs. There were wonderful times to grow up in. Which reminds me of my first nearly proper date. It was with one of the shop girls at Kilburns. Hilda Ellis was her name and she was a real cracker. At twenty-six years of age, she was in her prime. What I would have loved to do to Hilda was nobody's business. Oh boy, did I lust after Hilda. Well, Jack my boss must have known this and he and Hilda set me up. Jack told me that she fancied me something rotten and that she wanted to go out with me. Oh, my prayers had been answered at last, the lovely Hilda was to be mine! So a date was arranged: I would meet her in the *Chantry* Pub on Wood Street in Wakefield the following Saturday. I was enraptured. I couldn't sleep, I couldn't think. Boy, what was I not going to do to the delightful Hilda! I was ten foot tall. However, I had one problem, I didn't have a decent bloody suit to wear. So I had to sneak a flashy maverick waistcoat and my dad's best check suit out of his wardrobe, and away I tripped like a little lamb to the slaughter to do battle with the redoubtable Hilda. I certainly felt like the renowned Clark Gable. But at sixteen, I was hardly prepared, equipped or qualified to play the part, but at the time I thought I was the bees' knees, especially in Dad's best suit. So debonair. So elegant.

I swept - no, not walked - swept into the *Chantry* like Bat Masterson at the OK Corral. Boy, was I going to sweep her off her feet! I half expected her to fall into my arms as I came through the door, but Hilda hadn't arrived. I sauntered to the bar, gazing up into the ceiling, and I asked for a pint of bitter while I nonchalantly rested my elbow on the bar and looked down at my fingernails in the best Humphrey Bogart style. However, before I could complete the charade by slowly turning to look around the bar, a voice behind me said, "Now, you can just P*** off out of here, you little prat, and ask yer mam to send you back if and when she ever gets you out of those bloody nappies!" The pub landlord had spoken. Oh, was I ashamed! Oh, were my illusions shattered! Oh, was my ego deflated! You can just bet your beautiful bottoms they were. I had floated in like a petal on the breeze, but I quickly ran out of there like a proper little wilting violet.

The magnificent Hilda (the bastard) never did turn up. What a set-up! But I had learned an important lesson - never bite off more than you can chew. I realise now, I was lucky to be alive and I count my blessings. If Hilda had turned up and meant business, she would have eaten me alive and blown me (and my dad's best suit) out in bubbles. Dread the thought.

## HILDA

Hilda they called her, that was her name,
Inviting me out was her wicked game,
Like a lamb to the slaughter I was to go,
Darling dear Hilda, well she never did show,
Arrive she chose not to, she stayed home instead
And I'm glad she didn't do the business,
for I might have been dead

I arrived for our date at the chosen hour,
But I soon came away, like a wilting little flower,
Now I am much older and more worldly wise,
I realise she was a man-eater, a man-eater in disguise.

# I Meet My Waterloo

**RASC**
Remember Always Someone Cares

**R** stands for the Royal, Royal and true to the line,
**A** stands for the action we saw, down in old Palestine,
**S** stands for service, service by day and by night,
**C** stands for the colours we wore, blue, yellow and white.

At seventeen and a half years of age, in 1948, I was seconded, at His Majesty's Pleasure, into the Royal Artillery at Oswestry in Shropshire for six weeks' intensive training as part of the army's plan to make a soldier out of me. They couldn't have succeeded if they had kept me for sixty bloody years. What an experience that was. I was grinning like a bloody Cheshire cat when I first had the pleasure of meeting the junior NCOs. That was the last time I smiled for the next two years. They didn't actually welcome us by hitting us around the earholes with pick-axe handles; they didn't have to, did they? Their looks were enough. We were all made to feel as if we were something lower than the low that had just crawled out of the woodwork. We eyed our formidable opponents for the next six weeks with trepidation, tinged with a little terror. We dropped our eyes, shrugged our shoulders and decided that there was just no way were we going to win at their game, on their terms. So we just surrendered on the spot and were taken from our mother's arms and thrown, headfirst, into a den of iniquity like Christians to the slaughter. The lion's den could simply not compare with those first six weeks of army life.

Our Sergeant Major was not very thin,
Somebody threw a tomato at him,
Tomatoes are soft, wrapped in a skin,
But this bloody tomato was wrapped in a tin.

We all felt sorry for our Sergeant Major. He was born out of wedlock (a proper bastard) and we all thought that his mother must have been a part-time biology expert who had accidentally inseminated herself with the sperm from a redundant bloody crocodile. He would say. "You may have broken your poor mother's heart but you won't break mine." The bastard!

A lot of the lads were homesick during our early training and one could hear them sobbing into their pillows at night, crying for their mams. That training period was hell. We were confined to barracks for six weeks and had to run everywhere on the double. Up at 5.30am, beds made up, blankets folded perfectly and kit (that you had been polishing half the bloody night) laid out for inspection. If you were not out of bed when the guard commander came round, you were thrown out onto the floor. The rules were simple: you only spoke when spoken to, you did as you were told, you respected senior officers and NCOs and you stood to attention when addressed by them. The penalties for breaking any rules were simpler still. You lost your privileges, your time, your leave, your freedom and sometimes your sanity.

We were put into billets with twenty-nine other recruits and confined there for the duration of our training. We polished every piece of kit until it shone like gold (the brass work we received hadn't been touched since the First World War) and you could see to shave in the tips of our boots. Even the studs were polished. Civvy Nick had now't on the army in those days. The orders were as follows. If you can move it, pick it up; if it doesn't move, paint it; and if it does move, you bloody well salute it. I was transferred into the RASC (Remember Always Someone Cares) and posted to Taunton in Somerset. I was downgraded due to very limited sighting in my right eye and I was transferred because I could never have become a gunner I always did what I had to do, I was never just a gunner. I had in fact originally been put on a posting to go to East Africa, but that was not to be, because when I told Mam, she just didn't seem to take kindly to the idea. Well, she said, there is no way they're are going to send you to East Africa, or anywhere else for that matter. No son of mine is going to be eaten alive by them bloody wogs. Army or no bloody army. My mam had spoken and as usual, the world had to stand still. She wrote letters to the army, telling the top army brass about my bad eyes my rheumatic fever, my pain in the arse.

But it made no difference. The army persisted in their burning desire to send me as far away as possible. (Who could blame them, really eh?) But it was not to be and our Hetty, my mam, pulled her final stroke, played her last card and the army just had to unconditionally surrender without a fight. They hadn't of course, come across anyone quite like our Hetty before.

What she did was to go to bed and send for the doctor, whom she

64

convinced that she was at death's door, just waiting for God to let her through. Well, she kidded the doctor, who believed she was dying, and he in turn rushed off a letter to my Commanding Officer to request that I be given leave of absence to comfort my poor old mum on her deathbed. I came home on compassionate grounds on a month's leave, all paid for by the army. Mam couldn't get out of that bloody bed quick enough to welcome me home and minister to my needs. Pity I wasn't called into the army during the war, because my old ma would have taken on that bloody Hitler single-handed if there had ever been any danger of him hurting a single hair on her little darling's head.

I met all sorts of characters while in the forces, from all over the place. There were Geordies, Liverpool (Scouse) fly boys, Scots (so-called) hardcases and Cockney wide-boys. We were all rivals and tribalism was rife. It does rather make me smile when people talk about racialism today, because we all think that we are a little different from the next guy. If I come from, say, Yorkshire, then I am much happier and have a closer affinity with another Yorkshireman than I could ever have with, say, a Cockney or a Scouser. Natural common sense, I calls it.

My best mate came from just across the border from Yorkshire (I was best man at his wedding). His name was Johnny Oliver and he came from Widnes in Lancashire. We went into the army together on the same day and came out together on the same day.

I was posted to an RASC Food Supply Depot at Taunton in Somerset for further training.

Yes, I was in the army for feeding them, not when they were needing them!

It was there that I got my first real hiding and where I developed a completely new perspective on life. I was a big, strong, fit young lad at the time (well, I weighed in at all of ten stone seven pounds) and I rather fancied myself as a bit of a scrapper. After all, I had been the cock of the school before I left and was the kingpin in our platoon.

Well, one particular day we were having boxing lessons given by a PTI (Physical Training Instructor) who just happened to be an army boxer, and he was demonstrating a blocking move against a straight left. I was boxing with him. He asked me to let go with a straight left, which I did, catching him bang on the chin. He didn't like that at all and, being a boxer and an NCO, he could hardly retaliate, could he? But the bastard did the next best thing. He picked the biggest, roughest, oldest, meanest Scots son-of-a-bitch in the camp and he said (to this Scots git). "Right, you're Freddie Mills." He then said to me. "And you, my little petal, are Bruce Woodcock and you are about to fight for the championship of the world. Now, let's see what you're made of!"

This Scotsman started out by stalking me, feinting, bobbing and weaving and I thought to myself. "This is it, this fellow had done a lot of this boxing lark before," and he most certainly had. In no time at all, he had flattened me and Bruce Woodcock had lost his title. It certainly taught me a lesson. Not 'arf. If he could do me, how many more could?

I wondered if perhaps I wasn't so smart after all. I started to back off a bit. I was growing up and learning fast. Mind you, I wasn't too badly disgraced because I learned later that this same Scotsman was a boxer and he finished up in the Glasshouse in Colchester after he had flattened three sergeants in Germany.

I will never forget Taunton and that proper Taunton Farmhouse cider or, to give it its proper title, firewater. We lads thought that we could drink anybody under the table, until we came face to face with our ready-made Waterloo. Oh yes, of course we could drink it all right, and we could handle a maximum of two pints of the stuff without falling over in the pub.

But we eventually learned to call it the Landlord's last goodbye, because, as soon as we opened the pub door to step outside, the fresh air would hit us like an hurricane from hell and we would immediately fall down flat and then make an unsuccessful attempt to seduce the pavement.

Then, in sheer frustration and despair, we would quickly fall into a drunken stupor and complete oblivion. If we had dropped a few barrels of that Taunton Cider on Berlin during the war, it would have been over in a matter of months, not years. What a sly, sneaky, unexplored secret weapon that could have been.

I must confess that the road sweepers in Taunton got a little p....d off at having to constantly sweep us squadies off their pavements in the mornings!

So those were my memories of Taunton in Somerset.

After several postings to Farnborough, Aldershot and many other places in between, I finished up in Colchester. Here my problems really began. We were billeted in Victorian barracks, large, cold, uninspiring, dreary buildings that had been condemned just after the Crimean War (by Florence Nightingale, no less). But they had been requisitioned back into service in order to satisfy the basic needs of us lusty young conscripts, who had to scrub the bare wooden floors with our tooth brushes, before using them to clean our teeth.

We had one metal stove in the middle of the room for heating purposes, which was quite inadequate by anyone's standards (in other words:

bloody useless). We used to use the barrack room shovel to grill kippers and toast cheese on this stove. My only other memories of Bleak House were of Saturday nights when I was confined to barracks, usually on my own, listening to Radio Luxembourg, feeling sorry for myself, and terribly homesick, while all my mates went home on leave.

I was on jankers (fatigues) again for failing to conform to army regulations. I served a total of over ninety days on jankers at Colchester.

I remember once coming home on a weekend pass and I thought to myself, "Stuff this for a game of soldiers, I ain't going back." So I went to my doctor with a bad back and he asked me to bend over. Like a fool I did, and he told me to go back to camp and report to my medical officer. I didn't bother. I stayed in bed on the Monday morning and got my mam to send for the doctor. Oh, I was in agony. I couldn't move, could I? He gave me a note and I stayed at home in Mam's capable hands for five weeks. She looked after me much better than that bloody army lot. It was 'cos she loved me, didn't she?

Then one Saturday night, as I was walking home after a great booze-up with the lads in Wakefield, this military ambulance passed us. Of course, we all shouted and cheered. Little did I know that the ambulance was on its way to collect me. It had been sent to pick me up and take me into the CRS (medical facility) at Pontefract Barracks. Needless to say, as I wasn't home, I was later to be found hiding around the corner at the bottom of our street. So, as it wasn't quite convenient for me at that time, they had to collect me later. Ma, as usual, in the meantime had come up trumps. She made the ambulance attendants tea and sandwiches and gave them some good books to read, like *Lady Chatterley's Lover* and *Kama Sutra* and such like. She then proceeded to tell them what a good lad I was, that I had just limped over to see my dying grandma and would they please not bother me. They could call back when it was more convenient, which they did. My mam had spoken and the world stood still! Needless to say, they did collect me later.

The army once again had me in their clutches, but it was not for very long, because I sneaked out of hospital every night and came home to my mam. I was discharged on a Thursday to report back to my unit on the Friday. Mam seemed to think it was hardly worth going back until the Monday; I thought that was a good idea too and I agreed. Well, it was Mam talking, wasn't it, eh?

Needless to say, when I returned on the Monday I was immediately put on an absent-without-leave charge. I was hauled in front of the CO and while I was waiting to go in, a prat of a corporal, who was in charge of the guard, noticed my shiny boots and nicely-pressed trousers. "Looking smart - ain't we?" he said.

"I chuffing well ought to be," I said. "It cost me five bob to borrow this gear."

I was wearing my mate's best boots and trousers and that silly bloody corporal put me on another charge for borrowing. Later, I managed to get my own back on this corporal when he got demoted and posted to Thetford, where I had become a corporal (another lesson, eh: What goes around, comes around) and that bastard got his just desserts.

I think I got a total of three week's jankers for my absence-without leave. Was it worth it? Of course it was. I'd been and seen my mam, hadn't I?

Colchester Command Supply Depot was partly manned by civilians. It was a proper working unit that supplied the army and air force with their food supplies. We squaddies used to work hard and would do all sorts of silly tricks for a bet. Yes, young and silly we were. I might carry four hundredweight of sugar, one on each shoulder and one under each arm, fifty yards for a tanner (sixpence) bet, or I might carry a hundred and forty to a hundred and sixty pound chest of tea into the back of an army truck on my head. I could always carry more weight on my head than I could on my back. Why? Because it was the largest part of my anatomy in those days. Come to think, it still is.

We used to make some great tea in this supply depot at Colchester. One could stand one's spoon up in it. We would make it by the bucketful. A quarter of tea, two two-pound bags of sugar and two tins of condensed milk. You didn't drink it, you ate it with a bloody knife and fork.

After my adventures in Colchester, I decided I was spending far too much of my spare time on jankers and I was beginning to develop a complex. Perhaps they didn't really like me after all, or so I thought. I asked for a new posting and they very reluctantly let me go with a boot up the backside.

I was posted to Thetford in Norfolk with the sole objective of making my new commanding officer's life a complete misery. He was actually a great guy who had the sense to recognise that I was really just a little treasure in disguise and if he treated me nicely, I could rise above myself eventually fulfil my true potential and become a sweet little gem, and a great asset to the army in general and to him in particular. So he (or so he thought) got rid of his problems in one fell swoop. He promoted me. That's what the army does with troublemakers and it was one of the best (and worst things) he ever did. I worked my socks off for him and I got things done.  The rest of the lads really did work for me and I looked after them.  The trouble was, I looked after them too bloody well.  For instance, if any of them were on guard duty on Friday nights and they also had a weekend pass, and if I was guard commander, I would let them go home Friday night and cover for them.  Then when the orderly officer came round and asked where they were, he was told that they were either patrolling the depot, or that they were guarding the cookhouse whalas (workers) who were on jankers.

I do remember clearly one particular time when I was supposed to be on guard.  I'd decided to go to my billet and to bed.  I told the lads, the rest of the so-called guard, not to bother patrolling the depot or any of that old rubbish.  All I asked was that one of them should stay awake in the guardroom.  Not much to ask, was it?

But what happened?  Well, every one of the lazy bastards fell asleep.  Nobody in camp was awake.  The drivers, who were due out on early detail, were still in bed, the cooks were still in bed, in fact everybody in the bloody camp was nicely tucked up, having a nice little lie-in.  Including me, the whole camp was fast asleep in bed.  Nobody had any breakfast and no-one turned out on parade, in fact any enterprising villain worth his salt could have simply rolled into the camp with a fleet of trucks and cleared out all the bloody warehouses and nobody would have known.

Of course, I didn't know anything about all of this until the Staff Sergeant came and dragged me out of bed, screaming.  "Get up, you stupid bastard, you're on CO's orderly room at 10am!"  We marched in quick-time halt.

"Felt a little queasy, sir."  Funny turn came over me, sir."  "Just had to lay down in the peace and quiet of me own billet, sir.!  I was ready to pass out, sir."  Oh my, nearly had the poor bloke in tears, didn't I?  Well, I got another severe reprimand (making three in all) but I kept my stripes.  Unbelievable!

Mind, I do think, on reflection, that our CO probably rather fancied me on the quiet.  He did look a bit queer at times.  Still, who could blame him, with blokes like me to put up with all the time?

I should have been in front of a court martial and shot at dawn and yet this particular Commanding Officer gave me a fantastic testimonial when I left the army and he wanted me to stay on as a sergeant.  He should have been so lucky.

I remember twice every week I used to travel to an out-depot with a fleet of civilian lorries whose task was to issue supplies to army and

RAF units in and around the Swanton Morely area of Norfolk. I had some great fiddles going with these civvy drivers. I used to take lead weights out of the weigh scales, or I would rest my foot on the scale while I was weighing out and allocating the rations to the various units. You can bet your beautiful bottoms that those RAF erks, those Brylcreem boys with their slicked-back bloody haircuts (the puffs), yes, them who had copped for the soft jobs in the forces, the ex-grammar school lot, well that lot just didn't get fed so well as us proper men, us real soldiers, did they?

Well, not while I was issuing their bloody rations, they didn't!

The rationing of food was still on at this time and I had a moral duty to see the food I was distributing went to the people with the greatest need. A proper little socialist I was in those days, the proverbial Good Samaritan, especially if there should just happen to be a bob or two in it for me. So I looked after my mates (the squaddies), then there was a small consideration for the civvy drivers, then Mam got her share, then Mrs. Berry, our next door neighbour. Well, she got her share too, and then (and only then), if there happened to be owt left, those quaint RAF boys (or girls, I don't know which) got what was left. But it serves the daft bastards right. I just have no sympathy. The shouldn't have passed their 11-plus, the prats.

They could then have been in the proper forces, the army, like me.

The things some kids will do just to get a new bike!

It was so funny, really, because some of the food parcels I sent home to Ma included meat. I would post the parcels home. Yes, dear reader, bloody great joints of meat! Tea, sugar, groceries, the lot, all sent by post. Mam told me that the postman often delivered her parcels dripping with blood and he would exclaim "Ah, ah. Another bloody food parcel from your Charlie, I see."

My mam would wipe the blood from her hands and say. "Certainly bloody looks like it, don't it?"

Spot the pun, eh? Bloody marvellous!

It was while I was at Thetford that I got to ride a motorbike properly for the first time. Once again, I was the Guard Commander on a Saturday night. I always seemed to be the bloody Guard Commander on a Saturday night. I can't think why. They must have had a lot of faith in me after the last episode, or perhaps they were tempting providence, or perhaps somebody simply liked a challenge. Anyway, this particular Saturday, as Guard Commander I was in charge and I had all the keys to the various stores. I had arranged with a pal of mine, an MT (motor transport)

Corporal, that when the camp had settled down to sleep, I would fill up his motorbike with petrol (he was a dispatch rider), which I duly did. The next morning, he and I set off early with crash helmets and all, to go and see his girlfriend in Cambridge (I think). We had a great day out, even though the selfish bugger didn't let me have a go at his girlfriend. I always thought that proper mates shared and shared alike. Ah well, he might have been a little afraid that, if he had actually let me have a go at her, I just might have left her with a perpetual smile on her face and he, the prat might have become, from then on, a bitter disappointment to the young lady in question. However, he did let me have a go on this Royal Enfield motorbike instead. Big deal. His bird was better looking than the bloody motorbike.

But it was wonderful, wasn't it? Except that I had never ridden a motorbike before in my life. Oh yes, I had, like with sex pretended, I had sat on one when I thought no-one was looking. I had even pushed one for about two bloody miles without the engine running when I had worked at Kilburns (I still had the dent in my arse from my old foreman Jack's clogs to prove it), but I had never actually ridden one.

I was all right until I came to this bloody great roundabout in Newmarket, I think it was. I kept going around this roundabout for what seemed like forever. I just couldn't straighten the bloody thing up. My mate, the MT Corporal, was on the back shouting, "Turn left! Turn left! The next left, you daft bastard!" but I couldn't could I? The bike, for its part had just about had enough of our capers. It was getting dizzy, going round and round in a bloody circle, and finally threw us off. We flew through the air like the man on the flying machine and both landed in a bloody great heap in the middle of the road. We picked ourselves up, dusted ourselves down and picked up the bike which, in turn, gave us a funny look as if to say, "Gormless gits!" before we carried on our way. After a while we ran out of petrol, possibly because of the fifty two thousand times I had gone round and round that bloody roundabout in Newmarket. So we pushed that bloody motorbike for miles until we saw an RAF station.

We went in to see the Guard Commander and our MT Corporal was brilliant. He spun him such a yarn (something about our being on a special, secret mission attached to the SAS and we just had to get to Thetford within the hour), and after the guard had wiped the tears from his eyes, he requisitioned us some petrol.

We kissed him goodbye, completed our journey back to Thetford and then we had to bribe our Staff Sergeant back at camp to look out for the petrol voucher and keep it away from our CO. This particular MT Corporal was a brilliant guy who later took officer training at Sandhurst and passed out as a fully-fledged officer. The army should have been so lucky!

# My Second Date With Destiny

1950 was another watershed. Another phase of my life had begun. I was demobbed from the army, I had refused promotion and I had passed my driving test while still a soldier. I was now ready for the next step forward onto the highway of life, wherever that step would take me.

I was issued with a new demob suit and did I not look smart! Like bloody hell I did. I looked like something that had just walked out of Dartmoor Prison and, I may add, so did all my mates.

We had all of us just swapped our army uniforms for civilian ones. All the same colour, all double-breasted, all forty-two-inch bottoms, all the same style and, by the way, some of those suits fitted the same bloody size too. Did we look gorgeous? You bet we did. We all looked at each other and all of us at that moment wished we had stayed in the bloody army.

If they (the powers that be) had only had the sense to show us those bloody demob suits before they turned us out, I feel sure we would have all stayed in and perhaps signed on for twenty-two years, all prepared to go to Korea to boot. We certainly looked awful and, to add insult to injury, we all had to go home and show our mums our new suits. Mine wasn't a patch on the one that Ma had bought me for 2/6 from a second-hand stall at Wakefield Market in 1946, and it certainly was not fit to be in the same wardrobe as Dad's best suit. No, siree I had worn scout uniforms. I had marched like a peacock on a Sunday morning in my Boys Brigade gear, with the white belt and cross strap, my forage cap at a jaunty angle and my head held high, as proud as punch. Yet there I was now at the zenith of my career, having risked my life for king and country, and all they could give me was a manky third-rate suit that wasn't even good enough to go to the toilet in, or to use in the toilet, for that matter. We couldn't wait to get home as quickly as possible. All of us had but one intention and that was to get those bloody suits off and into a dustbin as quickly as possible.

My second date with destiny happened around this time. I had been writing to a female pen pal while in the army and we had kept in touch. So when I came out of the army, we arranged to meet on a blind date outside Barretts shoe shop in Leeds, where my sister Lenore worked. Well! I turned up and discreetly hid round a corner nearby. I took a furtive glance at this ravishing beauty who was stood there awaiting her knight in shining armour - me - to come riding by on a white charger, sweep her into his arms and carry her off to his castle in Wonderland. Boy was she to be disappointed! Little did she know that the cowardly wimp who had been hiding not 10 yards from her had decided not to take the risk (and apart from that he didn't fancy her, did he? He went scampering away as fast as his feet would take him, back home to the well-worn bosom of his mam.

Of course Mam was pleased, wasn't she, when I told her of my fruitless efforts. Because there was just no way she wanted to lose her number one to some overdressed, over-sexed, money-grabbing hussy. No, no way, no-one was good enough for me. So she said. "Never mind love, perhaps you'll be able to find the right girl one day. Maybe in about 50 years or so. Now just you sit down love, and I'll make you a nice cup of tea." Hee, them were the days with our dear old mums, before, like most of the males of the species, we all got married and stepped into that den of iniquity called marital bliss ah well. I digress, as is my wont!

Little did I know what was shortly to transpire, because my pen pal was in love, wasn't she? She was besotted, she had this irresistible urge to seduce me, I think, and she just couldn't wait to get to me. Anyway, she allowed her sexual feelings and latent, lustful thoughts to overcome her good sense in the pursuit of her unfulfilled desire for me. As I said earlier, my sister worked at Barratts shoe shop at this time and my pen pal knew this, didn't she?

Well, what happened? She went into Barratts and of course our Lenore was quite happy to make her comfortable until she had finished work. Then she brought her home to meet me; well, she would, wouldn't she? She wanted to spoil the wonderful relationship between me and Mam.

I think she thought it was rather pathetic really. Well, it probably was. Anyway, she must have wanted me married off, so the silly little cow brings my pen pal home. I ran upstairs, and says to me Mam, "Tell her I'm not in, I must still be in Leeds looking for her. Anyway, it happened. Our Lenore very tactfully shouted me down, didn't she, so I very sheepishly crept downstairs to meet my fate. I said to my would-be girlfriend, "Hello, love, how are you then? I just slipped upstairs to the toilet and I have only just got home myself from Leeds. Where were you? I was stood outside Woolworths for four hours waiting for you."

She said, "Woolworth's, me bum, you lying devil, you know damn well we arranged to meet outside Barratts, and you had me stood there like an idiot. Stuff you. I'm off home to me Mum." This ended what could never have become a beautiful friendship.

My mam said. "Never mind, love, come on sit down and I will make you another nice cuppa tea.

# Night Life In The 1950s

When I first came out of the army, my mates and me would do all the local pubs: *The Spread Eagle* and *The Angel* up on Bradford Road, *The Dog and Gun, Double Six, The Crown And Anchor*, all on Kirkgate in Wakefield. Sammy Herbert of *This Sporting Life* fame was the landlord of The Dolphin, where we used to have some great times. The *Gardners* and *The Angel* in Lofthouse and *The Drum and Monkey* in Outwood were all great pubs in their own right, and all provided free entertainment. There were talent contest in some, dancing in others and, believe it or not, waiter service in all.

You could buy a packet of fags (a full packet of twenty, too) from behind the bar in those days and a pint of beer only cost 11d. in old money. Today, we pay up to sixteen pounds a gallon for our beer and we don't even get waiter service, or free entertainment.

Today we stand and queue at the bar and we don't even bat a bloody eyelid.

The world has been turned on its head.

I had a mate in those days, Reggie Smales was his name, who was a right silly daft bastard whenever he got a smell of a barmaid's apron.

He also had a big gob which got me into more trouble than I had even bargained for. It was never trouble that I had caused. I always seemed to be fighting someone else's battles in those days - usually Reg's.

One time we were in *The Crown and Anchor* down on Kirkgate in Wakefield when Reg got into an argument with a chap who was going to flatten him. Well, big-hearted bloody Arthur me said to the other bloke, "Take no notice mate, he didn't mean it."

The next thing I knew, we were in the passage on the way out, and this bloke put his fists up. So I belted him, knocking him down the stairs, through the door and outside. When I went outside, this lad was there with all his mates who were holding him back while a bus was parked at the kerb. It was only a bus trip from Barnsley, wasn't it, and where was me mate, the redoubtable Reg?

Well, he, as usual, thinking discretion to be the better part of valour, had done a bunk, hadn't he?

He left me holding the fort. How I got away with that one I will never know.

The next time we had a spot of bother was at the *Embassy Dance Hall* down Market Street in Wakefield. The same thing happened again: Reg opened his gob, I stepped in to help him out and bang! I was in it again. The biggest mistake I made was not shutting Reg's gob for him every time he opened it.

We used to go dancing on a Sunday night upstairs at *Thornes Club* and at *The White Cross* in Guisley. Another great place was at Mark Altmans in Leeds. The Savoy up on Horbury Road was a great nightclub, too. I think that was where *The Grumbleweeds* got their first real start in show business. Yes, we had it all and entertainment was cheap in those days, too.

Around this time, I borrowed Dad's van without him knowing in a bid to transport me and my mates to *The Spread Eagle* in Gildersome for a good night out. Little did I know that Dad had not checked the engine oil for maybe two years. Anyway, away I went, belting up Bradford Road this particular night, with all my mates in the back of the van singing, "Here we go. Here we go!" when bang it went.

A bloody great rattle and the engine stopped. Oh my God! What on earth could have happened? We gingerly lifted the bonnet, glanced inside and there it was: a bloody great, gaping hole that you could have put your head in. Something was protruding out of the engine too. It was a con rod that had disconnected itself from the crank shaft and had decided to come out for a little air, hadn't it?

There was no way it was going to go back either. Well, what now? We managed to get a tow back home with a London Carriers van (which cost us all a fair bit of our hard-earned brass), but the biggest problem was the forthcoming confrontation and my feeble explanation to him-of-few-words, my dad. I went into the house and Dad was reading the paper. I sat down at the table (I had kept my raincoat on just in case), picked up a knife and started scraping it on a plate, looking down at the table.

I then plucked up courage and said. "Er, um, er, ah, er, um, er, Dad, I've got some bad news for you."

He looked up over his glasses and said. "Oh aye, what's that then?"

"Well, er, I, um, ah, mm, ah I've smashed your van up," I said.

He looked up again over his glasses, and said. "Nah then, tha's done a bloody good job then, asn't tha, little bit of business gone, no more work. Aye, tha's done a reight good job, then."

He then sat back in his chair and carried on reading his paper, as if nothing had been said! He-of-few-words hadn't said much, but, by God, he had certainly said it all. If he had smacked me in the mouth, kicked me out of the house or ostracised me for life he couldn't have done more than he did with those few words.

I remember the time I was once talking to him about politics, or whatever, and he said. "Well tha sees, lad, I don't bother me bloody head about things like that. They're all out for themselves, aren't they?"

Then, the issue of wasting public money was once raised, he-of-few-words replied. "Well, tha sees, it's the easiest thing int' world to spend some bugger else's brass, i'nt it?"

That was my dad, what a man. I do honestly believe that if he had ever been caught in a forest fire, he would have just stood there and the fire would have simply, had to go round him, leaving him untouched. Yes, indeed. What a remarkable man.

But, all was well that ended well. I gave him the gratuity that I had received from the army on demob, he bought another van and so the story continued.

# So To Work

What next, where to go, what to do. I didn't want to go back to butchering, nor did I want to offer my arse back to Jack at Kilburns for target practice, even though, in my heart, I knew how much he must have missed it (not that his aim was that bad anyway). I felt sure that he had probably sharpened the toes of his clogs in gleeful anticipation of a pleasant meeting with my arse again.

Ah well, Stuff you, Jack, I decided, he was going to be one off, wasn't he? I took my bum to a place where it was better appreciated: to a seat, a driving seat, in fact, of a butcher's delivery van owned by Jowetts the Butchers, who had shops in Upper Springs and in Kirkgate in Wakefield. I was to spend ninety per cent of my time at Jowetts poncing about in the back of the shop, making sausages and such. They wouldn't allow me in the front of the shop - something about putting customers off (whatever that was supposed to mean). The other ten per cent of my time was spent delivering orders, all for about two pounds a week and as much meat as I could pinch.

Well, meat, unlike beer, is non-alcoholic, so one can't get pissed on it, can one? It is not very pleasant to sleep with either, so at that time in my life, it was unable to satisfy most of my more urgent needs. So I upped and left, didn't I?

My next step forward (or maybe backward, on reflection I don't really know which) must have been a step in the right direction because I began to realise, very early in my life, that each move, each job, was part of a new learning process; a gathering of new experiences and a making of new friendships which all gave me a better understanding and a clearer insight into the ways of the world and the true realities of life itself (what a load of rubbish). But I was growing up and leaving Ma's apron strings and moving on into the real world, the world of real work.

As a boy of seventeen-and-a-half years of age, my weight had been ten stone seven pounds; now, at the age of twenty, I weighed thirteen stone two pounds and I had a head to match.

Yes, I was quickly developing into a man.

I had obtained a job at a local brickyard: Roper's Brickworks at Lofthouse Gate near Wakefield. It was owned by Aberford Quarries and managed by a great bloke called Cliff Farrer. Cliff lived in the big house nearby and had become the manager after marrying the previous owner's daughter. Yes, Cliff's wife was old man Roper's daughter. Cliff copped for a nice house, a cushy job and they lived happily ever after. Now, Cliff was a mate of me dad's and he allowed Dad to park his van at the brick-yard for free (of course). This favour often included a free tow off, usually every morning, by one of the brickyard lorries if it just happened that Dad's van failed to start, which was like every bloody day except Sunday when Dad of course, was down the pub.

Dad never, ever had a battery on that old van worth more than a tan-ner. The starter motor was usually knackered. The brakes, of course, were just a luxury because when he had worn the brake shoes down to the rivets, he had a hole in the cab floor through which he would put his legs and he would slur them on the floor to try and retard his forward progress.

He wore out more pairs of boots with this game than half the soldiers in the First World War marching into battle.

Father had a lovely arrangement with Cliff, the brickyard manager. Dad got all the perks and Cliff got all the aggro. Dad talked, or bribed, Cliff into giving me a job. I don't know if I was supposed to be grateful or not but Dad most certainly had not done me any favours.

The first job that Cliff gave me was working in the quarry. Yes, this was the same quarry in which I nearly died during the war (remember Ma nearly killed me). I was employed filling tubs with clay stone, which were then winched on a railway line up and out of the quarry and then they were tipped into a crusher at the top in the brickworks. After a while, I graduated to much better things and at last I got a job with a title. I was elevated to the position of "Muck chamber" "Shute beater" and "Unclogger", grade two. What a bloody awful job that was! The crushed stone, which had by now become a very fine dust, was conveyed up into the muck chamber and then it was transported down a shute to the brick-making chamber, to be mixed with water, moulded and made into bricks. Well, that was in theory; in practice this bloody shute was always getting blocked. So I was employed to keep belting this shute with a bloody great shovel to keep it free and unblocked. There must have been at least two tons of dust up there in that bloody muck chamber. I couldn't see. It got everywhere, in one's eyes, in one's ears, up one's arse, and it strayed around and tantalised one's goolies, if one wasn't careful. I was just like that proverbial abominable bloody snowman in disguise and my nose has never ever been the same since. I am sure that bloody Cliff Farrar didn't like me much, or perhaps he was getting his own back on me for the aggro that my dad was causing him. There were no such things as eye protectors, goggles, air filters, plastic helmets, or any of those countless other health and safety devices that seem to be so essential to the process of survival today.

My generation just had to get on with the job and most of us lived to ripe old ages in spite of - or because of - the abuse that we had unwittingly inflicted upon our bodies.

But what my generation had to do, and the way that some of us had to live, just does not fit in with today's so-called expert medical advice. Because by all the present day expert reasoning my generation should in theory all have died before the age of forty. The fact that we are not dead doesn't surprise or deter the experts, who just carry on expounding their clapped out theories, frightening everybody to bloody death in the process.

Back to the brickyard. I quickly applied for a transfer on medical grounds.

I couldn't see, I couldn't hear, me bum was red raw, and me goolies felt like they had been used by Joe bloody Davis, the snooker champ, on his last World Championship tour.

Cliff did eventually manage to hear my cry from the wilderness and he relented; he had to because I had threatened to go tell me mam what he was doing to her favourite son. Yes, she was still keeping a watchful eye out for me. Well, they do, don't they, even if they sometimes manage to live long enough to see their little darlings draw their own pensions!

I was demoted to the ground floor, where I took the green bricks off the brick-making machine and wheeled them on a single-wheeled barrow into the kilns, then progressed to loading lorries.

Then I graduated once again to the hardest job of all: drawing bricks out of the kilns.

There was no one single easy job in the brickyards at that time it was all heavy manual work. But drawing was the hardest job of all, it was literally donkey work. In fact, on reflection, I don't believe those bloody donkeys could have done it.

We had to strip to the waist because of the heat, and wear rubber pads that we had made out of old motor car inner tubes to protect our hands from the rough bricks. It was so hot that the heat used to burn the soles off our boots and, to cap it all, we were on piecework.

We certainly did not get owt for now't, we had to get out there and earn it the hard way. I never did have any special qualifications and I didn't know what 'A' levels or 'O' levels were. I was just a simple labourer that was all, but I had my youth, my strength, a big head, a big heart and a bucket full of pride. (Any man worth his salt had in those far off days). I had a job, I needed to prove myself, and I had the opportunity.

Two of us would draw between 15,000 and 18,000 bricks each day. We would load them on to iron barrows and push them out of the kilns to be loaded into lorries. There were 250 bricks to every ton, and we would move up to 72 tons daily, 36 tons each. I once stacked 125 bricks (half a ton) onto barrow and I lifted and I pushed that barrow outside the kiln for a tanner bet. I was as proud as punch, just as if I had won the heavyweight championship of the world, no less.

That particular job was very satisfying and it was real man's work. Those were the days when a man felt like a man and was proud of the fact. Mind, it did help that our wives were at home bringing up the kids, so we didn't need to go home and change nappies, like today's bloody wimps, eh!

In those days there were very few mechanical aids, just blood, sweat and tears to help stimulate and lubricate one's movements. There was plenty of work to go around: on building sites, in coal mines, in the steel works, driving lorries, and so on. There was quite a lot of manual work when I was young. Perhaps this was because a lot of the lads did not return from the war, and quite a lot more 18 to 20 year olds had to do National Service. Whatever the reason, there was plenty of work for everyone in the early fifties. Cliff, my boss, in his wisdom promoted me once again to an elevated position. He sent me up to the "burning chamber". To the uninitiated, the burning chamber is where the coal holes which feed the fires in the kilns are situated, right at the top of the building above the kilns. This was a dark desolate unfriendly place, Dante's Inferno had nothing on these chambers. Now my job (I was in charge, of course; well, there was only me) was to supply the burner (the man who fed the fires) with coal. I did this by shovelling coal into buckets on a conveyor on the ground floor, which then took the coal up top to the burning chamber. Then I would go up top and barrow the coal to the fire pots. This was no problem at all until the conveyer chose to break down, which was every other bloody day.

Then I had a real problem, because I then had to fill the barrow with coal, move back about 50 yards or so, then I would run like bloody hell (and I mean like bloody hell) up that wooden gantry at the side of the kilns, right up to the top of the building. That gantry was about 80 to 100 foot straight up, and if you stopped halfway up, you never made it to the top. I was all right for perhaps the first ten barrow loads, then I would become knackered, and someone else took over. On it went like that. That bleeding conveyer was a jinx. A chap called Charlie Hemingway used to be the kiln fireman on nights, and Charlie was a bugger for his ale. So on a night when Cliff Farrar went to the then up-market Sun Pub on Leeds Road, Lofthouse Gate, well, our Charlie would sneak into the *Traveller's Rest* next door to enjoy a pint or two with me dad and Bill Teasdale, the landlord. Now this would have been all right if Charlie had stuck to the rules and put what you call a "mend" on every 20 minutes; this meant stoking the fires every 20 minutes between his pints at the *Traveller's*. But this was too much trouble for our Charlie. What Charlie used to do was take off some, what we called "back caps" to create an updraft, then he would stoke the fires with four times the amount of coal needed. He would then spend all night in the pub, the temperature gauge would remain constant and nobody would know what he had done. But the bricks in the kiln were under cooked at the top and burnt at the bottom. Poor old Cliff Farrar scratched his head for years over this and he never found out the reason.

Cliff then moved me onto driving. At last I had arrived. I did eventually get to become a driver of sorts. I drove an old short wheelbase 'O' model Bedford, which was fitted with a 4cyl Gardener diesel engine. This was quite unique in those days, in fact Aberford quarries had some right odd ball vehicles. They even had some ex-First World War Associated Daimlers with long bonnets that had been fitted with Gardener diesel engines. They ran sand and gravel out of a quarry off Denby Dale Road in Wakefield for years. That sand pit was near where the Asda supermarket now stands.

The only problem with driving my little short wheelbase Bedford tipper was that the top speed was just 30mph, (though considering that the speed limit in those days was set at 20mph, this was quite adequate)

But nor for me. I discovered a way to make that bloody engine go faster. I would place a penny at the rear of the fuel pump governor rack to hold the rack open and make the engine go faster. Now this wasn't done to enable me to do more loads, oh no, it was done to allow me to spend time over a few more cups of tea in the transport cafe between loads.

Yes there was always more ways than one to skin the cat!

While on the subject of go-faster devices, apart from that extra gear that we used going down hills (which we proper drivers called the silent sixth, or the last goodbye, neutral), I employed all sorts of other sophisticated devices over the years to make them bloody motors go faster. I jammed cold start buttons closed with lumps of wood, and removed and reverse fitted low geared transfer boxes to make the motor go twice as fast; all done in the name of progress!

Yes, I had some great times at Ropers Brickyard, and I worked with some great blokes. There was Charlie Hemmingway, the burner; little Billy Sutcliffe, a setter; George Jackson, also setter; and Arthur Clough, a driver who lived at Hunslet Leeds. Arthur was to become the General Manager for Bayford Fuel Distributors of Leeds, who 30 years later tried to buy me out. Small world! They hadn't a hope in hell, but that is another story and another day.

I eventually left Ropers Brickyard for better prospects, or so I thought at the time.

I went to work for a chap from Jacobs Well Lane in Wakefield, who had a few tippers and used to deliver coal to Ropers Brickyard and various places in Lancashire. When he asked me to come and work for him, I thought, oh great, long distant work at last, all the way into Lancashire. At last I have arrived, now I am a big wheeler. Big deal! I was there just a fortnight and the man was bloody barmy.

He would say to me. "You must not slam the cab door." One had to close it gently. He used to follow me around, spying on me. I remember once when I nicked some coal that I had short delivered somewhere. I was just about to shovel it into the coal hole when I happened to look around; who should just happen to be stood there watching me, yes, that's right, my new employer. I couldn't have that, could I, so I gave him a rollicking and told him to stick his job. I could hardly work for someone who didn't trust me, could I now?

Cliff Farrar at the brickyard agreed to take me back into my old job, but I had to wait a fortnight before he had a vacancy. So rather than go on the dole, I took a job working for Harlow and Milner, digging trenches at the top of Thornhill Edge near Dewsbury in the middle of bloody winter. I stayed at Ropers for a while after that, then moved to Armitages Brickworks off Potovens Lane, Lofhouse Gate, opposite where I now live. I worked there with a great set of lads. There was George Stokoe, "Faffer", we called him, because he never swore. He would say, for instance, "I am faffing fed up!" He was a real hard case! Then there was Claude Steel, Johnnie Wright who used to drive the long wheel base Bedford delivering best bricks, and old Arthur Dickinson. Arthur, well, he must have been at least 90 years old and still working. He drove a 5 cylinder Gardener engined, high-sided Foden tipper. All the loads were hand balled on to the trucks in those days. I can well remember the times when two of us would load the high-sided Foden with 6 tons of bricks in just half-an-hour. We never looked at the wagon, just the pile of bricks on the floor: bend throw, bend throw. With men like that, who needed mechanical aids, eh? I also spent some time at the NCB Newton Hill Headquarters as a general labourer. My foreman was a chap called Jack Sharp from Wrenthorpe.

In those days on building sites and in brickyards, there were no washing facilities, and rarely toilets. We made do and managed. We ate our snap on the job with dirty hands and enjoyed every mouthful. Today's hygiene police would have had a bloody fit, but nothing ailed us. Our immune systems had a job to do and they did it well. Our bodies were looked after and they served us well. I also worked for C and F construction at Newton Hill. Harry Flavel was the gaffer, he was the son-in-law of Joe Fisher, a well-known Wakefield car dealer who built the Redbeck cafe on Doncaster Road. He also opened the Ace Club on George Street, Wakefield, for gambling and dancing, which was managed by stuttering Jack, his brother.

He was a great character, was our Joe, and a real gentleman, with his Trilby hat and black overcoat. All the car dealers in those days, Harry and Walt Rawson, wore their trilby hats and overcoats, they were like bloody uniforms and designed exclusively for car dealers.

Today's dealers walk about like bloody tramps, what with their jeans, mobile phones and cheque-books falling out of their back pockets.

But they are not in the same league as Joe and his mates. Joe had a garage on Ings Road Wakefield. All his engine oil came from the same barrel, and battery distilled water came from the kitchen tap.

One could buy a car from Joe in those days for no deposit and a few bob a week. He would just mark your payments off in a little black notebook he carried around with him, and if you refused to pay, well he just sent the heavy brigade round to your house to collect and, if you had any sense you would pay up. Now that was a much better system than the one we employ today, simple but effective; no embarrassing, time-wasting court appearances with an army of solicitors. No, it was so simple in those days and we all knew the score: pay up or else.

My wife's mam Irene used to clean for Joe. Another son-in-law of his used to work for C and F Construction with me. Eric Waller was the mechanic, his dad kept the Sun Inn on Leeds Road. Jim Connis, another pal of mine worked there with me. He lived in lodgings down Garden Street Wakefield, where my future wife Jean lived. At C and F again it was all manual work, loading the lorries by hand, all shovel work. I spent some time at Leek and Carney civil engineers as a labourer. Another nice chap I once worked for was Walter Small. He lived down Jacobs Well Lane did Walter. Again it was all hard work, civil engineering, digging trenches. I drove a Ford V8 for Walt. I will never forget one time, after digging trenches, loading the wagon at Middlestown and taking the load to the tip, I got stuck. And it was nearly time to go home, Walt came over to the tip and said to me, "Nah then lad, it's home time, we have to be off now, so do thee best and I'll see thee tomorrow."

And he buggered off and left me to it. That was Walt, it was sink or swim with him, either get thee sen out of that hole lad, or stop there all bloody night. I'll never forget that bloody Ford of Walt's. I once sneaked home in it for my dinner and the steering wheel came off in my hand, it broke in two, and I had to drive that bloody wagon from Lofthouse to Wakefield with a great moving spanner on the steering nut. Believe me, that wasn't easy!

Walter used to have a lock-up garage on George Street, or somewhere near there, where he kept the lorry. I had the key, didn't I? Now, that was surely tempting providence, I could never look a gift horse in the mouth. So come Friday and Saturday nights, I used to take me mates on a pub crawl in Walt's wagon, then down to the *Embassy* Dance Hall in Market Street Wakefield in the Ford Lorry. Then I would drive any willing damsel home after the dance. Quite a nice arrangement really, and very convenient and cost effective, for me at least because not only did I have transport to take me home on a Saturday night, I also had transport to take me to work on the Monday morning.

But it could not go on. At last Walt found out, and come one Monday morning he said to me, "Nah then, lad, we have come to the parting of the ways."

He paid me up, gave me my cards, shook my hand, wished me the best of luck and I still don't know to this day why he sacked me. He never said, did he, but I have never been sacked as nicely before, or since. He was a proper gentleman, was our Walt, a great character.

I worked for the Crystal Springs for a while delivering pop. They were down Calder Vale Road, near the Chantry Bridge. Apart from being hard work, it seemed at the time a rather uneventful job, apart from one or two minor fiddles with the returned empties. I then got a job at the steam laundry on Grantley Street, Wakefield, driving an Austin LD van, collecting and delivering laundry from and around Selby Whitley Bridge and the Methley areas. I was paid on commission and, being a new starter, I had to travel to the furthest distances. So in effect, the driver who covered the most congested areas, like Wakefield, could collect six parcels, while I was travelling to collect or deliver only one. But I enjoyed this job, meeting people, making new friends. The hours were long and the pay was low, but I really did enjoy working there.

The chap who owned the steam laundry was, I think, called Peter Pick or Peece. I wiil never forget that he had a beautiful 1947 SS Jaguar car at the time.

The Distribution Manager, or whatever his title was, was Percy Howe.

Mrs. Field, Stephen Field the car dealer's mam, worked there too. She repaired any damaged clothes from the wash, as she was a seamstress, no less.

It was there that I made friends with a guy called Albert Bolton and through him his brother Pete and his wife Lil. Albert and I had some great times together, boozing, dancing and so on. It was around this time that I at last met the girl of my dreams, my wife Jean. I will never forget the night Albert and I were out together in a steam laundry van, when we happened to notice Jean stood outside the *Strafford Arms* Hotel in Wakefield. I said to Albert. "I wonder what she's doing there. Do you think she could be touting for business?"

Albert replied. "No, she's waiting for you, you daft prat."

I said "Bloody hell, what day is it? I hope she hasn't seen us." And she hadn't, thank god. It was while I was working at the steam laundry that one of the worst things in my life happened to me. I was coming down Bradford Road towards Wakefield, past where Gordon's Tyres (another mate of mine) are now, up over the slight hill and down the other side (I think it is called Broomhall Avenue). Suddenly a small boy on a bike came out of this avenue, straight in front of me. I couldn't see him and he couldn't see me until I was almost on top of him. But it was too late. He was crossing the road half on and half off his bike. I tried to steer to the right to miss him, but he followed me across. I had nearly stopped when we collided. He slowly, as if in slow motion, toppled from his bike, and his head struck the floor. I think he was dead before he arrived at the hospital, and his mother saw it all through her front room window. What an awful tragedy. He was an only son, and his father was the manager at Jackson's Bakery down Westgate Wakefield.

The coroner's enquiry subsequently exonerated me from blame, but that was of little consolation to me at the time. I would have gladly done 20 years in jail if I had been found guilty and the worst thing was that I was not allowed to send flowers or express any sympathy for fear that it would be prejudicial. It took me a long long time to get over that, and sometimes I think that I never have really. I had taken the most precious thing of all, a young person's life.

Many months later, as I was driving through Wakefield, I saw the boy's mum and she recognised me. I will never, ever forget the look on that poor woman's face. I had killed her son. I often wonder, even today, about the meaning of life. Why was I allowed to live, and why did he have to die. Why?

Had he lived, he would have been in his fifties today, but it just wasn't to be.

I then moved from the steam laundry to Rawsons down Portobello Road, Wakefield. I drove an Armstrong Saurer for them; boy, were those vans big! They were huge, over 30 foot long, and that is some size on a rigid chassis that couldn't bend in the middle.

They even had some of these trucks built without roofs so that they would hold more products. They would then be sheeted over with a large waterproof sheet, all very ingenious.

Rawsons had an old hand-operated petrol pump to fuel the trucks. I enjoyed working there, it was easier work than what I had been used to, so I don't remember why I left. I either got sacked for some reason or left for some reason: I met another guy at Rawsons all those years ago, a chap called Albert Palfreman who was a driver at Rawsons when I was there. He was a young man who had just returned from Australia, and since then he has built up a very successful motor body repair business in Stanley.

Among the 23 jobs I had before starting my own business there was the time I spent with Peter Slater - two weeks. Driving his eight-wheeler AEC and Albion Tippers, I worked nights delivering coal from Slater's garage at Gildersome to Lansil at Lancaster. When I applied for this job Mr. Slater asked me if I had driven eight-wheelers before. Of course I said yes. He then said to me, "Now listen, lad, be careful wi' them brakes, because every time tha puts thee foot on that bleeding brake pedal it costs me half a crown. So keep thee left foot off the brake, and thee right foot flat down ont accelerator pedal.

Keep going and hope fort best."

I replied. "Yes, Mr. Slater." Having passed the statutory driving test that all prospective employers gave in those days, away I went on to the next stage of my learning process, and all for the princely sum of ten pounds a week. Boy, what a firm that was and what a reputation they developed in such a short time in business! Most tipper drivers in those days were known as hell drivers, or simply bloody idiots! Accidents happened every week and some drivers were injured. Most of the journeys we did were from Yorkshire, over the Pennines into Lancashire. The vehicles that we drove were grossly overloaded; and brakes were very poor in those days, mainly vacuum assisted, although the AECs did have air brakes on three axles out of four. Now with vacuum brakes we would jump on the brake pedal with both feet, close our eyes say a little prayer and just hope for the best. About two miles further on down the road, if you were lucky you managed to stop. Yes, those old vacuum brakes that were fitted to old ERFs, Maudsley's and the like, were very limited in there effectiveness. We as drivers had to judge our stopping distances, very carefully, because, with a vacuum brake there wasn't any progressive braking effect. Once the brake was applied, that was it and no amount of extra foot pressure would make a difference, because the vehicle would only stop in its own time, which could become very disconcerting.

Going up over the Pennines, we were down into first gear all the way up, and going down the other side we were still in first gear. We would apply the hand brake on three notches to help retard our progress - or so we hoped!

We never dared touch the footbrake, because the handbrake worked on the rear wheels and the footbrake on all four. We had to rely on the front brakes for emergency use only. The brake drums would get red hot with constant use and the brakes would fade, until you had no brakes at all. So we always left the footbrake and front brakes for emergency use only, unless of course, you worked for the redoubtable Peter Slater, as all his vehicles were fitted with an extra gear. Yes, the silent sixth, mentioned earlier. What we drivers used to do to gain a bit of extra speed was to throw the gear shift out of gear going downhill, close our eyes and hope for the best.

The only problem was that once the gearbox was in neutral, we could never get it back into gear again. The vehicle was travelling too fast, and you just hadn't a hope in hell of stopping.

See you later, Peter Slater. In a casket crazy basket. Those were indeed the days, before full air brakes and exhauster engine brakes. Writing about these particular episodes in my life reminds me of a recent, tragic accident involving an eight-wheel tipping lorry, which resulted in the deaths of several people at Hebden Bridge. The transport manager was unfairly charged with manslaughter and found guilty. Subsequently, on appeal the guilty verdict was overturned.

As is usual in accidents like these, which attract a lot of media attention, it became a very emotive issue (as Hillsboro was). The relevant facts were obscured, because the people who conducted the enquiry were not qualified to make proper judgments and did not, or dared not, ask the right questions. The questions that should have been asked are as follows:

How can a transport manager be held legally responsible (and he is) for the actions of an employee, be that employee a vehicle mechanic or driver, over whom he cannot exercise any actual physical control?

What experience did the driver have of driving heavily loaded vehicles down very steep inclines? (The driver in this case was a middle-aged, retired policeman)

What gear was the vehicle gear box in after the accident?

Was the brake failure due to brake fade?

How did the vehicle become totally out of control?

The basic problem with heavy vehicles is that their brakes are not up to the same standards as those in a motor car. But the biggest problem is that most drivers do not know this, because due to better roads, they have never experienced brake fade. The fact is that brakes are better today, but only in the sense that the manufacturers have applied better and more power assistance. But the basic problems still remain. Any brake is only as good as the brake linings that are fitted and after prolonged use these will get red hot and fade, until there is no braking effect at all.

But yet those so-called experts, the powers that be who introduced the Large Goods Vehicle Tests, didn't trust the drivers' own employers (who had the most to lose) to do the job and yet failed to ensure that tests were carried out with loaded vehicles.

Before I was even offered a job at Peter Slater's I had to pass a driving test with a loaded eight-wheeler and I was shown how to keep brake fade to a minimum. To quote Mr. Slater's immortal words. "Keep thee foot off them bloody brakes, lad, because every time tha press's that pedal, it costs me half a crown." How right he was! I will never forget that fortnight that I worked for Peter Slater. But I am grateful to the almighty for allowing me to survive.

Going to Lancaster overnight we travelled through Settle and the Dales. What an experience that was: little winding lanes, no power steering in those days and as one travelled along, one would be thinking to oneself: now where is that next double bloody hairpin bend? Then one would jump up, literally standing up in the cab to frantically pull the steering wheel round, shouting, "Bleeding hell, it's here?" Then one would sink back down into one's seat again, relax for all of ten seconds, until the next double bend hovered into sight. What a bloody nightmare! No heater's, headlights like candles, and brakes that were useless going downhill.

Mind you, we drivers didn't really need heaters, because we would sweat cobs pulling that bloody great steering wheel, with probably a ten-ton overload, round those beautiful winding roads up in the Dales. They once gave me an old CX Albion eight-wheeler for a laugh, which I didn't find very funny. But as I was the new boy (I was twenty-two years of age at the time), I had to live with it. Now this bloody Albion was about knackered, had no guts, wouldn't pull the skin off a rice pudding, and to cap it all, that prat of a day driver had overloaded it by about twelve tons. That's right, twelve tons.

The foreman driver said to me, "Now look here, lad, thee get into bottom gear as tha comes out of Settle and bloody well stop in it till tha get's ovver that bloody Bucker Brow, because tha knows what's going to happen. If tha try's to change down going up, and tha happens to miss a gear tha will shoot back down that bloody hill like a bat out of hell. Tha will demolish half of bloody Settle, and Mr. Slater won't be right pleased if he happens to find his wagon a pile of scrap in the middle of the square in Settle, will he?"

I said, "No, Mr. Foreman." And away we went merrily on our way, me bringing up the rear in that bloody old Albion. We gets through Settle, I puts the wagon into first gear, and hopes for the best! The bloody thing wouldn't even traverse the first small incline coming out of Settle, let alone Bucker Brow. I stalled the engine in first gear, stood on the brakes and waited in abject fear for my rescuer to appear over the horizon.

He came in the guise of the redoubtable foreman, who came at me like an avenging angel, a true messenger from God. To me he seemed like the Devil incarnate, smoke was coming out of his nostrils, fire out of his ears, and he was sweating blood from every pore in his body.

Ye, he was quite a formidable sight, especially at midnight on a moonlight night. "Now you, yer little prat, what did I tell thee about not changing gear?

I replied. "I never touched the bloody gear after leaving Settle, in fact if tha shuts thee gob and opens thee eyes, and looks tha will see the bloody things still in first gear. Go up Bucker Brow in this bloody thing, tha must be bloody crackers, it took it all its time to crawl out of Settle in first gear and that's all downhill. A notice tha didn't volunteer to drive this bloody wagon thee sen, did that, no tha dint, tha prefers one o' them fancy AECs beignt (being the) foreman an all that . Yer big mouthed git, tha's gorrer bloody gob on thee as big ast Mersey Tunnel, if tha can do any better, thee have a go."

Well, after this exchange of pleasantries had taken place and after we had both exhausted our substantial vocabularies, he said, "Well, I expect a shall have to give thee a bloody tow."

I replied. "Well tha expects right, unless tha happens to be a proverbial optimist, an tha thinks the bloody thing's going to walk over Bucker

Brow. But if tha thinks I'm going to push it over, well, tha's one off, and apart from that if tha takes a look at thee bloody wagon tha will see that rigor mortis is already slowly setting in."

To cut a long story short, I was towed over Bucker Brow. This particular hill was to feature in my life later when I had my own fleet of tippers. Talk about climb every mountain; that bloody hill became my Mount Everest!

The final episode which ended my short sojourn at Peter Slater's happened a few days later. We always stopped in Settle for fish and chips. I climbed back into the cab and happened to notice that the dead man's handle was up. This was a warning device, telling you that the air supply was faulty and the air pressure had dropped. This meant you had no brakes, so the dead man's handle came up and said stop! Well, stop was written on the handle. Of course, the fact that you couldn't see the bloody thing in the dark didn't seem to have bothered the designers, Westinghouse. Well, big hearted Arthur (me), instead of ringing the garage for assistance, thought to myself, if I start the engine, I may build the air back up. So I started the engine, knocked off the ratchet handbrake, put the vehicle into gear and off I went. Of course, I couldn't stop, could I? But I had the presence of mind to swing the lorry to the right up the side of the parade of shops in Settle, where there is a very steep hill. I stalled the engine in gear, applied the handbrake, jumped from the cab and frantically looked for something to put under the back wheels, because the wagon was slowly slipping back down the hill. The only thing I managed to find that was big enough was the foreman driver's bloody head, but he was reluctant to let me use it, the bloody wimp, so I used the next best think, a bloody great stone, weighing about two cwt!

The vehicle mechanics came out from Gildersome, repaired the brakes and away I went. It was dinner time the following day when I got back to Yorkshire. So I thought, stuff this for a game of soldiers, I ain't having this, and all for ten quid a week. So I went home in the wagon, and I courted the sack. If I had left without notice I would have got nothing, but if they sacked me they had to give me an extra week's pay. I stayed at home till about 4pm, then I set off to Slaters and on the way I saw the manager, who was out looking for me. He followed me back to the garage.

When I got near to Gildersome crossroads, I sped up to the traffic lights and then jumped on the brakes. The empty AEC skidded and juddered to a stop, it nearly stood on its head. The manager almost ran up its behind and very nearly had a heart attack. When we got back to the garage, he jumped out of his car, ran and said. "You bloody lunatic, you nearly killed me. I have never in my life seen a wagon driven like that. You're sacked."

I said. "Good, lick'em, and stick'em (my cards) and let me be off." The nightmare was over at last and another chapter was closed.

# At Last The Real Thing

It was about this time a few years later (1952/53 in fact) that I first met my future wife Jean: Her Highness, the virtuous one. She used to walk about town with her nose stuck so far up in the air that spitfire pilots had to swerve to miss it, after surviving the Battle of Britain and all that Hitler had to offer. She was so stuck up it was unbelievable. She would even cross over the road to avoid her mother and pretend that she hadn't seen her. Anyway, I wasn't to know all this until later, much later, when I had chosen the near impossible task of taming the shrew!

We lads (the likely ones, of course) used to tour all the dance halls in Wakefield: the *Music Saloon* up Wood Street, the *Embassy* down Market Street, the *Savoy* up Horbury Road, the *Unity Hall* above the Co-op in Smythe Street opposite the Opera House, and for good measure a few dozen pubs in between. This particular night it was either Christmas Eve or New Year's Eve 1952, I don't remember which, my mates and I had gone to the midnight dance at the Unity Hall. We always went there after attending midnight mass at the cathedral, where we would pray to be delivered from evil. We never asked the Almighty to give us this day our daily bread, but we did ask for something more stimulating and satisfying, like a luscious blonde who had forgotten to put her knickers in her handbag.

The objects of our desires remained completely inaccessible until our pent-up frustration got the better of us and we were forced to pop the question.

There was, however, one exception that I remember clearly, and that was when we did once use a condom. No, not as a blow-up balloon! We put tinned milk into a condom and left it in the back seat of a married mate's car for his wife to find. With mates like that who needs enemies? I also remember when one of the lads called at the chemists to buy a gross of condoms - 144. He was going off on a dirty weekend, wasn't he? On his return he went back to the chemists playing bloody hell. "Eh up," he says. "There was only 143 of them bloody condoms in that gross, there was one short." The chemist gave him another and said. "Oh, I am so sorry if I spoiled your weekend, sir." I digress. Coming back to the Unity, us sex-starved lads were out as usual looking for crumpet. We, of course, were the predators, the evil ones out to tempt and tantalise the female of the species, who was born to fulfil but one purpose, and that was to satisfy man's more urgent needs. She had to succumb to our attentions and be subjected to our desires of the flesh! Well, that's what we hoped, didn't we? We soon learned different, though. What stupid prats we really were. What we did come to realise in time was that God had made two fundamental mistakes when constructing a woman. Number one: he had fitted her with a gob to speak and drive us males bloody crazy; and number two, he had concealed the most important bit where it couldn't be got at. Well, not so easily anyway.

There she was, the girl of my dreams, Her Highness, in all her glory. The world stopped dead for me. Her name was Jean Willmer. I took one look at her and said to my mate. "By gum, she's a cracker, I'd love to give her one." Little did I know that it would take me nearly two bloody years to achieve that worthwhile objective and it was only possible then after I had succumbed to her blandishments and accepted her offer of marriage. I had to, or I would have got now't! I asked the girl of my dreams for a dance, including the last waltz and she allowed me to walk her home after the dance. I think, on reflection, the fact that she lived in Wakefield was a bonus, the fact that I didn't have far to walk her home did help to maintain our long lasting relationship.

I was going out with her for three months before I got to give her a peck on the cheek and another six months before I accidentally brushed my hand against her bosom on a cold frosty night in an alcove down Smythe Street. When she said to me, "what do you think you are doing?" and I said that I was just "warming my hands, love," she smacked me in the gob and said. "That's it then, that's all you want me for," and stormed off home.

She was that cold, she was like a bloody iceberg in disguise, and she could have sunk the Titanic any day of the week. I think Irene, her ma, must have been seduced by an Eskimo and Jean was the unfortunate result of that illicit relationship. Jean's dad Jack was a bit frigid too.

Real blood didn't flow in Jean's veins.

She had a heart of stone that was designed to pump ice and she would have made great company for a redundant sperm whale.

Jean lived down Back Garden Street in the back of the beyond, off Westgate in Wakefield. One of the penalties I had to pay for the dubious privilege of being allowed to go out with my future wife was that I had to meet her family. (I do joke, of course).

Jack, Jean's dad, worked at Kirkstal Forge in Leeds where he worked 12 hours a day.

He was also the man of the house, God in drag. He was served ham for tea, while the kids, Jean, her sister Kath and brothers David and John, had the jam, if there was any. Jack worked hard at his job and had to travel on two buses to get to work at the Kirkstal Forge. He liked a pint and a game of cards in the *Shepherds Rest* on George Street.

Jack had been a regular soldier and was a man of few words. Well, why use words when a crack round the earhole was all that was required? Those were happy days courting Jean. Jack would be belting one of the kids then Irene, Jean's ma, would step in and pull him off, saying, "Stop that, Jack, you'll hurt him (or her)." Then Irene would have a go, wouldn't she? Irene was a cleaner, she cleaned the Town Hall offices early mornings. She was a great woman, a real bundle of fun, always laughing. Jean had been a mistake (that I have had to live with for 43 years.) Jack got Irene pregnant when Irene was in service, and there had to be a wedding with Jean's Grandad Yonty holding a shotgun to Jack's head - Now, lunchtimes at Irenes had developed into an art form. Irene would go to Kath Gavies, a neighbour down the street, for a cal (talk) and probably play merry hell at something Jack, her husband had done, because Jack always kept her short of bras, (money). Anyway, at twenty to twelve she would look at the clock and say. "Bloody hell, Kath, look at the time, I've got to get our Jean's dinner ready."

She would dash home peel the tatties and cook the dinner, usually scotch broth and bloody chips, Irene's favourite recipe. (Jean was weaned on scotch broth and chips). Lo and behold, when Her Highness walked in at lunchtime, her dinner was on the table and that was every day. Quite a remarkable woman, was Irene. She would leave the ashes in the hearth until they crept out on to the rug and she would sit in front of the fire until her legs resembled a draft board.

They also had an old horsehair sofa at Jean's which had a funny smell, but I was pleased that bloody old sofa couldn't talk. If it had, I would have been dead. Jack wouldn't have taken kindly to my unsuccessful attempts to seduce his lovely daughter. But having said that, when I asked him eventually for her hand in marriage, he said. "Nay lad, I thought, tha would have asked for a better bit than that. Why not take all of her and be done with it?"

Then he says. "Bloody hell, lad, ah thought tha'd nivver ask, of course tha can, but don't thee ever dare bring her back!"

Great character, was Jack and I liked him a lot. Especially when I had to go back into the army for fourteen days training one year. My old mate Albert Bolton, the prat, was looking after Jean while I was away and Her

95

Highness, of course, was encouraging him. I knew he never got ow't that I hadn't as yet had myself but she of high virtue was playing games, wasn't she? Ducks and bloody drakes and all that rubbish, but she was also playing with dynamite too. Because Jack, her dad, says to Her Royal Highness. "Now see here, lass, tha had better make thee mind up who tha's going out with, tha is either going out with one ort other, not both, so that had better decide right now, ore else."

And she did. Whether she felt she made the right decision, I will never know. But after 43 years with her I know I did, and I know I have been very lucky.

But that's another story. When I met Jean she had already been courting for a long time. She was, in fact, engaged to a mate of mine called Frank Hemmingway, who came from Lofthouse too. He spoilt her bloody rotten. Whatever she wanted he bought for her. He spoiled her for me too, the silly prat).

She would play games with him, arranging to see him and not turning up. Ah, well. That soon changed, didn't it, when Prince Charming (me) sauntered into her life - by the back door, that is.

She thought I was simply marvellous, love at first sight, wasn't it? Although on reflection, I think it was my black blazer with my army badge on the pocket that did it! I think she thought I was an army veteran or a university student, or something. She most certainly must have thought that I was a little bit more up-market, like, than the usual plonkers she had been used to going out with.

I think in her own little way, she thought I could have been a proper little gentleman, you know, someone she could look up to and respect, and all that tosh, much better by far than the rubbish guys she had been used to in the past. Oh yes, there was the time a certain would-be bloody Casanova tried to seduce her in the back row of the Regal cinema, down Kirkgate in Wakefield. (No, not me, that was to come later, much bloody later). She smacked him in the mouth, gave him his money back and walked out. That was our Jean. No way was she going to sell her soul for the price of a back row seat at the Regal; even the Aga Khan with all his brass would have been turned down, eh!

But well, I mean, even if I say so myself, she just couldn't resist me, could she?

Against her better judgement, she dumped Frank and fell for me hook, line and sinker.

This was the start of a very tempestuous relationship. We were complete opposites, and she fought me every inch of the way, and has done ever since. I never, ever managed to tame my shrew. We fell out many, many times, and we parted many times too. It was a battle of wills, who would crack first. One or the other eventually did. We couldn't live with each other and we couldn't live without each other. When we fell out, I would sneak over to where I thought she would be. She worked at the *Double Two* on George Street, I worked at the steam laundry, in Grantley Street. I would go to the Civic Centre where you got cheap subsidised meals after the war in the hope that I would maybe accidentally bump into her, the little cow! And she would come up to Outwood pictures for the same reason. I couldn't get enough of her (still can't).

I would try to arrange to meet her, say on the following day and Jean Her Highness, would perhaps say. "No, let's leave it until the day after. I have to wash my hair." or some such rubbish.

She was, of course, trying it on with me, like she had with poor old Frank. She was playing hard to get, but this time it didn't work, because I would say in reply. "No, I have a better idea, let's leave it until a week next Tuesday."

I would then go out with my mates. I remember one time when we fell out and I went to the *Griffin* Hotel in Wakefield with my mates, where we would often go for a pint of beer, a sing-song and a dance. Lo and behold, who should be there with another bloke, yes, that's right, Her Highness, the redoubtable Jean. The little cow had pre-empted me. She knew, didn't she, that I would be in there with my mates and she had done it deliberately. The bloke in question is now my brother-in-law, Derek Coxsidge, a great guy. Yes, that's right, she didn't dump him like the rest. She introduced him to her little sister Kath instead and they are now happily married. Over the years we have shared some great times with Kath and Derek. Pity it couldn't last, but that is another story, another day.

Jean's brother David was a rebel without a cause. He played rugby for Yorkshire schoolboys and later for Batley. But although he was a hard rugby player and all that, his mam Irene, bless her, would always warm his underpants in front of the fire before Mighty Mouse was ever allowed to wear them. The little love David worked (sorry, was employed to work but never did) at the local council. He worked mornings as a plumber, then go home at lunch times for lunch. Irene would feed him, then put him to bed with a nice hot water bottle. She would tuck him in and he would sleep like a baby until it was time for him to shout for Irene to go upstairs to turn him over in bed. Much later he would get up and go out on the razzle with his mates, the lazy idle git. I remember one time he had been out with his mates boozing and he came home stoned out of his mind. He got out of his bed in the middle of the night for a pee, went into his dad's bedroom and opened the wardrobe door. His dad wakes up, doesn't he? And he hears a noise, tinkle tinkle, doesn't he? So Jack gets out of bed and there is David the little love, stood in front of the open wardrobe, peeing all over his dad's best suit. Jack nearly killed him. "You little bastard," he says. "Look what you just did to me best bleeding suit, I'll bloody kill yer!" Yes, quite a card, our David.

Jean's grandma was a witch, or so it was said, and after being married for 43 years to the reincarnation of one, I just wouldn't be surprised. Jean's ma Irene never had much brass to spend.

Jean's family, like mine and almost everyone else of our class, were poor in those days. Irene used to have to buy the kids clothes with what were known as Cleggs cheques. These were cheques that were brought from Clegg and Huntingtons in Wakefield, at a price. The loan was then paid back in weekly instalments, plus interest. These cheques could be exchanged for goods and services at the local shops. Poor old Irene was hooked on those bloody cheques and she never ever got out of debt. The only one who didn't have to use these cheques was Jean's dad Jack, him who looked after the brass. He could go to Leeds, couldn't he and pay cash for his clobber. Well, he was the man of the house and it would have just been too much of an embarrassment for Jack to walk into a shop to buy anything with a Cleggs bloody cheque.

I think Jack honestly thought he had paid his debt to Irene when he agreed to marry her and make an honest woman of her after he had got her pregnant. Ah well, that was how it was in those days. Shot gun weddings were the norm; you got married or else!

I will never forget the day that Irene bought Jean a new coat, a check coat no less, to wear with her tattered Gypsy Rose Lee bloody headscarf. All the girls wore headscarves in those days). Now Irene couldn't afford to buy Jean's sister Kath one as well, so she said to Jean. "Our Jean, don't you tell our Kath, will you?! But Kath got to know didn't she, and she told Derek, her boyfriend, who she was courting at the time. Well Derek just couldn't keep his gob shut could he, he couldn't help himself, he was in love, weren't he? Unlike me, who didn't say boo to a goose, just please and thank you. Well, I seemed to have this consoling effect on women, they thought that butter wouldn't melt in my mouth and were lulled into a false sense of security, beguiled by my humility, or something like that. But not Derek. Like Saint George who was going to slay that bloody dragon, the fearless Derek jumped in there with both bloody feet, didn't he? Right bang smack, straight into the lion's den. Just like a little lamb to the slaughter.

"Mrs Wilmer," he says in the bravest voice he could muster (which was just a little whisper). "Mrs Willmer I don't think it's fair that Jean's got a new coat and Kath hasn't." Well, this confrontation started in the living room, didn't it? He was 6ft 2in tall, was Derek, and before he had finished saying fair, Irene had him by the throat. She lifted him up off the floor and threw him into the hallway. "Fair!" She says! "Fair! I'll show you what bloody fair is." And she threw him out of the house. Poor Derek was petrified, wasn't he? Irene came back into the living room rubbing her hands. I was sat twiddling my thumbs and looking up at the ceiling ever so innocently, wasn't I? And of course, being the treacherous bastard that I am (I just couldn't resist it), I said to Irene. "I don't think Derek should have said that, Mrs Wilmer, should he?" Well, I'll leave you dear reader to guess the reaction to that one. Ah well, All's well that ends well. Didn't do me any harm, did it, because while Derek was in exile, Jean and I had full unrestricted access to the front parlour (I still got now't!)

Derek should have kept his gob shut. It took him ages to get his foot back in through that front door, and he never really got his feet back under Irene's table until he had married Kath. I felt really sorry for him, the daft sod.

Jean's best friend at this time was her cousin Sylvia, who worked with her at the Double Two Shirt Company in Wakefield. Jean and her cousin were like sisters and while employed at the Double Two in the 1950s, they were both invited to work at the Ideal Home Exhibition at Earls Court in London, where the Double Two were exhibiting their products.

The young Princess Margaret opened the exhibition and I do remember that both Jean and Sylvia remarked on how lovely the little princess was. She was, they said, just like a little baby doll!

I'm sure that in their own little way Jean and her cousin enjoyed their trip to London, but it can't have been much fun really, because they both returned home with their virginity intact. Well, at least they had a small consolation prize, they had seen Princess Margaret, hadn't they? Bless 'em, the little loves!

Sylvia's boyfriend, later to become her husband was a chap called John Snowden. We shared many happy times in our youth and I have fond memories of him. More about John later.

About this time Irene Jean's mam, worked with a friend at Wakefield Town Hall. This friend had a 1932 Morris Minor car for sale for £25, so

Irene told me about this little car and I went to look at it.

I thought it was absolutely marvellous and I bought it.

I decided that I was entitled to a bit of comfort in my old age. I was now 23 years of age, and I was bloody sick of Irene nagging me to catch the last bust at ten to eleven, which I usually missed. After all, it was rather difficult, after having left Jean with her virginity still intact, trying to run for that bloody bus with one leg stuck in the air, up back lane, across Wood Street and on to Northgate near Clayton Hospital in Wakefield. So I rarely caught that bleeding bus home.

Oh, the joys of courtship! Irene used to push me out the front door when she thought I was having it away with her darling daughter. Little did she know that her daughter was more than capable of handling me or anyone else, for that matter. No, no, I didn't meant it that way, dear reader! No, what I meant was that Jean was an artist, a master of deception. She could have started World War bloody Three any day of the week, and won it!

She taught me that anticipation was better than realisation, because I had to be ever the anticipator who never truly realised his ambition until later, much bloody later.

Back to the Morris Minor. We went everywhere and anywhere with everybody in that old car. We took our families off at holiday times - to the seaside, Bridlington, Scarboro, Blackpool.

My pride and joy, I called it. It had a top speed of 45mph (well, it had downhill).

We would have as many as six people in that little car. When we returned home from a booze-up on a Saturday night, the only trouble was every time we hit a bump the bloody body rubbed the tyres, and if you applied the cable brakes hard you were all over the bloody place.

Now, making love in the back seat of a 1932 Morris Minor is like a mouse climbing up an elephant's tail with the intention of rape; it is the height of impossibility, and Jean taught me that the hanging straps fitted into the rear corners of the car were not designed for placing her-of-high-virtue's feet into while her bum rested on the steering wheel. Oh no, she said, those straps are for holding on to with your hands. Well, one lives and learns, doesn't one, and to think I never knew! Ah well, we all make mistakes; pity I wasn't allowed to make mine. Well, just once would have been a bloody fine thing!

The most memorable moment I had with that car was when I was visiting Sylvia's mam, Aunt Lil and Uncle Alf on Eastmoor Estate. I was laid underneath this car adjusting the back brakes with my legs stuck out at the sides when this bus comes along and the bloody silly driver runs over my feet. Jean's Aunt Lil happened to be on this bus at the time and she says. "I thought I felt a bump."

I said. "So did I, they were my bloody feet." Anyway, little John, Slylvia's boyfriend at the time (he is only about 5ft 2in), picked me up and carried me into the house, and as we go through the front door, the silly little bastard bangs me head on the door frame, doesn't he? Now, not only have I got crushed feet, I've also probably got a fractured bloody skull and concussion too.

They ring for an ambulance, which takes me to Clayton Hospital casualty department. The doctor says to me. "Run over, run over by a bus, a double decker, hmm, and run over them sideways too, hmmm, remarkable." I think what saved my feet was the fact that I was wearing a pair of second hand shoes two sizes too big for me. My feet were black and blue, and my shoes were unrecognisable as such.

I think I claimed £25 from the Bus Company for a new pair of shoes and a week off work.

Today I could probably retire on the proceeds.

I suffered with me feet for years and could never get shoes that were comfortable. Strange as it may seem, 40 years later a foot specialist found that I had a dislocated toe which had grown on top of the adjoining bone. He had to cut the excess bone away and pin it into position. Not surprising when 15 years after the accident I dropped a 5cwt safe on the same toe and Derek Turner the rugby player came and bailed me out. But that's another story and another day.

# Part 2

## The Ramper At The End Of The World

In 1954 Jean and I decided to get married. She had sat me on her knee, and sang to me, *'Baby, Won't You Say You Love Me'*. How could I refuse? We had got engaged around a year earlier and had started saving for the big day. We had to cut down on many things to save money. Instead of going dancing or to the cinema, we spent our spare time looking in furniture shop windows and dreaming.

Kath, Jean's sister, and her boyfriend Derek were courting strong too and we used to fight over who got to use the front room at Irene's. My sister Lenore and Vic were also courting, as were Sylvia, Jean's cousin, and John. Everything in the garden seemed rosy. But it was about this time that I was taken ill with appendicitis and Jean walked from Wakefield to Lofthouse to see me as there were no buses running for some reason. I eventually had to go into Chapel Allerton Hospital in Leeds for an emergency operation, and I remember Jean coming to see me in hospital. I told her to wait outside till I got my clothes, sneaked out of the hospital, and climbed over the 8 foot railings to meet her. I still had the stitches in at the time!

What one will do for the love of a good woman, eh!

But it didn't do me any good; invalid or no bloody invalid, I still got now't!

Moving on to 1955, the big day arrived. My dad had managed to get us an old terraced house to rent from Saville and Kilburns, the Wakefield Estate Agents, for 11 shillings (54p) a week. It came complete with outside toilet and all the trimmings. There was, as was usual in the old terraced houses in those days, a set pot for boiling water in the corner of the kitchen, rising damp on every wall, a stone kitchen sink and the main feature was a conventional fireplace, complete with black hob.

It was our new home and we thought it was absolutely marvellous. With the help of Pete Bolton, my pal Albert's brother, we flushed all the house doors with hard board. Well everybody who was anybody in those days always flushed the front doors of those old terrace houses with hardboard.

102

Well, we had to make them doors look a bit better, or different from everybody else's hadn't we? The only trouble was that all us terrace householders thought the same, so every house in the bloody street had the front doors flushed with poxy hardboard!

Then, of course we had to repaint the whole house.

Now Sylvia's mam, Aunt Lil, helped us out in this respect. Jean's Aunt Lil was a lovely woman and an expert at decorating. She bloody well ought to have been, because she moved house every three weeks and every time she moved, she would redecorate. After a while this redecorating lark did become a bit of a bind, so Lil insisted that her daughter Sylvia marry a painter and decorator, which Sylvia obligingly did. Now John Sylvia's husband, redecorated for Aunt Lil 42, 000 times before she died, bless her. I dare say that Lil has by now just about driven that St. Peter crackers with her demands that he repaints the heavens red instead of blue, and I would just like to bet that she has been trying for years to get God to hang a bit of net curtain over the moon. (Here I go again!) Suffice to say, we had a lot of help from both our families and friends.

We had saved up the princely sum of £200 between us over two years and we had gone to the January sales in Leeds to buy our furniture, which consisted of a dining room suite, two fireside chairs, lino on the floor and a rug in front of the fireplace. A new bedroom suite completed the picture.

It was all ours and it was heaven.

The big day of the wedding arrived. Our Reg my cousin, was best man, Sylvia, Kath and my sister Lenore were the bridesmaids.

We got married at Wakefield Cathedral and I will never forget it cost me £5 to tip the verger. I had no change, and a fiver was a fortune in those days.

Jean's mam and dad had booked the West Riding Club down Market Street for the reception. Jack, her dad, had by this time left Kirkstal Forge, and was now working as a cleaner for the West Riding Bus Company. The West Riding club was for the bus company's employees' use, so Jack had managed to save us a bob or two. It was great. Dickie Day, a local character, came along to entertain the guests. Harry Thornton and Charlie Moss, the auctioneers from Laidlaws were invited, as was Ivor Applegarth from Saville and Killburns, the auctioneers. Well they had to be there didn't they, after all they kept my dad supplied with work. My ma provided lettuce, tomatoes etc, which she had bought from Wakefield Market, and she also made the trifles etc. Jean's ma for her part provided the wedding cake as our wedding present, and I paid the bills.

103

After, we moved into Pollard Street, Lofthouse Gate - or the Ramper, as it was nicknamed - for our honeymoon. We had to live on lettuce for a fortnight after the wedding; that was all that was left after those greedy guests had eaten all the ham and the jelly and custard. I wouldn't have cared, but they hadn't bought a decent bloody present between the lot of them. We were absolutely broke, we didn't have two halfpennies to rub together. I couldn't pay Freshwater, who had the garage on Leeds Road at Newton Hill, for the wedding car until four weeks later. But money didn't matter. We were together in our own little home, we had each other and it was heaven.

We would budget for all our yearly expenditure. Every week we would save a little for bills, food, clothes and insurance etc. We put our savings for various things into little cups in our front room cupboard. Those were wonderful days down the Ramper. We were young, we were happy and we were in love. The street down to our house was just a muck track, so in the winter we would be sludged up to the eyes, and in summer everything was covered in dust. But we had some really good neighbours.

From the top of the street there was Ernest and Annie Drake, a lovely couple. Annie would do owt for anybody. Then there was old George Winter and his wife, she who wore Mother Riley bloody stockings.

Now George was a real character who had originally come from Barnsley. All his life, he had pushed a barrow loaded with fruit and vegetables, which he used to sell from the barrow. Now, in his old age, he still had a barrow. But this time it was used to collect coal. The old bugger used to stand at the end of the pit lane, at the Lofthouse Colliery entrance on Potovens Lane, and he would wait for the loaded coal wagons coming down to the halt sign at the bottom. He would wave them out, then when they were nearly at the end of the lane and near the halt sign, he would put both hands up to stop them.

The drivers would brake hard, coal would fall off the back of the lorry and old George would sweep it up and put it into his barrow to keep the home fires burning.

Next to George lived the redoubtable, unforgettable Ken Petty and his wife Phyllis. Ken became my mate and he  deserves a chapter all of his own later. Like me, Ken had been everywhere and done everything. He was a brilliant mechanic and electrician, he could in fact repair almost anything, and did. He would stick two steel knitting needles into the live incoming electrically supply and bypass the meter to save on his electricity bills. He was fantastic with motorbikes and he achieved quite a lot during his career. (Motorbikes, I mean). If Ken took a fancy to a motorbike, he simply took one. He would file out the chassis number and then he would re-stamp a new number onto the frame; he was brilliant. Spotlights, too, were his particular forte. He couldn't walk past a bloody car with a spotlight on display, he just had to pinch it. I do remember quite clearly once when the coppers were after him and Ken got wind of this. He asked if I could fix him up with a bit of storage space. I agreed to let him use my spare back bedroom. Well, he filled that bedroom with dozens of spot lamps and motorbike bits. There must have been the equivalent of at least twenty bloody motorbikes in my back bedroom at that time! Jean nearly went stark raving bonkers.

The police did eventually catch up with Ken and he was taught the error of his ways.

They took him and locked him up, and if ever they had found all those other bits in my back bedroom then I would have joined him. (That reminds me, I never charged him for storage either.)

Ken and I were to become good friends (well, sometimes) and over the years he repaired my cars and trucks. He sometimes drove for me too if he fancied a change from his work at Lofthouse pit, taking a day off work to help me out. I was struggling to survive, and Ken played a major part in that process. It was about this time that Ken Petty punched Jack Proud, the greengrocer, on the nose, for pulling his overhead electric cable down with his lorry. Ken had this cable slung from his house window across to his garage and poor old Jack hadn't seen it, had he? Jack called the police, and Ken had to go to court.

Evelyn Berry, our neighbour, stood as a witness for Jack. Just to even things up a bit, a week later Ken put a brick through Evelyn's front bedroom window.

I had an improvised garage at this time, made out of bits of wood and an old tarpaulin sheet. Because my so-called bloody mate Ken was having to pay rates on his purpose-built garage, (the only garage in the street, I might ad) and I wasn't, he shopped me to the local council, the prat!

We had another fall-out over that episode. Ken Petty became my chief, well my only mechanic a few years later, on weekends, or when he chose to have an extra rest day at Tommy Mapplebeck's (the Lofthouse colliery Manager's) pleasure, Ken was also my best mate, would you believe.

Quite a guy, indeed quite a character was our Ken. He always had a nice car, the best car in the street he would say.

I well remember another incident from my days down the Ramper. One of our neighbours let's call him John, had a nice car and was a real dandy too, what with his double-breasted suit. In fact he was the only man in the street that had a decent suit in those days, and he sure impressed the ladies. He wasn't short of a bob or two either, he had a good job, and was good at it, was our John. He would do all the usual haunts, the *Spread Eagle* and the *Angel* up Bradford Road, and he had quite an eye for the ladies. I remember one Saturday night in particular, when he became an overnight sensation. He was out as usual doing the usual pub crawl and he returned home this night, drunk as a lord. He had been drowning his sorrows because his wife, bless her, was ill in Pinderfields Hospital in Wakefield. Anyway, John cops (got himself) a young dolly bird, doesn't he, and he offers her a bed for the night. He was a bit lonely, his wife being in hospital and all that, and he felt he needed a bit of company, a bit of moral support, someone to talk to, a shoulder to cry on. Today the state would have provided that support; female stress counsellors are available for free today. But they were not available to us in those days. So John had to provide his own and he was lucky to just happen to be able to drop on one while he was out, one who was ready willing and able to satisfy his needs. Now it wasn't often that one was able to find such an unselfish, caring, loving individual, who was prepared to rise to the occasion and minister to someone else's needs. But she was and she did, bless her. Anyway, after John's samaritan had eventually consoled him and managed to settle him down to sleep, there was a bloody great crash, the kitchen window was smashed in and through it staggers a raving lunatic, brandishing a chopper. "Where is she?" he shouts. "I'll kill the bastard."

Our John and his helper jumped out of bed. "What on earth can be the matter?" exclaimed John to his counsellor. Or it may have sounded like "What the...was that," anyway, same thing. It had been a rather warm night, hadn't it, so they were both in the nude. It had been just too hot to sleep in clothes, ah well. So there they both were, running around trying to put on their clothes, but it was too late. The lunatic came rushing into the bedroom, swinging his chopper (yes that's right, a small axe) round his head. I doubt if John's counsellor would have left her husband in the first place if he had been able to swing his own, chopper round his head. Yes, the raving lunatic, the wild bull of the Pampas, was indeed the counsellor's husband, and he had followed them home with the intention of killing them both. There was a mad scramble in the bedroom, John pushed the husband against the wall, jumped over the bed, and he and his friend fell over each other going down the stairs, closely followed by the mad axeman and his redoubtable chopper. They managed after a struggle to get out the front door. The girl ran down the street, chased by Evelyn Berry, our next-door neighbour, with a sweeping brush. The entire bloody street was out by this time. John shot up the street pursued by the mad axeman. Naked bodies were flying all over the place. I honestly believe things would have calmed down if someone had been given the opportunity to explain to the axeman that the real reason his wife was with John in his hour of need was because she felt sorry for him, and her only desire had been to bring him a little comfort. But it wasn't to be. The axeman after a while gave up the chase and decided on an easier target, John's car (his pride and joy). He started to knock hell out of it and that did it. That was the only thing that would have stopped our John in his stride, and it did. He came back down the street shouting, "Stop it, you daft bastard, leave me bloody car alone, it's done now't to thee. If tha wants to hit ow't, then hit thee bloody wife and leave me car alone!" By this time the police were on the scene and quickly arrested the mad axeman. But our John didn't get off scot-free either, because he made the front-page headlines in that Sunday's News of The World. But I do feel he was treated rather unfairly by the press. I believe his intentions were perfectly honourable, and he just wanted a little comfort and sympathy while his wife was in hospital. You can bet your bottom dollar that half the other blokes in the street agreed with me, and only wished that they'd had the guts to do the same.

What a man, what a character! But it was all's well that ends well. John's wife came home fully recovered from hospital, and her and our John settled back into their normal, happy married life together. But after that John became rather more discreet, eh!

That was the Ramper, all right. Peyton Place was a little more up-market, but couldn't hold a bloody candle to our dear old Ramper at the end of the world.

A lovely couple called Ernest and Pat Rowley were also our neighbours down the Ramper, and Ernest was a friend for many years. At that time he worked for a haulage contractor from Barnsley, driving a petrol engined Dodge tipper. He used to bring his lorry home of a night, which was a serious mistake, a real temptation. It was like giving a starving man a sausage roll and then telling him not to eat it. Because that bloody lorry gave my mate Ken Petty and me a real problem. We had to decide who would have the right of access to the petrol tank.

We, decided to compromise and agreed that we would each take our turn at having a go at Ernest's fuel tank. Unfortunately, we must have got the days mixed up one time, because poor Ernest ran out of petrol at Newmillerdam. Ah well, we can all make mistakes, can we not?

Next door to Ernest lived Peter and June Padgett. Peter worked for

Watson and Cairns the motor cycle dealers in Leeds. We used to have some good Saturday nights out with Peter and his pal Gerry Booth, the carpet man. The only problem was when Peter got a pint or two down him, he went potty, especially at driving. Peter is now the biggest motor cycle dealer in Yorkshire, (and he's still bloody potty!) Peter's business is at Batley.

George and Evelyn Berry were next. George had some land at Potovens Lane where he kept pigs (I was to rent this land off him later, to park my tipper trucks) until his wife Evelyn decided they ought to invest in something a little better, like a new bloody house. George and his brother Ray worked at Stone House's Mill down Westgate, Wakefield. Then there was George's dad and Kath and Jim Berry, who also lived down the Ramper. As friends and neighbours, the only problem that we had was perhaps when we fell out over the kids, whereas the kids, (the little bleeders) were usually as right as rain two minutes after they had fallen out with each other. Ah well, nothing changes. Bert and Margaret Hemmingway were also neighbours. I worked with Bert at Ropers Brickyard later, and Margaret used to come on a Friday to collect Bert's wage before he ever saw it! Bert also had a window cleaning round to help to supplement his income. He was a great lad, was Bert. My wife Jean at this time had her cross to bear, because our kids were born twelve months apart. My eldest daughter Susan was born in 1957, and my daughter Anne in 1958.

Jean produced our first daughter and I produced the second. Yes, that's right, we couldn't even agree on the reproduction process!

When Jean did her shopping, she had to do it with one child in a pushchair and one in her arms. So you can perhaps appreciate her struggles on and off those West Riding buses to and from Wakefield, loaded down with shopping, two kids and a pushchair. Nothing was easy in those days, there was no one-stop shopping for her by car, no, no sirree. And, I might add, the kids in those days were properly fed, washed and walked to school.

Unlike today, where they are given a quick wipe around the face with a wet cloth and a glass of pop, before being thrown into the back of a bloody car at 8.55am and driven to school.

There were very few mod cons like central heating, hot baths, inside toilets and instant hot water. But I do remember one rather special domestic appliance I acquired for Jean, oh yes, I do remember it well. It was an old Beatty washer which I had acquired from an old house that I'd helped to clear out with my dad when he worked for Laidlaw's auctioneers. It was as rusty as hell and we were going to scrap it when I said "Hang on a minute, let's try it first," so we plugged it into the power supply and lo and behold, with a clatter and a bang, it started. Her in-doors at last had her first and by no means last (because she wore them out faster than Hotpoint could produce the bloody things) electric wash-ing machines. When I presented her with it, Her Highness stood there in the kitchen wrapped in silence for five minutes, just looking. The washer for its part, bless it, stood there with downcast eyes and a wry smile on its face, staring back. I feel sure it gave Jean an imperceptible wink, as much as to say. "Come on then, I dare you." The washer I felt rather sorry for; it was in fact a little older than Jean and it did warrant a little respect from Her Highness. It didn't deserve to be scorned and looked at as though it was something the cat had just brought in, did it? Eventually Her High-ness says, "What is it then?"

And I say's. "What does it bloody well look like!"

And then she says. "Surprise me"

She then says. "Me mother had one of those 20 years ago."

I says. "Oh no she bloody didn't, this is a proper washer. It may look a bit rough now, but when you have learned to blindfold yourself before using it, then it won't look half as bad and besides that, you don't have to wind the ringer because it's electric." The washer, bless it, never said a word. It just stood there on its three rusty little legs, stuck out its discol-oured copper boiler of a chest and, displaying what looked like the largest sexual organ we had ever seen between its legs (the bloody great single phase motor), it just stood there. I think it was Jean's second glance that did it, because she just happened to notice Willy's, er, motor didn't she? Yes, the washer was now called Willy.

Ever been turned on by a washer? Jean was that day. She fell in love with it. She just couldn't leave Willy's motor alone, every day she was at it, until God forbid, Willy's motor started dribbling oil all over the floor. Well, it would, wouldn't it, all the use she was giving it! So what does she do? Well, now that she had worn Willy's motor out, she decided it was time she had herself a new washer! So she tried to get rid of Willy, she stabbed him in his boiler with a screwdriver, so that now as well as the motor leaking oil all over the kitchen floor, the bloody boiler was also leaking water too. So Jean says to me. "Now you will just have to buy me a new washer. I can't do with that mess all over me kitchen floor and besides that, all the bloody neighbours have got new washers. You will just have to buy me a new one, because there's a hole in the boiler."

I says. "I will 'ave a look at the bloody thing." Now the oil leak, well that was easy. I put a bowl underneath the motor to catch the oil. But the water leak from the boiler, well that was a bit more difficult, but I did manage to effect a satisfactory repair. I gets a match stick, wraps a bit of cotton wool round it and bungs it into the hole, and low and behold, the leaking boiler's repaired. "Now get on wi thee bloody weshing, yer miserable cow, and stop thee moaning," I said to my wife. Willy lasted for another two years, after I had fitted him up with a new set of false teeth (rollers).

We had two little rocking chairs in our house at this time, which was all we had room for in the living room. I used to love my little rocker, so did Jean. I would come home after a hard day at work and fall asleep in my little rocker and Jean would then rock me in my chair until the money fell out of my pockets, straight into her purse.

That bloody rocking chair cost me a fortune. It was better than any modern cash machine and she didn't need any card either. I wouldn't care, but she won all ends up. Here was I, struggling to survive, and the little money I had was spent when she charged me once every three months for sex. Now I even lost out on that little pleasure too; no brass, no sex, and that was that!

She was a right cunning little bleeder. I remember once when she went just a little too far, and I bundled her into the car and took her home to her mam's didn't I? I left her outside St. Michael's House flats in Wakefield where her ma Irene lived, and dumped her. But even her mum wouldn't have her back. Irene says, "I put up with yer for twenty bloody year, now it's somebody else's turn. You have made your bed, now go and lay in it." Quite a girl, our Irene, she had a lot of sense. If it had been my mam she would have welcomed me back with open arms and furthermore, she would have locked me in my bedroom and wouldn't have let that hussy anywhere within three miles of us. She would have made sure that all my pockets were full of money and not empty, bless her.

Anyway, that same night as I was dozing in my rocker, safe from that preying mantis and her wandering hands, there was a gentle almost inaudible knock on the front door. The door opened and a head appeared; it was Derek Coxsidge, my brother-in-law. I think he thought I was going to throw something at him, because he said in a whisper, "Er, um, is everything all right? For Mrs. Wilmer has asked me to bring Jean back."

I says. "Yes, she just would, wouldn't she, the silly old cow."

Derek grabs Jean, shoves her inside and he's off like the clappers. I think Irene must have bribed Derek. One thing was for certain, she sent her back home to me pretty sharpish! Marital bliss, the art of conquering, or learning to live with a woman! Yes, those were happy days, even though we were living in so-called poverty.

Yes, I will repeat it again. We did have to use outside toilets; yes, we did have to use old fish and chip wrappers to wipe our bums on, because we couldn't afford luxuries like proper newspapers; but we were very lucky because that outside toilet was ours and at least we didn't have to share it with everyone else in the bloody street like some of our less fortunate contemporaries had to.

I suppose by today's standards we were poor, but the nice thing was we didn't feel poor. We didn't know we were poor, because the people we worked and lived with were all on the same level in society, and we were all in the same boat together. We had to sink or swim and we chose to swim, so we survived.

This poem is by way of an introduction to our way of life in the 1950s

We were born into a real world, such a long time ago.
We worked long hours when wages were low.
We had no TV or washer and we didn't have a bath.
We didn't have a garden, so we didn't need a path.
We had an outside toilet, way, way down the yard.
We wiped our bums on newspapers, times were very hard.
There were no holidays abroad, or carpets on the floor
But we had coal on the fire and we didn't lock the door.

Children were born - no birth control pills were made.
And we brought them up on our own, without any state aid.
Our children could go out to play safely in the park.
And the old folks could go for a long walk in the dark
We didn't use Valium, there was no LSD.
And we cured most of our ills with a nice cup of tea.
But if we were sick we were looked after and treated at once,
Not fill out a form and come back in twelve month.

There were no vandals, no mugging - there was nothing to rob
And we were as rich as could be on just a couple of bob.
Most of us were happy in those far-off days.
People were kinder and caring, in so many, many ways.
The milkman and the paper boys used to whistle and sing
A night out at the pictures was our usual weekly fling
We couldn't afford to eat out and to buy our grub.
But at least we had waiter service, service in every pub!

We couldn't afford posh houses, we didn't have a car.
But we had the best of neighbours, yes, the best by far.
When we did the shopping, we had to use the bus.
But we just got on with things and didn't make a fuss
Stress counsellors and social workers, those we never knew
We just got on with life and did what we had to do.
We certainly had our share of trouble and our share of strife.
And we just had to face it, it was our way of life
But now as I grow older and look back through those years.
I don't think of the bad times, the trouble and the tears.
I think of our way of life and the things we used to do.
And those special shared moments spent with the people I once knew.

May I be allowed to stop for a moment to reflect on my life.

Some of us still had to work 12-hour days. We still lived, in the 1930s and 40s and 50s, in those old back-to-back terraced houses with old stone sinks and set pots built into the corners of the kitchens, to boil our water on Monday washdays.

We still had an old coal fireplace in the front room, with an oven to cook in and a hot water tank to boil water in. Yes, we still black-leaded the fireplaces, scoured our front steps with a scouring stone and aired our freshly washed clothes in front of the fire on a clothes horse, or a clothes rail hung from the ceiling. That was, of course, after they had been washed with dolly blue in a peggy tub, using a posser. We still had clip rugs on the floor made out of old clothes that were cut up into bits of cloth. We survived in spite of our outside toilets and ash middens. We had our unpasteurised milk delivered to the door in a horse-drawn milk float, straight from the farm, and it would be measured out for us and poured into jugs. Our coal came on a horse-drawn dray from our local coal merchant, who also moved our furniture when and if we had to move house. Most of our day-to-day necessities came by rail and were delivered to the door by an LNER horse-drawn van, or a Scammell three-wheeler and trailer. No, nothing much had changed for my generation.

From 1830 to the 1950s, we still worked just as hard and lived in the same conditions as our parents and grandparents.

But for all that, we had some really wonderful times. My town Wakefield was indeed the Merry City, in those wonderful days of our youth. When Jean and I were first married, I can well remember the odd Saturday night when we would go out on the town together in my little old 1932 Morris 8. We would go to Primrose Hill Club on Eastmoor, or to

Alverthorpe Club, where we danced the night away and had a ball. There was always entertainment at these clubs.

We would have pie and pea suppers at the club, or call for fish and chips on the way home, which we would take back to a friend's house. Then we would settle down to enjoy ourselves and play a few games after the meal, like truth or dare, kiss or promise, cheekies, touch cock for buttons, or pass the wife - which was a big improvement on pass the parcel!

The only problem with this game was that you couldn't keep the parcel, it had to be handed back. If things became a little boring, we would make do with a bit of wife swapping. Wife swapping is nothing new, in fact it was our generation that invented the bloody game, although we didn't call it that in our day. It was called 'just for lend', or 'let's pretend', or just 'playing cheekies with a friend'. The only bloody trouble was, we wife swappers always finished up going home with the same bird that we came with and it always used to cost me a few quid to boot, before anyone would do me a swap. Remember, my wife's mum had been seduced by an Eskimo and the result was that Jean could have sunk the Titanic, she was that cold. Apart from that, at the time she was practising to become a trainee corpse, so as you can well imagine, I was at a distinct disadvantage. I honestly believe that I would have had a much better chance of a decent swap at these orgies (sorry, parties) if I had in fact turned up with a pregnant bloody kangaroo!

This Is The Wife Swappers Lament.

Yes, we were happy, as happy as could be.
Happy little wife swappers, that was we
We would do a swop for a couple of bob
This wife swopping to us was just the job.

Yes, it was our generation, who started this new trend.
Swapping our wife for the wife of a friend.
We started by playing, just let's pretend
But we ended up wife swapping in the end.

We loved this game, oh how we liked to play.
And some played it well, most every day
But some didn't play fair, they hadn't much tact.
And when my turn came round, they wouldn't swap back.

I soon got tired and my wife back home I did send.
This wife swapping for me had to come to an end.
I decided to do my swapping on my own.
So I went a-swapping and left the wife at home.

Moral

Never play with fire, you only get burnt.
That's the truth of it, that I learnt.
If you go astray and you want to roam.
Then make sure you play away and not at home.

On a more serious note, we used to have some great times with so many of our friends. There was Jean's cousin Sylvia and her husband little John (the prat of the fireman's lift and fractured skull fame), Jean's sister Kath and her husband Derek, and their friends too, who also became our friends. We were young, not very well off, but we all had some really great times together in the 1960s. We would visit the Malt Shovel up Dewsbury Rd, Wakefield, with Jean's cousin Sylvia and her mam and dad, Jean's mam and dad, Irene and Jack, and sometimes Jean's grandma and dear old Yonty, her grandad, would come along too. We would all have a ball, listening to music, dancing and enjoying ourselves. But the real highlight of our lives was when Jean's Uncle Ronnie came across from South Wales, where he was a car dealer. He would arrive in Wakefield, just like John F bloody Kennedy, the president of the United States, (the one who got assassinated, pity it weren't Uncle Ron!) in a bloody great Yankee cadillac convertible. That was something really special in those days, and we would all fight each other for who got the first ride. Why?

Well, nobody at our humble level in society had ever seen a bloody cadillac, let alone ever ridden in one. Oh yes, I had a clapped-out 1932 Morris Minor, which I had bought for twenty-five quid; Sylvia's husband John had a bike; her brother-in-law Derek had a pair of roller skates; and her dad, well, all he had was a second-hand pair of boots from Wakefield market! But cadillacs, wow, they were like UFOs in our day, something from outer space. Uncle Ronnie, bless him, was about the same age as his nieces, in fact they had played together as children. He was conceived a little late in his mother Martha's life, he was, well, just a little afterthought, really, a bloody mistake in fact! Ronnie now lives in Canada, thank God, where he is no longer able to come along so easily to disrupt our peaceful, mundane, mediocre lives, the prat. Bless him! I must not close this paragraph without mentioning Sylvia's dad Alf and Jean's dad, Jack. We had some good times together and it was a tradition that every Christmas day we would all go to the pub together, which we did for years. Alf was a good mate and a wonderful man who always had a smile and a good word for everyone. Unfortunately he died from lung cancer, I believe. I will never forget the night just before he died. I picked him up and took him for a pint at the Whinney Moor Hotel on the Lupset Estate in Wakefield. No, I will never forget Alf Jack and all those wonderful people I once knew.

We used to have friendly arguments with two friends of ours about the relative advantages or disadvantages of owning or renting one's home. They would say. "Well, at least our house belongs to us, and at the very least, we shall have something to leave our kids; you won't."

I would reply. "Bugger the kids, I'm not depriving them or me over 25 or 30 years just to struggle to pay a mortgage and have a fine home, at the expense of everything else in life," and I would say. "Anyway, by the time you have finished paying for your house, you will be too old to enjoy it and apart from that you will never be able to turn it into money, because you will always need somewhere to live."

I was happy with my rented accommodation and no major debts. I only built my own house when I could well afford to and when I was really forced to move out of the council house we lived in, in the 1960s. Well, it wouldn't have looked quite right, would it, with 24 bloody great furniture vans parked on and up and down Potovens Lane in Outwood and me living in a bloody council house. Well, not really I suppose! I always remembered what my dear old dad used to say to me, about the people who lived opposite us on Sunnyside (that is what we called Johns Avenue, Lofthouse, where we lived when I was a lad) He would say, "I'm not pining (starving) myself to bloody death, just to 'ev a fine home." Great character my dear old dad!

# Hargreaves At Rothwell

Around this time I worked at Shawcross Pit delivering briquetts with an Austin Loadstar lorry, which unfortunately (for them) was fitted with a petrol engine. At the time I was running a 1934 Austin 16 hp car, which I could hardly afford to run. So I used to take a gallon can inside a small suitcase to work with me everyday. All my mates called me Doctor Murphy. But I had the last laugh because I used to coast down hills to save petrol, then siphon myself a gallon a day. I dared not let that bloody suitcase out of my sight. But I remember one day walking up to the canteen with my little suitcase and the yard foreman, when the bloody petrol can started to leak, didn't it? The foreman said, "What's that dripping out of thee case?"

I said. "Bloody, bleeding hell, that's another sodding flask I have just broke, and me on me way to the canteen to get it refilled!" It was a bloody good job he couldn't smell, and that he hadn't stopped to light his pipe and thrown his match anywhere near Doctor Murphy's bloody attache case; we would have both gone up in flames.

We had some great fiddles on that briquette job. I used to go to Keighley with an old salesman delivering our briquettes. Now this old guy was an artist at fiddling. By the time he'd had his share and I'd got mine, there was hardly any left for the paying customers! I eventually left Shawcross, as it became too far to travel to; besides, it was becoming too hot to handle.

By this time I managed to get a job at Hargreaves in Rothwell, driving their coal tippers. I worked 60 hours a week and was paid between £10 or £12 weekly with overtime. I never managed to work anywhere in my life where I got sick pay. Lorry drivers in those days were paid for one week's holiday a year, and usually we would work that week to earn an extra week's pay. We didn't feel like people seem to today: overworked, over-stressed, and complaining about so-called poverty, because we just hadn't time to think; we just got out and got on with it. Hargreaves was a good firm to work for and I was there for about three years.

I took an interest in trade unionism in those days. I was elected and became a member of the trade union committee at Hargreaves. At last I had arrived; I was now a real live trade union man, no less, I had taken another step up that ladder and I was soon to become an agitator and another bloody nuisance to the management. Oh yes, the words I used now were not 'mate', oh no, my mates had suddenly become 'brothers' and the firm I worked for was not a firm any more, oh no, it had now become 'management'. It eventually got so bad with this 'them and us' attitude, that the drivers couldn't even reply to a good morning from management without first having a bloody shop steward present! My nickname at Hargreaves was Midnight Charlie, because I was always late in at night in my attempts to maximise my earning capacity by earning extra overtime. The boss used to come round on a night to check who was still out, and he would pull my clock card out of the rack and say to himself, "That Walker, we can forget him. He won't be in until midnight!"

I was once coming through Rothwell one night at 8pm and the boss was on his way back home when he stopped me. "And where have you been until now?" he said. "Building sites close at 5 to 6pm."

I said. "Well I'm sorry but the first house of the pictures (cinema) didn't turn out until after 7pm," and he laughed, he thought it was funny. So did I, but it was true. I used to go to the pictures to earn my overtime. I was late for work every morning. But the boss nailed me one day and I had to report to his office. "Now, what's the meaning of this," he said. "You are always late for work."

I says. "Well, sir, I have made a New Year's resolution, I am going to change my ways and get to work on time."

He replied. "Yes, I've made a New Year's resolution too. The very next time that you're late for work, your bloody well sacked.

Oh dear, I had to do something about that. So I thought the best way out of this dilemma was to employ my own clocker on-er. I decided, therefore to employ my mate Harry for a few bob a week to clock me on. This was great because not only did he become my clocker on-er, he also became my knocker up-er. He would clock me on, then knock me up as he passed the Ramper. Now this worked fine except for one week. He came knocking me up, and said to me. "Come on you lazy bastard, I clocked you on over an hour ago." I opened the window and said. "Great Harry, but tha had better get thee sen back now and unclock me, because I'm on holiday today, yer daft bugger." (I had forgotten to tell him). I remember at Hargreaves, certain penalties were imposed if one happened to arrive late for work. For instance, if we drivers were booked to start work at 6am and arrived at 6.30am, then we were not allowed to start work until 9am and we had to finish at 5pm. The result was that we lost 3 hours overtime and we usually had to stay in the depot doing menial tasks, like sweeping up.

Well, I'll never forget one day I had arrived late for work as usual, (this was before I had employed my clocker on-er Harry, of course) and I had to go home until 9am, then return to sweep up etc. So me and another lad (he was called Harry too, as it happened) skivvied (malingered) all day and kept out of sight until after 7pm, and every time the assistant manager came around looking for us, we would see his legs from under the wagons and we would scarper. Anyway, next morning he has us in the office, doesn't he! Tommy Woolford, they called him, and he was a big softie really. He says. "Now then, you bleeders, what happened yesterday? You should have clocked off at 5pm, and didn't whilst 7.30pm."

I said. "Well, Tom, it was like this, me and Harry got so involved in what we was doing and we wanted to make such a good job of the top garage floor that we lost all track of time. I kept saying to Harry. "It must be 5 o'clock ." "No it can't be." Says Harry. . Anyway, Tom when we had finished and came down to clock off, well, what time was it. It was after seven, wasn't it, and I says to Harry, now look what you've done. Tom ain't going to like this, and we shall all get into trouble." And believe it or not, we got away with it. Well, I was the union man, wasn't I?

Hargreaves at this time had a large fleet of Albion, and AEC tippers and tankers, which were a throwback to Bulmers, the firm that Hargreaves had taken over, but as an added bonus (for us drivers, that is), they had some old petrol powered Albions too. It was so funny really, because all the lads that drove these vehicles were bringing keys to work every day to try and unlock the padlocks on the petrol tanks. But I had managed to suss this problem after only the second day at work. The locks were fitted to an asp and staple; all I did was knock the pin out of the asp and unscrew the tank filler cap and bingo, I had access. I could have, in fact, fitted a portable electric pump into the fuel line and extracted the fuel into a can out of sight inside the cab. Or, as a last resort, I could have unfastened the bung at the bottom of the tank. Who the hell needed a key in the first place? All that was required was a little logical thinking! Of course having, taken a few gallons of petrol, I then had to make certain that the vehicle returned a reasonable mpg. So I would coast down all the hills with the gearbox in neutral and for good measure, I would then add a few gallons of diesel from one of my mates' diesel tanks. There was not much of a check on diesel, and three gallons of diesel slipped into a petrol tank to mix in with, say, twenty gallons of petrol was never noticed. My vehicle always returned the correct mpg figures. In fact, I bet there were times, when I was getting more mpg than the rest and that was on part petrol and part diesel!

I remember once running out of petrol with my car in Hargreaves yard. My car by now was a 1939 Hillman 14 and in desperation, I had siphoned

118

some petrol out of one of the petrol Albions into a watering can. As I was walking up to the top car park, the yard foreman caught me and he says. "Now what's tha doing?"

I says. "Well, I'm about sick, Arthur, I haven't had that car for ten minutes and there's all sorts gone wrong with the bloody thing. The top hose is buggered and I'm having to fill me radiator up."

He was nearly in tears, he even offered to carry my watering can! I was glad he didn't and I'm glad that he couldn't smell either! I don't know what he would have thought if he had seen me five minutes later emptying the contents of the watering can into me petrol tank. That car was fantastic. I couldn't afford to run it really, but I soon devised a way to run it on paraffin. I thought to myself, well, a Ferguson tractor engine runs on paraffin, and that is the same engine they fit into Standard Vanguard cars to run on petrol. So what I did, with the help of my good friend, the mechanic Ken, I designed my own hot spot. I wrapped a load of copper wire round the inlet and exhaust manifolds, so that the exhaust manifold heat was transferred to the inlet manifold. The heat from this vaporised the petrol or paraffin. I then fitted an Autovac tank off of an old scrap bus under the bonnet. I then filled this Autovac with a gallon of petrol and fitted a two-way tap. I used to start the engine on petrol, then when the engine got warm, I would switch over to paraffin, and I always had to remember to stop a mile from home and switch on to petrol, or the bloody thing would never have started the next morning. But I do remember one of my little experiments that went wrong. When I tried putting a drop of diesel into the car's tank, I must have put a little too much in, because I bloody near poisoned everybody in Rothwell with the fumes, there was clouds of black smoke everywhere. I now know that a diesel engine will run on paraffin or petrol, but a petrol engine will not run on diesel. Yes, desperate measures had to be taken to overcome desperate straits. We survived because we had to. I used to take some of the other drivers on their holidays, usually to a caravan at the seaside in this car, to earn a few bob. One day the car had broken down. I had to fetch this party back from Morecambe, and I had another car that was knackered. I had paid £10 for it for spares, so I swapped the number plates and tax disc and away I went in the scrap car. But on my way back, as I was overtaking three or four cars, up what I think was called Pool Bank, I was confronted by another car coming the other way. He wouldn't move, neither would I, and he ploughed into the cars on his left. I kept going. Somebody got my number, so they, the powers that be, sent a copper round to examine my car. It wasn't even the same car, nor was it the same bloody colour either! I got done for dangerous driving. While at Hargreaves, the drivers had to take it in turns to work away in Hull for a week, running coke out of the gas works in Hull to the power station. We were paid a lodging allowance, of course, but most of the lads kept their lodging allowance and thumbed a lift home, didn't they? I tried this a couple of times, but there was too much aggro, too much uncertainty, and it took too long. So I thought, stuff this for a game of soldiers, I ain't having this. I simply drove the wagon back to Rothwell and parked it at the back of the top garage (the safest place to hide from the police is in a bloody police station, eh) and no one ever knew. The yard foreman after all, didn't know what job each vehicle was on. The time that I spent at Hargreaves taught me a lot and served me well, because the controls they had in operation there were pathetic, or simply non-existent. Hargreaves at the time were operating over 200 vehicles and they couldn't have been adequately checking fuel usage, mpg, drivers hours, or anything else for that matter, because we drivers got away with murder. I do believe that Hargreaves must have had a license to print money in those days. They seemed to have the CEGB contracts to supply coal to the power stations sewn up. Perhaps they were making so much money that they could afford to be complacent. But I learned from these experiences that controls and systematic checks are essential to any business, in order to avoid any unnecessary temptations. We would do just two loads a day to Skelton Grange Power Station in Leeds from Manvers Main near Wath. Ridiculous, but sometimes I would fall asleep in the lorry cab and I didn't make it to Skelton Grange Power Station before the 4pm deadline. Once we had arrived and got weighed off at Skelton Grange, we then parked our vehicles up after we had tipped the load and then we didn't go back over the weigh bridge until our eleven hours were nearly up. But me, well, I often missed the deadline and that would mean three hours overtime lost. I have engineered breakdowns, pulled fuses, and when the fitter came out, I would say. "Well, goodness gracious me, if I'd only known, eh? I could have repaired that. Well, we all live and learn don't we?" It is quite the hardest thing in the world to puncture a tyre, but I have managed it all right, to protect my three hours' overtime. I remember once I fell asleep at Prince of Wales pit and my mates, the rotten buggers, left me there. I woke up three hours later and the pit yard was deserted. How I got away with that I will never know.

As the unions increased their memberships during the 1950s and consequently their power, they began to make outrageous demands. I became very disillusioned with the unions during this time, when I became a TGWU representative at Hargreaves in Rothwell. The union committee of which

I was a member had become very militant, and as committee members they would dream up all sorts of bloody crazy ideas to foster their own feelings of self-importance. I began to realise that if you gave the average man a licence to think, once he started thinking, boy, did you have problems! That is what happened. At one time we were going to go on strike because a driver at Hargreaves Keadly Depot, near Scunthorpe wouldn't join the union. I thought they were bloody stupid. We had at that time just fought a World War to protect the freedom of the individual, and here we now were trying to force someone to do what they didn't believe in.

We had a great job at Hargreaves and were more or less guaranteed 11 hours pay a day for doing next to now't. Two loads a day from Manvers Main Colliery to Skelton Grange, that's all we did. Most of the day was spent asleep in our cabs while waiting to tip at Skelton Grange, a bloody doddle. Our union even wanted to report the tipper drivers of a local haulage company, Jackie Hansons, to the Traffic Commissioners, because they were speeding and earning bonuses.

The fact that they had to work for the bonuses while we were sleeping on our cabs didn't seem to have entered our union bosses' pathetic little minds, stupid bastards. They wanted that extra couple of quid that Hansons' drivers were getting, but didn't want to work for it. When you get a group of like-minded men together, all with tunnel vision, and incapable of understanding or accepting rational argument, then they create problems. Hargreaves' management, however, did recognise this fact, so they simply solved the problem by removing the two most militant union members from their jobs as drivers. (They just happened to be the Shop Stewards, Joe Turner and my mate Stan Hanson.)

They were given extra money and promoted to Transport Supervisors; so much for glorious union principles! We, the rest of the sheep, sorry brothers in arms, just went back to sleep at Skelton Grange Power Station.

While at Hargreaves, I got to know a lovely guy called Alan Wells. I will never forget him, he helped me to get started on my own in business. Alan was a great guy. He had a scrapyard, at Bolton on Dearne near Wath, and in this yard he had an old six-wheeler Sentinel Lorry. I thought to myself, how lovely it would be to have a motor like that to start up in business with. I was always a bloody dreamer! Well, Alan told me that if I found some work, I could take this wagon, and pay him later. So with this in mind, and while still working in Hull for Hargreaves, I travelled around all the big companies looking for work. Reckitts and Colmans, etc etc. I told them all I had a six-wheeler truck, and could they give me some work please? All this was going off while I was supposed to be delivering coke from the gasworks. I must have been very impressionable at that time, because the wagon in question was probably buggered; if not, why was it in a scrapyard, and how would I survive without money?

In 1958, I suddenly began to take stock of my life. I had been married for three years and I now had a lovely wife and two beautiful daughters. We had our own little home, even if it was rather primitive and lacking in the latest mod cons. I had a good job; well, I enjoyed working at Hargreaves, it was much easier than anything I had previously been used to. We had no debts, everything we had was paid for and we even had an old car. I couldn't afford to run a car really, but we had one. But was all this enough? I decided no, it wasn't. I had, up until 1958, been a butcher, baker, I had been a storeman in the army, I had worked on building sites, in brickyards, dug trenches, driven lorries, and after having worked for a total of twenty-three different firms, (not including King Geroge VI), I was running out of new employers. I realised that I might eventually become unemployable. So I decided to make the biggest decision of my life. I must have been crackers. A chap called Walt Wymer was a mate of Ken Pettys at this time, and he had started in business with two tipper lorries, an old pre-war Maudsley and a 1948 Austin K4. Now, Walt was probably paying more out in repairs on these vehicles than what they were earning, so he decided enough was enough; he'd cut his losses and run.

They do say that there is one born every minute, and dear old Walter recognised one immediately, yes that's right, a fool, me. Walt offered me the Austin for free; I could pay him when I got started. He should have paid me for taking the bloody thing off his hands!

So I started looking around for work. This time it wasn't work for a six-wheel sentinel flat lorry, but for a four-wheeler tipper. I found some, or so I thought, on the A1 at Doncaster bypass. A site foreman said he would fix me up with a job if I ever got a wagon.

Great, I was on my way, though I knew not where. I had £25 holiday pay, a few gallons of engine oil knocked off from Hargreaves, a clapped-out untaxed lorry, a heart as big as a bloody lion and no visible means of support. Where I was going to get my next week's wage from had never even entered my pathetic little mind. All I could think of was that I had at last been given an opportunity to better myself, to climb out of the rut I was in, and get on and build a better life for my family and myself. At the time there seemed no other way; I didn't have any education of any con-sequence, I was a nobody, a dreamer, a loser, and it did seem that this was my only chance to prove myself. So I took up Walt's offer and away I went, where destiny chose to take me.

# And So Into Business

I arrived at the site office on the A1 at Doncaster on this particular Monday morning at the crack of dawn, long before anyone else had arrived. There was I, sat in my motor, as proud as Punch. I was now a haulage contractor. It didn't matter that my motor wasn't taxed, I hadn't even paid for it, and I didn't know where the next tank of petrol was coming from.

I was suddenly awakened from my dreams by someone opening the cab door. The intruder into my thoughts was the site foreman no less. "Ah say, what have we here then, lad?" says he. "Now, tha doesn't call that a wagon, does tha, not a proper wagon surely? "Ah know we're a bit desperate for lorries, but we're not that bloody desperate, no way. Ah'll tell thee summat. Tha sees that big mechanical loading machine over there? Well, I do believe that if my machine got anywhere near thee clapped out wagon and tried to put a load onto its back, thee wagon would be terrified and collapse with fright. In fact I don't think that machine would even attempt to load that pile of scrap that tha's got there. Even machines have their pride, that knows! No, sorry lad, I can't give thee a start here, go on, take that bloody thing to the nearest scrapyard before it falls in bits around thee and then if tha can get thee sen a proper motor, come back and I'll give thee a start."

All my dreams were shattered, I had failed at the first hurdle: no job, no work, no future. Where would I go from here? I decided straight up the A1, where there were various contractors doing work, all the way up to Wetherby and beyond. I called at every one, all with the same result: sorry lad. I spent all that week searching desperately for work, but to no avail. I had to borrow £5 off Dad to give to Jean for her housekeeping money, so we could pay the rent and have something to eat. It was about this time that I started hand-rolling my own cigarettes, as I couldn't afford to buy them. I would empty all the available ashtrays to provide the tab ends to increase my tobacco supply. The most difficult job was drying them out after liberating a few from the local pub toilets! Ah well, I digress. Oh, what a week that was, it really was. Then, on the Saturday night I had a brilliant idea, or rather, an afterthought. While I had been employed at Hargreaves, I had got to know of a local company which was involved in the processing and haulage of opencast coal in a big way, and I had heard that their contracts manager was a guy called Farthing. So that was a start. I went into a phone box (we had no phone at home) and looked for Farthing (unusual name). I soon found it: Mr R Farthing, Queens Drive, Ossett. Nothing ventured, nothing gained - my last throw of the dice. I upped and went to see Mr Farthing, a man I will never forget.

I arrived at his home about 8.30pm on this particular Saturday night and tentatively knocked on his back door. When he opened the door, I apologised for disturbing him on a Saturday evening, and I explained my situation - that I had left my job at Hargreaves on the promise of an offer of work for my lorry; that I had a wife and two babies to support. I was desperate and please could he help me. I also threw into the conversation a little white lie. I said that the assistant manager at Hargreaves, who was a friend of mine, had wished me luck when I left, was sorry to see me go, and had suggested that if ever I needed help, to go and see Mr Farthing. Well, I think that this final onslaught clinched it. After I had given him my handkerchief to dry his eyes, and he had given me a cup of tea and a bun, he told me to report to the British Oak Screens on Denby Dale Road, Wakefield the following Monday morning to be employed on internal work. On this particular site, I would be loading under the excavating machine (we called them diggers) from the on site coal stock, then I would run onto the weigh bridge and, after the coal was weighed, I would then tip the load down a grate. The coal was then put through a screening process. For this, we budding entrepreneurs, we amateur, pretend-to-be-haulage contractors, were paid the princely sum of just 10 pence per ton. Now, my lorry could legally carry about five tons, but I would load seven or eight tons at a time. So at 10d. per ton in old money, when there were two hundred and forty pennies to a pound, I was earning approximately 28p per load in today's money. Great, big deal, but it was a start on my climb up that proverbial ladder. I was now a haulage contractor, I had stepped out of the make-believe and into the real world and I had now joined the ranks of the hell drivers. (That film *'The Hell Drivers'* had nothing on us - more on that later.

I was now well and truly out of the world of the sheltered innocents and out there in the real world. I was in a rat race, and believe me, it really was dog eat dog, or rat eat rat.

## THE HELL DRIVERS
### Or Those Drivers From Hell!

I struggled and struggled and fought to survive
Without the will to struggle, I would have been eaten alive
But I learned my lessons, oh I learned them so well
And will always be grateful to those drivers from hell.

The most important thing I learnt, and didn't find funny
Was that our employers were the ones, who made all the money
They subcontracted all their work, and they did it so well
With the help of those drivers, those drivers from hell.

As time passed me by, and I moved on to pastures new
As I built Walkers of Wakefield, I knew exactly what to do
I became a main contractor, with a service to sell
And I did it all with the help, of those drivers from hell.

They were the ones who provided the resources
I was just there to organise their forces
So that is my story, a story I do tell
It couldn't have been done, without those drivers from hell.

Yes, it was a real struggle trying to stay in business at that time against all the odds, and I couldn't have done it without my parents. Dad used to lend me money when I was stuck. He had so very little himself, but I always paid him back. When I got my monthly cheque, I would say to Dad. "How much do I owe thee, then?"

His reply always was. "Well bugger me, lad, if tha doesn't know, how the bloody hell does tha expect me to know?" He-of-few-words had spoken and we sorted it between us. My old Austin Truck served me well for about six months. But later the tipping rams came straight out of their sockets in protest at being forced to tip a load of about ten tons, when there were originally designed to tip five, and then the chassis bent in half and gave up the ghost. I thought my days as a budding entrepreneur were over. I couldn't afford to repair the truck, I was desperate. What could I do? Then my second angel in disguise came to my rescue. I had paid my first angel, Walt Wymer, back for his lorry, and now I remembered the next saviour in my life, whom, I will never forget - Alan Wells, yes, the lad who had the scrapyard at Bolton on Dearne, near Wath. It was Alan, you may remember, who would have helped me with the six-wheel Sentinel flat lorry had I managed to find the work. This time I had no money and needed another tipper. Alan didn't have ow't good enough, but he found me one, which he bought from another haulage contractor in Wombwell. I said I would pay him so much a month until I had paid for it. But Alan said, "Nay lad, tha won't, tha'll pay me when tha can afford to." I would have chopped my right hand off before letting him down. Salt of the earth, was Alan. Yes, mates I have had, some of the best, the very best. Alan had been and bought me a short wheel base Commer, which was fitted with a Perkins P6 diesel engine. Pretty Polly Perkins, I called it.

Alan fitted me up with some good tyres and a good second hand battery, and away I went on the second phase of my adventure. Back out there into the unknown, seeking my destiny.

That little old Commer that Alan Wells had bought for me was thirteen years old, unlucky for some. It was knackered really, and it might have thought to itself that I was taking it away to a happy retirement home, or maybe on a nice holiday. But that little Commer was to be sadly disillusioned, because it worked harder in those few months that it managed to survive with me than it had ever worked in its bloody life before!

The Commer was designed to carry five tons and it was fitted with 7.50 x 20 tyres. It had to work hard for me, because we were paid on tonnage: the more weight we were able to carry, the more money we earned. That old Commer regularly carried 8/9 tons from Temple Newsam screens to the British Oak Screens, and we the drivers from hell, fought for every load. Times were hard. We started work at 4 or 5am on a morning to be the first in line waiting for the digger driver. Then the day really started and the rat race began. After being loaded we would all go hell for leather and try to pass the guy in front, all in an attempt to get that extra load. I remember times when we would go up Stanley Hill to Wakefield two abreast, trying to pass each other. I used to have a trick or two up my sleeve. I used to go up this hill in an old 7 ton BMC 7.01 tipper, and as soon as I saw someone trying to pass, I would put my hand inside the flap in the engine compartment and push in the cold start button. This was an excess fuel device. Bloody hell, you couldn't see for black smoke! My motor used to prance up that hill like Red Rum at the Derby and the poor bugger behind, trying to pass, had to drop behind with his headlights on because he couldn't see, could he? Not very environmentally friendly and strictly against the law, but it worked and that's all that seemed to matter. That little old Commer blew 23 tyres in a month through overloading. I know, because I changed every one. The lad who had the scrapyard down Portobello Road, Sandal, used to stand these second hand wheels and tyres outside his office for me to collect and to save time. I remember once blowing two tyres in a day, so I had no spare wheel and I crawled up Stanley Hill, on past Eastmoor, down to the British Oak Screen at about 5mph. How I managed that I will never know, but I did; the bloody tyre was red hot.

That little old Commer was more economical on fuel than the Austin, simply because it ran on diesel instead of petrol, and I was able to obtain a drop of diesel out of the loading diggers every time the drivers went for a pee or for their snap. A pal of mine, from Barnsley, and I got this down to a fine art. We would come early on to the site, and take it in turns to have a go at the digger's fuel tanks or the fuel bowser. We were very adept at sucking diesel from those tanks, like two little suckling pigs at their mother's teet, consantly looking up and turning round to see if anyone was coming, then heads down again for another suck. We would sometimes bring a 40 gallon drum on the job, fill it and take it away, so our employers didn't have it all their own way. They may have paid us peanuts and made our lives hell by putting too many vehicles on to the job to fight for too few loads, but the more astute among us were amply compensated. We found the fiddles, and we survived. Funny how today people exploit the benefit system, but we made it into an art form. Shortly after this, in the early sixties, the Government must have got wise to our fiddles, because they ordered the fuel companies to put red dye into all diesel that was sold cheaply to farmers and plant operators. We now paid 4/6d (25p) a gallon or double the price farmers paid, so that put paid to that fiddle - or did it? The fuel we used was called DERV and still is: Diesel Engined Road Vehicles. If one was caught using red diesel, then one's wagon would be confiscated and one wouldn't have liked that, would one? So I eventually got hold of a 500 gallon tank and placed it on a banking at George Berrys pigsties which I was renting for a few bob a week near the bridge on Leeds Road, next to the Woodman Inn. If I now had to buy my fuel, I might as well buy in bulk! Well, I did, but I didn't buy diesel at 4/6 a gallon, not bloody likely. I bought a substance called Crystallite Burning Oil at 2/3 a gallon instead. This was used as a burning oil, very much like paraffin, a dry fuel. It was, of course, not designed or allowed to be used in diesel engines, and to do this was strictly against the law. But the Government had made an awful mistake: they hadn't dyed it red, had they, and apart from that, the powers that be didn't honestly believe that anyone would be daft enough to use it, because in its crude form, if regularly used in an engine, it would eventually bugger it up. Ah, well. What they hadn't realised was that I had no intention of using it in its crude form. I would put it through my own refining process. And that was easy, because engine oil was nearly as cheap to buy as fuel. So I decided that I would put one gallon of engine oil into ten gallons of my burning oil. Hey presto, no problems. This oilier substance now lubricated the injector pump and protected the cylinder walls and valves and I saved a bloody fortune. I ought to have patented my new product and called it Chasasoil or Crystal Derv, or something, and put it out there on the black market, which at that time was bigger than the bloody Common Market is today. Ah well, who knows, I may have eventually bankrupted Shell and BP. Well, I can dream, can't I? I mention the above purely to highlight that I was out there on my own and I had to be resourceful, one jump ahead of the system, to survive.

I got to know some great guys in those days. We were all struggling to survive, and we learned the hard way. One mate of mine had one of his motors taken from him, and he nearly got jailed by the Customs and Excise boys for running on red diesel. They used to stop us and test our tanks of fuel. But we often fooled them. Some of the lads had another spare tank fitted out of sight on the wagon, piped up separately, to run on red diesel. We had to adapt to suit the circumstances and to keep on beating the system, eh!

They were great guys I worked with, some of them became well known international and, dare I say it, reputable hauliers. Butter wouldn't melt in their mouths, or so one would have thought!

But they had, most of them, all been there on the floor and from humble beginnings they all learned their trade well.

I could go on and on. They all made it to the top because they had all been there, they knew every trick in the book, they were rarely outsmarted and they were students of human nature.

These guys were not lucky. There was no such thing as luck. They worked long hours, they struggled, they persisted until they had achieved their goals. They were resourceful, made their own opportunities and then they exploited them, and survived. They made it (some of them) to the top by sheer guts and determination and I am so proud to have been in there with them.

Those who fail in business are usually the sons or daughters of the founders, or the people brought up within an established, systems-controlled business. The real heroes are the ones who start and build the business from nothing, reach the summit of their own level of competence, and put in their own controls to build the establishment. They are then able to recognise their weaknesses and still succeed in spite of them.

The one thing that really does make me sick is hearing successful businessmen who have made it condemn and ridicule up-and-coming youngsters who are just starting out. Those kind of bloody hypocrites all have short memories.

People who have lived in glass houses should never throw stones. But let's go back to basics, and back to Temple Newsam, where it all began. I eventually wore the Commer out; it gave up the ghost and simply collapsed and died. Ken Petty, mechanic and mate, suggested I got something a little more robust, like a Sherman Tank or a bloody bulldozer. I couldn't afford either, so that was out of the question. We did, however, decide to go and see Stanley Hughes, the second-hand coach and truck dealer, at Drighlington. Stanley sold me an old ERF built like a tank (it needed to be) with a Kirkstall axle. David Brown gearbox, and an AEC 7.7 engine. It surely was an hybrid, I worked out of Coney Warren, an open cast coal site with this motor, which was rough work. Again I was carrying 10 tons on a 7-ton motor. It was a long, steep climb out of the hole in the cut up to the top and on to the main road to Wakefield. You had to put the vehicle in bottom gear and rev the engine like hell to have any hope at all of getting up that slippery bank of clay, and if you stalled the engine or got stuck, God help you and the wagon; because the site foreman would simply send a bloody great D8 Bulldozer with a lunatic of a bloody driver to shove you out of the way. I got stuck many times and one time this silly bastard of a dozer driver pushed me out and at the same time pushed both my rear mudguards off, complete with mountings and lights. Then, to add insult to injury, he ran over them with his bloody dozer. The bloody idiot! I'll never forget that motor. I remember to this day the registration number was DUS 504.

Why do I remember? Because I had to fit and nail two old pieces of pit conveyor belting onto the rear wooden cross member and I had to paint the number in white paint DUS 504 onto the belting. I found some old white paint but didn't have a brush. I used rolled up thin paper - what a bloody mess, with runs an all. I must confess, my first attempt at signwriting was a complete disaster, but beggars couldn't be choosers, and the show had to go on. For rear lights, easy, I hung a small red inspection light from a nail and fastened it to the battery with crocodile clips. As for stop lights, who needed stop lights when the bloody thing wouldn't stop anyway? To go on, my other memories of my pal the ERF are also clear, because it had no bloody brakes. I had to put a full tin of brake fluid into the master cylinder every day before I dare even think of running the bloody thing. Us hell drivers used to run from Coney Warren and Temple Newsom to Skelton Grange Power Station Leeds, Bowers Row Screens near Swillington, and British Oak Screens, Wakefield. Now there were many ways to get to The British Oak Screens and pass the wagon in front, of course: on Eastmoor Stanley Road, past Dysons Provision Merchants onto Kirkgate Ings Road, Denby Dale Road. Another way was to go down Warrengate, Market Street, Denby Dale Road three abreast, all trying to pass each other. I have even seen them with one wheel on the pavement in their attempts to be first. The best motors in those days were long-nosed Leyland Comets fitted with 350 Leyland engines. They were flyers, at least they did 45mph, which was fast when one considered that brakes were real luxuries, if you happened to have any at all. Vacuum brakes as fitted to Maudsley and AECs were bloody awful. You just jumped on the pedal with both feet, closed your eyes and prayed, and eventually you stopped. But my ERF with its faulty brakes was pathetic. There was only one way I could travel to the British Oak, and that was whichever way avoided the most traffic lights. I just couldn't stop. I went through so many lights at red it was unbelievable. I drove all the time on my nerves, that's all I had. I would be driving perhaps 100 yards in front of myself, having to change into lower gears. Everytime I saw the vehicle in front's stop lights go on, I had to pump the brake pedal up and down four times before I had any pedal at all. Crazy, bloody stupid, it wouldn't be allowed today, and quite rightly so. But I was young and silly, had no money and all that seemed to matter was to earn a crust, and keep going until I had the time or the money to repair the vehicle. Yes, those were hard times and desperate ones too. I remember we didn't have time to stop for the statutory breaks that the law demands today; no, if we were on road work, we would have our snap while stood at traffic lights waiting for them to change from red to green.

I can remember clearly a job came up somewhere the other side of Barnsley, on site work working 24 hours a day. Lots of the other lads managed to employ casual drivers for the 12-hour night shift but not your Charlie. He either couldn't get or couldn't afford to employ anyone. I will never forget one morning waking up and finding myself somewhere in Barnsley near some traffic lights, not knowing where I was. I was on my way home after doing 36 hours on the trot. Yes, bloody stupid, but it was there to be done, and I took advantage of the opportunity.

That ERF nearly killed me (I wonder why?). I was once on site at British Oak trying to change an injector, and I couldn't get the bloody thing out. So, in sheer frustration, I started the engine while leaning over the engine bay. That injector flew out like a bullet from a gun and hit me smack bang, right in the middle of my forehead. The mark is still there today and I have never been the same since. I was telling a pal of mine, Duggie Powel from Barnsley, the fuel injection specialist who used to repair my lorry, what I had done. And Dugg, he says to me, "You daft bugger, that could have killed you. I have seen them injectors come straight through the bloody cab roofs." Yes, Duggie Powell, what a character. Duggie always wore the same pair of overalls and he never ever got them dirty. Yes, a proper little gentleman, our Duggie. It did not matter if he had been laid under a lorry in a snowstorm, or crawling under a bloody bulldozer on a coal site! One thing was for sure, Duggie would always crawl out from under whatever, looking absolutely spotless. He never got his hands dirty. In 1963 his wife told me the reason for this. He had bought his overalls in 1953, second-hand off Barnsley market, and because they were by this time falling to bits, she only dared wash them once a year. She had threatened to kill him if he ever got them dirty, and I would just like to bet that those overalls are as clean as ever today, 36 years later.

I can remember oh so many, many incidents that happened to me in my early years in business, far too many to record here. It was certainly not a life lived from 9 to 5 nor was I ever employed in a protected occupation where you were paid if you were off sick, or whether you worked or not. No, sirree. I had to work because I was my own employer, and I couldn't guarantee myself a 40-hour week, or sick pay, or holidays with pay. No, that was just not available to me. I didn't have holidays for years; if I didn't work I got now't, it was as simple as that. So I got really annoyed by the silly buggers who used to come along later in life, look at my Rolls Royce or whatever and say, "Oh haven't you been lucky!" Not 'arf, I had. I never saw my kids grow up, I didn't have a social life for years. Lucky, no! Exciting, yes! A life lived to the full, yes; but lucky - never! There were times when I'd be out at 10pm on a freezing cold winter's night, on site at Temple Newsam, on my own. There I was a grown man crying with frustration (can you believe it), struggling to change a lay rub coupling on my Commer truck, lying underneath it in freezing water, and no one to even hold a light for me, let alone give me an hand. It was that cold I couldn't even feel the spanners, let alone use them, but it had to be done. There was only me, and it was a lonely life, too, yes, so very lonely, and when my wife Jean used to ask years later, "And where were you when I was bringing those kids up on my own?! Well that's where I was, at Temple Newsam, and at thousands of other places over the years, places that I would have gladly exchanged for the opportunity of staying at home with my wife and kids.

Ah well, again I digress. I remember the breakdowns that happened so often because of the heavy loads my trucks carried; they were always grossly overloaded. I would always carry a spare half shaft in the cab, because I broke them on a regular basis on coal sites. I remember times when I had to run with five-gallon drums of diesel perched on top of the engine, gravity feeding the injector pump because the bloody lift pump didn't work. Or the time when I would fit a pipe to the lift pump and stick in into the fuel tank, because the filter was blocked, or there was dirt in the tank. Oh yes, that happened too. Other haulage contractors who wanted to steal your loads would ground you by putting sand or sugar in your fuel tank. Sometimes, when driving under the digger to get loaded, if your vehicle was not positioned properly the digger driver would ask you to run forward and reverse a little closer. Oh yes, one had to be careful, because that bastard behind you who was waiting to load would drive forward and take your load before you had a chance to reverse into position. 'Hell Drivers' - that film doesn't even begin to tell the full story. Those drivers couldn't have lived with us, the proper Hell drivers.

I remember the time I did six loads from Temple Newsam to British Oak Screens without a clutch, as the clutch rod had broken in two. Oh yes, if you couldn't drive a truck without a clutch, you could never call yourself a proper driver, and that principle still applies. How many drivers today can do that, as they sit in their air-conditioned cabs, with their synchromesh gear boxes and air brakes? Not many, I guess and we learned to drive with crash boxes and no synchros in those days. I took engines weighing half a ton or more out with 5-ton jacks. If I wanted the tipper body up and the hydraulic pump didn't work, easy. You got two railway sleepers and wedged them at an angle, positioned at each front corner, and then drove the wagon forward. I had to be very careful, because if the sleepers slipped, they could go straight through the bloody body. When I got stuck, bogged down to the driving axle, which was like every day if there was no tow available, I would look around for stones, bricks, a railway sleeper or whatever, and stack them from the floor up to and under the body. Then I would send the tipper up and the back wheels would come out of the hole. The holes were then filled with rocks or whatever, then I would let the body down and the wheels came down onto terra firma and you drove away. Broken springs were not a problem unless they broke at the front at the fixed end, then the back axle would move. I have followed lorries many times that were running down the road like a crab, we used to say. The vehicle was out of line, with either a broken spring or broken centre bolt. If a spring was so badly broken the mudguard was rubbing the wheel. I would jack the chassis up and wedge a bloody great stone between the body and the spring, anything to get home. I couldn't afford to call garages out so I did my own repairs, and got on with the job. Today drivers don't even carry a spare wheel let alone know how to change one, yet they call themselves drivers.

If you had an air lock in the fuel system, one way to get home was to slacken off an injector pipe, so that air in the system was released along with diesel of course. That was all right, providing the diesel that was being sprayed over the engine didn't get near the exhaust manifold, which it did once when I had to slacken a pipe to keep going. I was the other side of Bucker Brow (of Peter Slater fame) at the time when the bloody engine caught fire. The cab was full of smoke, nearly poisoned me and all the bloody paint was burned off, all the plastic pipes burned out, before I was able to smother it. Ah well, another lesson learned. I could go on and on about breakdowns, mishaps, near tragedies and so on. But that would fill another two books.

Expansion, the ERF truck, like the other two soon wore out, and I purchased a BMC seven tonner, fitted with an Eaton two-speed axle. This was a much faster vehicle than any of my others, but it was prone to breaking springs and half shafts. After a while my pal Albert Bolton's brother, Pete, came to work for me. Pete worked for John Duddlings the fruit, veg, and potato merchants in Wakefield, so he moved up from carrying around 2 tons on a 5-ton Bedford, to carrying 10-12 tons on a 7-ton BMC. Quite a step up into the real world of commerce! Pete always complained about me having no brakes on my bloody motors, but the brakes were okay, it was the weight that was the real problem. Pete and his wife Lil lived at 11 Chantry Road, Lupset Wakefield, and in Jean's and my early years they became our best friends. We used to take them off at holiday times for day trips in our little old car. They were a little older than Jean and me. Peter had been a prisoner of the Japanese during the war, so life had not been easy for him. Lil worked at Paton and Balldwins Mill in Wakefield. They had a nice home and one daughter, Pauline. Pete and I worked together for a couple of years. Pete was a hard worker, and I think he wanted to become a partner in the business, but that could never have worked out for us. Pete was very assertive, and liked too much of his own way, so we could not have worked so closely together. In fact Peter eventually left after we had a fall out, and he went to work for Lyons Bakery on Thornes as a driver until he retired. I never saw much of Peter up until he finished work; I never saw much of anybody really. But after he retired and went to live in some flats off Thornes Lane I would visit him when I went jogging past his flat. Pete and Lil split up later which was a pity, they were two good people. There but for the grace of God go we.

It is 1962, and we are both working hard. One job we had was working on a canal bank, I think it was somewhere near Askern, Doncaster. We had a great fiddle going with the weigh man and the lads at the tip for a few packets of fags and a few bottles of beer. We would get two weigh notes for every load we did. My pal Johnnie and I both had two lorries working on this job, and every afternoon Johnnie and I would be parked up, and we would be in the pub watching the wagons go past through the pub window. Every time his driver went past I would say, "Another one for me - because every time his driver pulled onto the weigh bridge he got a weigh note for me, and Pete got a weigh note for him. The other drivers used to be as mad as hell. They just couldn't understand what the bloody hell was going off! I remember the times when one of Johnnie's wagons or mine broke down, which was at least twice a week. We would take each other off site and go for spares to repair the broken down vehicle, and at the end of the day we still finished up with two or three more loads than anyone else. Strange but true; that little fairy with her magic wand never let us down, did she? I remember times when I condescended to do the odd load or two, just to keep my hand in, like, and I would pull on the weigh bridge get a weigh note, pull off and go for a haircut, then pull back on with the same load, weigh it again and so on and on and on. I was on and off that bloody weigh bridge like a yo-yo weighing that same bloody load. I never tipped it, just kept on weighing it and getting weigh notes for my mate at the tip to sign. I was amazed: those fags and few bottles of beer worked like magic, and produced loads out of thin air. This just couldn't go on, of course, our little good fairy's wand began to wear out and one day there was whole hell on. We were on the site (for a change) and we heard through the jungle telegraph that the big site boss was at the weigh bridge. It had been said that there seemed to be more tonnage being booked, but not enough being delivered on to the job and he, the boss, was there to sort things out. Oh dear, what now? Well, as well as fiddling extra loads for each other, Johnnie and I had also only actually been carrying small token loads on our motors, about three tons, say, on our 7-ton wagons. Well no point in overloading and prematurely wearing our bloody motors out, was there? A point of view that was shared by our benevolent friend, the weigh bridge man. I think he had a soft spot for our old motors and didn't want us to abuse them. He perhaps also thought the world of his weigh bridge and was reluctant to put much weight on to its back. Anyway, Johnnie and I had a conference. What the bloody hell should we do now? Well, we must have sat there for at least an hour debating what to do. We dared not go anywhere near that bloody weigh bridge while his Majesty was in there. Anyway, we agreed we would have to make a move, or he would wonder where we were. So we tossed a coin to see who was going to be the first to step into that bloody lion's den and face him. I lost the toss. We also decided that we had better load the wagons to full capacity, didn't we? There was so much muck put on to our wagons. It dropped off the back, sides, front, out of the cab and even out of our ears, and when we at last struggled onto the weigh bridge, those wagons were on their bloody hands and knees with the weight we had put on to them. But for all that, the load on my motor still only weighed just over 10 tons, which was a far cry from the 12-ton plus loads that our previous weigh notes had carried. I walked into the weigh bridge whistling and decided to put on a brave face, although I didn't feel brave.

I said (I think): "Hello, Mr Big Boss, nice to see you and how are you today?"

His reply is echoed in this poem:

"Ah ah, now what have we here?" says he,
"I perceive you are Tweedle Dum and he must be Tweedle Dee."
"Well tha's perceived bloody wrong, does tha see,
Cos that's Johnnie Lax, and am sure tha knows me.

So don't be so bloody sarcastic, it dun't suit thee at all,
So climb down off thee bloody high hoss, before tha 'as a fall.
Give me that bloody weigh note, and a'll be on my way
I haven't time to bandy words wi thee, I haven't got all day."

This big boss, well, he happened to glance at the scale.
He says, "This weighs less than normal, now how did
tha manage to fail?"
I says, "I hope to carry a bigger load, I know I will again
So every night as I go to bed, I kneel and pray for rain."

The big boss he told me I had quite a massive gob
And if I didn't keep it shut, I'd be out of a bloody job
He pointed and said, "I know, I know you are the ones
Who have fiddled the loads and lost us thousands of tons.

With my hand on my heart I took a step back
With a tear in my eye I said "How could tha say that?
Johnnie and me, why, we have done our very best
And tha will see if tha looks, more loads than the rest."

"I know," says the big boss as he gave me a stare,
"Through your fiddling we're near bankrupt and tha just doesn't care"
A says, "Johnnie and me, why we don't owe thee ow't
And to show our good faith, we will do a few loads for now't."

The boss says, "I can't prove ow't, I have to sadly declare
Bur a'm letting you both know that I am fully aware
Your fiddles are over and they're over for good
I hope you get the message and that it's understood."

Johnnie and I hung our heads, our heads in shame
The powers that be had rumbled our game
The boss had made his point, oh so loud and clear
So we gave him our cigs, and the last of our stock of beer.

For Johnnie and me had worked the system oh so well
The weigh man for a few cigs and beer his soul would sell
And now it was all over, well it was for today!
The Boss man he smiled as he took our stock of cigs and beer away.

But the moral must be as my tale I do tell
Everyone has a price as their souls they do sell
What I have to tell is not very nice
But I learnt and I know, we all have a price.

We pay the price to smooth the way
And we pay the price, the price we must pay
Hypocrisy can be a virtue but people are apt to forget
That we only spend our money on the things that we get.

Now Johnnie and me have to live with our conscience,
as it pours its scorn
And our only consolation is to know,
an honest man has never been born
So as I tell my story and whatever your judgement may be,
Please have a little understanding for Johnnie, and for me!

This is the first verse on
Johnnie and me were haulage contractors that was our trade
We operated two tippers each, and a living we made
We became the best of friends as we tried to survive
As we struggled to earn a crust, a crust to stay alive.

Johnnie was a fiddler among the very best
And as he played his fiddle, he would corrupt all the rest
We both worked on site work, way back in '62
And Johnnie lent me his fiddle, as we had nothing better to do.

We would bribe all the weighmen and the banksmen too
With a few packets of fags, and maybe a bottle or two
For this we were given extra loads, boy we made it rip
We did more loads on paper than were ever took to tip.

But this just couldn't go on, it couldn't go on, oh no
Because someone shopped us, and our employers got to know
So they sent someone to the weigh bridge to see what it was all about
And the someone had but one intention, he was going to sort us out.

He sat waiting in the weigh bridge, waiting for Johnnie and me,
The Big Boss would sort the fiddles, yes he would, would he.
Johnnie and I were disappointed that we didn't have his trust
But if someone was there to spy on us, then they must.

So that was the end of that little tale, but not the end of the story. Oh
no, because Johnnie and I were to move on to much, oh much, much
better things. We had become true artists, and we made such sweet music
with our fiddles; but that is another story, to be told later.

It was a pity really that we had to move on because that job at Askern
had become really cost-effective, and economically viable. At last we
were the ones that were making the money as well as our employers. We

had even been presented with a wonderful gift by a digger driver on site for a few bob and a few cigs. He gave us a spare key and free access to his diesel bowser; well, it saved us breaking the lock didn't it? So we never had to buy diesel for our motors. This, of course, was before those nasty, selfish bastards, the powers that be, decided to dye it red and we were nearly prevented from trying to earn an honest living. Ah well, all good things must come to an end.

It was about this time that I had a vehicle written off, by my insurance company. Funny, today I will never make a claim, but I have had my share, I suppose. I ran off the road with my BMC into a ditch and smashed the mudguard and other odds and ends. The insurance company sent out a loss adjuster didn't they, and he says to me, "Ah yes, new mudguard etc. I estimate it will cost about £50 to repair." This was a lot of money in them days weren't it?

I says, "Whooh, hang on a bloody minute, as tha had a look at that bloody chassis."

"Why?" says he.

"Ah says come ovver here, sithee, just thee cast thee eyes ovver here, is tha blind or what? Look thee down that chassis, it's as bent as a dog's hind leg," says I.

"Oh my word, it would appear so," says he with the bloody pencil.

I says, "Nivver mind thee and thee £50, that wagon's a bloody write-off.

He says, "Well it certainly looks like it could be, doesn't it?"

I said, "Here, see thee, take this tenner it is."

He says, "Of course it must be a write-off."

I said, "Ah should bloody well hope so, and here's another fiver. I want paying out, and I want that salvage at scrap value, it'll heve to go for spares if now't else."

He says, "Certainly sir!"

Well! All of a sudden I have got a bloody knighthood haven't I, and it only cost me a tenner. I bet it cost some of our creepy, weepy civil servants and those knights in shining armour, our big chiefs in industry, a bloody sight more than that to get theirs.

Anyway, enough of my knighthood, back to my BMC and the bloody court jester, the insurance man. To cut a long story short he wrote it off and I kept the wagon at scrap price for spares. I was as happy as a little sandboy, it was the best tenner I had ever spent, well nearly. The next tenner I spent was with my old pal Alan Wells at his Bolton-on-Dearne scrapyard. I bought a second-hand mudguard, a set of number plates and a logbook for an old BMC that Alan had scrapped. Away I went with a spring in my step, a twinkle in my eye, a smile on my face, and a few hundred extra quid in the bank. Destiny rides again. I was back to work the next day.

That wasn't the first and only time that the hell drivers had used spare number plates. Because some of us had identical vehicles, all fitted with the same numbers and same tax discs, duplicates and originals, sometimes we had our number plates fitted with bloody zip fasteners, depending on financial circumstances, so that they could be easily removed. And as everybody drank bottles of Guinness in those days, we sometimes used Guinness labels for tax discs. The secret was to make sure you didn't happen to have an accident, or get pulled by the police on the same day with two vehicles bearing the same number. But the silliest thing of all about that particular insurance claim was that although the chassis looked bent, it wasn't really. (It was only me who was). What had happened was that my spring maker, Charlie Barnsley, had once fitted a new rear cross member to my BMC and he had made it too big. Consequently, the chassis was in effect splayed out at the back. I did suggest to Charlie that he ought to patent this idea and fit a few dodgy cross members to my mates' trucks and we would all make a bloody fortune. But for some reason he didn't like the idea!

That bloody BMC, oh I remember him well, Basil was his name. He caused me some problems, did our Basil, like say at 4am on a cold miserable frosty morning, when he didn't want to start did he, the lazy idle bleeder. I used to park him at the end of the terraced houses down the Ramper to keep the chill off of him, 'cos I loved him, didn't I? Well, I used to tell him I did and the bastard still wouldn't start. I would stroke him, whisper sweet nothings in his ear, kick him. All at four o'clock of a morning, and still he wouldn't bloody go. I used to park him on a slight slope, but sometimes, well many times, in fact, I misjudged things a little and he just wouldn't roll off and down the hill. Either that or the stubborn bastard just didn't like me and he left his brakes on a bit, which might have been it, because the things he did were absolutely unbelievable. There were mornings when I would get a bloody great lump of wood under his back wheels to lever him off and as soon as he started to roll down the hill I had to run like hell after him, jump into the cab, throw him in gear and start the engine. This, of course, didn't always work, did it? Sometimes I had to brave the elements, go back inside and get Her Highness to arise from her slumbers to give me a push. And that wasn't a pleasant experience either, after she had given me a bloody rollicking for waking her and wakened half the street with her shouting in the process. Apart from that, Jean wasn't really a pretty sight first thing of a morning, was she, with her hair in curlers and in her nightdress. Oh no, sirree. Her nightdress wasn't one of those skimpy, short, see-through things designed to keep the husband in bed of a morning, oh dear no. It

was a right bloody passion-killer, a Victorian nightgown, yes gown, not dress, presented by Jean's grandma, the witch, on our wedding day. It reached the floor, with long sleeves, and buttoned at the neck. What a bloody sight, enough to frighten poor Basil my BMC to death, especially first thing of a morning! I decided it wasn't such a good idea after all to ask Jean for a push; it wasn't doing poor Basil's nerves any good. All the excitement didn't do me much good either, having to climb into bed with that bloody nightgown. It used to put me off, not turn me on. As I say, her grandma was a witch, and she had cast her spell.

Back to Basil. Sometimes, when he had a flat battery, Basil's engine would only turn over slowly, so (and this, dear reader, takes some believing, but is perfectly true), if I couldn't roll the wagon down the slope, I would have the starter button wires out and bared ready. I would then put the starting handle into the starter dog at the front of the engine and join the starter wires together. These were long enough to save me climbing into the cab. Basil's engine would grunt and groan, slowly turn over, and I would run to the front of the wagon, grab the starting handle, and swing like hell, as hard as I could. This usually did the trick, and Basil's engine started. I would run back to the cab door and pull the starter wires apart, then tape them up until the next time. Oh, I had some fun with that bleeding BMC! On reflection, it was probably a good thing that I had weigh bridge men, digger drivers and such bailing me out with free fuel and extra loads, because that bloody wagon couldn't have made it on its own. I am now 66 years of age and why, I don't know, but I still dream about that bloody BMC. It was a nightmare really. But I suppose it must have been because we went through so much together that I still have a soft spot for it. The good times, the bad, the pneumonia, the slipped disc; it was a bleeding jinx. I bought a new Ford Thames Trader in the early sixties. I got 10% discount, paid 10% deposit and the motor was mine - well, not really. And who got to drive it?

Well, Pete did, didn't he. I was still stuck with Basil, but that's another story.

# The A1 And Me

As I mentioned earlier, Johnnie and I were removed from our lucrative fiddles at Askern. I suppose it was thought that we may have been an undesirable influence or summat. Can't think why, because there was no way we were ever going to corrupt those other contractors by introducing them to and teaching them how to play our fiddles. Not bloody likely; we had earned our spurs the hard way, and we had earned our brownie points too. Apart from that, we hadn't had the opportunity to register our fiddles at the Patents Office, although new patents had been applied for. So the powers that be moved us to the other end of the Earth to Ferrybridge by the sea, no less, and we were employed to move fly ash from Ferrybridge Power Station to various sites on the A1, which was being upgraded at the time. Now this job had been going for many, many months with no problems. Everything was straightforward, weigh bridge at the power station under control, everybody on the job had been security checked and cleared. Our employers even had their man (who soon became our man) on site monitoring every load that came off of that site. In fact, all they were short of was a few bloody SAS men to complete the picture. So, dear reader, everything was in order, comfortable and correct. Those guys, the Hell drivers, were up and down that A1 like bats out of hell, and in and out of that bloody power station like yo-yos. So there they were, all happily working away like bees in a honey pot, no problems - well, not really. Not until Johnnie and I came on the scene with our redoubtable fiddles. We had become so good at our fiddles that we were too good for the likes of Ferrybridge Power Station. We should have been playing them for that London Philharmonic Orchestra, no less.

Well, there we were, and within just one week the bloody place was turned on its head and we began to inject a small measure of common sense into the people who were running the show. Purely to make some much-needed improvements of course, and to satisfy our own mad desire to increase our profitability. So Johnnie and I, well, we decided to make a few changes. We had a word with the weigh men, who were very understanding chaps, especially after we had bunged them a few packets of fags.

We all agreed that it would be much better, for us, that is, not to run from the site onto the weigh bridge to weigh the load. We would all save a lot of time if we simply rang through on the telephone from the site to the weigh bridge and gave the weigh man our estimated weight. He could then enter it into his records to be cross checked with our weigh notes and the site man's records.

What an absolutely brilliant idea, wonderful! We saved time, got extra loads, the weigh man had less work to do and the man on site had a few extra bob in his pocket to spend. Fantastic! We were all happy. Now wasn't that nice, to be able to bring a little sunshine and pleasure into other people's lives? Johnnie and I did get a lot of satisfaction from helping others; nice to have such an unselfish attitude eh? And our initiative and enterprise knew no bounds. We had, in fact, changed the system for the better; it was now much easier to operate, and far more profitable for Johnnie and me. But we didn't really think that the main contractors would have appreciated our efforts on their behalf, so we thought we had better not tell them. Ouch! We would now get loaded on site, be given our weigh note by the site man, fill it in ourselves, go to the phone and ring Billy the weigh man. The conversation would go something like this. "Hello Billy, this is Charlie, Charles Transport." I would go on to give him my registration number and the load weights, 9-ton 6cwt, 10-ton 3cwt, or whatever, and Billy would enter the details into his records. We would sometimes say. "Oh Bill, the last two, or sometimes three load we have just done were so and so."

Bill would say. "Bloody hell, yer gerring through some work, you two buggers! You had better bring me another packet of fags next time you pass me weigh bridge, on yer way home that is."

So there it was, all perfectly honest and above board. The site man issued the weigh note on site, checked the number of loads that were loaded, the weigh man weighed the loads filled in the note and away we fled, sorry - went. And when we tipped the load on site on the A1, the site checker signed our note. So the powers that be had thought of everything. All the checks were in place, the weigh man's records were reconciled with the site man's records and the chap who received the loads on site confirmed receipt of aforementioned loads. Nothing wrong there, everything thought out properly and the system was foolproof. Except they hadn't made any allowances for human nature. Johnnie and I had calculated these human resources, and we had harnessed and conditioned (no, not corrupted) them to our way of thinking. We had in fact seen and exploited the fundamental weakness in the whole of the human behaviour and that is greed. The only other motivator that comes anywhere near to greed is fear. We had recognised in this instance that greed had overcome any element of fear the men might have felt at the possibility of losing their jobs. We knew that greed usually prevails and thanks to us, it did.

While on the particular job, some of the fly ash would be cancelled because it was too wet. No problem to us, that; oh no, we would run onto one site, get the load cancelled, wet or not. The checker signed the note. We would then call at another site, tip the load and get a spare note signed - two loads for one. Sometimes we got paid for non-delivery of returned wet loads and subsequent deliveries of the same load to another site - wonderful! The site security system was fantastic, so good in fact that I remember clearly one time when I had broken down with Basil, for three full days and nights. Yet at the end of the week, Basil had still done seven loads more than those other silly buggers tearing up and down the A1, and he had been asleep for three days and nights. Wonder how he managed to sleep with all the noise from those gormless prats, tearing up and down the A1!

But all good things must come to an end, and Basil my BMC and I moved onto pastures new. The only thing that spoiled my little interlude at Ferrybridge was that the man on site, that bastard, the site manager, had been given the right to get a few, note a few gallons of petrol for his car on my account that I had at South Yorkshire Motors, now Calderford on Barnsley Rd, Wakefield. He wasn't satisfied with just a few gallons for services rendered, was he? Oh no, the thieving git must have had all his friends and family running into Calderford for freebies. I stopped that account sharpish like though I couldn't do a lot because he was to become useful later.

I just don't know, one cannot trust anyone these days, can one?

On reflection, I seem to have more memories of the times I spent with Basil of any other vehicle or times in my life. Perhaps it was because I was young and in my prime; perhaps it was because, at that time in particular, there were so many happy moments to share. I was happily married with two lovely kids; I had wonderful parents who stood by me; we were living in a generally happy environment, a close knit community with good friends and neighbours; and I was doing a worthwhile job, trying to build and build a stake in the future for me and mine. It was hard, but it was also satisfying. However, I also think that this particular part of my life, with Basil in the early 1960s, was the loneliest, the hardest, and the most frustrating.

There were constant breakdowns. They seemed to never end: broken springs, half shafts tipping gear, blown up engines, blown out tyres. On

144

and on, never-ending. Repairs by night, and back to work next day, if I was lucky. It was during this time that my mam developed cancer; she was 57 years of age. What an absolute tragedy! My dad and mam, it seemed, were at last getting on together reasonably well, after my sister Lenore and I had got married and moved out. My ma was two years dying. How I got through some of my days at work, I will never know. She used to lie in bed in that front room at home, still booking removals, and pushing my old man out to work, and Dad, bless him, would still go about in his usual laid-back manner, he was a bugger. He would promise the earth. "Yes, love," he would say. "Don't worry, I shan't let thee down, yer can rely on me. I shall be there on the dot to move that furniture." Oh yes, and he had no bloody intention of doing it, had he?

My old man could tell a lie, and prove it. The only other man that was ever nearly, only nearly, capable of licking Dad's boots was my signwriting friend Geoffrey Victor Reeve who was also really laid-back. How they ever managed to hold themselves upright and walk in a straight line, I will never know.

Neither of them ever seemed to have a problem, oh no they didn't. They just gave the problems to other people, they couldn't care less, and they ambled through life without a care in the world. But more of that later.

There was our Hetty, pushing and shoving our Wes, my dad, out to work as if she hadn't enough problems of her own, eh! About this time Ted Berry our neighbour died suddenly. He was a great chap, always pleasant and a laugh for everybody. He was the chief underground engineer at Lofthouse Colliery, and he was in competition with my other pal, Ken Petty. They had a race to see who could crawl the furthest up Tommy Mapplebeck the colliery manager's bum. I think Ted won with a short head, because his head was two sizes smaller than Ken's. I joke, of course; I thought the world of both of them. When Ted died, Mam used to say it ought to be me, not him. She was eventually taken to Cookeridge Cancer Hospital in Leeds, and I used to visit her most days, sometimes straight from work with my BMC. I took Mam with her clothes into Cookeridge and when she died I came away with a plastic bag with her bits and pieces. That was all that was left, - a bag full of now't. Now't left to show for 59 years of her life, except memories, and memories are made of this. We all have them, treasure them and make the most of them. For that is all life is: only a series of memories, so guard them well. The only time I ever remember kissing me mam was when she was dying and maybe she never even knew. I held her hand and she whispered. "Don't worry." We stayed at that hospital all night. Dad wiped a tear from his eye and said. "Well come on, lad, there's now't we can do here nar, time we buggered off." That's how it was, you tried not to show your feelings. That's the way we were brought up, but it didn't change the way you felt, and it didn't always work either.

We broke the news to my sister Lenore and tried to get on with our lives. Thank God I had my wife Jean to fall back on. Yes, those early sixties were traumatic, that's why I remember that bloody BMC so well. It was about this time that Phyllis, Ken Petty's wife contracted cervical cancer. She went to the doctors and was told not to worry. My mam had said to Ken before she died. "Bugger that for a tale, Ken, thee go get a second opinion." Ken did and Phyllis got the proper treatment. She is still very much alive today. Ken always said. "If it hadn't been for thee mam, our Phil would have been dead." Our Hetty had spoken.

I remember well the time that my BMC had broken down with serious engine trouble, and I had fallen out with my mechanic, the prat Ken Petty. We fell out many times. I remember once we had fallen out over whose turn it was to explore the petrol tank on the lorry that our good friend and neighbour Ernest Rowley used to bring home for our convenience. Anyway, whatever the reason, this left me with one of he biggest problems of my life: how to get Basil's engine out. It weighed in at nearly half a ton and all I had to work with was a few rusty spanners, a knocked-off ex NCB 5-ton Jack, a few scaffold poles and some block and tackle. Around this particular time, Jean and all our neighbours had been pestering the local council with doctors' notes and complaints about the insanitary damp conditions we lived under. I think the final straw came when the Housing Manager threw in the towel. That was after Jean or one of our neighbours had him pinned by the throat up against the wall in the Housing Dept, and was threatening to pull his head off and stick it up his bum, or something like that.

Anyway, to cut a long story short, we all got council houses, which left all the houses down the Ramper empty, thank God. If they hadn't been empty, I would have been knackered. I still rented the pigsties near the Railway Bridge, at the side of the Woodman Inn on Leeds Road. Lofthouse Gate. So what now, and if I did ever manage to get Basil's engine out, what then? I hadn't a bloody clue, but my pride wouldn't let me admit that even to myself. I took the cab off - that was the easy bit, first I took the steering wheel off, box off and rolled the cab forward onto some old tyres. Now the engine just sat there looked at me and said, now wot? I said. "Thee just wait and see." I stood back, looked this way and that and then I decided to fetch Her Highness from her cosy little world indoors into mine, the real world outside. Now that was probably my hardest task, dragging her with the gob away from her best friend, the bloody TV. My next job was to rig up the scaffold poles, three legs they call 'em. I mounted the block and tackle onto the top of the three legs. I unbolted the engine off its mountings, and away I went, with Jean the little love holding the engine steady. I pulled Basil's engine from his chassis - so far so good. Basil says. "Now what."

I said, "Hang on a bloody minute, give me time to think." Basil says, "Well, while tha's thinking, stick summat under me engine, because if that bloody chain breaks, me engines going to come a right proper cropper, ain't it.

I said, "Basil, dun't be so bloody impatient, it's alright for thee stood there doing now't except bloody criticising." Now what? While Her Highness was stood there holding the engine, yawning and dreaming about her favourite TV soap opera or maybe fantasising about that wonderful he-man she adored so much, Rock Hudson (who was actually the good fairy in disguise) I skipped away sharply while Jean was keeping Basil company to fetch my car. I hooked the car up to Basil's back end and gently, while she of ill grace hung onto Basil's engine, I pulled the BMC backwards and clear of the engine. Wonderful! Basil says, "Now what?"

I says. "Shut thee gob and get back to sleep yer useless bleeder." I then had another brilliant idea, I borrowed Dad's sack car, lowered the engine to the deck, put it onto the sack cart and pushed it, all half a ton of it into George Berry's pigsties, while her of little imagination says, "Well, can I go now, seeing as tha's just made me miss Coronation Street?"

I says. "Yes, love." Well, I think that's what I said. I couldn't use rude language in front of Basil, could I? Basil just stood there and said now't. So I says. "Now what?" I hadn't a bloody clue. I decided to go see the service manager at the local BMC dealership, Westgate Motors in Wakefield. He was a mutual friend of Ken and mine, so having already known Ken for a long time, he was well and truly corrupted enough to be of great assistance to me. I bunged him a few quid to borrow a few specialist tools, a few ideas and a workshop manual. I don't even remember what was wrong, or what I did to repair that bloody engine, but I did it. I had to, there was no one else, only me, and besides, I wasn't going to let that prat Ken Petty think I was stuck without him - which I was. Now what? I put the engine back in the chassis the same way it had come out. But how the bloody hell could I get that cab back on? I couldn't lift it high enough.  Now what?  Well, I had another brilliant idea - needs must!  I realised suddenly that because I had no-one to turn for help, I was beginning subconsciously to put my thoughts into logical order, and to apply common sense to my problems.  I was using logic.  I'd been forced into becoming an original thinker.  I was relying more and more on my own thoughts and ideas, and putting them into practice.

Now, between the empty houses down Pollard Street in between George Berry and Peter Padget's old houses was a passageway through to the backs of the houses.  Above this passage was a bedroom.  Could I put ropes inside the bedroom round the joists and then fasten the block and tackle to them to pull the cab up, and then lower it onto Basil's chassis?  Could I?  I had no bloody choice.  I had to try, hadn't I?

But how the bloody hell could I get that cab from George's pigsties, to under that window?

I went and borrowed Dad's piano bogey.  I put long planks across the bogey, rolled the cab onto its roof, then juggled it onto the piano boogey and roped it on - with, of course, the little woman's help  God knows how but we did it.  Now for the tricky bit.  I towed that bloody piano bogey with the cab on it across that rough track at about one mile an hour, with Jean holding on to that bloody cab like grim death, and yes, we did it together!  We lifted and lowered that bloody cab back on to its chassis.  Today's generation wouldn't know where to start without a hydraulic lift and a dozen pairs of hands to help.  I have taken engines out with 5-ton jacks and put the bloody things back - we had to.  So don't anybody tell me I have been lucky.  I have, but not in the way they mean.  I have been lucky in obtaining a priceless gift, the gift of knowledge.  I am not a specialist, I never wanted to be, but I have learned a hell of a lot about many things, and I can apply common sense.  So now, at 66 years of age, I can get impatient with the young specialists and the tradesmen, who tend to lose patience with me because I don't understand their speciality as well as they do.  Well, they don't really know what it's all about, do they?  I wonder how they would survive on their own in a jungle?  What price their bloody speciality then?  They wouldn't last for 10 bloody minutes on their own.  I have spent half of my life cleaning up after tradesmen and the other half admiring, envying and paying homage to specialists.  I must have been bloody crackers.  Their brains are conditioned and focused in a straight line, looking down the wrong end of a telescope.  Many of them who are brilliant within their chosen speciality are complete dummies out of it!  I am, of course, digressing again, because it has taken all these years for me to realise what we went through to arrive where we are. At long last I have, after writing this, achieved a little pride in what we did. An old soldier must have had a similar feeling, a life that was full to bursting. Now I know how they built the pyramids - with a little common sense, persistence and determination.

Back to Basil and me. I finished up with a slipped disc when I was lifting an ERF rear spring from out the back of my car. I was supposed to be off work for months, but I couldn't afford that, so I used to draw my sick pay. I also had an insurance policy for accident and sickness benefit, which paid me about £12 a week. After a few days of lying on a board, I went back to work. I would call at Pinderfields Hospital for stretching exercises as I was passing in my lorry with a load for British Oak Screens, but I finished up back in bed in agony. I had been nearly 12 weeks on and off with pneumonia and this bloody slipped disc. Apart from the money that Pete Bolton was earning with the new Ford Thames Trader, the only other income was sick pay from the insurance company. I was having to pay HP payments on both lorries, at that time, so there wasn't a lot left, with only one truck working to pay the bills. I was laid up in bed in the kitchen with my slipped disc during one of the worst winters we have ever known. Coal had to be delivered all over the country by road, because at that time most of the rail trucks were frozen solid. When a load came up for delivery to Worthing in Sussex one Friday, Pete loaded the BMC but there was no-one to deliver the load to Worthing except me. I got out of bed, took a flask and some sandwiches, called at a chemist in Wakefield and bought some pep pills. I also took some pain killers with me and off I set like a bloody idiot on a Friday afternoon to Worthing on the south coast. My intention was to get down there as fast as I could, tip the load and then travel straight back home and crawl back into bed. But it didn't quite work out as I had planned. Travelling down wasn't so bad, apart from the pain in my back. It seemed to take an eternity to get there. The people at the coalyard I was to deliver to had been waiting all night to receive these desperately needed coal deliveries. I arrived there around 9.30pm I think. I tipped my load and set off on the return journey home. I had perhaps travelled 30 or 40 miles to Horsham when I heard a noise coming from the front wheels. I stopped and managed to crawl out of the cab, to find the nearside front wheel was aglow. It was apparent that the wheel bearing had seized up. I was lucky that there were houses nearby. I staggered to the back door of one of the houses and asked for a bucket of water. The woman took one look at me and she said. "My God, what's the matter with you?" The householders put the fire out, then the lady of the house called the police. A police constable came along and took me to the police station. I would not let the police call an ambulance. On arrival at the station, I had to sit on a bloody hard stool all night. That was the longest night of my life. They never even asked if I would like to sleep in a cell, and my pride wouldn't allow me to suggest this to them. So hour after never-ending hour, in agony, I waited for dawn.

The next morning, I managed to get out of the police station to a fruit stall in Horsham, and I had a couple of bananas for breakfast. That was all I had to eat until I eventually arrived back home at around 10pm on the Saturday night. The police had arranged for Basil to be picked up by a local garage, who fitted a new wheel bearing and repaired the vehicle. I left at 3.30pm for home, and boy, I just couldn't get home fast enough. I hardly saw any signs or roundabouts, passing the Wakefield turn off on the A1 before I saw one. I travelled further on to the Barnsdale Bar Pontefract turn off. Again I nearly missed the turn off. I was travelling too fast, I mounted the kerb, ran over some grass, hit a low stone wall with my offside front mudguard, and carried on like a bat out of hell to Pontefract. I simply did not care, I was in agony, and all I wanted was to get home and to bed. I had been 38 or 39 hours without sleep. I drove through Pontefract to Methley, missed the Stanley turn-off and as I sped round the left hand bend past Methley Church on the left, there were some people crossing the road. I swerved to miss them, they scattered like a flock of chickens in all directions and I carried on home. It may sound funny now, but it wasn't then, it was just bloody stupid as I was in no condition to drive.

On reflection, 37 years or so later, I am not proud of episodes like that. I was a fool. I am ashamed to admit to stealing, fiddling, cheating and to having done so many wrong things in my life; even though at the time these things happened, my actions did seem to be justified in my desperate attempts to survive - there just didn't seem to be any other way! At this particular time in the early sixties I was in serious trouble. I had HP payments to pay on vehicles. I had been off sick for around 12 weeks and things were desperate. I had to sell the nicest little car I had ever had, a Morris Cowley, to buy a new engine for our Basil, my BMC, but even this wasn't enough. I was really desperate. I went to see my Bank Manager. I will never forget his name, Mr Jones of the Midland Bank in Wakefield. He said. "Right, Mr Walker, I will give you the money, get off and buy your engine, and we will talk about the details later."

Wonderful, another angel in disguise, and strange to relate that man was still my bank manager 20 years later when he gave me an overdraft of over £90,000 to buy my warehouse at Flanshaw. That was an absolute

Every picture tells a story.
Sister Marris
my dear old Mam.

Mum and Dad in 1955.

Me Gran and Bruce - The dog's on the right.

i

Me Uncle Clarence,
The Small Bore Rifle Champion of the World in 1939.

My dear old Auntie with Lady Mason and the
Mayor of Barnsley, the day she got the BEM.

Blackpool 1944.
Family day out with my sister and
him of few words, with her of many.

Me in 1937 aged six.

Hilda the maneater and me the butcher boy.
At Kilburn's at the top of Queen Street in 1945.

iii

And so into business, me and the Bradford Jowett van outside
7, Johns Ave, Lofthouse in 1948.

My sister, Frank Heppy and me in 1948.

22149354 L/Cpl Walker RASC.

Demobbed.
I couldn't wait to get that bloody
suit off and into the dustbin.

Showing off! I'm the prat in the middle, with all brawn and no brains.
Oh boy didn't I think I was just marvellous. Until some Scottish git
proved me wrong. By beating hell out me! If I had told me Mam, she
would have killed the bastard, and my C.O. too for allowing it.
Ah well that's what Ma's are for!

## Meet The Wife's Family...

Jean's friend, Her Highness, and her cousin Sylvia, resplendent in their tattered Mother Riley headscarves.

Yonty, Jean's Grandad, who's shotgun was responsible for Jean being born in wedlock!

Jean and her Mam at the back with young brothers David & John in front.

Jean's Dad Jack enjoying a pint of Bevereley's Best Bitter.

1939 Hillman 14.
1956 down the Ramper.

My pride and joy! No the car not the wife.

1954 Wedding Day. Dad, Mam, Sylvia, Our Reg, Me, Jean, Kath,
Derek, Lenore, Vic, Jean's Mam & Dad

1955
Him and Her

My first ever new vehicle, a Thames Trader.
My first time in debt too!

How Walkers of Wakefield started in 1967, on the back of a Gypsey!

Into the 1970s, we had expanded to nearly forty trucks of our own and were probably sub-contracting work to twice that many too.

Range Rover Recovery Vehicle.
When fully equiped it probably weighed in at about 5 ton and
did about 2 mpg. So it didn't stay around too long, it had to go!

My secret weapon, me Rolls Royce Silver Shadow 1
that I cherished for 20 years.

Walkers Gargages Ltd.
Fleet of Recovery Trucks in the 1970s.

The young ones!
With Ken and Joan Moorhouse in the Primrose Hill WMC in the 1950s.

And the not so young ones!
With our very dear friends Ron and Vera in a bar in Spain in the 1980s.

One of our Albert's upmarket 'do's. My wife and I on the left with
transport manager and his wife. Whilst opposite sits my general
manager and his wife. The vacant chair is Alberts. He had
disappeared, it was time to pay the bloody bill!

My dear friend Albert and his wife Jean.

My pride and joy...no, not the wife, our Dennis, me Fire Engine!

'Charlie The Champ' leading RA Memorial Parade, Wakefield 1996.

Big time Charlie in all me glory.

Better days, my wife and I.

fortune in those days, but that is another story. At this time, things were still desperate. We were short of work. I had even diversified by putting one vehicle on contract to a well-known Leeds fuel distributor, Sydney Glover.

These new enterprises didn't work out either. I stayed three weeks. I was being paid peanuts by Glovers; we earned next to now't.

The best thing that ever came out of these learning experiences was when I came to realise that the only people who made the real money were the ones who had control, who were pulling the strings and making us their puppets. I would commercialise on these truths, oh yes, later, much later.

I survived, oh yes, but only just. I often think that it was only with the help of Mam, who of course was sat at the right hand of God and who was looking after my finances during these troubled times. I thought that she must have had a quiet word with the Almighty, because she was still up there looking after me, though why I can't imagine. I had, (or so I thought at the time) been forced by desperate circumstances into temptation and was so ashamed. I had exploited the system and done whatever it took to survive.

I can try to excuse my actions by telling myself that everyone to a greater or lesser degree, tries to obtain something for nothing, be a child at school who steals a pencil; a public sector employee who takes a day off work sick when he or she is fit for work; the people who fiddle the social security systems by working and claiming benefit; the so-called disabled who cheat the system; the professionals, doctors, civil servants, solicitors in particular. They all do it. But despite this, I am not excused from the wrong things I did. They just weren't right, but I did them anyway. I can only hope that in all the years since those early days when I was starting out in business, I have redeemed myself somewhat, in that I put more back into the system than I took out. I was never on the dole; that would have been a disgrace in my day. I don't now owe anyone ow't, nor do I want ow't for now't. I have given and still give to dozens of charities. I care for my fellow man and in my own way I do try to make up for and pay for those early mistakes. But it will never alter the fact that I was wrong to do what I felt I had to do.

I am still a selfish, egotistical hypocrite. I am, after all, just another human being with all the usual human failings, but even that fact doesn't excuse me. But I will temporarily close this, my confessional box and move on.

The time had come at last for the partings of the ways. Basil had to go.

He was sorry to leave me, but his time was up. He had had a very hard life with me, I had certainly abused him, and he must have earned a record for the most weight ever carried, on a fourteen ton gross four wheel vehicle. He had been fitted with extra heavy duty rear springs by Charlie Barnsley and boy did he need them because one of the last jobs we ever did together was carrying stone from a quarry between Normanton and Castleford, onto the A1 at Brotherton. We had to weigh our loads at the Laporte Chemical Works weigh bridge in Castleford. Well, this particular day, as Basil and I were loading under this digger in the quarry, I was busy telling the tale to the other drivers who were waiting to be loaded. I could hear Basil give a sigh, every time a bucket full was dropped onto his back and he seemed to be going a little red in the face too. After a while Basil says to me. "Is tha going to stand there all bloody day calling then, while this bloody silly digger driver breaks me bleeding back or pulverises me into the bloody floor?"

I looked round and Basil was nearly on his knees. I shouted "Christ!" And to the digger driver, "Whoa, stop, yer daft bastard, can't tha see Basil's just had a bloody heart attack, yer daft bugger?" (I saw that same digger driver recently in a pub and we still laugh about that incident.) I just had no idea how much weight was on Basil's back, because he was a high-sided coal tipper. Now I could judge loads of coal no problem to within a few hundred weight, but stone was a different commodity altogether. It's a good job the incline out of that quarry was only very slight, because Basil crawled out of there on his bloody hands and knees. We travelled at a crawl onto that weigh bridge at Laporte's in Castleford. Now this is perfectly true, unbelievable but true: when Basil and me pulled onto that weigh bridge, the weigh man nearly had a stroke. He ran outside and shouted to me, "Get that bloody lorry off of me weigh bridge, is tha trying to break me bloody scales or what?" The bridge only weighed up to 20 (tons). I backed Basil off the scales and I had to weigh him twice. I drove the front wheels on to be weighed, and then we weighed the rear half, and believe it or not, the gross weight vehicle and load weighed in at just over 23 tons. Basil weighed in at around 4 tons 10 cwt; that meant Basil had just over 18 tons on his back. Bloody hell, I was frightened to death and it was nearly as far to go back to Normanton and tip some off as it was to go to Brotherton. I decided to chance it. I said to Basil, "Bloody hell, we're all right now."

Basil said, "Are dost to meen we, 'we', he says, tha meen's me dunt tha? I am the one ast got 18 ton on me bloody back, not thee and all tha has to do is drive me there, and send my bloody tipper up and get this bloody load off of me back, so let's be off."

152

I stopped every half a mile to let the tyres cool, and how we got to Brotherton I will never know. How I managed to get Basil's tipping gear to lift 18 tons I will also never know. I still have nightmares today. Needless to say, in that same week I had a rear spring broken, a centre bolt break, and a tyre blow. Basil got his own back and he told me straight that he had had enough. So he was put in part exchange for a 1950s AEC Monarch fitted with a 7.7-litre engine.

This vehicle had originally been an ex-Regent Oil Co Tanker. Jack Robinson, who owned A1 Transport at Gildersome, fitted a tipper body and gear and away I went to my next adventure.

After my overloading episodes with Basil, we were doing more and more quarry work, and we were less restricted on weight carried over private weigh bridges, which we used on this kind of work. So I decided to move into the big league and buy a more substantial motor, which the AEC was. It was a lot slower than Basil, but it weighed over a ton more , and I dare not say it could handle bigger loads than Basil, dare I, because that load he carried from Castleford to Brotherton should have been noted in the Guinness Book of Records. Ah well. All I will say is that the AEC was a better built vehicle, and made to stand up to harder work than a BMC. The AEC's spring shackle pins were as big as Basil's kingpins. What a motor it was, built like a bloody tank! So away we went. I loved that AEC, it was an old motor, a proper motor, a man's motor; but I never ever forgot Basil. We had shared too many memories and magic moments together. I ran this AEC for a few months on open cast coal sites and out of quarries where I wasn't restricted to carrying legal weights of up to 14-tons gross. I was carrying 10 and 12 tons on that old AEC, and its unladen weight was 5 tons, 10cwt at least, so I was grossing 15 half 17 half tons. Great! I was earning good money with my AEC when all of a sudden this work came to an end and I was found some work running out of collieries. But here was the crunch. When we loaded out of and were weighed on NCB (British Coal) weigh bridges, our vehicles could not carry more than their legal permitted weight, which was 14-tons, wasn't it? So my AEC, which weighed nearly 6-tons unladen, could only carry a load of coal weighing just over 8-tons. Bloody ridiculous! Come back Basil, all is forgiven. I had just fallen out of the frying pan into the bloody fire. My BMC Basil had been perfect for roadwork over NCB weigh bridges at legal weights, but was not up to site work. The AEC was perfect for site work but wasn't allowed to carry sensible loads from NCB collieries. What a bloody state of affairs, but that was the law.

So I made a decision, I swapped the AEC for a brand new 702 model BMC, four-wheel chassis and cab. I searched for and found a scrap BMC, which had been fitted with a Boye's trailing axle and an extended chassis, which had converted the original BMC four-wheeler into a six-wheeler. It was also fitted with a Edward's double ram tipping gear and an aluminium bulk coal body perfect. I fitted all this second hand gear onto my new BMC chassis and cab, and hey presto, I had a new 24 Ton gross BMC six wheeler, which had just had a complete respray. The vehicle weighed in at probably 8-tons. I now could carry a payload of around 16-tons great, except that the engine was designed to pull weights of 14-tons gross and was now expected to pull loads of around 24-tons gross. Our Basil would have turned in his grave! I had to drive that bloody motor like Malcolm Campbell with Bluebird. I had to keep those revs up, going down hill out of gear at say 60mph or so, then slip back into gear uphill and hope I would climb over the brow of the hill before those bloody revs dropped. We managed. If I hadn't got the speed up the hills, at least I was getting bigger loads over those bloody weigh bridges. I did all right with that motor and lo and behold two years later, when I sold it I got more for it than the price I'd paid new. Why? Well, I bought a four wheeler chassis new, fitted it with second-hand gear and I sold a six wheeler tipper two years later. From then on, when I bought new vehicle chassis cabs, I always looked for and attempted to buy good second-hand bodies. Because after a year or two the chassis cab looked as old as the body. I learned another lesson eighteen years later when I bought 24 second-hand Penman demountable exchangeable bodies for my fleet of Bedfords, but that's another story, for another day.

The BMC proved so successful that I decided to convert the Ford Thames Trader, and Ken Petty had a pal called Reg Walters, who had a garage opposite Elland Road Football Field. What a character Reg was, he looked just like James Robertson Justice, with his bloody great flowing beard. He was an engineer, but not just any old engineer; an engineer with contacts. He was so dedicated he slept in a bed at his garage. Pete had had an accident with the Trader - very convenient for me. We gave Reg the vehicle to repair, and he offset some of the insurance claim costs against the fitting of a third axle. As the accident wasn't Pete's fault, I could claim loss of use of the vehicle while repairs were being undertaken from the offending party. All the time Reg worked on my vehicle I was being compensated for loss of vehicle earnings. It made sense, of course it did, and I was also being paid to help Reg fit me extra axle - wonderful! Reg bought an old Albion CX rear bogey complete from Sammy Luckman's scrapyard up Bradford Road (CVS). He shortened the prop shaft and strengthened my Ford Trader's chassis. Now I had another six wheeler tipper; the only problem was the Albion had been fitted with Lockead brakes and the Ford had Girling brakes. The other problem that the redoubtable Reg had not allowed for was that the Ford master cylinder was not big enough to serve the bigger braking system, which was now fitted with two extra brake drums. Because of the extra brake piping, that master cylinder had to push the brake fluid a further distance and it just couldn't be done. With one push of the brake pedal...oh dear, it was too bloody late now to change our minds, we had done it. Pete, the bloody wimp, wouldn't drive it. He never did like a challenge. Someone had to and that someone was me. What a bloody game that was, in between changing gear, with or without the clutch. My left leg was employed pumping that bloody brake pedal up and down to build up the brake pressure, just in case. If I happened to have to stop in a hurry all the time my right foot was flat to the floor on the accelerator pedal. Experiences like that certainly taught me how to drive. I must have been absolutely bloody crazy! Young and stupid.

I remember one job we used to do, taking coal to Lancaster for 25 shillings a ton, so it made sense to try and get the biggest load possible over to Lancaster to make the job pay. That's what the redoubtable Peter Slater was probably thinking when he overloaded that bloody eight wheeler Albion for me to drive, but there was a difference this time: Peter Slater's AECs and Albion's were fitted with 11-litre engines. My converted six wheeler BMC that I was using at the time was fitted with a little 5-7 litre engine, it was a bloody dinky toy compared with Slater's motors. But not to be deterred, I loaded my BMC with, I think, about 16-tons of coal. Nothing ventured and all that. So away I went to face that bloody Bucker Brow. Through Leeds, Skipton, Settle I went, putting that gearbox into first gear low as I got near to the Brow. I had the engine flap open inside the cab. I had my finger holding the cold start button in, and there were clouds and clouds of black smoke, all the way back to bloody Settle. That BMC huffed and puffed, and shuddered to a stop just on the brow of the hill. I thought, "You lazy bastard!"

I set off again (which was stupid, I was to find out later.) I gave the engine full revs, let out the clutch, the front end of my motor jumped over Bucker Brow. Now, talk about the Grand National: that Red Rum just couldn't have lived with my BMC over Bucker Brow, that Beachers Brook, why, that was chicken feed, eh! But I was to regret my day as a steeplechase jockey sooner than I expected. I managed to deliver the load to Lancaster, but there was a nasty noise coming from the BMC's nether regions. I found out why the next day. When I took the gearbox out and the bell housing off, the bloody clutch plate fell to bits in my hands as I was removing it. I learned all right, I learned the hard way: never send a lad to do a man's job. Those bloody BMCs were not good enough to be four-wheelers, let alone to be converted into six-wheelers.

I had by this time built up a fleet of four trucks. I had started in business, working on a contract A licence. I had what I think was called a limited B-licence granted by the Yorkshire Traffic Commissioner. I was able to obtain this licence with Sydney Glover's support when I started work for them. I now had something to sell because the B-licence enabled me to work within certain limitations for other people. In those days you just couldn't go out and buy a truck, and then set up in business oh no. The big boys, the old established hauliers, were the only ones who were allowed to work for anyone and to travel anywhere, with their top-of-the-range A-licence. These A licences were worth a fortune; new ones were never issued by the Traffic Commissioners, it was the established hauliers who increased their fleets and therefore their A-licence capacity. These A licences, once issued, could be sold along with the lorry to which they applied. The A licence was worth far more than any lorry, it was a right closed shop at that time and far more privileged than any setup by the unions!

Jean's Uncle Ronnie, as I mentioned earlier, was a car dealer in Cardiff South Wales. He built up a good business and seemed to be doing well for himself. I came to know and like Ronnie. We had a lot in common as we had both started in business with now't.

Anyway, Jean's Uncle Ron got himself into trouble in Cardiff with the Inland Revenue, I think, and he left his wife, did a bunk and came and settled in Wakefield, at no fixed abode. My dad, bless him, managed to get him and the girlfriend he brought with him, Pam, a little house to rent from Laidlaw's the Estate Agents. The house was near the Carlton Cinema off Kirkgate Wakefield. We helped him to decorate and get fixed up with some second-hand furniture from the salesrooms. I even fixed him up with a little driving job, and helping to repair my lorries. So that was Ron and his bird settled.

At this time I had bought a beautiful Mark 9 Jaguar from Reg Walters from Leeds. He told me that the car had once belonged to Billy Cotton, the band leader; it ought to have been gold-plated and belonged to bloody Liberace for the price he charged me. The robbing git. Anyway, I thought this car was the bees' knees didn't I? Friday nights, one night a week, my mates Pete Bolton, Ken Petty, sometimes Ernest Rowley, and others used to meet up with Alan Storrs and some of the other contractors, and have a night out with the lads. We used to go all over. I remember once we were in the Tin Hat, WMC in Mapplewell one Friday and we had just half-an-hour to get to the Ace Club on George Street Wakefield. (Joe Fisher's gambling club) before the doors closed at 11pm. We left the Tin hat at 10.30pm and arrived at 10.50. That old Jag could certainly motor. But one Friday in the middle of Winter, when it was freezing cold, we were in the pub at Horbury Bridge which belonged to the dad of one of our mates. Anyway, when the time came to leave, Alan Stores ups and sets off like the clappers in his new MG Magnette. I says to my mate, "Come on, we'll catch him and pass him before he gets through Horbury." So we ran outside and jumped into the Jag. I flew up the hill after Storsie, through Horbury, and as we came down the hill at probably 90mph towards Wakefield, we came up to the left hand bend at the bottom of the hill out of Horbury. I don't remember touching the brakes, but that bloody Jag spun round in the road and carried on at the same speed towards Wakefield, but this time in reverse, although the car was still in forward drive. We had just hit a patch of black ice and we shot across the road completely out of control. We were terrified. The car mounted the pavement, shot along the pavement, just missing a concrete lamp post by about two inches. Still going backwards it ploughed through a fence, and finished up in the mid-dle of a rose bed in someone's front garden. We were out of that bloody car like a shot and away. We eventually recovered the car, my insurance company compensated the householder and all was well, except I couldn't claim for repairs to my Jag because it was only third party insured and I couldn't afford to repair it. So I decided to park the Jag up for a few months, then re-insure the car (fully comprehensive), and then engineer another accident, or live in hope that someone would do me a favour and steal it! After all, one of our new neighbours who had a Citroen and couldn't keep up with the HP payments had consulted a friend about his particular problem and this friend had suggested it could be a good idea if the car just disappeared. The neighbour agreed, gave his friend a few quid for his advice and, lo and behold, overnight that car just vanished, never to be seen again. The neighbour got paid out, and everyone was happy. So I knew that there would be no problem with my Jag.

The opportunity to deal with that problem came sooner than I thought, because Jean's Uncle Ronnie had decided to move onto pastures new; he wanted to go to Australia to start a new life. He would go on his own and then, when he got settled, he would send for his girlfriend Pam and their child (yes, they had a child.) As it turned out, he never did send for her, did he? The problem he had was that he had no money, but what he still had was a Trader's Insurance Policy. So we agreed between us to arrange an accident. I was coming up Leeds Road Outwood, past Outwood Picture House. I stopped near Church Lane to turn right, and Ron, who was behind me in a lorry ran into me and wrote my Jag off - at least, that's what we told the Insurance Company. What really happened was that I backed that bloody Jag up against a steel gate post at George Berrys pigsties so many times, it was unrecognisable as a car, let alone a Jaguar. Ron's insurance company paid me out. I claimed loss of use too, and while the insurance companies were arguing, Ron got a few bob to take him to Australia, and I got a few bob for my car. Now't wrong with that, is there?

As I attempt to get my thoughts into focus. I think it was at about this time in my life, just before we moved into the council house at 29 George Street, Outwood in Wakefield that I developed pneumonia, and I was laid in bed hallucinating. Jean and my dad were getting the new house ready for us to move into. They had been to Beaumonts, a furniture wholesalers in Huddersfield, for the furniture, and when I had recovered enough to move, everything had been done, bless them!

All our old neighbours from the Ramper had moved into the council estate, along with many more who had moved out of various condemned houses in the Stanley and Outwood areas into new homes.

We had some great neighbours. There was Eric and Rene Roe who lived next door. They had been childhood sweethearts, and they had done everything together. Their leisure time was spent walking and cycling together. Unfortunately this very happy state of affairs was not allowed to continue, because Eric fell in love with a girl from work, and they parted in due course. Pity really, as they were such a lovely couple. Our other immediate neighbours were Eric and Bett Brook, who were a little older than Jean and me. They were a wonderful couple, who looked after us and did an awful lot to help us. I used to work every hour that God sent at this time, and Eric would help Jean with the garden. He was a great guy I will never forget. Eric worked for the council, I think he was a boiler man and he would finish work every day at 4pm, then he would hurry home to get out into either his or my garden. Betty and Eric's favourite meal, was bacon roll out of a tin; when it was fried it was really lovely. They hadn't much money coming in and I paid for their help by giving them odds and ends that I had acquired on my travels. Higher up the street we had Edgar and Shirley Sharp, who became our good friends. Edgar and I are still mates after 37 years. Tragically Shirley contracted cancer and died young. Jean had lost her best friend and coffee maker; Shirley was a lovely woman. My two eldest kids, Susan and Anne, spent many happy hours playing in Edgar and Shirley's back garden with their two kids, Karen and Julie. They used to play in a Wendy House at the bottom of the garden. Karen married another chap who became a great friend of mine later in life, David Wilson. A little higher up the street were Bert and Margaret Hemingways. I worked at Roper's Brickyard with Bert. Then there was Brian Clayton and Meg, his wife; Brian came to work for me later as I became established in business, as did another of our neighbours, Don Briggs. Kath Berry lived at the bottom around the corner of Andrew Crescent, and George Berry at the top round the corner on Andrew Crescent. My mechanic, the bleeder Ken Petty, lived round the back. He and I fell out many times, but we always remained good friends at the end of it all. I remember one time in a fit of temper going round to see him. We had had a fall out and he had been having a go at our Anne. I told him to have a go at me instead, and I threatened to throw him through his bloody kitchen window. He threatened to call the police. Happy days!

I have one regret - that my language to Ken was a little too profound to be used in front of Phyllis, his wife. Councillor Ken Steaples who was also a good friend and neighbour, lived on Andrew Crescent too. He was to prove a friend indeed later, when his influence as a councillor was used to my advantage. (More of that later.)

At this time I was still renting land off George Berry down the Ramper to store my lorries and operate my haulage business. I was paying George cash; we had no legal binding agreement, only a gentleman's one based on mutual trust. Some hope! George's wife Evelyn wanted out of the council house, and to move into an home of her own, so George sold his land suddenly to a fireplace man, who built the showrooms on Leeds Road. That was just past the Woodman Inn, and there they stand today, as an up-market Italian restaurant!

In 1962 I was in serious trouble. I was in business, I had trucks but I had nowhere to keep them. In desperation I moved onto some waste railway land on Potovens Lane and I applied to British Rail estates dept for permission to rent this site. They agreed, so my bacon was saved again.

# W 'Walker And Son'

The period 1962 to 1963 had been traumatic. I had lost my mother, I had lost my operating base and I was 31 years of age, married with two kids and living in a council house. My dad was still struggling on, doing a few removals and working for Kilburns and Laidlaws the auctioneers. He was 66 years old, the same age as I am now! He still parked his old vehicle at the local brickworks, he would get his vehicle repairs done at a wooden hut at the side of the Elephant and Castle at Lofthouse, very convenient of course, while Ivor Oldroyd the garage owner was doing his repairs. Dad was in the Elephant doing a few pints of beer, all very convenient like. Ivor was to later build a purpose built garage opposite the Elephant, and there it stands today.

A young lad worked for Ivor at this time as an apprentice mechanic. His name was Frank Armstrong.

Frank quickly learned what things were really about when he started doing cash-in-hand jobs for my dad! Frank later owned a Renault Dealership, where Charlie Browns are now based in Northgate Wakefield, and later a Mitsubishi Dealership on Leeds Road at Outwood, now a Toyota dealers. Again I must say it's a small world. Derek Turner was the captain of Wakefield Trinity Football Club at around this time and he had just started in business with a 30cwt Morris Van, doing a few removals and furniture shop deliveries. Although Dad and he were competitors, they also became the greatest of friends. Derek had a lot of respect for Dad; besides, my old man used to lend Derek his larger van if Derek had a big job to do. Around this time there were a lot of furniture removers in Wakefield. There was Smiths up Dewsbury Road, where my brother-in-law Derek Coxsidge's father Ernest worked; there was Harold Smith at Ossett, who did all the prison warder removals; Ernest Marsh, who became another mate of mine; Ronnie Tucknot of Proctors Removals, who had used his gratuity money when he came out of the army to start in business; Fred Hoyle, another of Dad's mates, operated several vans based near Kirkgate station and, of course, Pickfords, who had bought old Mr. Gilbeys removals and storage business in Tootal Street, Wakefield - quite a formidable crew.

At this time around 1963, Dad was using a 1200 cube old 1946 Bedford furniture removal van, which was painted leaf green. He traded from 7 Johns Avenue, Lofthouse, Wakefield as W Walker and Son, and I was the son. He would charge his customers 25 shillings an hour for his services. Dad was, however, 66 years of age and was becoming a little tired. He was really too old to be doing house removals, which after all was one of the hardest jobs around at that time. In those days, when people died and Dad cleared out the house and moved everything to the salesrooms, he was moving real furniture, furniture that had been handed down through the generations. This furniture represented a family's life: the sideboards and dressers were magnificent specimens made of solid mahogany, usually fitted with a bloody great mirror, which had to be unscrewed from the back. It would take two men to carry the mirror on its own, so I will leave you to guess, dear reader, what the sideboard weighed. Wardrobes were the same, mahogany walnut or oak. Some of these wardrobes were built like forts and would have repelled any invaders. They were solid and had to be split into five separate sections. These were either carried downstairs by two men in the conventional way or, if there was a bend in the stairs and the wardrobe wouldn't go around it, then Dad would have to take the bedroom window out, borrow a ladder from a neighbour and, balancing the wardrobe, he would shove it out the window for nearly its full length before lowering it onto the ladder and eventually to the floor with a rope. But the real clever tricks were saved for 4-foot wardrobes, which had to be shoved and pulled up that ladder on their backs, so that you did not scratch the polish. Incidentally, you could not cover the wardrobe. If you did, then it would not slide up the ladder. Those 4-foot wardrobes, on reaching the top of the ladder, then had to be turned in midair on to their sides to allow them to go in through the bedroom window, and all this without putting a mark or scratch on the furniture. While Dad or me or whoever was turning the wardrobe in midair, we were also trying to hang onto the window sill or that bloody ladder with the skin of our teeth. People today wonder why I am nervous of using a ladder. It is because I have fallen off far too many in the past.

Now Pickfords, of course, didn't have this problem, oh no, they could afford to used the proper window tackle which would fit the frame, and then they could used block and tackle to complete the job. Oh so easy, but we couldn't afford this gear and we just had to manage. If Pickfords or any of the other big removal firms had a five, seven or ten cwt safe to move, they would probably send six men with an appliance called a staircat. This staircat was like a heavy-duty sack cart fitted with caterpillar tracks. Wonderful! All we had was a rusty old sack cart and two men: sorry an old age pensioner and a lad, because they were cheaper to employ than real men! We just had to manage because we couldn't afford those luxuries. It was down to us, the job had to be done and it was. Pianos, well they were easy. They were nearly all German over strungs, Pianolas were a little different; they were tremendous things, very, very heavy, fitted with bloody great electric motors, but we managed, I could write a story on its own about Dad's and my exploits at moving furniture, but again I digress.

I will for the time being leave it to your imagination, but it must be said (and I will be the one to say it) that in those days, all furniture was real. Pianos were proper pianos and not bloody dinky toys like the ones produced today. Furniture was not made of chipboard, it was made of real wood and moved and carried by real men. Oh dear, here I go again! I suppose on reflection the people of today and the quality of the products they produce, sell and move deserve each other. (Oh and lest I forget, no, we didn't wear bloody plastic helmets on building sites! Why not? Well, there were fewer pigeons around in our day, and our heads were a bit too big to wear them anyway!)

Dad wanted to retire in 1963, he'd had enough. Who could blame him, he was on his own. Mam had died in 1962 and now all he wanted was for me to take over so that he could relax a bit in his old age. But unfortunately it just wasn't to be, and the fact that it wasn't still haunts me to this day! I still dream in my old age of working with my dad, but now it is much too late and just a little sad. I'd have helped Dad with removals on Saturdays if I hadn't been working at my job at Hargreaves. I would love to have taken over his business while he was alive, but unfortunately Dad's business didn't produce a regular income, and I dared not take the risk, I had a wife and two kids to support. I also hadn't realised that my Dad was getting older; he was very fit and I thought he would live forever (don't we all). So Dad carried on with the odd removal, and I struggled on with my own business.

We used to invite Dad down to our new council house to watch boxing on television. He loved his boxing, in fact in his youth he had been a very good amateur boxer, though he never talked about his past. In fact, he never said much at all, except when he really had something to say, which wasn't often. I remember once when he became ill and we made him stay with us a few days while he recovered. On the third day he was off home and he didn't come back.

He would sometimes confide in my wife Jean, (they always got on well together,) and tell her how he felt about being on his own. He would say "Nobody knows what it's like having to come home to an empty house." About me he would say, "Our bloody Charlie! Well, he's all talk."

162

He was probably right too, because I think I'm like my ma, all gob. My sister Lenore is quiet and more like Dad. I would see my dad nearly every day. Our Lenore and Jean would clean for him, and he seemed to be managing all right. It was in 1964 that we took him on holiday with us in a caravan that we had hired at Bridlington for a week. How we managed to do that I will never know, because he liked to do his own thing and on the many occasions at holiday times we would ask him to come with us for a day out and he would reply. "No, bugger off, I'm all right," and that was that. I think fate works in mysterious ways and that holiday just had to be because it was his last!

We went to Filey for the day and he wouldn't come down on the beach with us. "Leave me here, bugger off and enjoy yourselves," he said. He loved our kids, all kids; he couldn't pass a child without giving it a copper or two. "Our Anne," he would say, "that kid's wonderful, she never stops laughing." He was right! We came home from holiday and he was having medical treatment for I know not what. His Doctor was Doctor Kershaw (great guy) from Outwood Surgery, who had given him some tablets, and he had said to Dad "Now then Wes, when you run out of these tablets call and see me at the surgery, and I'll give you some more."

One Saturday morning Dad was at the surgery before it opened, at 8.30am. At 9am, when he was allowed in, the doctor's receptionist, the old so and so, I forget her real name, but all the patients knew her to be a real arrogant, self-important bitch, she asked Dad what he wanted. He replied, "Doctor Kershaw told me to call for a new prescription for my tablets.

"Have you made an appointment?" she asked. Dad said, no, he didn't know he needed to make an appointment.

The last time he had seen a doctor was 25 years earlier, when he had broken his ribs playing football for the Farm Stores, and you didn't have to make an appointment in those days. She of ill grace refused to let Dad see Doctor Kershaw without an appointment, so he said to her, "Well, bugger you then, and stuff you and your prescription," and he walked out.

He never got or took another tablet and three weeks later he was dead. He took ill on a Saturday. Jack Berry, our neighbour Mrs Berry's lad, got in touch with me. I was working in Wakefield doing a removal I think and he said Dad had been taken bad I dashed home, Doctor Bottomley had been and diagnosed Dad's severe pain, as congestion of the lung. Dad was sat up in bed, and he said to me, "Bloody hell, lad, I thought me time had come." I think he had collapsed and Jack said he had been asking for me. Jean came up and we made him comfortable and some-

163

thing to eat. I had a look at his garden and decided that I had better tidy it up a bit as it was getting neglected. We realised too that the house needed decorating, and we planned to see to that too - but it was too late. It always is. I had decided to stay with him that night and he asked me to fetch him his Capstan full strength cigs up to his bedroom so that he could have a 'spit and a draw', as he called a smoke. I fetched him his cigs and a pot of tea to bed, and I said, "I think I'll have a bath, Dad." He said, "Reight lad, there's plenty of hot watter." As I was in the bath, I heard a noise from Dad's bedroom. I rushed in and he had collapsed. I said, "Don't worry, Dad." I fetched Mrs Abbey from next door while I phoned the doctor. Doctor Bottomley, our own doctor, was on call, attending to his patients needs (not like today with deputy doctors on call). He gave Dad an injection of I know not what, but it was too late. Dad was doing his last removal from life to the kingdom of Heaven to sit at God's left hand with my ma; they both deserved nothing less. If Dad had been able to carry on with his tablets, if his illness had been properly diagnosed, would he have lived longer? Who knows, I certainly don't. Maybe the powers that be do, the people who are just two steps away from being God, who have the power of life and death; the ones who are responsible but who are rarely held accountable; the ones who should never assume but often do; the ones who cannot afford to make mistakes but often do.

They are the ones who think they know, but they are answerable to no one except their consciences and their maker.

So there it was, 1964. Dad had led a very contented life, a simple but a contented one. He never lived long enough to properly retire from work. He had worked hard all his life, never had proper holidays, never gone abroad (The army wouldn't take him to fight in the First World War). I doubt if he had ever been on a train more than twice in his life. He had never had a car; my Uncle Clarence once offered to give him one but he wouldn't take it. He had once been on a bike of course, when he had cycled from Barnsley to Selby and Scunthorpe looking for work. Dad was cremated at Leeds Crematorium which is where my mam's ashes are too. Derek Turner and all his mates paid their respects, even Tom the Greenhills Packy man was there too. Yes, Tom had still called to see Dad every Friday night after Mam died, even though Dad didn't buy anything from him. He called for his tea, didn't he. Dad's house was like a second home to all the local traders, and anyone in need.

Dad would make Tom his cup of tea, and he would say, "Get what tha wants, Tom, out oft pantry." Tom would help himself and that's how it was. But now that they're gone, my mam and dad and a generation of

164

doers, givers and carers, have gone with them, never to be replaced, because they have taken with them most of all that was good and right in life, a life that I knew and was grateful to have shared with them.

They were a part of a breed that I was proud to have called my own, a breed that truly knew sorrow, hardship and real poverty, and triumphed just the same; a breed that were caring, unselfish, who had pride and integrity, who didn't expect ow't for nowt, a breed the likes of which will never be seen again.

Which leaves me feeling ever so humble, grateful for having known them, but just a little sorry too, knowing that today's generation won't be as lucky. A little poverty for all cannot be such a bad thing if it helped to make people like the people that I once knew!

As I dream of the past and what may have been.
But now it's too late, and I can only dream
I think of the things that should have been said.
But it is all too late now and my dad is now dead
I could never have known what was to be his fate
And when I did, it was just far too late.

# Part 3

## The Beginning Of A New Adventure

When Dad died, there began another turning point in my life. I felt that I owed him something, which I did, both to him and to my mother. They of course had started W Walker and Son from nothing and a part of their lives had gone into that business. They had started from scratch with nothing and they alone had planted the seeds and had cultivated what was ultimately to become a nationally known haulage and distribution company. W Walker was my dad's name, I was their son and I honestly thought when Dad died, that in fairness to Mam and Dad I ought to at least try and carry on where they had been forced to leave off. I thought this was what they would have wanted me to do, to carry on. So I found somebody to buy my tipper lorries, my B licence, and Charles Transport, which I had started from now't in 1958. The lad that bought Charles Transport was called Pearce and the firm that I started and passed on to him, is still in operation. I know it was recently, because I have seen several vehicles with the name M Pearce on contract to Darrington Quarries on the side. Small world, eh?

So there was I in 1964 stepping out once again onto the Highway of Life, knowing not where it was likely to take me. But this time I wasn't alone. Ma and Pa were both up there or out there or wherever, looking after me. As it is written in the scriptures: 'The sun always shines on the righteous' and the sun most certainly did shine for me and mine and has done ever since. Dad's turnover in 1964 was £1500 a year, he was doing odd jobs for the salesrooms, and an occasional removal in between. I couldn't survive and bring up a family on this small turnover. So I had to find some more work. I needed some regular bread and butter jobs. I'd got to know a chap called Norman Court, who lived at the bottom of Potovens Lane, Lofthouse Gate and Norman just happened to be the warehouse manager at Cavendish Furnishes in Kirkgate. I was able to convince him that he ought to recommend me to his branch manager as a possible candidate for their furniture deliveries in the future. I was cheaper than their existing carrier and employing me could be to their financial advantage. So I became the main contractor for the first of many furniture shops that I was to work for within the Great Universal Stores Group, in Wakefield and the surrounding area. I was eventually to work for shops in Kirkgate, Upper Kirkgate, Westmoreland St, Castleford, Pontefract and God knows where else. The crack was that I'd do two days' house to house shop deliveries in one day; I'd get paid for two days work, but I'd give half a day's pay back to the shop manager. In effect, the cost to GUS, was no more than it had been when the work was being done by their previous furniture removal contractor. The only difference now, of course, was that I was working twice as hard and having to pay the managers for my extra half a day's pay, but that's how it was then and probably still is today.

'What's in it for me?' was usually the shop manager's first question on his introduction to a new supplier. One either paid and got the work, or refused and eventually went bust. I chose the former and survived.

We had at last acquired a 'new fangled' device called a telephone, which of course was to become essential to the business. So my wife Jean would, wherever possible, book me a house removal for 7am, before I went to my shop delivery work at 9am. Think for a moment about that dear reader: I had just two hours to empty and move the contents of a full house, no matter how big that house happened to be!

In those days most people had the equivalent of one-and-a-half bedroom suites, and if they happened to live in an old terrace house, which most people did, then the bedroom furniture would have to come out of the bedroom window, down a ladder, because it wouldn't come down the stairs. Funnily enough, when I cleared out homes for Saville and Kilburns and for Laidlaws the auctioneers, to save time the whole of the bedroom furniture came out of the upstairs bedroom window. It was thrown out to my mate waiting at the bottom of the ladder: beds, bedding and soft furnishings. All the rest of the bedroom furniture then came down the ladder.

It became rather upsetting at times though, when we would have to clear out homes after the owners (of the furniture) had died. Sometimes the homes had been left just as they were when the owner was alive and it was awful to think that most of the furniture that these people had owned and cherished over the years would have to be taken to the tip, or be broken up and destroyed. There would be beautiful mahogany sideboards, and horse hair sofas and they all had to be dumped, because people wouldn't buy these items from the salesrooms. I began to wonder after a time what a life was really worth.

But life must go on and our modern mums in the sixties preferred to buy their new utility furniture on hire purchase. Rather than a bit of good second-hand gear, for a few bob, from the salesrooms, like my mam would! They had pride you see, not much common sense, but they had pride. In those days our mums didn't ruin their furniture by using spray polish on it. They would use warm water and vinegar and a wash leather instead.

But back to those mercenary shop managers! I would sweat cobs on those early morning removals. It would drip from my forehead like water from a tap. I would run up those bedroom stairs two at a time and come down six at a time if I was empty handed. Washers, spin dryers, fridges and bloody great tea chests full of heavy crockery, all of these items I would carry out single handed, including the three piece suites. While my mate carried out the 'smalls'. No (silly Billy) not the lady of the house's knickers, the small items of furniture. Those early morning house removals had to be done quickly, because we just had to be at those furniture shops for 9am or else!

The furniture shop managers in those days were like little tin gods and those shops were like Ivory Towers. All the managers without exception were called Mr. But I called them supercilious, silly egotistical prats the lot of them (behind their backs of course). I used to say that the laziest people that it was ever my misfortune to be associated with were furniture salesmen-cum-shop managers and the only reason they became sales people in the first place was because they were born to be lazy idle gits!

Now these amateur salesmen would promise the earth to a would-be customer to obtain a sale and because a lot of their lady customers went out to work, deliveries of furniture had to be made after 6pm. Yes that's right, silly bugger me had to do the delivering. I would sometimes find myself with two-thirds of my daily deliveries to do after 6pm. Those working women were to become a bloody nuisance; it was usually only the ones who went out to work who could afford to buy their new homes and furniture.

The rest of us - me included - who chose to stay at home and look after the kids had to manage in an old rented terrace house or, if they had been lucky enough, in a council house and make do with second-hand furniture.

One could buy a beautiful second-hand solid mahogany bedroom suite in those days for 30/-, whereas a Beutility Suite with a bloody plywood back would cost say £50 pounds. But that was just what most of these working mums desired and it just had to be a Beutility!

It was funny really because everybody in those days just had to have a fancy new bedroom suite. The fact that it stood in a corner and never moved, or that it was only used to hang clothes in, simply did not matter. Nor did the fact that the lady of the house never got to see it, well not really, except when it wanted dusting. Because if she was doing her matrimonial job right, then all she would be admiring would be the bedroom ceiling, while he of ill repute was having his wicked way with her! I joke of course, because it was usually the man of the house who was to lay there in bed, hour after endless hour, sulking, and admiring the bedroom ceiling; while she lay in bed, at the side of him, (pretending to be asleep).

Now after our working mums, had gone and spent an absolute bloody fortune on these up-market, semi utility bedroom suites, they would then usually have to economise on the rest of the household furniture: the more important things in life, like chairs. But non of these things seemed to matter of course, as long as they all had their Beutility bedroom suites, which even had they been made of cardboard, would have still lasted a lifetime (for hanging clothes in.) Not for them my working mums lino and a clip rug, made out of old clothes. No sirree, fitted carpets no less for them! What was good enough for their mams, was certainly not good enough for them. They were going to have it all and the sooner the better. Not for them Clegg's bloody cheques, or Greenhill's packymen on call, oh no, only the best from Cavendish, John Henry Taylor or Woodhouse's furniture shops.

Mind you, if they should just happen to have won the football pools, then they could maybe and I said only maybe, (just about) afford to buy a suite from our local Gibsons, the up-market furnishers, near the Playhouse picture house, down Westgate in Wakefield.

Everybody, or so it seemed, started to move up-market a bit, when they got rid of their old tin baths from the wall outside the back kitchen door and things were never quite the same after they got rid of the 'Jerries' from under the bed and moved into their inside toilets.

Since Jean's mam Irene couldn't even afford to buy a Jerry, Jean and her sister Kath had to manage with a two gallon metal bucket at the side of the bed. For years Kath would be woken from her slumbers by a noise in the dead of night that sounded just like the Niagara Falls in all its glory. Kath would then be heard to murmur: (quote!)

Tinkle Tinkle little star,
What's that noise I hear afar?
Rest ye quietly, says Jean it's me
Now go back to sleep, while I finish me pee.

Mind, having a bucket had its compensations, because it would only need emptying every six months, or if it had started to smell a bit maybe, or when and if it happened to wet their bums, eh!

Because of these after 6pm deliveries, I found myself having to work until 9 and 10pm at night and to add insult to injury, some of the recipients of my after six deliveries became upset if I should just happen to roll up at 10pm, just before they had decided to go to bed, or in some cases after they had in fact retired. Oh yes it did happen, I would find myself doing the daytime deliveries and then I would have to continually double back to do my after six deliveries. The awful truth was that all the people who had asked for an after six delivery expected me to arrive with their furniture at ten past the hour. Now it was just physically impossible to be everywhere at ten past six and those dizzy, silly bloody salesmen just hadn't got the common sense to ask the customer to leave a key next door. Oh no, of course not, that would have been too bloody simple wouldn't it?

The one thing that really did upset me about these so called sales-men was their attitude to a customer. Oh, they were wonderful at the point of sale, but when a purchase had been made, oh then it was goodbye and bugger you. I just could not ever understand this short term, live for today approach to business. If I had been a salesman, I would have checked the furniture before it left the store so that in the event of any defect being found, it could have been rectified before the delivery had taken place and not later. I would then have either phoned or written to my customer, to check if eve-rything was all right with the furniture. I would then have sent cards occasionally, in an attempt to establish if I could be of help in the future. This would have helped to ensure continuity of customer relations. But the silly bit of course, was that these so called salesmen had plenty of time to cultivate such good relations. More especially mid-week, when there was very little customer activity and these lazy bastards would be sat on their bums doing now't, except telling each other how good they all were! It was through these early experiences that I was to learn other lessons in my life, which were to serve me well later. I learned never to take people for granted. I also learned to appreciate every oppor-tunity to be of service and that the customer in my business just had to be King or Queen. Because he, or she, were the ones who paid my wages (of sin).

Another lesson that I was to learn was that we really only got out what

170

we choose to put in and that principle applies just as much in life as it does in business. I had to work for twelve and sixteen hour days and most times for seven days a week. I remembered those lessons over the years. I was to get most of my future business through recommendations. The reason of course, was because I very rarely let anyone down. I had an absolute commitment to my customer; I owed everything I had, or was to ever achieve, to my customers. When I was doing removals I would always put the customers' furnitures into the room where it was destined to go; I would always put the carpets onto the van last and then unload them first. I would put the carpets down in their new home, if at all possible. I always put the beds together, with the bedding on top. My philosophy was, that if the beds were up, then if the customer should become tired after sorting out their personal effects, well then at the very least, they could go to bed. There were many times after I had done a job and I had in fact been paid, that I would then spend time, for no charge, helping the customer to sort things out. But why?

Well, because I truly cared, and it was to pay off over the years. Care was the operative word and the secret of true success. I would never do what some of my contemporaries did: to practically throw people's furniture on and off the van. For me, the furniture that I handled had to be stacked, wrapped and handled properly. I didn't leave my furniture covers all over the van floor. The furniture wraps were folded and stacked away, ready for the next job and if I should only be moving someone perhaps just one hundred yards away, then that van had to be packed properly just the same. I could only do a removal one way and that was the right way. There were many times that I had to move full houseloads of furniture, with an 800 cube trailer, so I learnt my trade well and it paid off. For years, I would have the friends and relations of the people I had moved in my earlier days phoning me up to do their removals. Some would say, for instance: "Do you remember, you moved my mother or next door neighbour twenty years ago?" How could I possibly remember?

I had in fact moved thousands of people but it was oh so nice to be remembered and it was very much appreciated. Yes, care, that was the word. I can pass hundreds of houses and still remember what the insides were like, which in turn helps me to remember certain removals that I did all those years ago. I must confess that I do tend to squirm, if I just happen to pass one of today's so called furniture removers, carrying out a house removal with a bloody great van and three men, who are trying to load, or unload furniture, with the van parked facing up a hill! I can see the furniture inside strewn all over the floor, or loaded and tied off from side to side. That was not my style at all, oh no. My style was just me and a lad and a 1200 cube van, parked down hill, so that the furniture stayed in place and of course it was that much easier to walk down the hill into a van than having to struggle up hill to load the bloody thing.

My style was to pack the furniture, from front to back, and from the floor to the ceiling. I often wonder how some of today's so called furniture removers would have managed to pack and deliver up to 36 three piece suites, with a 2200 cube Furniture Pantechnicon, without doing any damage?

Or how would they attempt to deliver 160 to 200 washing machines with a van and trailer on multi-drop shop delivery work around the South Coast of England? That's right, sometimes 40 to 60 drops with a 3600 cube van and trailer, but my lads did it and they didn't have a mate either! More about that later.

# Mrs Coe's Pianos

So I did my furniture delivery work, my early morning removals. Then I was to move on to collecting and delivering pianos for Mrs Coe, of Wakefield, just as a little fit in job like and to make life just that bit more exciting. Mrs Coe was the wife of Charles Coe, a well known musical instrument dealer in Wakefield around that time. Charles had died and so Mrs Coe, who was a lovely woman had decided to sell the shop in Wakefield. But she had also decided to keep the piano sales, restoration and the hire side of the business going. So she acquired premises down Howard St, off Northgate in Wakefield, which in fact was an old terrace house that she was to convert into a small shop selling sheet music etc. Now at the side of this shop was a passageway, or ginnel as they were known, which gave access to the back of the houses. Above the passageway was a bedroom and part of this bedroom floor had been converted into a trap door! Why?

Well, the trap door was used to get the pianos in and out of the bloody bedroom wasn't it, yes that's right! The bedroom!

All very ingenious, but how the hell that bedroom floor ever managed to stand the weight of all those pianos I will just never know, but it did. I am of course, dear reader, talking about proper pianos and not the bloody dinky toys that some call pianos today. Mrs Coe's pianos were the real Monty. Bloody great German overstrung Beckstiens and the like. At the top of the range and just to make life more interesting (or difficult depending on your point of view) she would store several pianolas and a Baby Grand or two. Just to give the place a bit of class like! She would have an occasional full Grand piano, no less, in her store and  guess what? All those bloody pianos had to be pulled or lowered in or out of that upstairs bedroom with a piece of rope. All very exciting, believe me. My old friend Derek Turner, the footballer, had done this job before me and even he had got a little peed off. Either Mrs Coe didn't pay him enough, or he got sick of pulling those pianos into that bedroom, or perhaps one had inadvertently fallen on his head. Who knows? Whatever the reason, I got the job of delivering Mrs Coe's pianos.

173

It may be right at this stage to mention the best 'little big man' that I was ever to have working for me. David Purnell was his name and he came from the Mountbatten Crescent Estate, off Coach Road, Outwood. David's dad was one of those miners who had, like a lot of other miners in those days, been forced to pull up his roots in South Wales. He had moved to the Wakefield area in search of work in the local coal mines. David was just fifteen years of age, when he was to come knocking at the door of my council house at 29, George Street, Outwood, looking for a job. I took one look at him and said to myself, oh no he won't last ten bloody minutes on this job. He looked just like a tuppenny rabbit, but I was wrong and David was to work for me for many years, until he eventually decided to get married. John Bruce and his brother Harold, who were David's mates, were also to work for me, until John got pissed out of his mind one Saturday night, and demolished a public toilet with one of my Tractor Units, but that's another story. John was years later to start a Plant Hire business and Harold now has a coach business in Rothwell.

David and I moved hundreds of pianos for Mrs Coe, to clubs, pubs churches, upstairs, downstairs and into me lady's chambers. We used to get some bloody awful jobs and when we were delivering pianos upstairs, I always took all the weight at the back, while little David at the front struggled and pulled those pianos up the stairs. I remember the times when David would run out of steam, and me too for that matter, and I'd have great difficulty in holding some of those bloody monstrosities (that Mrs Coe called pianos). My legs would start to tremble and I would shout to David: "Pull you silly little bastard, pull!" and that last little effort usually did the trick. And, I might add, a bloody good job too. For if we'd failed, I was the one who could have been dead or injured.

One of the worst jobs I ever did for Mrs Coe was near Bishopsgarth, the police training college. I was conned into moving a piano for a friend of hers. Now this particular lady had moved from an old house on College Grove Road into an upstairs flat at Bishopsgarth and the removal firm had been told there was a piano to move. So they were prepared and three men were sent to do the job. They did the furniture removal all right, but move the piano, which was upstairs, no way. Those bloody wimps just left it on the landing. Now this piano was something else, it was jet black ebony, what a monster! It most certainly was not, one of your everyday run of the mill pianos, oh no, this one had character. It was fitted with ornate candlestick holders and had nostrils that breathed fire. A caricature of the devil himself was carved on the keyboard. After the devil had finished with it, he had passed it on to the *Crown and An-*

*chor* pub, down Kirkgate, where it had spent most of its life. I took one look at this monstrosity and wished that had stayed there. On reflection, I actually think it was a pianola; it was just far too heavy to have been an ordinary piano. I think it was fitted with two bloody great electric motors, because it was the heaviest upright I'd ever moved in my life. I stood and stared at it, the piano in its turn stared back at me. It grinned as it said to me: "No way!"

I replied. "Just thee wait and see, if tha doesn't go down them stairs the proper way, then I shall just have to throw thee down. Then all that tha will be good for is bloody firewood." I don't think he liked that, so David and I lifted him up and carried the lazy bastard downstairs. That was the easy bit!

We took him across the road to Bishopsgarth on our piano bogey. When we arrived, I discovered that the piano had in fact to go into an upstairs flat. I decided there was just no way that piano was going up those outside concrete steps. If ever we reached the top, then it would have to be turned on its axis before it would go through the door. But because of the iron railings that were fastened to the concrete steps that piano just couldn't be turned. What a dilemma!

So the piano says to me: "Nah then, what's tha going to do?" It was born in Germany, but due to its time at the Crown and Anchor, it had developed a broad Yorkshire accent.

I said, "Now just thee wait and see and try and have a little patience Paul." Since we had got to know each other, I had christened him Paul the p——, sorry the piano.

I left Paul where he was, sulking, and went home and got Eric Brooke my next door neighbour, the one who had been nourished on fried spam, to give me a hand. I took some tools with me and returned to the piano. I dismantled those railings, we picked up that piano and we huffed and puffed and we sweated cobs, but we pushed that piano to the top of those stairs.

The piano then says to me, quote, "Nah, then clever bugger, nah what?" un-bloody-quote.

Now came the tricky bit, I must have been crackers. I had to balance that piano over the edge of a 15 foot drop, pull it over on to its end and then put it on to the piano bogey and spin it on the top platform. All this time the piano was hanging over the drop and at the same time I was trying to keep my balance. I was petrified, but I did it, and Mrs. Coe, bless her, had been vindicated because she had told her friend not to worry and that I would move her piano for her. I just had to put two fingers up and stick my tongue out at that bloody Paul, the redoubtable piano, before I left the flat. That was another job well done, but it does not alter the fact that I was stupid to even attempt a job like that. The same job tackled today would have probably been done with a crane and probably six men fitted with hard plastic bloody hats.

From then on, I was to move hundreds of pianos and with the help of Mrs Coe's man, I was to eventually design my own piano skid for moving grand pianos. I also designed a piano bogey, which was fitted with a longer chassis and a higher than normal frame so that it was able to negotiate higher door steps. My poor old dad used to have to manage with his little single axle bogey, which was useless. He always believed that when you turned a piano round a corner the keyboard went first, which was totally wrong. The back of the piano, always goes round the corner first. But I could never convince Dad that I was right. (I suppose in theory he was right, but in practice he was wrong.)

There are tricks in all trades. Furniture removing was always a bit like painting and decorating I suppose. Everyone thinks they can do it, but like everything else there's an art in doing it right. If I couldn't, even today, as old as I am, get a piano into, or out of a house and onto a van on my own, with a piano bogey, then I would go and eat hay with a bloody donkey! And I dare not call myself a furniture remover, well not a proper one anyway, dare I? The last time I was to move a piano on my own was when I was in my sixties. I do remember one particular incident well, in the early eighties, when I sent two fit young men, one a football player, to Leeds. I'd sent them to move a pianola, and the bloody wimps were useless. They didn't even have hearts as big as a pea. I had to go and move the thing for them. They had just looked at it, seen its size and then phoned into the office for extra help.

I was eventually to graduate on Mrs Coe's recommendation to become the piano remover for Mike Terry. Wonderful! I believe his first name was Mike, anyway he played piano just like Winifred Attwell and he was terrific as a honky tonk pianist. He had two pianos; one was as usual a German overstrung, which was tuned up for the job. David and I took this piano all over Yorkshire for Mike, on and off stage at The City Varieties in Leeds like a yo-yo, and to Bradford Alhambra. There was only me and little David, the poor little bugger. Mike was to become a TV celebrity, a Captain something or other, I think he appeared on some children's TV shows. He may have been quite happy (and famous) as a star on stage, but I hated having to go on stage with that bloody piano!

# Christmas 1967

It was all non-stop, go, go, go. We did removals every Saturday, sometimes long distance some overnight. Then we were back to the shop deliveries the next day. I remember once coming through Wakefield one Saturday when there was an annual miners' gala, and there were the miners, who got paid six days for doing five days' work, and some of them were as drunk as Lords. They were shouting and waving, all enjoying themselves and for once in my life I began to think that I must be bloody crackers. Here was I working every hour that god sent, with hardly any free time and very little social life. I didn't manage to see my kids, because they were always in bed when I got home and it was then I started to ask what life was really all about.

I remember those Christmas times very clearly, because we were always so busy delivering furniture and we had to make sure that it arrived with the customer before Christmas Day. It was funny because people would spend weeks or even months deciding whether or not to purchase some item of furniture and then, when they'd finally decided they'd expect it to be delivered yesterday or even sooner. Everybody in those days just had to have a bit of new gear during the festive season. They had to impress their friends and relations like, didn't they?

The season of good will really did apply in those days and although people didn't have much money coming in, there was always a warm welcome, a drink of something and a nice piece of Christmas cake or a mince pie. And we were the lucky recipients of all this good cheer. We'd walk away after doing our delivery with a spring in our step, a smile on our faces and usually a bloody great hangover the next morning! I joke of course, but these things happened before all the 'repressive' new laws of today were forced upon us. In those days we did seem to have more freedom as individuals. We didn't need to worry about drinking and driving when I was young! My generation, well those at the level that I lived at in society, didn't have much to spend, but we all saved a little bit during the year to help us have a Merry Christmas. There would be Christmas clubs where one could save a few bob a week, so that there would be that little bit extra, to make Christmas just that little bit special. Chickens were luxuries that no-one in my circle could afford under normal circumstances. But everybody saved their coppers so they could have a little bit of chicken at Christmas time and the man of the house always got a leg and a bit of breast, as was his right! Well most men like to see a nice leg and a bit of breast, don't they?

My generation had never heard of turkeys, let alone seen one. Turkeys, I was to learn much later, were a protected species that were fattened for Christmas, to be sold only to the very rich. So there it was: All through the year we lived on neck of mutton stew, tripe and bloody onions, or a bit of cow heel and shin beef if we were lucky, but at Christmas we all had a bit of chicken just to make things that little bit more special. One particular Christmas that I will never, ever forget, wasn't so special. I was working as usual for umpteen furniture shops, and I had probably delivered half a dozen pianos for Mrs Coe in between my other jobs. I suppose I always like a challenge. Anyway, this particular Christmas Eve I had flown about all day like a bloody racing pigeon doing deliveries here, there and everywhere. I was coming out of Pontefract around 7pm and I had decided to drop my mate, a young lad, off at his home in Featherstone.

David was not there that Christmas, the lucky little bleeder. On reflection, I don't quite remember where my old mate was at this time. I can only imagine that he had developed a little common sense as he got older and had decided to opt out while he was still alive, because he probably knew in his heart of hearts that I would have worked him to death, given half a bloody chance. Or maybe the reason was much more simple. The bloody fool had just got married hadn't he and perhaps he needed to conserve his energy for those precious few moments or days that he was to spend between the sheets with his new bride (the mucky little git!)

Bless him, (with a seven pound hammer). I still had a van load of deliveries to do in the Wakefield, Earlsheaton, Dewsbury, Morely and Leeds areas. When I arrived at Earlsheaton it was pitch black and freezing cold. I had to strike a match to see the numbers on the house doors. I was lucky because I had learned years before that when one went into a street, the odd numbers were always on the left and the even numbers on the right, or were they?

I parked the van at the top of the street I wanted and to save time I picked up a bloody great thick 4 foot 6 inch Divan base, which I could only just get my arms around. I struggled down the street to let's say Mrs Jones at No.13, unlucky for some put the bed down and knocked on the front door. The lady of the house answered, I says hello love, to her, "I've brought your bed."

She says. "What bloody bed?"

I says. "The bed that you ordered from Cavendish, Mrs Jones."

She says, "Jones, they dun't call me Jones, my name's Smith."

She tells me that the street that I wanted is the next one further down the main road. Then she says to me: "Nah lad, tha will just have to do what Jesus said won't tha?"

I asks. "And what were that then?"

She says. "Take up thy bed and walk, or words to that effect!

Now bugger off, I've just missed me favourite TV program through thee."

I picked up that bed and struggled down the garden path. I slipped on the pavement edge, I fell arse over whatever, and the bloody bed went one way and I went the other. I was to finish up sat on that pavement edge, nursing a sprained ankle and a deflated ego. I must have sat there, for at least half an hour, feeling sorry for myself. Now dear reader this next statement may take some believing, but it is perfectly true, though it shames me as a grown man, to have to admit to it. There I sat on that pavement, on that Christmas Eve and I was sobbing my heart out. I had my head in my hands and I felt so alone. While my friends and family were either out enjoying themselves, or perhaps sat indoors, around a nice cosy fire, enjoying a nice Christmas drink. I felt as if the whole world, which I was no longer a part of, had deserted me. I was just a little lost soul, lost in time and I was crying from frustration and I thought to myself: "What on earth am I doing here?" (or something like that).

This was just another of so many instances of where I was and what I was doing. My dear wife Jean used to say. "And where were you then, when I was bringing them kids up on me own?" Well, for the record, that's where I was. Sat on a cold pavement in Earlsheaton, one Christmas Eve, feeling bloody sorry for myself.

It was my own fault of course I didn't need to be there. I could have refused the work. But I just wasn't built like that. I appreciated the fact that I'd been given the work and it wasn't because I was greedy, (not much). I was working because I was frightened of losing a job. I was very insecure. I had no built in guarantees, like most people today have. I couldn't guarantee myself 40 hour working weeks, or holidays with pay. I didn't even know if I'd be working the following week and I had responsibilities. I had commitments, a wife and children to support and I had to grab what was on offer, while it was there. Yes, I was motivated all right, by the greatest motivator of them all, fear! Don't anybody ever dare tell me that I've been lucky, at least not where money is concerned. I've earned a lot of money over the years, and earned is the operative word. No-one gave it to me. I had to work and I struggled. I was to sacrifice the most precious commodity known and that was time. But it will all have been worthwhile, provided my kids are able to appreciate the true value of money and able to understand it has to be treated with respect. That it has to be managed properly and, last but not least, it doesn't grow on bloody trees. Somebody at some time had to work for it.

So I picked up my bed and I walked, well I hobbled back to the van.

When people ask me today what it takes to be successful in business I would say one has to care, one must persist against all the odds. Including sitting on a bloody cold pavement on a Christmas Eve in Earlsheaton!

# Dear Arthur

Norman Court from off Potovens Lane was the chap instrumental in getting me started in the furniture delivery business and I'll never forget him. He was a wonderful man, always with a smile and a laugh for everybody. Norman was the warehouse man at Cavendish Furnishers in Wakefield, which once belonged to Jackson's Furnishers. At the time I was working for Cavendish, I got to know another character who was to become a great pal of mine. Arthur Green was his name and he lived at and owned Springfield Farm . Now Arthur lived on his own and he was very poor. He had half a dozen cows, an old Ford tractor, about 100 years old, and a few hens. He also had a heart like a bloody lion. He just had no money and when his parents died, he was left on his own with only his livestock for company. To supplement his income he would do whatever he could to earn a few bob to survive and that is how I got to know dear Arthur. He became a furniture remover par excellence. He was as rough as a bear's bum, but what a bloody wonderful character! He helped me no end when I was just starting out and I helped him of a night during his harvesting in the summer months and what a bloody job that was forking those bales of hay onto the top of his trailer. I never did quite get the hang of doing that bit properly.

As time went on, Arthur in desperation had to rent some of his land off a chap called Malcolm Oliver whose mother had the shop at the bottom of Lingwell Gate lane.

It was while Arthur was working for me that he fell in love. Arthur had never had a girlfriend, at least I don't think he had, but our reluctant Romeo was smitten. Head over heels he fell for the cleaner at Cavendish. Her name was Ethel and she'd had a very hard life with her first husband, struggling to bring up her lovely kids alone. So their meeting was a blessing for both of them. Ethel and Arthur would do the week's washing together every Saturday afternoon in a bloody old washing machine in the cow shed. They were just great for each other. Arthur at last had a family and Ethel had a man who cared and looked after her. Wonderful! But Ethel would never leave her council house in Wakefield to stay with Arthur permanently and even today, now that they're in the twilight of their lives, I'm still not sure if they're together yet, in Arthur's new bungalow at East Ardsley. Arthur was to sell Springfield farm to John Wright the coal man. John's dad was an old pal, we used to see each other at Road Haulage Association (RHA) meetings in Wakefield park, years later. Small world!

We had some memorable moments at Springfield Farm. Like the times when we would call at Oliver's shop for bread and then go to the farm for our dinner, which was usually Finney haddock and bread. Arthur would get this great iron frying pan off the wall at the side of the kitchen sink. Now this pan was blacker that Paul Robeson the soul singer's bum. He would half fill this bloody great pan with water, throw in the haddock, turn up the gas and while the fish was cooking or rather, burning, he would butter the bread. I'll swear by all that is holy, that was the best Finney haddock that I'd ever tasted in my life. And this tantalising tasty creation was washed down with a beautiful pint of hot steaming tea, no less. All this to the accompaniment of six clucking, (yes you read it right,) hens, singing and dancing in harmony and bent on entertaining us, while we ate. That bloody Bolshoi Ballet had now't on Arthur's hens! Arthur just loved to play happy families with his flock and when he chose to eat, then so did his livestock. I'm just bloody pleased that his cows were too big to come through that back kitchen door, or we would have been sharing our dinners with them too. Mind you, it made sense really, because as Arthur said, he didn't need to spend money, on a bloody vacuum cleaner, did he? His hens picked up all the crumbs for him!

When we worked at Cavendish, we had to take second-hand three piece suites in part exchange for most of the new suites that we delivered and when I worked for the furniture salerooms, a lot of old furniture had to be dumped, because people wouldn't buy it. Then Arthur in his wisdom decided that all the old walnut or mahogany furniture could be used to keep his own home fires burning. He decided the three piece suites could be burned in his yard, but only after he'd broken them up first so he could retrieve all the money that had dropped down the backs of those suites over the years. What Arthur was to find down the backs of those three piece suites was just amazing. It was a bloody good job they couldn't talk, if they had, they would most certainly have had a good tale to tell!

That furniture was to come in very useful one winter's night (and the following morning).

*All Through The Night* I'll never forget that particular carol. Again it was Christmas time and I was attempting to remove a diesel engine with a 5-ton jack, from an S Type Bedford. Again it was freezing cold, it was that cold I couldn't feel the spanners. I was on my own, and those three piece suites were wonderful. They kept the cold off me for a part of that night, while they were burning. Around this time the greatest miscarriage of justice took place. Arthur had got to know another lovable rogue through me. He was a guy called Philip Swain, a scrap man, who came off the Lupset Estate. Philip was also a mate of Ken Petty. Now Philip was actually a nice chap and a fair dealer, and he asked Arthur if he could rent his yard to store some scrap cars. Arthur agreed. I don't know if he was to receive any rent or not. But he did have the option to take any spare parts he might need, from the cars in his yard. Either way, it was a blessing for Arthur, because he never had much of anything throughout his whole life. Philip, however, had got himself mixed up with a gang of real crooks, who were stealing cars and storing them in Arthur's yard, then swapping the number plates and moving them. The police were soon on the trail. They got the thieves, caught and prosecuted Philip for receiving stolen cars and Arthur was prosecuted too for, well I know not what. They all of them got convicted and sent to prison. Arthur got two years. Now a two year sentence for a man who had never knowingly done an unkind, or a really wrong thing, in the whole of his life, was simply unbelievable, and how Arthur managed to survive that sentence, I'll just never know. I used to take Ethel to Thorpe Arch Prison near Wetherby when I could and that was bloody awful. I was lucky because I nearly joined him. The police called at my home one Sunday afternoon and took me to Wood Street Police Station. What an awful experience that was. I was sat in the back of that bloody police car between two burly coppers, who were to question me in turns, for four hours. I had nothing to do with the stolen cars, so they released me and brought me back home and I thank God for that. I wouldn't like another experience like that one. I think what helped was that I had a pal who was a Detective and it was he who got me released.

# Darling David

While working at Cavendish I also got to know Don Vines, the rugby player and wrestler, who became a friend. He too had come from South Wales, to play rugby for Wakefield Trinity. Don was the debt collector for Cavendish and other shops in the group, and he also took part in the film *This Sporting Life*, filmed in Wakefield. The first proper van that I ever had was a 2200 Cube Bedford fitted with a Perkins R6 diesel engine. This particular engine was the worst ever designed and manufactured by Perkins in Peterborough. In fact, it was the worst bloody engine ever designed and manufactured by any manufacturer. Where I purchased this van I don't even remember, but I do remember that bleeding engine and the trouble that it was to cause me. I remember the time I did a removal for our local policeman with it. He was another of Mam's waifs and bloody strays. She'd adopted him years before when she'd invited him into our house one cold winter's evening and introduced him to her bloody teapot. I moved this young copper from Outwood to Blackpool, and returned home via Brighouse, of course before the M62 motorway was built I had to stop at the traffic lights in Brighouse and when they had changed to green, I set off. Thump, this bloody great articulated lorry ran into the cab of my van, striking my vehicle sideways on. I was pushed completely round in the road, so that I was facing in the opposite direction. The lorry driver had tried to beat the lights and came through at red. I had to go to court and the driver tried to suggest that I'd been working over my hours. How right he was, but that didn't alter the fact that he'd come through those bloody lights at red!

I claimed from the driver's employers, and the insurance company for repairs to my vehicle, and I also claimed for loss of use of my vehicle while repairs were being carried out. I actually don't think that I even bothered to repair this particular vehicle, not with the problems that I'd experienced with that bloody awful Perkins R6 engine. Anyway, I'd probably received more from the other parties' insurance company than the motor was worth. That bloody van had received its just deserts, for all the aggro it had caused me! It was about this time, (down the Ramper) that my pal Ken Petty broke his arm while he was trying to start a Standard Vanguard car, belonging to darling David, Jean's brother.

David he was a right lazy little idle git and while Ken and me were trying to repair his bloody car, where was lover boy? He would be out birding, or at home in bed, wrapped up warmly with his bloody hot water bottle and his mam there with a nice cup of tea, as and when required. The prat! If he needed to turn over in bed, he'd shout for his mam and she'd dash upstairs and turn him over. He was so bloody idle, he was once sat in front of a roaring fire at home and he says to Irene: "Mam, come and move me, I'm burning." He would go out (only if he had to of course,) when it was raining without a coat, then he would say, "Oh it's raining! I wondered why I was getting wet!" The thick pig. Where was he when I needed a hand with my vans? Either in bed, or out on the Town with his bird. David, the little love, would work perhaps three months in a year, providing that the work wasn't too hard of course, then he would spend nine months on the pan crack (the dole).

He was supposed to be a plumber, or a pipe fitter, (sorry heating engineer) but he was never on the job more than two bloody minutes. I mean proper job, work like. He couldn't ever hope to get to know ow't could he? He was never there. He bloody nearly bankrupted Church's the heating engineers in Wakefield. He had in fact to move out of the country for a while on account of a so called contract job. If he hadn't, one of Church's sons would have castrated or killed him. I think killed to be the most likely, because I don't think he had any of the others. It was eventually to get so bad in this country, with all the dodgy jobs that he'd done, that he had to emigrate to Australia. He got a job over there as a handbag salesman, the poof.

David once came to do a job for me in his capacity as a plumber. There was a leak in our downstairs toilet and Dave came along in a van, with his big box of tools, a screw driver, a wrench and a rusty pair of bloody pliers, that he had pinched from Church's. He also brought along three of his mates to talk while he passed the tools. It took them three days to complete the job, it was to cost me two thousand pounds and when they'd finished, I had to call the local fire brigade to pump all the water out of the house!

That, was my brother-in-law David. If he couldn't make a balls of a job, then his mates could for him. (I joke of course, because he always made a balls of it himself, David I love yer really. While on this subject I can recall an unpleasant incident, or was it an accident, that happened to me, when attempting with David to remove a safe from a big house on Manygates Lane.

Now this particular safe was very, very heavy and as usual, we didn't have the proper equipment to do the job, like the glorious Pickfords might

185

have had. Like six men, a skid cat and maybe a mobile crane! Oh no, the only resources that I could afford at that time was a second-hand single axle piano bogey that Dad had pinched from the salerooms, a rusty bent sack cart, with a buckled wheel and of course, the wife's brother, David Rocky bloody Willmer. He was nicknamed Rocky when he played rugby for Batley. Only God knows why. His bloody head may have been like a rock, but his heart was like a bleeding jelly, the wimp. Well there we were the two of us, or one and a bit of us, I could hardly call David one of us could I? He was there as a bit of company like, in case I should just happen to get a bit lonely. He certainly wasn't there to do any bloody work. Anyway, I had tried to move this safe with the piano bogey and it was just impossible. You can't balance a 5-ton safe on a single axle piano bogey not by yourself.

So I decided in my wisdom, while Rocky was having a little rest in the guest bedroom, that I would put the safe onto the sack cart, then lower the sack cart handles onto the piano bogey and strap the cart to the bogey. This would give everything (except David) more stability. We pushed the safe outside, no problem. Having got it outside, it then had to go across a bit of lawn and up the van tailboard, into the van. I managed to find a plank from the back of the house and we tried to pull and push that safe into the van. The problem was that I shouted to David to pull, and the daft bastard pushed! The next think I knew the safe had shot off that bloody tailboard like Stevenson's Rocket and dropped on my poor bleeding foot. David came across to help, sat on the safe and asked me how I was. Well, after I had removed him and the safe off my foot I told him, but he couldn't understand French. Then the silly daft bastard went and stood on my foot, didn't he, just to add insult to bloody injury. The casualty department in Clayton Hospital found that I had two broken bones. They set the bones and put my foot in a pot. I wrapped an old scarf round it and away I went, or so I thought, to move that bloody safe. But I was too late. My old pal Derek, the real Rocky Turner, had been and moved it for me. That's what real friends are all about, they're there if needed, and Derek was that day and I'll never forget him, or his kindness. I would do anything for that man. While I'm talking about safes, I may just as well recall another incident that involved a safe removal. Safe removal, that's a bloody laugh! Now this particular safe was to be taken into Laidlaw's salerooms if I ever managed to get it downstairs and out of the Halifax bloody Building Society in Westgate. So away we went, Marvellous bloody Mighty Mouse and me with our bent little sack cart, to move it. We managed to get it out of the upstairs offices and onto the landing. We then wrapped a rope round it, a bit of clothes line no less, and attempted to lower it down the stairs. Well I did! Mighty bloody Mouse, well he just let go. That safe shot down those stairs like a world war V2 rocket, with me following behind, clinging on to my bit of rope. We shot down those stairs, straight through the door at the bottom, across the pavement, just missing a double decker bus. We finished up in a bloody great heap, in the middle of Westgate. I mean the safe and me of course. 'Mighty Mouse,' he was still sat on the stairs, having a little rest. I feel sure that by now dear reader, you'll have become more than convinced that my brother-in-law and I had become proficient at the safe, removal of safes, hah, hah, bloody hah!

It was the best thing that ever happened to me when the little darling decided to emigrate to Australia.

# The Yellow Peril

It was about this time that I bought my first yellow van and from then on all my vans were to be yellow. I bought this particular van from a firm (I think) was called McIntyre from somewhere in Lancashire, Rochdale. The chap that owned this firm had a large fleet of trucks, mostly vans, and he worked for one of the large tyre manufactures. Now part of the deal was that he would paint this van whatever colour I wanted and the colour I chose was yellow. This chap nearly collapsed. He just couldn't believe I had chosen yellow. In those days there were blues, reds, greens and even black, but yellow no. Nobody had seen a yellow vehicle, especially a yellow van! (There were yellow submarines of course, but vans, oh no). I chose this particular colour because it was different and set me apart from the rest of the riff raff. I like to kid myself that I set a precedent because ten years later the GPO and British Rail changed their colours to yellow. Why? Well for safety reasons because the colour was noticeable. My motives were purely commercial . I was later to acquire a proper stuffed stags head, which I had pinched from the salerooms. I mounted this at the front of the van, at the top on the Luton and as I passed by, little kids with their mams would laugh and point. But they were also noticing and maybe remembering the name and that, dear reader, was the cheapest form of advertising. Just like Liberace, with his fancy suits and his candlesticks. He was noticed and he was remembered, more for his gimmicks than for his actual musical talents. Gimmicks were all he needed to make him famous. Yes, my stag's head became worth its weight in gold! Everybody needs a gimmick. This yellow van did well for many years and although I had to top the engine oil up every day with a gallon of oil, it gave very little trouble. It was sign written by a very good friend of mine, Ken Moorhouse, who lived in a large terrace house on Leeds Road, Newton Hill. Ken was employed as a sign writer at Charles Wensleys the Bedford Vauxhall main dealers on Ings Road. As well as supplying Bedford commercial vehicles, the firm were body builders painters and sign writers. Ken was to work at Wensleys for a short time and for Comberhill Motors (the Atkinson Dealership) a little higher up Ings Road. Westgate Motors were the Austin Morris dealership in Wakefield, sadly no more. Charles Wensley were taken over by Glanfield Lawrence and Westgate Motors and Comberhill went out of business. The area on

Ings Road has now been taken over by a retail shopping park. Westmorelands the vehicle bodybuilders, at Alverthorpe were taken over by Bonalack and have now disappeared. South Yorkshire Motors, the main Ford dealership on Barnsley Road, still exists as Calderford. Nothing stays the same, everything seems to have its place and time, then disappears forever! But that first yellow van was the start of it all!

# Expansion

I was still working all hours, I would still do that odd removal to maybe Redruth in Cornwall over seven hundred miles and then turn around and travel straight back home and that was before the motorways were built. This journey, and many more like it, was done in a 1200 cube 1946 O model Bedford, at a top speed of probably 40mph. Thank god there were two drivers, my mate and me. But it could not go on. The time had come to expand. I was getting too much work and I just couldn't cope, so I'd bought the big yellow van as a second vehicle. I still had Arthur working for me on a casual basis after he came out of prison and I also had Geoff Reeve, the sign writer, helping out. Now would be as good a time as any to write a few words about Geoffrey Victor Reeve.

In my whole life I've only ever known one man more laid back than Geoff and he was dead, my dear old Dad. Geoff simply did not have a care in the world. He left all his problems to his wife Brenda, who was the one who had to try and make ends meet. Brenda had gone out to work most of her life. Geoff had owned shops and built up a successful window cleaning round. Brenda would go with him and she'd clean the bottom windows while our Geoff did the top ones. He was a wizard on a ladder was our Geoff, he had no fear at all. In 1966 Geoff and Brenda lived in an old bungalow in what we called Nook Lane, up an old muck track at the side of the old Lofthouse Colliery pit stack, only fit for use by a bloody packhorse, or maybe a Sherman tank!

That's how Geoff managed to get the bungalow in the first place, because the bungalow was inaccessible; nobody could get to it, let alone live in the bloody place except gypsies or maybe a few ferrets. Geoff had a scrapyard (sorry, metal trading business) up this lane where he played around with scrap cars. While Brenda would be grovelling on the pit stack, scratting for coal! Geoff wouldn't buy coal, no way, well not while he remained married to a mobile coal screening plant and not while he lived next door to that bloody pit stack!

I originally got involved with Geoff in a little business venture. We would buy and sell second-hand cars. At least Geoff tried to sell them and if he couldn't he would give them away, or swop them for an old guitar (which neither of us could play) or a few bloody marbles, or cigarette cards. As you can imagine, that little venture didn't last long. I was running out of money and Geoff had far too many potential customers waiting for a few free cars. As a businessman Geoff was a bloody walking disaster. He was a lovely guy (wouldn't hurt a fly) but in business he never charged enough, he was a soft touch who always fell for a sob story. It was a shame, because Geoff was a brilliant tradesman and could do almost anything except make money which was the most important thing.

Brenda must have had a heart like a bloody lion to have put up with him for all those years, but for all that they were made for each other. She's got a lovely disposition, always a smile and so full of life, while Geoff's so contented and lives his life as only he can, to the full. I admire them both, they live life as it was meant to be lived, bless 'em.

While Geoff lived up the Nook I used to pick him up on a morning to do a removal booked for say 8am. I daren't book them any earlier, because Geoff was never noted for being an early riser. He rarely got out of bed before 11am, and would usually require a stick of bloody dynamite stuck up his bum to blast him out!

Geoff as well as being a skilled painter, decorator, sign writer, scrap man and car dealer, was also a brilliant drummer. He played drums for Joe Fisher at the Ace club on George Street and the club didn't close until 4am, did it? So Geoff was to become a night person, a moony in fact. He was a bloody vampire in disguise, who stayed up all night to prey on little innocent old ladies and then slept all day. The only problem was that even after he stopped working nights he still wanted to stay up and then sleep all day, the lazy idle git. And it wasn't a quick wash round the face and a cup of tea on his way out through the door for him (oh no, not for our Geoff.) He had to have a proper wash and a proper breakfast. Grapefruit for starters, yes, bloody grapefruit and he always had to have a second cup of tea. It was a ritual every morning. I would sit there like an idiot feeling so frustrated and helpless. He may have been a pauper, but he lived like a bloody king. There were times when I would tell him to stuff it and go and empty houses on my own. Talk about Nero fiddling while Rome burned, well that was our Geoff in reincarnation, Nero no less. He was a law unto himself. In fact, he'd been working for me on and off for maybe three years, driving my big removal van, before I found out he didn't even have a driving licence. He would say. "What do I need a blooming driving licence for?" (he didn't swear like me, proper gentleman, our Geoff.) That was our Geoff. Not a care in the world, a full blooded nonconformist, a real live bloody Beatnik, Flower person and red nosed Hippy, all rolled into one. But more about Geoffrey Victor later.

Now that I had two vans, I was employing more people.

I had also decided to expand my family and had a new baby daughter to support. 'Catherine the Great' we called her. She'd been conceived by accident when my wife Jean was caught bending over the washer. I now had three daughters. It was funny really because I'd always wanted a son to help run the business but on reflection I'm glad we never had one. First, I'd have probably killed him for not conforming to my standards and second, he'd have stood no bloody chance with my three daughters. They'd have eaten him alive.

Now that I have grandsons of my own I'm ever so grateful, and give thanks to God every day that I didn't have any lads. They'd have driven me stark raving, bloody crackers.

Lads are aggressive, vindictive, selfish, egoistical and worst of all they just happen to have been born with mothers. And that dear reader is the worst thing that can happen to any lad. Having a mother to spoil the little bleeder rotten. They should do with lads what they used to do with girls in China: the little bleeders should be smothered at birth! Or at the very least castrated to prevent them doing any further damage, to society.

Back to business. I was also now working for Heppers, the auctioneers in Leeds. Ivor Applegarth, who'd been the auctioneer at Saville and Kilburns in Wakefield, had moved to Heppers and he took me with him. When Dad died I told Ivor I wasn't working for 25/- an hour like Dad had. I said I'd get the jobs done quicker but I expected to be paid accordingly and this arrangement was to work quite well for both of us. On some jobs, because the value of the furniture wasn't much I'd receive less than I'd earned, but Ivor would make up the short fall on the other jobs, so I didn't lose out.

At this time there was also a lot of house building going on in Wakefield and the surrounding areas, something I took advantage of. I'd done my own market research and then developed my own marketing strategy. Simple really! I had some nice colourful brochures printed, advising people, of all the do's and don'ts when arranging their furniture removal. I also included reason why they should employ me to do the job rather than anyone else. I'd plant these brochures with my friendly estate agents, the caretakers of new flats and last, but not least, with the general foreman on all the new house building estates in the area! I'd then bung them all a few bob for every house removal they got for me. It worked a treat and again I'd exploited the motive that makes the world go round: greed!

Now at my level in society, bunging a client to obtain an unfair advantage is known as bribery and corruption, but the higher you climb up that social ladder, the more refined become the words for this practice. So much nicer and far more acceptable to the higher echelons. To them it is simply a discount (we all like a discount, or summat for now't eh!) or a commission, a small gratuity, or something spent on lunch with a client. But I prefer to call it by its proper name: bung. It was a shame really, because the estate agents weren't too impressed and very little work came from them. But if they'd ever woken up to the potential for exploiting the house removal market, they'd have made a bloody fortune. Unfortunately their heads remained buried in the sand.

Exactly the same problems apply with buying and selling houses. Millions of people have to wait until they've sold their house before they can move on and purchase another, which can sometimes take years. Why on earth can't houses be bought and sold like cars? After all some cars cost more than some houses, and houses don't usually depreciate like cars do they? It took somebody like Laurie Barratt, the UK's biggest house builder, to take the industry by the scruff of its neck, inject some common sense and move it into the 20th bloody century. As well as taking houses in part exchange, he offers his own removal service and the systems that he employs today to revolutionise the house building industry should have been used years ago. Still, I made do with my site foremen and my flat caretakers, didn't I? As I was to become more established in the business of furniture removing I got to know my competitors and joined the various trade representative organisations like the Road Haulage Association and the British Association of Removers.

One of my good friends was Ernest Marsh, of P Marsh and Son, situated at the bottom of Dewsbury Road. Ernest had several vehicles, including tippers, and we'd attend association meetings in Leeds together. Ernest was to give me some of his surplus work and at the time I thought it was marvellous to be able to catch a few crumbs from a rich man's table. I did a few jobs for Ernest for a carpet manufacturer in Halifax. They were subcontracted from a firm called Hopkinson, based out Dewsbury way. Hopkinson had a fleet at that time, well in excess of 20 vehicles, which to me seemed out of this world. They were really in the big league. Little did I know that within just a few short years this same company would become one of Walkers of Wakefield's main contractors and that I'd be passing a lot of work to them. I was also able to pay Ernest back for work he passed on to me and I helped his son John get started when he had a fall out with his dad.

I came up with what I thought was a brilliant idea at that time. I organised a meeting in a little pub in Westgate. The Little Bull I think it was called. I invited all the furniture removers in the area to attend with a view to setting up a central removal agency to administer, organise and distribute all the available removal work in our Wakefield area. This would be on behalf of the shareholders of the company, ourselves no less. My argument was that there was only a certain amount of work to go round in our area and we furniture removers had to undercut each others' rates to get work. So our charges were restricted by supply and demand, or to use the new in words of today, market forces. My solution was to set up our own agency, pool our resources, and channel all the available work through the agency, to each contractor depending on the size of his shareholding. This way we could increase our charge out rates and create a monopoly situation, virtually charging what we liked within reason. If the government could nationalise that coal industry for the benefit of the people who worked it, then we ought to have been able to do the same.

But it was not to be. These friends of mine preferred to carry on the old way and to fight each other for the available work. So I went away and worked on my own. I had three vans and still I couldn't cope with the work on offer, so I went out and bought a 12 foot single axle little box trailer, which Jean's brother John converted for me. One Saturday afternoon we got some plywood and lengths of wood and extended the roof. Bingo! I had myself another removal van, at least that's what I called it. Actually it was a right bloody abortion, it was awful, but it worked and I did hundreds of removals in that trailer with negligible running costs. I did full house removals with it and I'd put 4 foot and 3 foot wardrobes on the drop down tail door. I used to frighten myself to bloody death with that trailer, many times coming down hills too fast, the tail wagging the dog, the trailer floating from side to side and the towing vehicle all over the bloody road.

I pulled that little trailer with cars: a Mark 10 Jaguar painted yellow, with my coats of arms on the door, that Jean would never ride in. (It was a right bird puller).

I also used a Vanden Plas Princess with a Rolls Royce Engine and a Ford mini bus, in fact anything I could lay my hands on and everytime that loaded trailer weighed in at probably twice the weight of the bloody towing vehicle. Now as I grow older I daren't do a fraction of the things I used to do to earn a crust. Thinking back, I must have been crazy. But it happened and it worked. I decided to put me dad's old Bedford van out to grass. After all, it had been bought from a scrapyard in the first place and was now well over twenty years old and was suffering from arthritis in both its axles. So I parked the old Bedford up on the waste land that I was renting now from the council on Potovens Lane. This land had been bought from British Rail by Stanley Urban District Council, and thanks to my friend Councillor Ken Steeples, they had agreed to carry on renting me the land. So Dad's old van was put out to grass, and used for storage. I would store all sorts in the back of his old van, including oil and diesel. I had a couple of 40 gallon drums in the back and a hand pump fitted to the drums. I also had a hole in the side, through which a pipe protruded! Everything in the garden was rosy, until one day a fire engine came tearing past me down Potovens Lane, with flashing lights and sirens going. I laughed and said to my mate. "Bloody hell, they're in a bit of a hurry, I wonder what's up?" I was soon to find out. A little further down Potovens Lane, there they were and so was Dad's old van, blazing away like Dante's inferno. Some of the local kids, the little bleeders, had set it on fire and it wasn't even bonfire night, nor was it insured. It burnt away and there was hardly ow't left. My oil, my stock of diesel, all gone up in smoke, the little bastards!

# Walkers Of Wakefield

That small box trailer proved to be so successful that I decided to buy a new trailer. I got a firm of body builders at Morley Ace Products to build me an 18 foot x 8 foot x 8 foot aluminium two axle box trailer. It was painted white and I changed the name of the firm from W Walker and Son to Walkers of Wakefield Ltd. There were two reasons for this: a limited liability company meant I could protect my personal assets, whatever they were and the name made the geographical association with Wakefield. Years later, I was to put a map of England on the back doors of all my vans, saying, 'From the crossroads of England, we put Wakefield on the map and the 'Great' back in Britain.' Thus Walkers of Wakefield was born in 1967 on the back of an 18 foot box trailer. My van trailer was nearly 1200 cube, it carried as much futniture as the old 5 ton Bedford that my dad had, but there was a difference: my running costs were reduced to less than half what they'd been with the Bedford. The Austin 4X4 that I'd bought was doing over 20 mpg compared to the Bedford's 10 mpg. I was only having to road tax one vehicle, because the Gypsy doubled as my car transport and trailer tow and was taxed at the same rate as a car. Insurance was half the cost, so it was more profitable. That first little trailer used by Walkers of Wakefield Ltd towed by the little Austin Gypsy in 1967, certainly played their part and were instrumental in stimulating my imagination in the years to come.

1968 was another watershed in my life and for the transport industry in general. That was the year Barbara Castle (labour MP and Minister of Transport), decided to introduce more competition into our industry by bringing in a new system of licensing, known as Operator Licensing. This meant that the old System of A,B and C licensing (based on a proven need), was to be abolished and a much fairer system put in place.

The new criteria was to be based on satisfying the appropriate Vehicle Licensing Authority that the applicant for a licence was financially stable, could provide adequate vehicle maintenance facilities and last but not least, was of good repute. (This ought to have ruled me out for a start) So no longer did we have to show proof of need. Providing you were capable of doing the job, you could compete on equal terms with everyone else in the transport industry and all this from a labour government, bless them. This dramatic change in government policy was to be the making of Walkers of Wakefield Ltd. They were to take off and play among the stars and they never looked back. The company developed a completely new concept in the way that return loads were obtained and organised. Their prime aim in business was to satisfy the customer's needs. They developed a total commitment to their customers. Walkers of Wakefield recruited an army of subcontractors throughout the whole of the UK to help to meet customer requirements and they developed an obligation to those contractors and also satisfied their needs, as well as there own. The principle we operated on was that Walkers got work directly from a customer and then found a subcontractor to do that work.

Once the subcontractor had done the first load for a particular customer, he couldn't morally make a contract with that customer to obtain work for himself. In effect he was stitched up! And while he was doing Walker's work, he wasn't in a position to do any other work for himself. His wings were clipped! The secret was to keep the contractor supplied with work all the time and thus reduce the competition.

Once again, I learned lessons that were to serve me well. I learnt from my first customer in 1958 that it's rarely possible to make a lot of money within the obvious limitations of one's own efforts or resources. It has to be done by utilising others' resources. It was to be other haulage contractors, some much bigger who could have eaten us alive, who were to provide the finance. They bought the vehicles, taxed and insured them provided the drivers, and paid their wages. They were the ones who were in trouble during the recessions of 1974 and 1979. It cost me nothing, but it worked so very well!

In 1968 I also bought my first proper up-market pantechnicon and it was a beauty. It was a 1500 cube Bedford integral van, fitted with a 300 cube Bedford diesel engine, 5 speed gearbox, and four front seats. Wonderful! I bought this van from my now old pal Alan Beaumont, chief salesman-cum-bottle washer at Syd Abrams, the main Bedford dealership in Manchester. Alan had been thinking about starting up in business for himself for some time and I gave him his opportunity, because I ended up buying my first new van from him, instead of from Syd Abrams. I was his first customer and I gave him his first repeat order. After those humble beginnings we both moved on to much better things, oh yes much better! I was to buy all my vans from Alan, right up to my retirement in 1988, twenty years later. I never bothered to obtain other quotes, because Alan would have the chassis bought and the body built and painted long before I received any other quote. Over the years, as I increased my customer base, I was able to introduce many of them to Alan and they in turn bought vans from him.

The new van that I bought in 1968 was of course painted yellow and it had a caricature of Andy Capp on the side with his cap on back to front. He wore a furniture remover's apron and had a picture of a house in his open hands. The caption said. "It's safe in our hands." This was just another one of the many slogans I was to put on to my vans over the years. They were all original and all my own work.

I'll never forget the first long distance removal I did with this van, nor the character that gave me the job. He was a man who lived up Bradford Road, in a big house near where they built the motorway later on. Now this chap had a fair bit of land where he kept a few livestock. If my memory serves me right, this fellow was the main removal contractor for the Prison Service. How he copped for this privileged position I'll never know, (and dare not guess!) because the Prison Service at that time didn't ask for quotations for individual removals. The chap just did the bloody lot and he must have made an absolute fortune. I don't wonder he was to become one of the landed gentry up on Nob hill, because he certainly had a monopoly all right. Thinking of it makes me turn stinking green with envy. Anyway, to continue, this lad got me to do a removal for him to Glasgow. I think his van may have been out of action, but how or why I never found out because he was one of our up-market removal contractors, were he not? Well this fellow didn't have a TK or an O model clapped out 20 year old Bedford van like us lesser mortals. Oh no, he had a proper motor, a Commer no less. It could well have been that he just wanted a rest from driving like, I don't know, but I got this job. We loaded up out of one of this chap's furniture depositories, a stable no less.

On reflection, I think I could well understand this chap's thinking. We all advertised our non-existent storage facilities as proper heated storage and in truth, this chap was the only one in Wakefield, that did have proper heated storage. The horses kept the furniture warm, that is if they didn't eat the bloody stuff first! After we'd loaded my van we set off for Glasgow around 4pm. On arrival my friend and a prison officer went upstairs, as it was a block of flats. I was to unload the van, including a piano, into a lift and then send the lift up to the fourth floor for the other two to empty. Great, I did all the bloody work, while my mate got all the tips. He did at least buy me a cup of tea on the way home when we stopped for a snack on the A1. Boy, what a character, one I'll never forget. He was just another of the many wonderful people it's been my pleasure to have known over the years.

We all learn from our mistakes (sometimes) and from others' too and this chap was to teach me from his own experience when driving for extended periods of time, more progress can be made at 30mph than at 50mph and he was right. I've never forgotten his advice. A much lower level of concentration is required at lower speed and it's better than having to bump the kerb to shake yourself awake. This chap had removed prison officers all over the country so he knew, he had been there. But we must all of us have been bloody crazy.

Another time I'll never forget was in the late 1960s, when I refused to do what a customer demanded. I believe this was the only time, I'd ever done something like that in my business life.

The customer was one of the furniture shops in Pontefract and the manager was a right little dandy, who always got his pound of flesh. The incident happened during the pre-Christmas rush, when it was all hell and no notion. I was flitting around like a blue arsed fly and finding it very difficult to complete all my deliveries. I'd already delivered one full van load, and had returned to the shop to deliver a second when the manager came out of the shop, throwing his weight about. He wanted me to double back over the same route and deliver something to his mother. I said, "Bloody hell, I've already been down that route, I'll never get the rest of these deliveries done at this rate."

He exploded "You'll do what you're told!"

"Like bloody hell, I will," I replied.

He said. "If you don't do as I've told you, you'll never work for Great Universal Stores (GUS) branch again."

I replied, "Oh won't I, right," and then proceeded to unload the van, and left him with a full load of furniture on the pavement in front of his shop. His final words were, "I don't think you'll be in business much longer."

I never forgot those words and two years later, to prove him wrong, I had fifteen vans a day operating out of British Mail Order Corporation depots in Lancashire, all a part of the GUS BMOC group, which also just happened to own Woodhouse, the house furnishers, where this chap worked. So much for his threat!

Sir Isaac Wolfson did me proud in the 1960s.

# My Bit Of Waste Land

It was around 1968 that I was to buy the piece of waste ex railway land on Potovens Lane, near Lofthouse colliery, from Stanley Urban District Council. My old friend councillor Ken Steaples was the chairman of Stanley Council and they'd agreed to sell me the land for a few hundred quid. Great. Now I'd become one of the landed gentry no less. I hadn't as yet started riding to hounds but I'd at least managed to get a toe in the water, hadn't I?

I decided to build a garage on this land. I was now a fleet owner and I needed a proper base and facilities to service my vans. The garage was 60 foot x 25 foot x 13 foot 6 inches. It was fitted with a vehicle inspection pit, three phase electricity, a sink and a hot water geyser in the bottom corner. My old pal Geoff Reeve, he of the many talents, built me a lean to, shed out of old railway sleepers, bits of wood and roofing felt. Geoff then built some portable shelving as storage space and funny as it may seem, nearly thirty years later, some of that portable shelving is still there in the same place, but it now serves a different purpose. It's in my potting shed and is used for storing plants. I honestly believe that if Geoff had got the job of building the Government's latest silly bloody project, The Millennium Dome, then it would last well into the next Millennium and probably only cost a couple of quid to build too! Back to my garage. A lad from Crofton built it for me at a cost of £1200, yes £1200! Four years later, I also bought the railway cutting from the council and built a house on the land that was to cost £12000 and a little later I built an extension that was to cost another £12000. That same house, in 1988, was worth well over £120,000. How values do change eh? And not always for the better either.

Back to my bit of waste land. At the start; I'd used a few loads of knocked off shale or red ash to make a semi reasonable foundation for my yard.

My bit of land had now achieved a bit of status, had it not?

It was now a yard and at last I had a lorry park. But after a while I began to get a little peed off with having to keep filling in the ruts left by my vehicles' wheels and I was pig sick, at having to constantly pull my vehicles out of holes. I decided to arrange a director's board meeting with myself and I came to a momentous decision. I agreed I could not continue with the present state of affairs. So I decided to elicit the help of a few of my mates, who just happened to be ready mixed concrete truck drivers. For a few bob they agreed, to deliver me several loads of surplus concrete. Well, that's what they told me, and I'd no reason to doubt their integrity, had I, as they were all fine, upstanding individuals. Slowly and systematically, I was to concrete my yard. I didn't use rubble as a base, oh no, that bloody concrete was over a foot thick in some places, and I laid it myself. Believe me, it wasn't much fun at 9pm on a fine summer night, having just done twelve or fourteen hours' hard graft, then coming home and laying a load of bloody concrete., which some daft bastard of a driver had decided to drop on my pavement. There it would be a bloody great dollop of concrete, sat waiting for me to finish work. Wonderful! But it had to be done, needs must and all that. I eventually built a wall at the side of the garage placed a second-hand diesel tank on the wall and with the help of a few hard up tanker drivers proceeded to fill it up, with diesel. I now had a small fleet of vehicles, a garage, a bulk fuel tank and regular fuel supplies. I was on my way at last.

# My Council House Removals

Around this time the labour government had decided to modernise most of the local authorities' housing stock. They were to fit gas central heating and upgrade their pre-war council houses to modern standards and it was assumed by our local authorities that each house renovation would take about three weeks. In fact, it took six bloody months in some cases and the tenants had to move out while the alterations were being done. Their furniture had to be removed, put into storage and then returned on completion of the house improvements. And who was to get the job of removing and storing all this furniture? Why me of course! At least for our local areas. How I ever managed to get this job, I'll never know. Perhaps I had a good friend on the council.

Or perhaps, as is more likely, there was just no other removal contractor in Wakefield bloody daft enough to take on the job! Or maybe nobody else in Wakefield, apart from the mighty Pickfords, had big enough storage facilities and even they wouldn't have coped with the amounts of furniture that I was expected to handle. Oh all of us had an old van body, a lock up garage, an old shed at the bottom of the garden, or a handy old bit of tarpaulin sheet to throw over a bit of furniture when required. But, proper storage facilities, oh no, nothing like that. Of course we all advertised our services. We were all known as local and long distance Furniture Removers and Storers and some of us (like me) were also supposed to be experts in overseas removals too. Although Christ only knows what I'd have done, had I actually been offered a proper overseas removal. Apart from subcontracting it to those people at Pickfords, of course!

If we, the so called bloody experts, did happen to get a bit of furniture to store,, we'd always find somewhere to store it. It wasn't quite so bad in winter, mind because we could always find a pal with an empty greenhouse or an old rabbit hutch at the bottom of his garden.

You will by now, have gathered that in my day removals were the easy bits, whereas the storage of furniture was rather more difficult. And the reason for this was that, most of us did not get enough furniture storage jobs to justify investment in a proper, heated furniture depository. After all, most people who lived in our area at that time were council tenants like me. Which reminds me, that must have been why I got this particular job in the first place, eh, I was one of them - one of them who

202

lived in a bloody council house. Yippee!

So there it was, all of us furniture removers managed to offer a limited storage facility to our customers, but it was to be very limited indeed. But because I'd kidded the powers that be that I in fact had storage facilities, all those council house removals for Wakefield, Stanley, Rothwell Morley, Featherstone and every other local authority in the area. I'm bloody pleased they didn't choose to come round on a tour of inspection, to see my up-market storage facilities, because apart from a burnt out old van body and a spare garage, they were non-existent.

I bought two extra old four cylinder Bedford 1000 cube vans from John Henry Taylor, the furniture store in Northgate. And away we went. I had six vans doing three and four removals every day. The drivers and porters were on bonus and boy could they throw that furniture on and off those vans, you bet your beautiful bottom's they could. They were wizards with a bloody shovel.

Those experts at the British Association of Removers would have been proud of me!

As I had nowhere to store furniture, I had to rent accommodation wherever I could find it and quickly. I finished up storing the bloody stuff all over Wakefield. I stored furniture in my bedrooms at home, in an old van body, in my sister-in-law's front room, in my mother-in-law's back bedroom, here there and anywhere that I could find an empty room or coal house to rent for a few bob a week.

It was hilarious trying to find all that furniture when it had to be re-delivered. I think my ma-in-law flogged the furniture she had in store and my sister-in-law kitted out her front room with some of the better stuff she had in her care!

It just couldn't go on. I had furniture stored all over Wakefield and I still couldn't cope. I just didn't know where the bloody hell I was. I bought a chapel down Long Causeway in Stanley. It wasn't big enough so I put another floor in and still it wasn't enough. I rented another chapel at Normanton. Still not enough. I put another temporary floor in my garage and still not enough room. I rented space at the old Symbol biscuit factory at Newton Hill off a pal of mine, Terry Hammond, who worked for H+G Northerner, a London Haulage Co. What a bloody mess I was in! I had furniture coming out of my ears. But we managed and we did what we'd promised to do even if it did cost me more in insurance claims than I'd earned. I honoured my commitments and if the insurance company didn't pay out, then I did.

Some of these council house tenants made a bloody fortune on these claims. We had no idea what was packed into tea chests. The sky's the limit, anything goes, and it did! Gold plated dinner services, silver condiment sets, crystal glassware, Wedgewood china, you name it, they had it. And all these claims were being made by my friends, the council house tenants, half of them on the bleeding dole anyway, would you believe!

## Our Albert And The British Association
## Of Removers

Now to my old pal Albert  Massey of  Ravenscroft Removals, Levenshulme, near Manchester.  Our Albert used to do a bit of furniture removing and storing as a hobby when he was a lad, (about 120 bloody years ago!)

He used to have a few problems with furniture storage, just like I did. He too would have to store furniture in his coal cellar, which of course, after he had been through all the drawers and packing cases (tea chests and orange boxes) looking for any little trinket that he could take to the pawn broker's shop.  I can well remember the odd, or very rare times when he happened to get a bit busy.  When he and their Jean, the woman he lived with, had to take it in turns at sleeping in the bloody bath, when every room in their house was filled with other peoples' furniture and two or three nests of mice for company too.  Oh yes, we've all been there.

We were, all of us at that time, or at least all of us who could afford to be, members of that great, formidable and fine illustrious body of wonderfull upstanding men known as: 'The British Association of Removers', or BAR for short.  My definition was: 'the Bloody Association of As-beens, Rejects, Dead-beats, and Never-wases'.  I do joke of course.

Talk about the unions, with their closed shops, they had now't on these bums at the BAR.

They'd spy on each other and check up on each other.  Well they had certain standards to uphold, you see.  And one could never hope to become a member oneself unless one could find a couple of other members, who one could bung a few quid to.  So that way you could be assured of being sponsored.  Oh yes, it cost you a bloody fortune before you got to become a member, and after all that, not one of those BAR members could do a proper bloody removal anyway!

I'd just love to stand up at one of those BAR meetings and tell those illustrious members about the time that Albert, me old pal Massey took me round his shed, sorry, his 'furniture depository'.  I had to help him move three piles of scrap and an old iron bedstead before we could get through the bloody door to feed the horse, collect the eggs, move the bales of straw and wade in our wellies through three puddles of water and two dollops of cow muck!

We never did find the furniture. We found an old pre-historic 1932 15cwt Bedford that Albert took off the road in 1940, when he retired, the lazy Idle git! We found three soiled furniture inventories, that some one had used as toilet paper. (I think it was Albert's tenants at the time, a couple of Gypsies).

There were two comics, the *Dandy* and the *Beano*, an empty woodbine packet, an old pair of their Jeans, corsets and last but nor least, two used condoms. They had probably belonged to his son Paul.

But we never did manage to find the furniture. Perhaps their Jean had sold it, for a bit of pocket money, without telling our Albert!

When Albert took over councillor Jack Barber's furniture business. Jack was on Manchester council. He was a great councillor and a really wonderful man, who I admired a lot. But he couldn't do both jobs and as a furniture remover, Jack would have made a bloody good window cleaner! I joke of course! I remember at the time Albert asking me about, among other things, half a dozen ESA school desks, that he'd found in Jack's shed, sorry, furniture depository. They should have been delivered ten years earlier to some school or other in Lancashire. Jack had been working for Walkers at the time and I dared not for the life of me, send those desks back to the ESA at Stevenage, as I had no record of them.

They probably finished up as pigeon lofts, or maybe our Albert was to convert them into, up-market hen huts, or what ever.

Whilst on the subject of the BAR and its members, I'm reminded of a removal estimate that I had to give, alongside our local Pickford's manager. It was for the weekend removal of a large local iron monger in Wakefield. There were literally millions and millions of parts. I was to spent hours and hours doing my homework in compiling my quotation. Later when I spoke to the Pickford's manager, I asked out of curiosity what formula he'd used to arrive at his quotation. He replied that he always worked out a price, and then to be absolutely sure, he just trebles it, to be on the safe side.

So much for the bloody experts!

I'll now move on. Talk about bloody Steptoe and Son, they had now't on our Dear Albert and his son Paul.

It was about 1972/73 that I first got to know my old pal Albert Massey, him with the obscure storage facilities. He was a pal of Alan Beaumont, my van supplier. Albert was running a fleet of vans at the time and he worked for Bowater Packaging and several other large manufacturers in the Manchester area. He was also on contract to the BBC, the BBC no less. He moved props all over the country for the BBC's top Saturday night show in those days, *'It's a Knock Out'*. Well, he had the BBC transport manager for a friend, didn't he?

Albert was one of the first haulage contractors to start operating draw bar trailers, after deregulation and he set a precedent. When the Ministry of Transport, in their wisdom, allowed us to operate draw bars without a trailer mate.

Before the war, the trailer mate was the one who used to operate the trailer brakes on draw bar outfits by pulling a bloody great hand brake in the lorry's cab.

Albert was a bit like his old dad who operated trailers after WWI even if he'd become a big wheeler. The two of them were so tight they'd cut a bloody half penny in two. Albert's draw bars were unique because he would go out and beg, borrow or steal, small redundant 24 ft semi trailers.

He would then go round the local scrap yards and he would buy for a few bob, the rear ends off old scrap tractor units. Albert would then weld the chassis ends together to a point and he would then fit a tow eye. He would then shove this the half of a tractor unit, complete with its fifth wheel coupling, underneath the semi trailer and eh presto the tight bastard had himself a ready made draw bar trailer. Absolutely brilliant! I copied Albert's idea later, though it was to cost me a few quid. I had to pay him for every conversion I did, something to do with patents, or copy right. It was through Albert's enterprises with the draw bars that we first met. The tight git was using little poxy Bedfords with 300 diesel engines to tow his trailers and even his three month old grandson knows that Bedfords are no bloody good for pulling their own weight empty, let alone a loaded van and trailer. So Albert had a brilliant idea he would fit Eaton two speed axles, but there was no way that tight old git was going to spend money on new axles.

We approached our mutual friend Alan Beaumont, who in turn approached silly billy me. Alan knew that 'droopy snoot' the van he'd just sold to me for £60, was fitted with a two-speed bloody axle. It was arranged that Albert take my van to Levenshulme one weekend to change the axle. I paid for the fuel to Lancashire and back and when my motor was returned I had to fit a new rear axle. The one that Paul had fitted only had three bloody teeth left on the crown wheel! That, was the beginning of a 'disastrous' friendship that has managed to survive for the last twenty-seven years.

I'll just never know how, though I do believe it might end if ever Albert gets to read this bloody nonsense! Over the years we've had some great times together with Albert, Jean and their family. We've attended and enjoyed the many events that have taken place over those years. Our kids' weddings and Albert's celebration of his firm's 100 years in haulage, which we celebrated together at one of the hotels at Manchester Airport where his son Chris just happened to be the chef in charge, so it cost him now't, of course!

I remember those wonderful weekends over the years when Albert would invite us to his local BAR dinner dances, (not withstanding) the times I got lost on the way. We enjoyed every single moment up until the times when Albert would give me the bill and I had to pay for the bloody lot. It wasn't too bad, though, at 2/6 a head for fish and chips eaten out of a paper with your fingers.

Yes, credit is due, those BAR dinner dances were something really special. They were very up-market like, with all the frills, and were always held at the Levenshulme WMC no less. Everybody managed to enjoy a nice bottle of pop with their fish and chips and there was always somebody who managed to bring along a wind-up gramophone so that we could have a dance in the ladies' loo.

The one really special occasion that I'll never forget, was when Albert invited Jean and I to stay overnight, somewhere very special indeed, well that is what he said! They say anticipation is greater than realisation, and me being the proverbial optimist, I was really looking forward to our special accommodation. I honestly believed our Albert had surpassed himself this time and that he'd maybe come into a bit of brass like, or else he'd had a bloody brain storm. Perhaps he'd decided, just this once, to bend the rules a bit by booking us into a decent hotel, somewhere like the Grand, Savoy or even the Imperial at least!

We were, however, sadly disappointed, because he hadn't had a bloody brainstorm. Oh no, he stayed true to form. It took us about three hours of driving around Manchester before we arrived at our 'hotel' for the night. We arrived at the 'reception', the front door of a bloody council house, and were welcomed (well grabbed and shoved inside) by Albert's son Paul, Steptoe in disguise. Before we had a chance to say 'hello' Paul, he had thrown our cases in the dustbin, had me by the throat and says, "You do know that it'll cost you £100 per person per night for bed and breakfast?" I was gob smacked. I says "Oh all right then Paul, show us to our room."

Paul says, "What bloody room?" and shoved us into the shed. That night at Paul's was the worst night I'd ever spent anywhere and that includes the night I slept on a bloody clothesline after Mam locked me out

208

all night. Jean didn't do too badly, she slept in an old tin bath in the cellar!

Oh yes, Albert and Paul's hospitality was overwhelming and I'll never forget that weekend in Paul's council house.

To be serious for a moment, Albert Massey, Alan Beaumont and I have been friends for years and we've been through so much together. We've shared some of our little pleasures and a few of the heartaches too, including the time I paid for Albert's recent heart transplant. The tight old git then went and asked the consultant for a discount, because he was a BAR member, would you believe?

But through it all we've been true friends. And we were there for each other if needed and who could ask more from a friend?

# Expansion Or Exploitation On A Large Scale!

After my fiasco with the council house removals, I bought a 2000 cubic foot furniture van from Chris Preciouse a local haulage contractor for £120. I intended to keep it as a spare van but that was a laugh, because the vehicle went to work immediately and so did the next five vehicles that were to follow. The whole fleet had only cost me £600. I'll never forget one vehicle that I bought from my old pal Alan Beaumont for £60. We christened it 'droopy snoot,' and there was a very good reason why.

The Luton compartment, the area above the cab, had dropped and was able to move around. It had a mind of its own, completely divorced from the rest of the vehicle. These erratic movements (up, down and side to side) were disconcerting indeed for the luckless driver, who very occasionally turned out to be me. As you sat in the driving seat of this particular vehicle, you would see the whole of the bloody dashboard move one way and everything else around and above would move the other way and I'm not talking just a few inches either. The whole bloody body was on the move, creaking and groaning over every bump and round every corner and all the time you wondered when the body would decide to leave the chassis. It had once belonged to Bevan Funnel, the continental furniture specialist, and they'd probably sold the bloody thing to Alan because it wasn't fit to be on the road. When I bought it there were no rear lights (perhaps it was afraid of the dark) and it wasn't fitted with a tail door either so I made one out of a few old bits of wood. What a bloody mess, but this old van was certainly to prove its worth, because it never broke down and it was to travel the length and breadth of the country, doing thousands of trouble free miles. I'll never forget 'droopy snoot'. He was the ugliest bloody van ever built and he'd scare every other road user out of their wits. But boy, what a motor. That was the best £60 I've ever spent in my life.

This was when I got to know a chap called Peter Holt who worked for a local firm called Rawsons, he is still an occasional friend twenty-five years later. Peter had been a driver and then became the Transport Manager for Harold Wood, the tanker man.

I'll always be grateful to Peter for, he was the one who gave me my first opportunity to step up into the real world of big business. We became friends and used to go out together, but unfortunately he lost his job at Rawsons and finished up doing the job that he always loved, tanker driving. Peter was a first class manager and if the circumstances had been different, I'd have loved to have given him a job. But this wasn't to be. We lost touch and I was on the point of selling my business at the time. Peter gave me some work at Rawsons and I moved on from doing local work, to doing their long distance deliveries all over the UK. My vans were loaded overnight at Rawsons so that my drivers could be away at 4 or 5am before the daily traffic flow increased around 8 or 9am. My company policy then was that drivers should start early enough to arrive at the customers' premises before they opened for business. Rawsons' haulage rates weren't very good, but I did have an advantage. The fact that my vehicles were loaded overnightwas a bonus. This meant in effect that the rate paid by Rawsons was worth an extra 20% compared to conventional day time vehicle loadings.

The other advantage was that Peter would try and send my vehicles to the areas I wanted to go. In the event that I had a customer, say Lebus in Reading, I could arrange a return load from Lebus, before I had even received a load into that area and this was possible because Rawson's, delivered the raw materials for the manufacture, of their suites to Lebus everyday. As a result my vehicle would deliver the load, into the goods inward department and then travel to the other end of Lebus factory, to reload three piece suites for delivery to the North of England.

Usually the return load haulage rate was worth three times the rate paid by Rawson's for the delivery of their load South. I made this point years later, when I was chairman of the Road Haulage Association Area Committee. There was discussion about what a load from A to B, ought to be worth. My argument was that the question was irrelevant because one man's outward load was another man's return load and the advantages I enjoyed working for Rawsons far outweighed the rates they paid. I used Rawson's as a stepping stone purely to get me where I wanted to be. This strategy paid off and helped me build a business with a multimillion pound yearly turnover. In the years that followed, I was to be amazed at the incompetence and lack of enterprise of most of the distribution departments within my customers' businesses. Without exception, the prime areas of importance for them were sales, sales and more sales. Production came second and then, from somewhere in a little wooden hut at the bottom of their yards, out of sight came distribution, the poor relation! The transportation and delivery of finished products has always been secondary to sales and production and always been judged as a necessary evil. For this reason people as a rule didn't understand the essentials in operating haulage vehicles cost effectively. My customers' vehicles, distributing their own products, were only ever loaded one way, so that productivity was reduced by 50% Whereas we had to maximise the vehicles' full potential to remain profitable. I learned the hard way that profit can only be made three ways:

Increasing sales.

Increasing prices (which the market won't always support).

Cutting costs.

The last is the quickest way to achieve results because ways of cutting costs can always be found. Increasing sales usually results in a price cut! So there we were in 1970, jumping off from Rawsons into the distribution departments of Lebus Sleepezee, Dorlux, Silentnight, Hackney Bedding Slumberland etc, to name a few. From there I was able to tout for business throughout the UK. Electrolux, Hotpoint BMOC, Gus, Thorn EMI, Burco boilers, the list went on.

I was now in a position to plan my loads and, sometimes be arranging a fourth load from a customer before I'd jumped off with my first load. I'd pre book a load, out of say Christy Tyler in South Wales, for a Wednesday. My first load would be say, from Rawson's to Lancs, I'd load South, tip and then run into Plysu at Woburn Sands and there I'd get a load for South Wales. It was certainly challenging and exciting, walking that bloody tight rope every day and I didn't often fall off. Whatever my customer wanted he usually got. I was once asked to supply a fuel tanker. Now I didn't know the first thing about tankers, but I found one. Good job that Saddam Insane weren't around in those days. I'd have made a bloody fortune supplying him with Challenger tanks! As time went by, I finished up providing most of the vehicles that Rawsons required. They sometimes phoned as late in the evening as 5.30 or 6pm for vehicles that had to be provided the same night and I did the rest. If I didn't have sufficient vehicles of my own, then I'd use other hauliers, from all over the country. Over the years, I talked Rawson's and other customers into letting me find work for their vehicles.

I'd then load my customers vehicles, sometimes from their own customers with return loads back to base. What a bloody stupid crazy situation. Every return load that I found for a customer's vehicle, would result in the loss of that vehicle to the customer for maybe a day, which would in turn give me an extra load from that customer.

The more loads I found for my customers vehicles then the less vehicles they had available, to carry there products, so I had in turn to provide them with extra vehicles.

I won every time the whole concept of vehicle operation and utilisation was stood on its head. I often would ask myself, this question over the years, why oh why if I could do, what I was doing. Then why the bloody hell, couldn't they the customer, or indeed the haulage contractors, who I was employing do it for themselves. Most of those firms were distributing there own products, (and that was all that seemed to matter to them) all over the UK. They had the vehicles they had the resources, they had the contacts. Why on earth couldn't they have utilised these resources better and allowed them to work for and to realise there full potential. But while ever my customers continued to have their heads buried in the sand, like proverbial bloody Ostriches I was to exploit there inherent weakness.

At this time there was a chap working at Rawson's called Terry Hammond, who worked under Peter Holt, the distribution manager as a supervisor, another chap now a neighbour of mine Neil Weatherhill was the night Foreman at Rawsons. Terry Hammond was to become a personal friend of ours over the years and we would spend many happy hours of an evening at his home in Sandal Wakefield, playing cards. Terry always won of course, (the cheating bastard) that is why he loved to play! Terry was to eventually move onto better things, when he left Rawsons and moved into the old Symbol Biscuit factory off Leeds Road at Newton Hill Wakefield. Where he was to work for a West London Transport company called H&G transport. Terry was to set up and manage H&G Northern.

Now I think I am right in saying that another chap that I got to know well, Alex McDade was to work as a driver for H&G transport. Alex was later to become a competitor of mine, both for customers and for my ex transport business. Alex started hisown business, Mac's Transport, opposite the NALGO offices on Bradford Road at East Ardsley. He sold out in the late 70s and now runs a successful commercial vehicle sales business. Alex was always a perfect gentleman. Terry Hammond was also to start his own transport business (we were all at it) he called it LPD named after his three children. Unfortunately Terry and his wife Barbara were to split up and the last that I heard was that he finished up as a travel agent.

Neil the night foreman at Rawsons also moved on to become the Transport manager at Perfecta Bedding at Wombwell near Barnsley (now a part of the Silent night group).

In the meantime I was expanding rapidly, I was doubling my turnover every year and I was now buying new 2200 cube capacity vans, those vans in 1970/71 were to cost between £2,500 an £2,700 pound. I often laugh at the thought that only fifteen years later, those same vans would cost over £30,000 each. Each new van that I bought was fitted with a radio and spot lights, the driver was given a set of tools and supplied with a small suitcase, to put his snap in! Funnily enough, years later, I was to even buy, my drivers, 24 volt electric blankets, to keep them warm of a night, in there Penthouse suites, in the Luton compartment above there vehicles cab.

Yes that was certainly a far cry from the days, when I used to try and sleep on top of the engine, with the gear lever stuck halfway up me bum, in the cab of an Albion Clydesdale, freezing to bloody death, in the middle of winter in the 1950s. Yes times had certainly changed!

I had some great lads come to work for me. There was Malcom Gunson, Alan Malloy, Brian Chivers, Joe Jones the tattooist, a little lad called Norman Gayford, and a big lad called Brian from Altofts. He was fantastic at handling and moving furniture. Brian was a member of the TA and I knew he'd always attend the drill hall in Wakefield every Friday night. So if I should just happen to have 23 three-piece suites to deliver around the North East of England, who did I send? Brian, of course, and he'd deliver the bloody lot so he could be back at the TA for 7pm. I believe sometimes he even came to work in his uniform, just to save time. Then there was little Barry Audsley, who I'll never forget. Barry died tragically young, from cancer. There was gentleman Don Pearson, who always came to work in his best suit (well he only had one). His next door neighbour, another smashing bloke, used to work for me as a furniture porter. Don used to live next to Jean's mam, down Garden Street. Don was to cost me a bloody fortune in back dated NHI and social security payments. He, like many of my employees at that time was on the dole, but I didn't know that did I. I thought they were all self employed. The officials from the Social had been spying on Don for months and as a result he was required to pay over a large sum of money. In PAYE taxes and NHI contributions. I, of course, paid it for him. Such a pity really that Don was prevented by the powers that be from earning an honest living! Once those powers had stopped a man's dole they'd also taken away his incentive to work!

Another chap I'll never forget was Pat Deac'y. Pat was an Irish lad who'd worked for Lebus upholstery as one of their northern based drivers. He was absolutely fantastic at delivering furniture. And quite easily did five day's work in three. He'd spend two days a week boozing in the pub, then he'd set off and still do more work in three days than anybody else could do in five.

Unfortunately for Pat one Saturday afternoon, as he was going over a crossroads, the van he was driving was struck in the side by a motor cycle, travelling too fast. The rider was thrown off and later died in hospital. Pat was charged with manslaughter and banned from driving. I went with him to the Crown court in Leeds to plead for mercy, but it didn't make any difference. He went to jail. When he was released he went to work as a labourer and I never saw him again until 25 years later. I'd retired from work and was out walking the dog, when I had a conversation with him.

By then he'd built up a successful haulage business and was in fact doing work for two of my old customers. Over the years there were hundreds who came to work for me including a convicted murderer and Arthur Scargill the NUM leaders chauffeur, no less!

I've had them all, the long the short and the bloody tall, bless them all!

I could fill ten volumes, but it's enough to know that I couldn't have accomplished what I did without them.

# My New Up-Market Office Facilities

Back to my garage and my bit of waste land on Potovens Lane. In 1972 Geoff Reeve built me some new offices down the side, inside the existing garage. They were built on two floors, about 6 foot high, so we had to duck down to miss the bloody light bulbs! The accounts office was on the ground floor and the traffic office was upstairs. Now that I was employing office staff, I had as an afterthought to build a toilet block. We didn't have separate toilets, or silly bloody signs to say ladies or gents in those days. The toilet key was hung at the back of the office door. But we did have a sign that just said 'the bog' and 'don't forget to wipe yer bums'. We couldn't put a sign up saying 'wash yer hands,' because we didn't have a sink, did we, and besides, one must get one's priorities right.

Now that we were moving into the big league we needed an accounts manager, or at least someone who knew what they were doing, because my wife Jean didn't. She was there just to make tea. I joke of course. So we employed a double entry bookkeeper called Claud Oxley. What a character Claud was. He was as straight as a die, as honest as the day was long. He was in charge of the petty cash box, and the drivers always had a battle trying to claim their travelling expenses from him. They'd never get paid until Claud had checked their claims and given them a bollocking for having the temerity to ask him for money.

Now if our Claud had ever aspired to become Chancellor of the Exchequer, we'd have had the best economy in the world. I do know that my drivers were frightened to bloody death of him. It was like trying to get blood out of a stone, getting any money out of Claud.

While Claud was ruling the roost downstairs, I was upstairs trying to talk on four phones all at the same time, in my attempts to obtain ever more business from around the country. In the meantime Geoff, my painter and sign writer, was repairing, repainting and sign writing my vans as I continued building a bigger fleet.

What a wonderful situation, there we were, with the offices in the garage workshop, along with the vehicles and the fumes from their exhausts, and to make things even worse I was to come up with an absolutely brilliant idea. Well, I thought so at the time. Geoff was marvelous with a paint brush and he could paint a 2000 cube van in a day, but this wasn't good enough for me, I wanted the job done in half a day or sooner. So I suggested that Geoff throw his paint brush away and used a spray gun instead, which he did. There we were, not only coping with dust, noise and diesel exhaust fumes, but also with spray paint all over the bloody place. We didn't have any spray paint extraction equipment, or luxuries like that, in those days. There was yellow paint everywhere: invoices, statements, letter heads were tinted yellow. We had paint in our ears, up our bums, in our noses, we were coughing yellow paint out of our lungs, and eating it with our sandwiches. Yes, that was a bloody brilliant idea of mine, absolutely brilliant!

We had dedicated work force, either that or they were just incapable of finding anything better. They must have been bloody crazy putting up with the conditions as they were then. Those Health and Safety and Environmental Health people would have had a bloody fit if that had happened today, but that's how it was, needs must! On reflection, I must have got the ultimate utilisation out of the existing floor space and know that if I'd been able to fit an office in that bloody outside toilet I would have done.

Geoff, the painter and bloody invoice decorator was a regular customer at the Central Motor Auctions in Leeds. He'd buy an old banger for a fiver, with a bit of road tax left, then run it until the tax ran out or longer, then he'd throw it away.

I remember very clearly the time I decided to buy my dear wife Jean a little car to learn to drive in. She was really looking forward to having her own car, so I went to the car auctions to buy her one, but while waiting for the cars to go through, I had time to think and that was dangerous, because I thought "What the hell does she want a bloody car for anyway?"

She'd only be gadding about here, there and everywhere, when she should be doing her job. So I decided to buy her a van instead, a Ford Anglia, and to add insult to injury I painted the bloody thing yellow. It made sense really, because besides working fourteen hours a day, bringing up three kids, doing the cooking, washing, working in the accounts office, making tea and satisfying my needs, she could collect a few spares, go to the bank and perhaps do an odd delivery in between! If she just happened to pass her driving test that is. Jean decided it wasn't such a good idea after all, so she failed that bloody test! The selfish bitch.

I remember one incident while Jean was learning to drive. We were coming up Leeds Road at Newton Hill with our three kids in the back. Jean as she changed gear, let the clutch out sharpish, stamped on the accelerator and the van jumped up in the air. Our Anne, my middle daughter, was sat with her back to the rear door, those doors flew open, Anne fell backwards hanging onto the rear doors, as if her life depended on it (which it did). Her bum was scraping the tarmac and that was one of the worst moments of our life. It may sound funny now but it wasn't at the time.

# Whatever It Takes

At the Central Motor Auctions, we bought an old short wheel base Commer Tipper lorry for a few bob. Geoff removed the body, reversed the tipping gear and made a recovery truck. We now had a fleet of vans, an operating base with offices, an office manager, a garage recovery truck and also a proper outside toilet. Who could ask for more? Well I could. I needed more work, more vehicles and now I thought I needed some real help from a proper transport manager, no less! I got to know (or more likely he got to know me) a chap who lived at the top of Potovens Lane at Outwood. He was a driver for Lebus Upholstery out of Reading. He talked me into giving him a job, he was a right go getter and he could charm a bird out of its nest.

We were expanding rapidly and our turnover doubled every year. We now had a customer base of 40-50 customers all over the UK, carrying furniture, upholstery, beds, bedding and domestic appliances for British Domestic Appliances (now Hotpoint) out of Mexboro, Manchester, North Wales Pereboro and Nailsea.

We had 14 to 20 vans working every day for Electrolux, between 10 and 20 vans working daily for BMOC out of their depots in Lancashire plus we carried bedding, furniture, plasics and domestic appliances and we did become one of the main contractors for Pilkingtons fibreglass out of St Helens Plysu Plastics out of Woburn Sands, BMOC and many more. It would be impossible to remember and record all the customers that we were to work for over the years. Suffice to say that we had a very large customer base throughout the UK. We also employed more than 80 other road haulage companies to carry our customer's products. Some of these hauliers ranged from the biggest who were the likes of BRS, Ackworth Transport, Ridleys of Allendale, Harrison & Jones, Blue Dart etc, to local contractors, like Thomas Masters and Andrew Hodgson of Barnsley (me dad and mam would have been proud, of there ex Barnsley Boy eh!) There was Richardsons of Leeds and Hopkinson of Mirfield and Carrs of Morley and oh so many more, yes we had certainly moved on.

I had a simple philosophy based on persistence. I truly believed that if I tried hard enough and that if I should rub a table long enough then that table would wear away and that is what I did to build up my business. I'd look, I'd listen, I'd digest information. I'd go to the public library for information on prospective customers, then I'd target the areas I wanted to exploit. I would then bombard that company on a daily basis with telephone calls. I would always start the conversation with, for instance, "I am sorry to be a nuisance, but I wonder if you could help me please. I'm rather desperate. I have an empty van in your area tomorrow and wonder if you're able to find me a load. The important word was 'help' and I found that those distribution managers would and did help. The silly thing about these conversations was the fact that I did not, more often than not, have one of my own vans within two hundred miles of that particular customer's premises. But nonetheless I rang that future customer every day until at long last (it took me three months to get into Pilkingtons) I would be given a load to move. This usually happened when and if his regular haulage contractor had let the customer down.

Once I'd received that first load, I had at last got my feet under the table, so to speak, and I was away. If I didn't have one of my own vans in the customer's area, I would phone every haulage contractor I knew and some that I didn't, until I found one. There was always one who'd have a van in that particular area. I began to realise that no haulage contractor, no matter how many vehicles he was to operate, could ever guarantee a vehicle of a given size and type in any specific area at any given time.

So I exploited this situation by offering a total service to my customers. As time went by these customers would come to rely on the service I offered. They didn't need to make contact with any other haulier, because one phone call to us was all that was needed to satisfy their requirements  The next move was to build up and cultivate customer relationships. The customers had to like me and they also had to feel a little sorry for me. So I learned never to roll up in a Rolls Royce, if a Ford Popular achieved a better result, or impression! I set out to give them what they wanted and I developed over the years many intimate relationships with my customers, some that still remain, even today: Ray Gill, who died, worked for BMOC and his family still send Xmas cards; Phil Thompson of ESA Stevenage, built me a model boat when he retired; David Boone, BMOC Geoff Holland, Morphy Richards and so on and on. It was one thing to obtain a new customer, but quite another to keep that customer happy. I had to work hard to satisfy my customer's demands but we did it and it was to pay off. I had to do whatever it took to get a job done and the strokes that I had to pull seem just unbelievable now. I had a serious problem getting upholstery returns back to customers. We would collect full loads of furniture for delivery and there would always be a certain percentage of cancellations. Unfortunately our vans were always fully loaded so there was no room for the returns and I was reluctant to send a van, to say London, with just a small amount of furniture on board.

So what I did was go onto the commercial vehicle car park, down Westgate, and look for a driver who was going home to the area where my returned furniture was destined. If the driver was away from his vehicle, I would leave a note on his windscreen, asking him to ring me! This practice worked so well that not only was I getting rid of my returns, I was also for a few bob (a small commission, no less!) getting these drivers to bring me furniture they couldn't deliver, for me to re-deliver. I was also getting these same drivers to tell all their mates and their transport and distribution managers what a wonderful chap I was! All of which brought in new business. I finished up again with vans and loads coming out of my bloody ears. I even had some of these drivers doing full loads for me on the side out of Rawsons. Yes, indeed, whatever it took, I suppose I helped in a small way to make Wakefield 'The Merry City' in the 60s and 70s, because all the drivers who had to park up overnight in the area, always stayed in Wakefield and we usually had a drink in The Wine Lodge, before some of them went off to a dance, or night club. We were to eventually subcontract up to 90% of all the work that we obtained. Walkers of Wakefield's own vans were now being used more and more, as a front, a shop window in fact. My vans were fast becoming props, to be used as an emergency stop gap! We always tried to send one of our vans into a new customer, for the first few loads, until we'd established a relationship. This would mean a fair amount of empty running for our own vans. But it worked! I always insisted that my own vans were top notch, well painted and noticed. I tried very hard to establish the right image. My vans were me, they were my first contract with my customer and my customer's first introduction to Walkers of Wakefield. They were the cheapest form of advertising and that's why I employed my old mate Geoffrey (Victor Reeve) to sign write my vans on a full time basis.

To move on I now had my base, my offices, my bookkeeper, my outside toilets and my new transport manager.

I had done my market research (although I never knew what the bloody work meant in those days) I had been on a BAR course on selling, AIDS they called it in them days.

Grab the customers Attention, cultivate his Interest, establish a Desire, then Sell to him. Well it were summat like that, now't about determination, persistence and bloody common sense. Today AIDS means something quite different; it means 'Add It Done it S.....it I've got it!' Sorry, dear reader (I couldn't resist that final quip). Mind you on reflection, how the hell I ever managed to do those 43732½  removals before I did that British Association of Removers course I will never know, by the way the half a removal I nearly did, I didn't finish, I got booted off the job!

I don't think it would be possible for someone like me to achieve the same results today, as I was to achieve in the 70s  What with all the stringent requirements that are imposed, like the need to have A levels or bloody O levels, whatever they are. You would also need a Certificate of Professional Competence, an Operator's licence, a degree in social engineering, an understanding of all aspects of sex discrimination, the Health and Safety at work legislation, racial discrimination and a full understanding of the 164000 bloody regulations enshrined in The Ministry of Transport regulations. Only when you had become proficient in these and, if one still had the time, or the inclination, and a bob or two would you perhaps be allowed to establish a road haulage business. And then only if one just happened to be able to recruit the services of one of our new breed of stress councillors to help sort out your employees and their work related, problems. My employees didn't suffer from stress; they were too busy and hadn't the time to think about it! You'd have no bloody chance today, unless you chose to break the rules and it always takes one to know one, eh! I made it, in spite of, not because of.

In the early 70,s we were certainly expanding fast. (Too bloody fast.) Our turnover was nearly £500,000 a year. Now if you consider that the cost of a furniture van in those days was around £3500 and today that same van would cost at least £40,000, then the equation to today's values becomes a turnover of £6,500,000 and I don't reckon that was too bad, for an ex butcher boy-cum-labourer and his wife who couldn't even iron bloody shirts properly when she worked for the Double Two Shirt Company in Wakefield. No, not bad at all! I must ask to be forgiven for my expressions of grandeur, I know it does not become me. Ah well, I always had a big head.

Due to this rapid expansion we were rather vulnerable. Our customers (in general) were owing us vast sums of money and they were taking longer and longer to pay. It was the 1970s when most big companies moved away from the old practice of paying bills by the 20th of the following month and extended their terms of credit to payment at the end of the month. That meant that we were owed at the end of the second month probably more than our total asset value. So I decided to form a new company. I bought a ready-made company called Pegmire. I changed the name to Walker's Transport Agency Ltd. In addition to our other limited facilities we had two limited companies. Walkers of Wakefield Ltd was to work exclusively for Walkers Transport Agency Ltd The Transport Agency had no assets other than four telephones, but if the Agency had ever gone into receivership, it stood to lose very little. More importantly Walkers of Wakefield Ltd, with all the assets, would have remained secure and unaffected! And all this before anyone had even heard of Robert bloody Maxwell! Common sense I called it.

At the age of 42 I was becoming too big for my boots, fast reaching my own level of incompetence. I'd been a humble labourer, a removal man, motor mechanic, warehouse man-cum-transport manager and now I'd become a Managing Director and all in such a short time too.

# My Management Consultant Bites Back

I'd never in my life been a foreman or supervisor, let along a bloody Managing Director. I was now not only responsible for my wife and family, but also for two businesses and the people who worked for me and their families too. I had to make sure they got paid. I was now accountable to my customers and the law of the land for the actions of all my employees. Could I cope? I decided not. I'd learned all I knew the hard way and I was to realise much later that it was the only proper way. I read every management and motivational book I could get my hands on, I read all our trade journals and if I didn't know what I thought I ought to, then I'd ask about, until I got to know.

But it wasn't enough. I had to be sure that my way was the right way. I had no yard stick, no measuring tool, no guidelines. I introduced a few systems of control, I designed the paperwork to implement them and if they didn't work, I tore them up and started all over again. It was a long, hard, lonely struggle. I was making mistakes, but I was learning. Perhaps because I had to learn this way, with no preconceived ideas, no established practices and procedures, I did have in the long term, an advantage. When I had to use my initiative to deal with a particular situation, I became innovative and I wasn't bogged down with out of date applications. What's more I could change course quickly as circumstances demanded. But for all that, I felt isolated. Oh yes, I had Jean, who was a great help as my own ready-made sounding board, but I felt like a bloody fairy at the top of a Christmas Tree. I wondered how on earth I'd ever got up there in the first place and looking down I thought I had a long way to fall.

I decided to get some help. I had seen an advert in one of the trade papers by a firm of management consultants looking for work and as one of my main areas of weakness was the accounts office, I decided to call them in. Claude and Jean with their double entry book-keeping system, simply couldn't cope with all the extra work. Even the Kalamazoo duplicate system we'd moved onto, was comparatively modern at the time, had its limitations and couldn't cope with the ever increasing volumes of work. Apart from that, we needed better accounting controls. I also needed operating statements and management accounts to enable me to better understand what was going on. I needed to control my costs and expenditure. We were also moving into a situation where we needed to establish cost centres and be able to isolate individual items of expenditure, along with the earnings, to arrive at a true profit. In other words, we just needed to know what the bloody hell we were doing and where we were going.

This firm of consultants were to spend three weeks full time sorting out our accounts. They sent three men to do the job and the man in charge was a chap called Paul Bernard, who was to become a friend. Paul did a brilliant job with our accounts department. We introduced financial controls and he was to teach me a lot. Later Paul left the firm that employed him and started his own consultancy business. He eventually moved to Wakefield and I was his first customer. I really am indebted to that man and I'll never forget him. He became my friend, my mentor and maybe even my saviour. Unfortunately he died a few years ago but what a man!

It was about this time that, my new manager, left my employment. We'd spent a lovely Christmas together, wished each other all the best and he'd said that he could never do me any harm. We were mates, weren't we? Two week's later he was off to Richardson's removers. Richardsons was owned by two brothers, and one of those brothers, Arthur Burridge, ran the business. Richardsons were the biggest removal firm in Leeds, real big wheelers in fact. Arthur was the chairman of the BAR at the time. It would seem on reflection that I must have been doing too well and was becoming noticed. Who was this Walkers of Wakefield?

Who was this young upstart from nowhere who was able to pass on work to the likes of the mighty Richardsons? That, was a serious problem that I had to live with for years. I was giving work to these big old established haulage firms all over the country and they took it because they were desperate, but they didn't like it. In 1974 in particular, they didn't have much choice. There was a depression and vans were stood doing nothing all over the country. I was even employing some of British Road Services vehicles out of Manchester and I was still expanding. Yes, I was certainly resented by a lot of the big boys, they didn't like me moving in on their territory. I don't know if I mentioned that Sir Marcus Fox was in the employment of the BAR at this time, as a consultant, (although he'd probably never done a proper removal in his life) and at one particular meeting in Leeds, the members were spouting about the cowboys starting in business with clapped out, untaxed, or not properly licensed, Ford transit vans and taking our work and I had to remind him that virtually everybody in that room at the Queens Hotel in Leeds had been a bloody cowboy at some time in their lives, including me! I give him credit when he had to agree that in an enterprising society with free competition, everybody has to be entitled to equal opportunities. But what short memories they all had.

Back to my manager and Richardsons. Arthur started sniffing around, got to know my manager and invited him out to lunch. The upshot was that, the treacherous bastard was promised the earth by Richardsons and as the grass is always greener on the other side, he went to work for them. Within one week he'd phoned all my customers. Thank God, with most he stood no chance, but he parked a van in Alstons yard at Colchester for two days until he received a load and it took him six months to get into Fibreglass at St Helens, but he succeeded. But long term it didn't do him or Richardsons any good. Richardsons were to go out of business. The manager moved on and had to keep moving on. He went to work for Jimmy Ball at Butchers Removers in Leeds. Something happened at Jim's, so he then moved on to Alex Mc'Dade at Macs transport. Alex used him for a while, then he had to leave there. It does somehow seem rather ironic really, because if he'd chosen to stay with me, he could have finished up owning Walkers of Wakefield, but he couldn't wait, he wanted it all there and then. (In 1987 I had to sell Walkers of Wakefield because I had no successor.)

I became the main haulage contractor for GA Moores at Boston Spa and myself and a chap called Brian Galloway became good friends. We used to go out together with our wives in tow. Brian was the transport and distribution manager at Moores and he was also a great guy, very intelligent.

He came to work for me as a transport manager, but not before he'd helped me move up in the world. Brian was to sell me my first second trailer. But this time the trailers that I bought from G Moores were not 12 x 8 x 8 dinky toys like my first little box trailer, that I had towed behind a car, no these trailers were huge, they were high cube, drop well, Taskers four in line Queen Mary's, oh yes now I had a bit of Royalty working for me eh. A Queen no less. I went out and bought some tractor units and I was now a big time bloody Charlie, these trailer were ideal, for the collection and delivery of new furniture to shops through the UK, because those trailers were low loader vans. I was to use these tractor and trailers for a couple of years then I sold them to another haulage firm at Ossett a chap called Richard Simm's, who owned Thomas Simms Haulage, Richards firm did a lot of work for us and, he was to continue working for us, with the trailers that I sold to him. This practice was to continue over the years as I expanded and I would sometimes sell to other contractors vehicles and they would run in my colours. I do remember oh so many of these lads who helped me to expand and develop my business. They in there turn, well some of them grew with me. There was the Malloy Brothers (Alan Malloy had been a driver of mine) who were to do all my removals and all my Freemans mail order work, there was the Liversedge Brothers who were to take over Richardsons, which in turn became Liversedge Richardson ah well.

Brian my manager was to eventually leave my employment for better prospects. He went bus driving! And eventually he was to start in business on his own, I will never forget him I believe he split up with his wife, he came to see me a couple of years ago. Paul got my accounts into shape he had introduced the necessary financial controls and I was now obtaining the management information that I needed, to run a business successfully. I had promoted Malcolm Gunson one of my drivers to traffic controller and Malcolm was helping me in the traffic office. Yes the bloody rabbit hutch that I worked in upstairs above the accounts office was now called a traffic office. I had also promoted little Barry Audsley another driver, as the foreman, now these two lads were great they were loyal and were totally dedicated to the business.

But for some reason Paul, my consultant, had suggested it was time I had a General Manager, a professional no less! He placed advertisements in the usual trade press and we got a lot of applicants for the job.

After rejecting a few unsuitable applicants, it was agreed that we offer the job to a chap from Huddersfield.

This chap had been a manager most of his life. He'd worked for many large local transport firms, so he had plenty of experience.

Paul's dream was slowly coming true. He was, or so he thought, going to take the company forward, onto another plane like, by introducing a bit of professionalism. We were to be given a new image, a bit of a status like. Gone would be the days of old, when I'd have to interview an applicant for a job in the back of my car. Mind you there was more room in the back of my car than in that bloody rabbit hutch of an office and what with those four phones ringing all day, it was quieter! As for all the female applicants, I'd take them onto our local Common for their interviews. All very exciting really and yer can bet that even if they didn't get a job, most of them did limp away with a smile on their face afterwards!

So I now had a General Manager, but where the bloody hell was I to put him? I didn't have a spare office did I? I had a spare toilet, of course, but this would hardly have been suitable to accommodate someone in the exalted position of General Manager, not a proper one anyway. What with his collar and tie, his nicely polished shoes, his umbrella to keep the rain off and of course his briefcase, for carrying his snap, (sorry his flask and sandwiches!) So we decided, Paul my consultant and me, to put him off for a bit, while we found somewhere a bit more suitable for a proper General Manager.

We agreed, that he would start work three months later. It would have suited me if it had been thirty bloody years later. How the bloody hell was I going to cope with a General Manager?

I remember, later on, when we moved to Flanshaw Trading Estate, there were times when we'd have a visitor call while I was outside on a Friday afternoon in my overalls, helping the lads to wash the vans or to transship a load. The visitor would ask me where the manager was and I'd say, "Oh him, he's in there, where he belongs, in his office. It was funny really, because all the lads would call me Charlie and my manager was always addressed as Mr. I couldn't help the way I was and wouldn't have wanted to change, but in some ways the arrangement worked to my advantage. I would use my General Manager as a front, which suited me just fine.

While on the subject of exalted positions, I always used to believe that all Managing Directors were people who spoke proper like, wore bowlers, pinstripes and carried brollies and wore bloody kid gloves too, (that was until I'd met a few). I was to be pleasantly surprised when I found the more successful ones, were just like me. They were all on first name terms with their staff and they too would have a sandwich at their desk for lunch, or jump on a forklift truck if there was no-one else available. In fact, I've had the pleasure of meeting some splendid chaps, in my time. Aubrey Appleton, the MD of Giltspur Bullens, had been a removal van driver. Archie Struthers, MD at the Oliver Rix Group, who'd wanted to take us over, had been a driver too and so many more without qualifications had pulled themselves up by their boot laces and climbed to the top of that bloody Christmas Tree so my old friend Martin Isherwood, the MD of Hardman Isherwood, the biggest independent UK white goods distributor, used to say. I just love name dropping, eh? But I'm also making a point that I hope the youngsters will understand, which is that special qualifications are not always necessary and can sometimes be an hindrance to success, if they encourage a blinkered approach to business. An open receptive mind can be a far greater asset than the best of qualifications! I had been happy on me bit of waste land in the late 60s early 70s and I was sorry to leave. My life had been reasonably simple and I had coped reasonably well with the usual problems that one experiences in business.  I was employing some really good hard working people, we were all of us involved together in making a success of the business.  We had good working relationships, there was no such thing as them and us and we were just one big happy family.

What effected one affected us all, be it problems at work or a problem at home.  It was so good we were all on first name terms and every Friday night we'd wait until everyone had finished work at whatever time that might be.  Then we'd all go together to our local pub, the old *Drum and Monkey* on Potovens Lane, and enjoy a drink or a game of cards.  We'd really take the mickey out of each other.  Yes, those were memorable days spent with some wonderful people.  We were all closely involved and we were good mates and I could always get those lads to work for me.

When I moved to Flanshaw with my new General Manager, my traffic manager and later my Co. secretary, I was to feel somewhat divorced from those special relationships.  Thing became a little more formal and rather remote.  The personal involvement wasn't there any more, the same excitement didn't exist.  I felt as if I was no longer a part of this great adventure that I'd begun fourteen years earlier.

We continued expanding the business and were to become very profitable.  In fact it was so good, it was as if we'd acquired a bloody great printing machine to churn out £5 notes.  But it was never to be the same as those first few years spent on my bit of waste land.  The essential ingredients that had made those times so special weren't there anymore.  Perhaps it all had to change, when we ceased to be Tom, Dick and bloody Harrys and became instead just Misters.

I was also to realise as time went by you can't buy respect, just because you happen to have an inflated title, or your own special named car parking space.  No, real respect has to be earned and comes from the knowledge that the man is always more important than the title he holds!

I'll never really know if I earned the respect of the people who worked for me.  I can only hope that I did!

But I do know as a fact that I'd never ask of someone else what I wasn't prepared to do myself and they all knew that.  I may have been Managing Director, but if there was a van to unload and no one else available, I'd unload it.  If there was a vehicle breakdown and only me available I'd jump into my recovery truck.  I would sweep the yard, I would stay and work late on a Friday night and help to, load or wash the vans, so that we could all of us, the drivers and me finish work as quickly as possible.

Maybe those things used to happen perhaps, because I was never designed, or ever had any inclination to become one of the Misters of this world.

The only Misters that I truly recall in my life, were to be, the older people, who I was brought up to respect, the Real Misters!

I was to remain as always, Charlie, just simple Charlie bloody Walker!

I was talking to one of my ex drivers a short while ago, who'd worked for me in 1973. He was a lad called Joe Jones, an ex driver I'd stolen from Rawson's and he'd come to see me when he found out from a friend of mine where my regular watering hole was.

It was lovely to see him 24 years later and Joe reminded me of how if I wanted something doing, I'd say "do me a favour, Joe" or whoever. He also reminded me of one instance in particular when he'd been working away from home all week and was looking forward to being with his wife and kids on the Friday night. But when he rolled into the yard Friday afternoon I was there sat at my desk, head in my hands, waiting for him. I had said to him that a load had just turned up for scotland, "Oh Joe, will tha, take it and I'll give thee extra night out money. It was so funny that Joe remembered after all those years. It seemed that the lads all had me weighed up and I never knew. He said, "Oh aye and I remember that tha always said thank you very much too, yer bloody con man."

Yes it was special. I attended their anniversaries, I knew their wives and kids, they helped me and I stood by them. I knew what made them tick, what to expect from them: Norman Gayford, Brian Chivers, Barry Audsley, Brian Clayton, Malcolm Gunson and the rest. I was their father, mother, and stress bloody counsellor and I do believe if I could have changed sex, I'd have been their mistress too!

I loved it and even years later when they'd moved on, they still came or phoned for advice or a job reference. That's what friends were for, yes they were everyone of them a friend. I remember the times on Saturday nights when we'd go to the *Jacobs Well Tavern* on Jacobs Well Lane, when a chap called John Hopwood was the landlord. I think Jean's brother played rugby for Batley with John's son. We'd meet some of the drivers and their wives, Jean's sister Kath and Derek, her husband, too. We'd play cards and have a ball. One of the lads, gentleman Don Pearson, who lived down back Garden Street, near to Jean's mother, was a real gambler and he'd gamble his week's wage away. We'd play blind brag. Now there can only be one winner at that game and that's the man who can afford to double up and at the time that was me. I used to take Don's wage off him most Friday nights and then I'd give the daft bugger it back. I had to, or his wife Jean would have bloody killed him and I needed him back at work on the Monday morning!

230

# My New Up-Market Image

Around this time, I decided to build a four bedroomed house on my bit of waste land. Well, I had to have a property that befitted my new up-market image didn't I, and I had to have somewhere where I could impress and entertain my customers wives.

The four bedrooms were there just in case I ever fell on hard times and then I could have filled my new boarding house with 123 lodgers! (one thing's for certain I would have survived:)

So I filled in the old railway cutting with rubble and I built my new house, complete with double garage. To put my second-hand Mercedes Coupe in, that I had just bought off Morrison, of Supermarket fame. Oh oh, here I go again. I swapped this car later for a Rolls Royce Silver Shadow which I cherished for twenty years, although I do remember several embarrassing incidents with this car.

One in particular was to affect my dear wife Jean. Around the early 70s I'd decided to go on holiday to the Yorkshire Dales with an old caravan that I hadn't used for years. To brighten it up a bit I'd stuck a couple of Road Haulage Association stickers and my own coat of bloody arms on the sides (of the van). So you can perhaps imagine that even before I'd hitched up my Rolls Royce, the caravan was looking like a bloody great mobile advertising hoarding. So off we set on our little weekend adventure, (or so I thought). We pulled onto this caravan site in the Dales and it was just as if Billy Smart's bloody circus had arrived to give a show. All the kids on site came rushing across to greet us. General exclamations were; "Is it real mister, is it a proper Rolls? Oh give us a ride mister!" By this time we were surrounded by kids and their parents. Mothers were coming over with babies in their arms, cameras appeared from nowhere and one or two sat their babies on the bonnet of the Rolls. I was (as usual) being asked to hold their babies, while they took photographs of their bleeding kids and me and the Rolls. The situation was becoming hilarious. Jean had by this time decided to hibernate, by diving into our caravan and hiding in the bloody wardrobe, where she was to stay until we drove off that site, all of two minutes later!

Thus our little adventure and our weekend away was over. Her with the long playing record of a gob suffered with a touch of verbal diarrhoea on the way home. The outcome of our one-sided conversation was that she had never felt so humiliated in her life before and she wasn't going anywhere near that bloody Rolls Royce again and that I could shove that caravan, along with the stickers on the sides, as far up my bum as possible! She was true to her word too, because she never rode in my Rolls Royce again and it was to take over twenty years before she could be kidded into a caravan. But the next time it was a motor caravan, able to travel under its own steam without needing a Rolls Royce to pull it!

I didn't mind really, but I would have appreciated a little more support from her with the gob. The least she could have done would have been to sign a few autographs for sale, while I was holding the bloody baby. As for her not riding in my Rolls Royce again, well that weren't a problem really, because me and my Rolls were becoming a little peed off with her Highness's habit of sitting on the back seat, wearing her bloody head scarf. After all, Rolls Royce rear seats were made for proper people to sit on, Royalty and such like. They certainly weren't designed for people who dressed like Old Mother bloody Riley and who wore one of those silly bloody head scarves! Oh dear no!

I must just mention two more incidents with this car, which I thought were so funny at the time and made me realise just how people's minds really work when they come across something that doesn't quite fit! I very rarely used my Rolls, in fact I only ever travelled 62,000 miles in the twenty-six years that I owned the car. So in effect I only used the car in emergency situations. Then I would use it as my secret weapon! I remember once I had been somewhere in it and I called into the tap room at the *Drum and Monkey* on Potovens Lane for a pint and I got into a good conversation with a chap at the bar. Anyway, after we had finished, we walked out of the pub together and as I was getting into my car, this chap just stopped dead. He says. "Is that thine then?"

I says. "Aye".

So he says: "Bloody hell, tha must have some brass!" That chap's attitude towards me completely changed. He just couldn't believe that the chap he'd met in the tap room could ever own a Rolls Royce. The other episode happened when a builder was doing some alterations at my home. He noticed my car and he thought he was going to take the pee out of me. So he says. "Nah then, what does it take to get a bloody car like that then?"

I says. "Well I don't really know, but I will tell thee what it doesn't take. It doesn't take coming to work after the bloody streets are aired at 9.30am and it doesn't take tea breaks at 10.30am, dinner breaks 12 until 1pm and going down to that bloody cafe at Lofthouse Gate at 3pm, before tha knocks off at 4pm! No sirree, it doesn't take any of those things. Because a will tell thee summat: if I had been doing thy job, it would have been finished by now and I would be on or ready for the next job to come along. I certainly wouldn't have had the bloody time to stand here wasting my time talking to thee." (As a matter of interest a new Rolls Royce cost £6000 in 1968).

Yes, I suppose most people found it difficult to come to terms with what they saw in me. I didn't quite fit into the frame that they had chosen for me, I wasn't what they expected. In fact, I suppose it's always possible to stick a Rolls Royce on a pedestal and admire it. But a peasant like me, in my dirty overhauls, with my Yorkshire accent and my bad manners, oh no. I would certainly never have been invited to one of Her Majesty's garden parties, like Auntie Phil was, but it didn't matter. When invited to posh dinner parties I'd choose, as I once did at a big do at the Queen's Hotel in Barnsley, to make a sandwich out of my bread roll and while the other male guests were enjoying their cigars and wine, I'd be enjoying my pint of beer and a roll up.

To move on, everything in the garden seemed rosy. But there was a bloody great cloud looming over the horizon, in the guise of Stanley Urban District Council no less, or at least the council clerk; sorry, 'Clerk To The Council.' In his wisdom he had decided that I was (actually) becoming a bloody nuisance to my neighbours. How dare they! All right, I'd taken over Potovens Lane as my own commercial lorry park and this was a main road. Okay, I'd knocked a few lamp posts down, but that was the council's own fault, for putting them too close to the pavement edge. Oh yes, I had to admit that some of my less tolerant neighbours were becoming a little pee'd off with my vans setting off for work at 4am on a morning, but nuisance, oh no, no way!

Anyway, the council as they do, had sent a mini deputation of about eight officials to see me in an attempt to resolve this problem. So I had to interview this bloody lot outside in the rain. Served them right, what did they expect, I hadn't even room to accommodate my new up-market General Manager, let alone that bloody lot. I don't think they took kindly to this, or the fact that they were not offered a cup of tea either. Well, we had certain standards to uphold and tea and coffee were reserved for special visitors, like Tax Inspectors and VAT officials and not for the likes of council employees. Yes, we had certain standards to uphold; at least that's what my poxy consultant Paul kept telling me.

To cut a long story short, they wanted me off my bit of waste land and as quick as possible.

They also said they'd never have granted me planning permission, had they known I'd be running all those vans. But to add insult to injury, the council clerk asks me why I'd bought all those vans when I'd nowhere to park them. I told him: for the same bloody reason that tha goes to work, to earn a living yer daft bugger!" But it were no good trying to argue with them bloody bureaucrats. I had to try and find somewhere more suitable so I suggested Outwood Park, right next to the council offices. I don't think they liked that idea somehow.

All I needed was another bit of waste land to park my vans on, a portacabin for my office staff and a little garden shed for my new up-market General Manager and somewhere to put his snap (food) bag in.

Unfortunately the powers that be didn't take too kindly to my various propositions. I'd have been perfectly happy to move under one of those redundant railway arches, but it wasn't to be. I did, however, manage to find somewhere semi suitable eventually at Flanshaw Trading Estate, which had been a cash and carry warehouse. There was just about enough room to park my vans, providing I could set fire to all my drivers' bloody cars! Anyway, I managed because most of my vans were away most of the week. The only problem was the size of the warehouse. At 20,000 square feet and with a row of offices across the front it was far too large for my modest requirements. All right, I could accommodate my council removals in a little more comfort, but they were now slowly coming to an end anyway. But I had no choice. I was backed into a corner, so I took the lease at 45p a square foot, with seven year rent revues, on a ninety nine year lease. Stop and think about that for a moment, dear reader, for the first time in my life I was trapped. Ninety-nine bloody year, I'd be lucky to live nine bloody months with that mill stone round my neck. And to add insult to injury, because Walkers was a limited company, I had to sign a personal guarantee too.

Yes, my poxy new warehouse had stitched me up right good and proper. All my carefully made plans, my determination never to be in debt, gone up in smoke. I was terrified at what the future held in store. I'd taken another tentative step into the unknown. One consolation: I did, of course, have room to accommodate my new up-market General Manager and his snap bag too! I give thanks to God that in the long term I was eventually able to purchase the warehouse from the owners, Food Securities, for the sum of £90,000 and at last get rid of that millstone from around my neck.

In fact the warehouse turned out to be one of the best assets that I'd ever had, and not the liability that I'd first thought.

While on the subject, this could be just the time to mention that shortly after moving in, I was to write a letter to Maggie Thatcher, the then Prime

Minister. At this time rates and water charges were paid on rateable values, which in some cases amounted to more than the rental charges. The Conservative government was encouraging business people to move onto new trading estates, where they could receive concessions, like rent free accommodation in the early stages, and all kinds of other benefits. These measures were designed to help us new thrusting breed of (new word) entrepreneurs to succeed and create new jobs!

We were no longer ordinary businessmen and women, now we were all entrepreneurs and I never knew what the bloody word meant, let alone able to spell it. The only problem was that there were thousands of old properties vacant all over the country after the former users had gone bust. In effect, we had a situation where there were only very limited opportunities available.

I therefore wrote to Maggie to ask her if she'd taken the trouble to consider people like me.

I sat in my empty warehouse, worrying about having to make some of my loyal staff redundant and all because I was having to compete, unfairly as I saw it, with people who were being subsidised by government handouts, or something to that effect. In the letter I also mentioned the fact that I had taken the outrageous annual cost of my water and sewerage charges and divided it between my six office staff; I had discovered that rather than use our own in-house facilities, it would be cheaper to have provided a Rolls Royce Phantom to take my staff to the public toilets in Wakefield four times a day and to have used The Savoy Grill in London for our tea and coffee breaks. I said it were bloody disgusting.

Believe it or not, I got a reply sympathising with my predicament. And (this is perfectly true) sometime later, when Maggie was on TV, with her red worn out snap bag, sorry briefcase she announced to the country that changes were to be introduced in the system of charging business rates. And that is perfectly true, a coincidence no doubt, but I still think I should have collected a bloody Knighthood. Mind you, I wouldn't have had the time, or the inclination, to grease up the right people's bums, or to go to Buckingham Palace to collect one!

> The government charged us a fortune to have a pee
> They made exorbitant charges for a cup of tea
> Because I was the one who had to pay the bill
> I decided instead to use the Savoy Grill.

# Part 4

## I Meet My Second Waterloo

There was I around 1974, sat in me empty warehouse, with me new up market general manager and his snap bag. We had a new accounts office with proper tea and coffee making facilities, we also had a new toilet block, with separate toilets for the ladies and for the gents, or us and them who sit down to pee.

### My Waterloo

Well there was me manager and of course there was me
And the other lot who were there, who sat down to pee.
There were toilets for the ladies and toilets for the men,
Yes toilets for us and there were toilets for them.

There was room for a crèche and swimming pool too,
Maybe a leisure centre could be built, if we had had now't else to do.
The potential was fantastic, who could ask for more,
But we hadn't a bloody thing on the warehouse floor.

It was decided that I had to fill that warehouse space,
I was fast becoming sick and fed up with the place
But I sailed forth to find work, I had a job to do
And I got some work at BMOC and from Freemans too.

At last I had arrived, and had obtained what I sought,
And I was now in the big time, or so I thought.
I had at last filled my warehouse, well that were a laugh,
Because me warehouse were full, but I had no proper staff.

So now I found my troubles, my troubles would start
I had no co-operation and I was soon to lose heart.
I began to despair and wished I were dead,
So I decided to sell out, to sell out instead!

But to sell out wasn't the answer, the answer to be.
I was forced to hang on, to just wait and see.
I was to just hang on and didn't know what to do,
I had arrived at Flanshaw and met my Waterloo!

Yes we had most certainly arrived and my problems were now to start. In the accounts office we had my wife Jean and our new accounts manager, he was a Mr, (yes now we had another proper Mr working for us) he was called Mr Walker, my namesake. And he was a proper gentlemen too, a nice old gentleman in fact, who had been in business for himself at one time in his life. Old Mr Walker did at least try and produce some proper figures for us. There was also a nice girl called Brigitte who had been with us on my bit of waste land, so she knew how to rough it, and there was also Jenny who helped Brigitte, but she was later to run off with one of my own drivers and with him she tried to start up a business in opposition to us. This was to happen many times over the coming years with people who I had set up in business, but they nearly always failed when they came to realise that certain sacrifices have to be made to succeed. Claud, my first bookkeeper who had been at Potovens Lane with me, for some reason wasn't at Flanshaw. On reflection I think he must have got bloody fed up with our modern new-fangled Kalamazoo system, or perhaps he didn't quite understand it. Whatever the reason, Claud had left. Maybe he didn't like me new Mr, the new general manager eh!

Malcolm Gunson an ex-driver was still the traffic manager and Barry Audsley another ex-driver had been promoted to yard foreman and warehouse manager combined - well he didn't need to do much in the warehouse did he, except sweep the floor, because the bloody place was empty! The new general manager very quickly changed things. He sacked Malcolm and brought in his own man from Archibould Transport, Leeds. Malcolm had probably deserved to be sacked after he had allowed one of our removal porters, young John Bruce, to go home in one of my tractor units one Saturday night and John, stoned out of his mind, had wrapped the vehicle around a brick toilet in Stanley. John was under age and didn't have a driving licence at the time. Would I have sacked Malcolm under those circumstances? Well, I don't really know!

There was probably a fair amount of resentment on both sides between Malcolm and my general manager, who I think had wanted to bring in his own man, but I did miss Malcolm. He had been in at the start of things and I was sorry to see him go. Apart from that I had also lost my chauffeur, because Malcolm would drive me all over the country at Christmastime to see my customers and drop off their presents.

But for all that our new traffic manager turned out to be superb and was a wonderful man who cared and did a great job for us. However, he was expected to keep an eye on the warehouse activities as they developed as well as doing his own job in the traffic office, because my general manager of course was a great delegator, and so he eventually became fed up and left our employment. He came to see Jean and I on the Sunday morning to say goodbye and he had tears in his eyes when he left our employ. Unfortunately he was to die shortly after, what an awful tragedy. No, I will never forget that man, he was a great guy!

It was a short time later that I had the unpleasant task of sacking my general manager's son. I had been away on holiday and returned to find a new driver working for me, my general manager's son. My general manager had waited for me to go away before introducing his son into our company. I think he had ideas to groom his son for better things to come, perhaps he had visions of him becoming our new transport manager, I don't know. Suffice to say he became a furniture remover driving one of our small vans on local removals. I must confess that I didn't particularly like the idea of my manager's son working for us, not for any other reason than the fact that there was a little resentment from the other drivers and a feeling that he may have been getting special treatment. Precisely the reason why, when years later my daughter Catherine came to work in the office, that she was paid less wages and had to work much harder than anybody else. More was expected from her and it had to be seen by everyone else that she did not receive any special privileges; in fact I deliberately made it harder for her and I expected more from her, bless her. I have always had a fear of spoiling my kid's and I never did, they had to stand on their own two feet, accept responsibility and make their own way in life, which they have and I am very proud of that fact!

As time went by and I was considering subcontracting the removal side of my business to other contractors, my general manager was to suggest that his son start up in business and take over the removals and mail order distribution. I needed time to think about that one, but I didn't really think it was a good idea for my manager to be running a business within a business, especially as he seemed to be struggling with the management of my business. Anyway, it wasn't to be because in the meantime his son and his mate had asked to borrow a van one Saturday morning to do a removal for a relative. It was company policy at the time that any employee could borrow a van for free providing they needed one to move their own, or their family's goods. Under no circumstances were they allowed to use the company's van to do work for hire or reward, because if I had allowed this to happen I would have had a situation where they company and employee would have been in competition for the work available, but of course the employee would have all the advantages because the van he used was for free! Well this was exactly what happened - this chap had in fact borrowed the van to do a removal for money, and when I found out I had to do something about it. As my general manager didn't feel the need to sack his son, I had to do it for him.

Then my troubles really started. The son could not accept that he had been caught out and he took me to an Industrial Tribunal in Leeds. He was funded and represented in court by the Transport and General Workers Union no less, and I had to pay my own legal costs. But the really annoying part in all this was that I was the one who had paid all my drivers' union dues, so in effect I was funding this driver's claim against my company for unfair dismissal. I won and his claim was rejected, but I still had to pay my own legal costs as well as the driver's! Yes, I have to say it again and again, the world has gone bloody crazy!

The worst thing about this particular incident was the dilemma that my general manager had to face, his loyalty to the company that employed him, as opposed to the love he had for his son. I personally felt very sorry for him, but he should never have placed himself in that position.

This just may be the right time to mention my own philosophy towards the people who worked for me, as this applied to them ever been caught fiddling. It was simple really. If they were caught and other people knew, then I had to be seen to be doing something about it and they were promptly sacked. On the other hand, if I was the only one to know, then I did a balancing act. I would have to balance what I had to lose against what I had to gain if I decided to sack an employee. I did not dismiss anyone for what they had done, but for the fact that they had been caught out. I had been far from perfect during my early life and I had many regrets, but I learnt to accept the fact that people are but human beings with all those normal human failings. And it was my job to prevent them from being led into temptation and it was up to me to make things as difficult as possible for them to exploit me. My job was to reduce those possibilities for exploitation to the minimum and if I failed then I deserved to be taken advantage of. Just like the silly bloody welfare state deserves to be exploited today if it be incapable of protecting itself. The only difference being of course was that I had the added incentive that I was protecting my own interests whereas the welfare state is spending other people's money.

239

I remember when I would order a supply of engine oil or antifreeze in the winter, I would always order plenty so that the drivers had enough for use in their cars. Yes, they could take what they needed for their own cars, but God help them if they sold any for profit! I deduced that if I gave them what they needed then they perhaps did not need to steal from me.

I knew that my drivers fiddled extra nights out subsistence money, when in fact they were at home in bed, and I accepted this practise as normal behaviour. But they all knew that if they had been caught they would be sacked. I also knew that some of them fiddled their expenses, but providing they didn't get too greedy, I paid them and accepted that too. In fact in the case of one particular driver, Alan Durnell, bless him, I had to increase Alan's expenses because Alan was that honest he was losing out to the other drivers and Alan never even knew! I considered all these things as normal drivers' perks; they had probably been away from home all week and to me if they had done a fair week's work, then they were entitled to their perks. I suppose in fact I must have become a student of human nature. I had been there, I had done it all and more than my drivers were apt to do to me, and I accepted them for what they were, born opportunists. Simple really, I just didn't provide the opportunity to be exploited! But the most important thing was that I knew most of what was going on; those drivers may have thought they were kidding me, but they weren't. And providing I knew what was going off, then I could handle it as I chose. I even developed an instinct for knowing what was going to happen and what to expect because it had generally all happened before.

I can recall many instances, when I have driven round Wakefield on a night and seen my vehicles parked up for the night, here there and everywhere, and I have pretended that I haven't seen them! This when the driver in fact had booked off in, say, Sheffield or wherever, and claimed an extra night out allowances as expenses. But the most important thing was that I knew what was happening and therefore I had the opportunity to choose to do, or not to do, whatever I thought was required. It was for them to do and me to know, eh!

I wrote a poem about Alan Durnel in 1997, over twenty years later, for his 50th surprise birthday party organised by his dear wife Kath, which I attended with a lot of the other lads and lasses who once worked for me. The get together after that was rather tragic, when we all attended the funeral of another ex-driver and dear friend, Bob Fawcett. Wilf, another driver, who was there, just happened to mention at the time that for some reason Bob had not managed to attend many of our get togethers in the past, when we had all worked together and that it was rather tragic and ironic that he wasn't there that day either. It was all very sad because Bob was still only a young man and it didn't seem all that long ago that we had attended his wedding, bless him!

### An Ode To Alan Durnel On His 50th Birthday. Always A Winner.

Alan crept into all our lives, as gentle as a lamb
Like a petal on the breeze, or a, just well here I am
As we got to know him better, we found him really great
No one could have had, a much better mate.

Daring, oh no he wasn't, that he could never be
Underestimated and so unassuming, he was there for the world to see
Reckless, *no* way, he had never heard the word
Never say never was the one that Alan heard
Eating he would go on eating, eating his humble pie
Lovable he remained, a great and wonderful guy.

Alan started out in life as a farmer, bold and true
He talked to the pigs and sheep, to the cows he just said 'Moo'
As he ploughed the fields and furrowed, as he talked to the plough
Oh how he wondered, how he wondered, how he wondered how.

How could he move on, move on to better things
When along came his Guardian Angel, with a flutter of her wings
She had a talk with Alan, and promised to do her best
And soon our dear Alan had passed his driving test.

And now we may well ask, for whom the bell rings
As Alan was on his way, to achieve many better things
He applied for a job at Walkers, he was surely grasping at a straw
They would employ a cat or dog, if they touched a steering wheel
with a paw
As he went for his interview, the office door opened wide
He was grabbed by the scruff of his neck and quickly pulled inside
They gave him a few expenses, he was told you can drive,
we know you can
And then he was pushed outside and bundled into a van.

241

Now this old van was a Commer and at least 20 years old
Be in London in two hours, now off you go he was told
So Alan set sail on his long voyage to discover
A voyage from which he would never really recover.

Honest and trustworthy he was rather obsessed
When I checked his expenses, I became rather depressed
Because other drivers spent five pounds and then claimed ten
And our dear honest Alan, well he was subsiding them.

His claims for expenses were all so very small
Some weeks he didn't bother, to claim any at all
I had to increase his expenses, so he got a fair share
But Alan didn't know, he simply didn't care.

Wage packets unopened were thrown into his cab
They shared a bed with Lucy, in his wagon and drag
For Lucy his dog and Alan travelled throughout the UK
And they shared there lives together day after day.

But little Lucy died, and it all came to an end
With Alan now heartbroken at the loss of his dear friend
He was devastated and at a loss, and now so alone
A tramp he still was, but a tramper on his own.

But the sun shines on the righteous, and all that gaff
For waiting in the wings was his future wife Kath
She stepped into his life, took him by the hand
And she took him on a journey into the Promised Land.

She brought him into reality, she taught him how to live
To take a little more from life, and not as much to give
Kath was a cracker, a sex kitten in disguise
And the things she did for Alan, made his esteem rise!

As she took him into Paradise, and as she lead the way
Alan got more from life, with a little more to say
She stole his virginity, she put a smile on his face
And she brought our dear Alan, into the human race.

Now as they go on together and their life becomes more complete
A nicer finer couple, we could never hope to meet
It has been a privilege to have know them, what more can I say
Except good luck, God Bless and Alan, Happy Birthday!

**And Now A Personal Message**

I remember those shared moments, from the days we first met
They are the memories that I cherish and I will never forget
Those memories are there forever, as I was helped to do
what I had to do
And whatever I achieved in my life, was due to people like you!

So this was Alan's story and it has now come to its end
It has been my pleasure to have told it, in honour of a friend
On this Alan's 50th birthday, I wish our Alan well
So let's drink a toast to Alan, to our dear Alan Durnel.

But for now we struggle on.

I set about finding some work for my new warehouse and I was to use some of my friendly transport and distribution managers who were employed by my customers, to help me with this task. My first port of call was to the British Mail Order Corporation headquarters in Manchester, to see my dear friends Ray Gill the transport manager and David Boone who had been the PA to the managing director, but who was then the distribution manager for BMOC. My visit was to prove very fruitful indeed, because I was already supplying up to 15 vans each day to BMOC and after my visit I was introduced to a few of their suppliers, who had been told to receive my offer of service most favourable or else, whatever that meant!

The Great Universal Stores Group did have quite a clout with their suppliers, so as a result of my meeting with one of these suppliers, I went on to become the main distribution contractor for a large manufacturing upholsterer in Bicester and this in turn was to lead to national distribution work both for Barrats of Bicester and for a company called Nu Trend, out of Hinkley. We now had three piece suites coming out of our ears. The warehouse was nearly full to bursting. I had certainly moved on since I had moved off my bit of waste land. As well as being local and long distance removers and long distance carriers, we were now warehouse men and distributors too.

I had also at this time, and after a lot of effort on the telephone, been able to make an appointment to meet two chaps who were to play a large part in my future expansion. They were Peter Batterbee and Charlie Baxter, from Freemans Mail Order Co. at Peterborough. Now Charlie had been the former distribution manager at Silentnight Beds at Barnoldswick, who just happened to be another of my customers at the time. Charlie had become the distribution manager at Freeman's and Peter became his transport manager. So, eventually, I was to become the distributor of Freemans Mail Order products throughout Yorkshire and the North East. This along with my deliveries of ESA school furniture into Yorkshire and Lancashire, my ten or so loads every day out of Fibreglass at St Helens, ten or more out of Rawsons Wakefield, fifteen plus out of Plysu at Woburn Sands, twenty or so out of BDA (now Hotpoint) depots in Manchester, Peterborough, North Wales and Mexboro, plus a few loads a week from Shaw Carpets at Darton and Dunlopillow out of Leeds, High Wycombe and Harrogate, Hardmand Isherwood out of Normanton and God knows whoever else at this time, I wasn't doing too badly. But I was having a serious problem trying to cope! In fact I had to refuse a five year dedicated contract doing national distribution work for United Bedding and Upholstery.

Much later I also had to refuse a dedicated distribution contract when offered similar work by Geoff Holland (still an old friend) at Murphy Richards in Mexboro when they decided to contract out all their distribution work. This particular work was to go to National Carriers. I did, however, continue to do a lot of haulage work for Murphy right up to my retirement in 1987. And I did in fact have one vehicle with an owner-driver working full time for Murphy Richards doing all their collections. Steve Liddle was his name and a great guy too. It was so funny really. Steve worked for Murphy for nearly ten years and he had his own name on his van doors, my name was on the sides of his van and 'on contract to Murphy Richards' was somewhere else on the van. So nobody really knew who owned the bloody thing!

Another offer that I had to refuse was from David Isherwood at Hardmand Isherwood when that company decided to go the contract hire route. I decided to stay with my spot hire business.

# I Had At Last Reached My Own Level
## Of Incompetence

I had refused all the offers of regular work because I didn't want to commit the business too deeply into dedicated distribution. I did feel that with the staff that I had and with my own accepted failings, I would not have been able to cope. Was I right? I will never know, but what I do know is that I was never to find it too difficult to find new business. I could always find myself new customers, but my main area of weakness was that I had a soft nature. I could not handle people, I did not have that ruthless streak where people were concerned. I always found it difficult to sack anyone and as a result I was to pay dearly. Because of my particular problems the business was to suffer and was in fact held back for years due to my own inherent inadequacies and failings.

Over the years I have given away or lost more money than most people have probably ever earned in a lifetime. But that's how it was; like a tiger doesn't change its spots, I couldn't overcome my own self-inflicted problems. In fact it was to take me all of ten years and almost the loss of my business before I had the courage with the help of Paul Barnard, my trusty management consultant, to make my general manager redundant and ask him to leave. I would like it to be known that I unreservedly accept the blame for the things that went wrong, after all I had the ultimate responsibility, I was in charge although not in control, so if I couldn't hack it, how could I blame someone else? At first I thought that perhaps I was too demanding, had I expected too much from people? And I often wonder what I could have achieved, what could I have become, had I been able to recruit the right people, if I had only had the right support. But it wasn't to be, because of me. But I do often wonder. However, I will never know and it is far too late to even care - was it in fact all that important?

I made a hell of a lot of mistakes during my journey through that great university of life, but I had also learned a hell of a lot in the process! I had done what I had set out to do, but was never to reach the level of perfection that I had fought so hard to achieve. On reflection though, I doubt if any of the satisfactions, or any sense of personal achievement, could ever have been a substitute for the failures, the heartache and tears, but I had to go and do what I had chosen to do.

It was to take me a long time, too long, before I slowly began to realise that perhaps my general manager was a little too old for the job...or perhaps he just wanted a quiet life...perhaps he was afraid to completely take over and do the job, in case he upset me. Or more likely, perhaps, he just couldn't, or wasn't even allowed to, do his job. But the worst thing of all for me was that I couldn't handle the situation!

Things were to eventually get so bad that I was in trouble, serious trouble and I simply could not go on. I didn't have the help that I so desperately needed and we were going from one crisis to the next, just simply muddling through and I for my part was going through hell in my attempts to overcome my frustrations. Even the most basic systems of control were not being applied and the place was in chaos.

We eventually did decide to employ a yard foreman to help take the pressure off and to try to implement some sense of order. In fact he was a really great guy, who had been a foreman at Hansons of Newmillerdam, who ran a large fleet of tippers at the time. But he didn't have a hope in hell of making a difference without the right help and control from the top. There they would be on a Friday afternoon, my new yard foreman and my general manager, sat on the desk in the reception office swinging their legs and pontificating on the inadequacies of the drivers as they returned into the depot. Whilst all hell was breaking loose outside in the yard, the people of responsibility were sat in the office complaining at what was going wrong. Vans were being parked up any old how, no priorities given to vehicles to allow ease of access on the Monday morning to facilitate an early start. Drivers who wanted to sneak off home early were allowed to go and those that stayed on had to do all the work. This state of affairs just couldn't be allowed to continue. I was ultimately responsible and I should have booted the pair of them out the door, but I couldn't because I was still blaming myself. And so I did the next best thing, I went out into the yard and sorted the problems myself.

Funny, my foreman had said to me that I wouldn't sort that lot out and I had replied that if I didn't sort it out within three weeks then I would close the bloody place down and they would all be without a job, including him! I did sort that particular problem but there were so many more problems. I was, as usual, working long hours, visiting, entertaining and trying to find new customers. I was organising the yard and the warehouse, designing a new office set up, laying down proper practices and procedures, systems of control, rules and regulations, terms of employment and whatever else was required to run the business and at the same time I was trying to do my general manager's job too. I was trying to design a complete new paperwork system for every department to enable the separate units to function as a whole. All this without any previous experience in this field whatsoever, but I tried, I improvised, I put things into practice and if they didn't work, they were torn up and I started again. I had no one to turn to, but that was what had to be done. I did it and I learned by trial and error. And in my spare time (that's a laugh!), I was trying to ensure that my customers' needs were being satisfied too. I was doing all this whilst my general manager along with the yard foreman were sat on that desk in the reception, swinging their bloody legs and complaining to each other. As I have said, I couldn't blame them, I should have made sure that they were allowed to, or were at least capable, of doing their jobs!

Without any of the advantages of established laid down practices and procedures or properly controlled paper flow systems, we were in fact muddling through like a boat without a rudder or a ship without a sail, not knowing where we were going, or even how to get there if we did. Many years later I was to say that I would have loved to have been given the opportunity to manage a business, employing experienced staff within a set of established rules and systems of control. I came to believe that I could have managed a business like that stood on my head and blind-folded too. But I had to do it the hard way, from the bottom up. Build in those systems and controls from scratch and try to employ the right people to help manage that establishment, and whilst all this was going on, try to run the business at the same time without any professional help. An almost impossible and soul destroying task. And that, dear reader, is a glimpse of what my life was really like. As you read of my futile attempts at trying to catch a feather on the breeze or trying to pee against the wind, I was in fact going nowhere fast. I do tend to think that some of the people of today's generation, supported as they are with their cosy index-linked early retirement packages and their protected occupations, have a bloody cheek to complain about their so-called stress related jobs, when they can have no true conception of what the word really means.

**Well what is stress?!**

Stress! well I really do wonder what that word means?
So I asked can it really be all, just what it seems.
I then decided to explore a little and what did I find.
I discovered stressto be really, all just in the mind?

Stress is just a condition, that is allowed to develop in the mind.
From an obscure thought planted, there for the brain to find.
It is in fact but only a word, just a word of a kind.
That is part of imagination, and all happens in the mind!

I had once become corrupted by life, by what I was forced to do.
And I became very disillusioned and I became a cynic too!
I was to became a reformed dreamer and a realist as well.
I had been born to live, to go through my own personal hell.

I adapted to circumstances, as my battles I once fought.
And I cried alone in my wilderness, as help I once sought.
But it wasn't forthcoming and I was out there alone.
And I was to struggle on regardless, all on my own.

I had to get on with my life and I sorted out the mess.
I was never brought up, to know the meaning of stress.
I was born into a real world, with the people I once knew.
Who just got on with our lives and did what we had to do.

I discovered stress is an unresolved problem, that is all that it be.
And that no other life form on earth, was born to cope as well as we.
I learned we are here to deal with problems, that was how we evolved.
And  that stress is but another problem, just waiting to be solved!

We must get on and deal with it, that's what we were born to do.
And all of life's little problems, we have to see them through.
For if one has never had a problem, one has never dreamed of hope.
For it is the solving of life's problems, that helps us all to cope!

Stress  is just an unresolved problem, that's as plain as can be.
And sometimes problems are not really problems, as to some they seem to be.
A problem is but a problem whilst it remains unresolved.
And a problem ceases to be a problem, once a problem is solved!

# Opting Out And Opting Back In Again

I decided I just simply could not go on so I told my managers that I was thinking of closing the business. I had to do something drastic if I was to retain my sanity and not go stark raving crazy! It was then that I did manage to get some reaction. My general manager, in all fairness to him, offered to work overtime or whatever it took to put things right. But it was a bit too late - I had just had enough. I had lost control and could not go on. I had reached a plateau in my life and felt that I could climb no further.

I had in fact reached the pinnacle of my success, the peak of my endeavours. I had at last reached (or so I thought) my own level of incompetence, and like to many other young and bubbling, struggling businessmen who had been there before me, I thought I was now heading for a fall from the top of that bloody Christmas tree.

The early seventies were amongst the worst years of my life. I went to hell and back in my attempts to survive and the biggest tragedy of all was the fact that it wasn't due to lack of work, but was probably a result of too much work. I was fast becoming a victim of my own success and I felt I did not have the professional support that I so desperately needed. Of course, my wife Jean was always a pillar of strength, my sounding board, my comfort and my port in every storm. We would spend our days together in the process of survival, and our nights, or what was left of them, were spent agonising over our seemingly wasted desperate efforts to succeed. I knew that if I had given Jean her head, she would have sacked the bloody lot of them. Oh yes! Nobody, but nobody, messed with our Jean and at one time she did in fact actually sack my general manager, but I, the wimp, reinstated him.

With the culmination of problems that I had to face, not least of all my own inadequacies and inexperience, Jean and I decided that enough was enough, and the business was put on the market. Amongst the interested parties was a firm from Lancashire called North West Farmers who owned a company called Howley Transport run by a chap called Geoff. Now at this time, Walkers of Wakefield were providing most of the work for Howley Transport's vehicles and we were in fact in a small way responsible for the success of that company! The upshot was that North Western Farmers wanted to buy me out whilst I would remain employed as the manager of Walkers of Wakefield Ltd., whilst this lad Geoff who I was giving all the work to, would become my immediate superior and the general manager for both companies! Many others showed interest in my company and I received many offers, but I came to realise that they all wanted me to stay on to run the business whilst all I wanted to do was to sell the business and run. So it wasn't to be, I turned them all down. I decided that if all these prospective purchasers, without exception, wanted me to stay on to run the business for them, then I may as well stick with it and carry on running it for myself. This was to prove a good move because although I had been offered around £200,000 for the business at that time, when the business was eventually sold some ten years later I was offered £1.8 million. So much for inflation!

It was funny really. Howley Transport, who had wanted me to work under their man Geoff were to go out of business and Geoff, who was incidentally a very nice guy, later went to work for Alex McDade at H&G Transport and for Carrs of Morley as their manager. As a result of these moves, Walkers of Wakefield were to keep a substantial number of Carrs of Morley's vehicles employed too...so all's well that ends well, and a small world too, yes indeed!

So I decided to bite the bullet, and I picked myself up once more, dusted myself down, and got back into the fray and I was to carry on the struggle regardless.

# Those Professionals And Their Specialities

My accountant of twenty years standing, Malcolm Dixon, advised me to employ a company secretary to take care of the office, legal and administration problems. Again, the object was to introduce a little more professionalism into the enterprise. I was actually becoming a little peed off with all these so called professionals. We now even had professional bloody drivers who had to pass an MOT (Ministry of Transport) driving test before they could qualify to drive our trucks, and this in turn created a driver shortage in the 1970s.

That's why we in fact had to employ Alsatian dogs and stray cats to drive our trucks in those days, the only criteria was that they could reach the steering wheel with their paws! Yes, I knew all about bloody professionals alright, including some of the solicitors I was forced to employ who always got paid irrespective of whether they got results or not. But I went along with my accountant, and we did employ a company secretary. I think he only stayed with us for about six months, perhaps he couldn't take the pressure! Or perhaps he just wasn't up to his job spec. which included cleaning out the gents toilet at least once a week! Or maybe, perhaps, our standards were just a little bit higher than his previous employers, The Storehouse Group, had been. Oh, he looked the part alright, sitting behind his new desk in his own private office, but doing the job, well that was another matter.

We would hold monthly board meetings to discuss, define, or simply sit on, bloody problems. What a complete waste of time. I soon began to realise that group meetings were usually just a talking shop for like minded people to hold forth on their favourite subject or their own vested interest, and didn't achieve much benefit really. So I stopped having them. During my company secretary's brief period of employment we were to be owed more money by our customers than ever before. He was supposed to produce monthly accounts, which he did, but they never added up! So I would produce my own weekly accounts on the back of an empty cigarette packed, which gave me all the information I needed to manage the business. He would say to me, 'Now, Mr Walker,' (yes, I had suddenly become a bloody Mr too), 'the company is worth . . .' such and such, and I would reply that no it wasn't until he had collected all that money owing to us out of our customers' banks and into mine! Then and only then could he say what the company was really worth.

And I would say. 'So go away and I will give thee some credit for what tha's done, if tha can get me credit control under control!' He didn't of course - well, he were one of them professionals, weren't he?

When he left I promoted my wife Jean to become my new financial director (debt collector for short) and that was the best, well nearly the best, move I ever made. Within six weeks all the money owed to us was in our bank. But she did go a little too far when she refused to pay the other haulage contractors who were working for us. She nearly bankrupted the bloody lot of them! Quite a girl, our Jean.

# The Theory Of The Principle
## Is Easier Than The Practice

Well, what is a manager? There have, over the years, been many definitions, but I have always believed in but one. He or she is a person capable of applying themselves to any given situation to achieve certain desired results.

I tried to introduce **M**anagement **B**y **O**bjectives, which was all the rage and the in thing in the 1970s. I had read all the motivational management books that I could lay my hands on, including all of the Drucker's works and the works of Vincent Peale and many, many more. I really did try to implement some sense of order into the business.

I drew up a MBO plan which at the time I thought was brilliant and would solve all my problems!

Without An Action There Can Be No Result.
Without A Result There Can Be No Progress.
Without Progress There Can Be No Conclusion.
Without Fear There Is No Motivation.
Without Motivation Comes Stagnation!
Planning
If I Know Where I Am Going, The Road That I Travel Matters Not!
Planning Bridges The Gap Between Where I Am Today,
And Where I Want To Be Tomorrow.
Supervisory Staff
Should always be expected to plan, to determine, and interpret, what each segment of a group must do. They should be capable of providing clear cut policies, for the guidance of their personnel. They ought to be able to anticipate problems and to take corrective action. They should be capable of exercising the necessary controls to achieve the desired results. Be able to plan their daily schedule, establish priorities, determine who does what and when. Avoid detailed supervision, by training and controlling subordinates. Be able to identify problems. Maintain a list of objectives, a diary of fact book. Plan and project and review results and plan whenever there is a need to develop a plan of action.

What is my business? What business and I in?

I read everything that I could get my hands on and I had absorbed, digested and recorded all this information in an attempt to assist me at managing the monster that I had unwittingly created.

Yes, the business had become a monster, far more potent than any Frankenstein could ever be, and it was out of control!

# I Revert To The Application Of Common Sense

After a time when I did begin to slowly introduce some sense of order and control into the system, and every time that my general manager went on holiday, I would systematically change things for the better.

We no longer had a petty cash box; drivers were all given a £20.00 float as expenses and they would then claim their expenses on their newly designed weekly work sheets, and then they would be paid a week in arrears along with their wages. Wonderful. No more queuing by drivers on a Friday night waiting for the paying out of cash expenses. No more listening to all their problems, when they would bare their souls and open their hearts to us, their self-appointed father confessors, hidden as we were behind our security screen.

We also had the extra bonus that because everything was better accounted for, mistakes were less likely to happen. This was just one of the many changes that I introduced, but it got so bad that my manager dared not go away on holiday. Claud, my first proper bookkeeper and ex-Chancellor of the Exchequer, would have been proud of me, oh yes! I was lucky I had been there. I knew all the potential fiddles and I was systematically to close all the loopholes. I knew exactly each individual vehicle's running costs, exactly what each vehicle's mpg should be and I let all the drivers know that I knew too. I also knew exactly what the gross profit on each load we carried was worth.

I was able to do sales, costs and profit comparisons, weekly, monthly and eventually cumulative comparisons yearly. I had pillar graphs, bar graphs, and individual unit, sales and cost comparison tables plastered all over the office wall (we couldn't afford proper wallpaper). I was slowly beginning to control the business and I knew and could measure the value of each of my customers' contribution to my sales and profit figures.

Yes, I was growing and learning fast. I knew my own limitations and my inherent weakness, but I also knew my strengths and how to exploit them too. I was probably a walking disaster when it came to understanding and controlling people, and I have suffered for years with my lack of understanding of human behaviour, but I did know my business and what made it tick.

I had eventually set out the basic systems and controls for running the warehousing and distribution aspects of my business, but I knew that I was only as good as the people who worked for me!  And due to my past and present unhappy experiences with the so called professional managers, I had become very disillusioned and had simply lost confidence in the lot of them.  Or, as I oft repeat, perhaps I was just too demanding and expected too much.  Whatever the reason I was therefore either very reluctant, or just frightened to death, to offer employment to any more of those sacred cows, the professionals.  I preferred to struggle on like a bull let loose in a china shop.  And when my star man, my traffic manager, left me, I was in a dilemma, but his leaving did give me an opportunity to find my general manager something useful to do.  A proper job no less.  I promoted him and made him the new traffic manager.  Then I decided that the receptionist was surplus to requirements and as it couldn't get any worse, that my manager would have to attend to his own calls.

So now he had become traffic manager, transport manager, general manager, and receptionist too!

256

# Another Venture With A Little Gained

I decided to attend a management training course sponsored by the Road Transport Industry Training Board at Livingston in Scotland. I had to go out and buy a second-hand BMW SI, or I would have never made it to Scotland. I was at this time running an old banger Hillman car with patched wings, which I had bought for a few quid from a second-hand car dealer from underneath the railway arches in Parliament St in Wakefield. I think I was running this old banger for spite, because I was heartbroken at having had to sell an S2 Bentley, my pride and joy at the time, because her from indoors, with the mouth, had been carrying on about my pretensions of grandeur.

Which reminds me of another incident with this Bentley car. I had been and bought this car, with my old pal Ken Petty, from a Leeds University Professor no less, and while this supercilious little prat was taking us around Leeds on a test drive, he pulled straight out of a side street in front of a line of traffic. Of course Ken and me shouts, "look out, yer daft bugger, where doe's tha' think tha's going?"

This prat of a Professor replies, "I am driving a Rolls Bentley and all the other motorists know that and they give way to me and rightly so!" Well, after that I just had to buy the car, didn't I?

Back to this management course that I attended. It was primarily a course designed for coach operators, I did in fact learn a lot, met some nice people, including Billy Connolly, who was entertaining in a WMC up there. (Though I couldn't understand a bloody word he said!)

Partly through my learning process at Livingston and partly due to necessity, I started a new business. When I returned from this course I had decided to convert a part of my warehouse into a garage. In the meantime, I still had my old pal Geoff Reeve working in the garage, on my bit of wasteland at Outwood and I was, as well as finding him work to do on my own vehicles, also providing him with repainting and sign writing work, from some of my customers, who were Rawsons in Wakefield, Meredew in Pontefract Hotpoint and BMOC out of Manchester etc.

So Geoff was busy and I was making profits out of these little ventures on the side...

So it did make sense really to start a new garage business; after all, it was complementary to my main business. I needed vehicles, which in turn needed servicing and repairing, and as a bonus I had customers who needed vehicles too. As an added bonus, other haulage contractors who worked for me also used vehicles. I deduced that with all these contacts, I should have been supplying, leasing, servicing and refurbishing commercial vehicles in a big way. Oh, what potential there was out there, just waiting to be exploited, and I had the keys to the doors to unlock these new markets.

But I realised that I could just not do it all on my own and I was still having to live with my earlier bad experiences. As current thinking is always controlled by past events, I decided against any further ventures on such a large scale. In fact I had decided to cut back on my new distribution project, because of the aggro it was causing.

Little Barry Audsley, my warehouse manager, was colour blind, and he was dispatching the wrong three-piece suites to the wrong mail order customers. Apart from this we did not always have a set number of vans employed on dedicated mail order distribution.

Oh no, we would send suites out as part loads say with a load of washing machines, or whatever, but the biggest problem was when we would, reload a distribution vehicle from the London area, for example, with a bulk load for Lancashire the North East or even Scotland and this particular vehicle would have maybe a couple of suites on the Luton for return to the customer at Bicester or Hinckley, or wherever. The problem was, when the vehicle was emptied in Lancashire or Scotland, it was reloaded again for delivery perhaps down South, so in effect we had those customer returns stuck on the front of a van for maybe two or three weeks. It was, in a word, absolute bloody chaos, so I decided because of the aggro to give away my distribution work. I employed Alan Malloy, an ex Rawsons driver, who I had set up in business with his brothers to do all the Freemans distribution work and removals and some of the work I gave to Tony's removals of Wakefield on a commission basis, of course.

I moved away from furniture removals and delivery, because that was where all the problems were. I applied the 80-20 rule; 80% of my insurance claims and problems came from just 20% of my work. It was all right when I was doing removal work on my own, but now that I was employing other people to do the job, I had lost control. So I decided to concentrate on what I did best and that was national haulage, where there were fewer problems. You know, on reflection, if I had been just as capable building the right team to work with me as I was at developing ideas and new business, well, who knows, maybe just maybe, I could have built an Empire. But it wasn't to be, and it doesn't really matter!

One Step Up Two Steps Down.

So I concentrated on my next new adventure, the formation of Walkers Garages Wakefield Ltd, which was a company set up in my children's name, for tax reasons and to enable us to juggle the profit figures. The new company did become successful and it did prosper, but again I never quite got rid of the aggro, nor did I ever get the right people to run the operation. Again as far as customers were concerned, we had some of the best. To name but a few: British Beef, Weddel, Mattesons Meats, Federated Brewery, Frozen Food Value, Sleepezee, Hardman Isherwood etc.

We also had four recovery trucks which worked for Walkers of Wakefield and our other customers, as and when required, and we gave a 25 hour recovery service to all our customers.

(We worked through our dinner break). Well, we just had to be just that little bit different from everyone else. We were to provide a service for all the national recovery organisations : National Breakdown, BRS the Police etc. This business was also to become a success story, but it took an awful lot out of me and I never did quite get things right. But at least I had control over my own maintenance facilities. Gone were the days when I would be getting my vans serviced by any Tom Dick or Harry.

My vans in the past had been serviced at Wallace Arnolds in Leeds at Rowland Wynns of Batley, Frank Wall of Bradford Road Wakefield and by Archibalds of Morley, and as a result of some of their failures, I had received some GV9s. Now these are prohibition notices issued by the Ministry of Transport vehicle examiners and on receipt of a GV9, a vehicle has to be taken off the road, and cannot be used again until any defects have been rectified. I had to appear before the Traffic Commissioner in Leeds and give reasons why my vehicle operating license should not be revoked. The outcome was that I had my vehicle capacity reduced to 30 vehicles, which wasn't a problem really because most of the work that I was given was subcontracted to other haulage firms and I had provision on my license for an extra 30 vehicles anyway. But I did care, because I am a stickler for and I believed in the practice of preventative maintenance facilities myself. It was at about this time that my now old friend Frank Kimbly came to work for me. (Frank, who I once had to sack; well, I gave him three months notice and told him to find a new job! I took him back three months later.) He was a brilliant mechanic, auto electrician and paint sprayer. He could in fact do most anything on a vehicle. Frank was to become the foreman mechanic and he stayed with the company for the next 25 years. Now that I have retired, he still works on my cars in his spare time, at the weekends, I would be lost without him as I would be if my gardener Jack, who has been with me from my business days, left me.

Jack retired from work at 65 years of age and has not stopped working for me since.

Another dear friend, Ethel, who was our office cleaner and is well turned 70, still cleans for my wife Jean, after all these years. Salt of the earth, all of them and as long as they are able to crawl through our gate at home, even if it is on their hands and knees, there will always be a job for them. Then there was our dear Dennis, Dennis Moffet, or Captain Birdseye, as the police patrol drivers called him, when they called him out with one of our recovery trucks to do a breakdown at night, because he always wore a peaked cap with a white top. Dennis came to work for me as a driver from Rawsons, now Peter Holt the manager at Rawsons told me to make sure that I always kept my right foot on Dennis's jugular. Unfortunately, I was to forget his advice. I gave Dennis a job in the garage as a semi-skilled motor mechanic because he told me that he didn't want to be away from home as a driver, since his wife, who I had once worked with at the Steam Laundry, was going blind. I believed him; yet she still has better bloody eye sight, than I will ever have. But oh boy, did Dennis cause me some aggro. The trouble was he honestly believed he was as good a mechanic as Frank, which he wasn't. He could not work without supervision. So when things became quiet in the garage, I had to put him onto driving jobs to keep him employed and the aggro I got was unbelievable. The moaning and groaning. In the end I told him that if he kept on complaining, he would force me against my will to sack him. He carried on with the aggro, so I sacked him and offered him a redundancy payoff.

Oh no Dennis, didn't want this, he wrote to the local paper, telling them how he was being exploited and made to break the law by working over his hours on recovery work. He reported me to the Licensing Authority, who sent an Inspector (a pal of mine, who I always treated to a bottle of whiskey at Christmas time!) to check and inspect all my drivers log books. He, of course, found nothing untoward!

So Dennis's next move was to enlist the aid of the mighty TGWU, to take me to an Industrial Tribunal in Leeds.

The Union Area Secretary, who I had got to know through a wining and dining session with the distribution director from Hotpoint, rang me and said. "What the hell is going off, Charlie? We know you are not a bad employer, the muck has hit the fan and I have to be seen to be doing something." We agreed that he would try and convince Dennis to accept my offer and as I was going on holiday, he promised to ring me while I was away, which he did. No way was our Dennis going to surrender. So we went to the tribunal and I took along, as a bit of added security, Dennis's work mates, who spoke on my behalf. Dennis lost his case and I paid my solicitor with the payoff that I had offered to Dennis. I was to meet Dennis over 20 years later, when we finished up as the best of buddies, both having suffered heart attacks in intensive care at Pinderfields Hospital in 1995. He was a lovable character and a guy who I have always thought a lot about. He was very loyal and a good worker, but if things weren't going his way, he could certainly become a bloody nuisance. I remember it was only a month before we had our spot of bother that I had given Dennis my entire miniature classic car collection, along with a model gypsy caravan, bless him.

The ungrateful prat! Another chap who did a hell of a lot of work for me over the year was Pete Rudge, the auto electrician from Ardsley. Peter made all my removable trailer dollies when I copied my pal Albert's brilliant draw bar trailer ideas. Peter was another one, who could do anything and would help anybody, but like Geoff, my sign writing pal, he never charged enough and often never got paid at all. I am proud to say that we have stayed friends for years and now, in the twilight of our lives, we still occasionally go out for a drink together and reminisce over those halcyon days gone by.

When I started the garage business, I converted 5,000 square feet of my warehouse into a garage, with a 30 foot vehicle inspection pit, vehicle wash bay and degreasing area, with all the necessary tools needed to do the job. It was indeed a far cry from those days of old, in the late 1950s when I was operating clapped-out trucks bought from scrapyards that were under powered, constantly over loaded and without brakes or decent tyres! Yes, I suppose I did feel just a little proud of my new enterprise, though my pride was tinged with a little sadness too, at what I felt I had lost when I left the Ramper and my bit of wasteland. I had certainly moved up and on, but I had left behind some great, close, friendly working relationships that I had shared with some wonderful people. They had shared the same adventures, the heartaches, the hard times and the good times too. Yes, I had left them all behind and it was all rather sad!

Now that I had built my garage, things had to be right. I even employed the Freight Transport Associations' fleet engineers to carry out independent spot checks on my own vehicles and on my mechanics' quality of work too!

Yes, we had certainly moved on.

# The Unions

As I have mentioned earlier in this story, I had been very involved with and supported the unions in the 1950s when I became a union delegate for the TGWU at Hargreaves Motors in Rothwell. At that time they employed something like two hundred drivers but I became very disillusioned then and more so in the 1970s when I had expanded my fleet of vehicles to over thirty. There was a serious driver shortage in the 70s not least due to the fact, that the silly bloody government of the day had decided in their wisdom to introduce heavy goods vehicle driving tests, notwithstanding the fact that every operator of heavy goods vehicles in the country already carried out their own driving tests and would never allow a driver anywhere near their trucks until they had established that he or she was capable of driving one. The nanny state, of course, as usual thought we were all bloody idiots!

The resultant driver shortage was like a gift from heaven for the brothers from the TGWU. They just loved it and so they began to flex their muscles and created mayhem. At last they had the ultimate power without the responsibility and were soon to exploit this fact to their advantage.

The background to most of the problems that some employers faced with the unions was the fact that they, the employers, had expanded their business by taking over other haulage businesses. They had then created a semi monopoly situation, grown too big and probably become divorced from their roots and more importantly, they had inadvertently lost touch with their employees.

The relationships, the alliances, the partnerships, the friendships that had previously existed between the employer and employee, within the transport industry in particular were suddenly lost forever. The worker became divorced from the company that employed him; he was no longer made to feel a part of it instead he became just a number, a nothing, a nobody.

So he fell into the welcoming arms of the brothers from the unions, where he found himself a new identity. He recovered his self importance, as he became allied to and became a part of the rapidly expanding Trade Union movement. And the unfortunate employers had only themselves to blame. I remember well in the 1950s that Jack Robinson, of A1 Transport, built up his substantial fleet of lorries by buying A licences

262

from hard-up hauliers. Jack at the time was a main contractor, working out of Temple Newsome Screens, near Leeds and he would employ owner-drivers with A licences as subcontractors to do the work. If they then became too hard-up to continue in business, he would buy them out, along with the vehicles' A licence. Jackie Hanson, who had hundreds of eight wheeler tippers at Seckar Garage Newmillerdam near Wakefield did exactly the same. (He was to later sell out to Tilling Stevens, the bus people.) Over the years this practice continued, with more and more large hauliers growing larger, and then they in turn would be taken over by bigger firms like the Transport Development Group and the like.

This practice created and still does today ever larger monopolies in transport, which in turn led to employees becoming just numbers and of little consequence in ever larger organisations.

The result was that instead of these employees becoming an important part of an employer's small business as in the past, they were now just unimportant numbers who no longer felt that they were a part of the business. They were therefore easy prey for the unions. It was really tragic that these drivers (and I was one of them) were rejected by their employers.

Some small firms did exploit their workers, but there were a hell of a lot out there who did truly care and looked after their employees, who in turn became a really important part of their employers' businesses. Some of these small family businesses were great to work for and the worker was usually on first name relationships with his boss. In those early days in my life, one could tell the boss what one thought of him in no uncertain terms, and he replied in the same tone. Problems were sorted then, face to face, and if you wanted a pay rise you asked for one. If you didn't get one you could leave, but if you were that good and your boss knew it and didn't want to lose you, then you got a pay increase - simple. And after you had settled your problems with your boss, after a week's work you all went out for a drink together. A fair day's work for a fair day's pay.

Today, unfortunately, wage negotiations are settled within committees and everyone within a group is entitled to the same rate of pay, irrespective of each individual's capability. So we find that as a group one may find one or two people who are capable of doing a first class job and do make a much larger contribution to the business than the others within their group. But the crunch is they all get paid the same. It wasn't always like that. At one time people were generally paid what they were worth, and rightly so. When I became an employer I had to deal with strikes by my drivers. I even paid the drivers' Union dues for them to avoid certain problems, for example when a driver didn't want to join the Union. I worked for many customers at this time who had been taken over by the Unions, especially on Merseyside. Pilkingtons at St. Helens, a major customer of mine, was just one example of bloody mindless Union Bolshevism. Our drivers were not allowed to load at Pilkingtons until they produced their Union cards. Those Unions at Pilkingtons at St Helens even stopped me using subcontractors, and forced me to use my own vehicles only. The result was that my daily output of loads from Pilkingtons dropped from around fifteen to two, if I was lucky.

Management had lost and the Unions were in charge. They were the ones who decided company policy and this was a serious problem, as nearly all our customers throughout the country had capitulated to the Unions. They had conceded more and more to Union demands, and had simply lost control. It was the big companies who were to blame, not the Unions, because as they became bigger and more remote from there work force, they became more and more vulnerable and lost control to the Unions.

A classic example of this incompetence and mismanagement was the way that most distribution companies years ago allowed themselves to be exploited by the unions and made to pay their staff exorbitant salaries over the years. The best example of this was the big oil companies, who had to concede to their drivers' enormous wage increases over the years. But they are now being forced to pass the whole of their transport and distribution enterprises over to specialist tanker companies, who know how to do it cheaper and better! The oil companies had created a semi monopoly situation over the years for their products, and because there was very little competition they were able to absorb their costs within customer price increases. But they forgot a very important principle and that is to think very carefully before one gives. Because, having given, it is virtually impossible to take it back! I did eventually become a reluctant hostage to the TGWU in the 70s, when I had to conform to union demands, because most of my customers had surrendered to their respective Unions and I could not obtain loads from these customers without my drivers being fully paid-up members of a trade union! I couldn't beat them, so I joined them, (very reluctantly).

I appointed a shop steward, Arthur they called him, and a nice lad too until he started taking the job a bit too seriously, like! I remember one day he came to see me, as was his wont. He would keep me informed of any possible problematical disturbances amongst my employees, you see. He was, in fact, a spy, a proper little Mata Hari in disguise, weren't he.

Oh yes, I had infiltrated the enemy camp and I was able to know what could happen before it happened and stop it from happening. Does that make sense? Ah well, nonsense it is. Anyway, Arthur says to me, "I have come to see you, Charlie, on behalf of Ray Mein (a driver)." Before he got any further I said, "Nah look here, Arthur lad, if the time ever comes and a situation ever develops here, whereby Ray Mein or any of my drivers, can't come into this office on their own to see me to sort a problem, without having thee hanging on their bloody coat-tails as the union rep, then, I shall sack the bloody lot of you and pack this job in! My office door is never locked (except when I interview female job applicants) and anybody can come see me anytime. So go away and tell that Ray Mein if he has a problem, to come and see me, and without thee as his bloody nursemaid." And I meant every word.

It was shortly after this that our friends in the TGWU decided, as they had not got much better to do, to call a national strike. This happened one February in the early 1970s.

Yes, it happened just as we, all the staff and Jean and I had celebrated our works Christmas party together. The staff had received their hefty Christmas presents and they in turn had clubbed together and bought me a replica model van and trailer, which Geoff the sign writer had painted and lettered. We had wished each other all the best for Christmas and a Happy New Year.

Several weeks later, they were all on bloody strike and none of the silly buggers even knew why!

It was actually really funny, because although the Union had called a national strike for higher wages, my drivers were in fact receiving more pay than their Union was asking for. Although a national strike had been called, not many drivers supported the union. But on this particular Monday morning, as my drivers reported early for work, there was speculation as to whether they should strike or not, notwithstanding the fact that they would not have even been in the bloody union, if I hadn't been paying their union dues! So in jumps big-hearted bloody Arthur, Captain Birdseye Dennis Moffitt, my garage vehicle recovery foreman, who had nothing to do with the strike, as he was employed by Walkers Garages Wakefield Ltd. Dennis says. "Leave it to me, I will sort this out. I know the Union branch secretary and I will give him a ring at home." So he did, and on my bleeding phone too, I might add! So not only were these daft buggers ringing the Union at my expense, after I had paid their Union dues and although I was currently paying them more in wages than their Union was striking for, they were now also asking the Union official if they ought to be on strike.

Of course he said yes. So strike it was, it didn't matter about me, the business, the customers, their own livelihoods. No nothing mattered except that Big Brother had spoken and they were on strike.

I thanked God that most of my subcontractors' driver's were still working and they did all my work during the strike. They also saved my own driver's jobs; without these other drivers, my silly bloody drivers would have had no jobs to come back to! I never forgot this incident and I could never be quite the same ever again towards my workers. I grew rather bitter, disappointed and disillusioned and this came about because of two men, Ray Mein, a driver who I thought a lot of and Dennis Moffit, who just could not mind their own business. They needed to be important and the rest followed like bloody sheep!

While my drivers were on strike, they decided to hold union meetings in a local club on a semi daily basis. This was probably to give the strike some sense of purpose and to give Arthur, the Shop Steward, a sense of importance, or maybe it was just an excuse for a good booze up. Either way, it was fast developing into a bloody pantomime! One day Alan Durnell, one of the nicer, less militant drivers came across from the club to see how we were getting on. Either that or the other silly prats had sent him across on a spying mission. Anyway, at this time I was in the process of redecorating my new house and I asked Alan if he would go to Sheffield to pick up some architrave for me. Alan replied: (bless him the little love)

"Well I don't know, Charlie, if I am allowed to do that, as we are on strike you know!"

I replied, "Oh are you, I can't honestly say that I have noticed."

To cut a long story short, Alan said: "I had better go and see Arthur the Shop Steward, to see if it is all right for me to go."

I replied, "Good idea, Alan, and while tha's talking to the Union tell that bloody lot over in't club that the next time any of them wants a favour, to go and ask their Union, and when you next wants to borrow a car to go to a wedding, don't ask me, ask the bloody Union. And tell that Peter Childs the next time he is going to lose his driving licence and wants somebody to speak up for him in court, to go ask the Union. Tell Wilf Mattinson the next time he loses his licence through drink driving and he needs a job until he gets it back, to go ask the Union for one." And so it went on and on. Every driver, including the Shop Steward, owed me a favour at sometime.

My drivers strike quickly came to an end after that. Perhaps they had run out of money!

266

I proceeded to sack the lot of them and offered them re-employment on the new Union terms, which were less than they had previously received. They all started work as new employees and lost any seniority benefits they may have accrued. Serves the silly sods right!

# We Move Into The 1980s

In the late 1970s we were doing quite well with both business's. The garage had acquired some major national companies as customers. We had also introduced another lucrative fiddle (sorry, sideline) to our business: we had started to sell fuel to some of our customers.

I had at the time fitted a fuel key system of control to my fuel tank (to prevent my drivers from taking advantage of my good nature). Each driver was issued with his own fuel tank key, the keys were numbered and any fuel that was drawn from the fuel tank, was metered and recorded to each key number - quite a foolproof system really. I issued these keys to my drivers and to my customers drivers too, which gave me another lucrative income at little cost. All this happened before self service pumps came onto the scene. The warehouse, too, was now full and bringing in a good income.

We were storing products for the local Yorkshire Purchasing Organisation courtesy of our good friend Lucy, a wonderful woman, who had been brought up in the old school, no less. Lucy was the warehouse manager at YPO and did a terrific job! We were also shipping around forty loads or more daily in and out of our warehouse. We were at this time also storing other products, such as sugar, Christmas hampers etc.

We were approached around this time by a Freight Forwarding Co, who wanted to rent some office and warehousing space from us. I fitted them up with the space that they required; I moved out and rented them the space in my office. I probably moved into one of the spare gent's toilets! Whatever it takes to earn a crust eh!

It was so funny really, because as well as renting to Johnar (that was the name of the firm), 1500 square feet of warehouse space, I was also charging them for the hire of our fork trucks and any casual labour that they may have required from time to time, while Graham, their manager and his assistant, were sat together in my former cosy office doing nothing except playing kneesies under the table together. I (if there was no-one else available) would be unloading or loading one of their trucks and getting paid for the privilege - they even had a cleaner to clean their one office. Bloody ridiculous, I called it. I think they eventually went bankrupt. I do wonder why!

I must also mention that we were to became sometime semi-international hauliers, with our weekly deliveries to Northern Ireland for G A Moores Kitchen furniture manufactures of Boston Spa and for Meredew furniture out of Letchworth. I sometimes wished that I could have sent the whole fleet to be blown up by the IRA, but it wasn't to be. I mentioned earlier that we had started working for Robert Hardman out of Leeds, who were eventually to become Hardman Isherwood and they were later taken over by Asda, the Supermarket chain. They traded out of a large warehouse on the Normanton Industrial Estate.

I became very friendly with Martin Isherwood, who had helped to start the company, and David his son. When they eventually took over and bought the business back from Asda and started to build up there own fleet of delivery vehicles, I helped David with this exercise. We were to eventually do an awful lot of business together. I carried their products all over the country and in turn, during quiet periods, I would load their vehicles from their own supplier of white goods, Hotpoint! I had some good times at David and Martin's Christmas parties. Those were good, unforgettable times we shared. We eventually looked after and serviced their fleet of trucks - H and I are now the largest independent supplier of products in their field in the UK - good luck to them.

We were also at this time running seating components out of Dunlopillo at Harrogate and Leeds, into the car plants at the Ford motor Company at Daggenham, and to BMC at Cowley. We employed a local Haulage contractor and friend to do most of the work, Arthur Brownridge out of Leeds. We also used many other hauliers on a return load basis. So there we were in the late 70/80s, still rubbing away.

We were not only finding and giving work to other hauliers larger than ourselves; we were also loading our customers' vehicles too. We were back loading Rawsons, Harrison and Jones, Hardman Isherwood and many more besides.

It was about this time that I became friendly with Gordon Wood, theWakefield tyre man. We entered into an agreement that he would look after my body by taking me training with him at the local health clubs, and I in turn would look after his mind and help to promote his business.

Over the following years, I gained four stone in weight and Gordon gained four new tyre depots. Gordon really had done remarkably well in business, bless him.

Gordon eventually got to service the whole of Hotpoint, Hardman Isherwood, Jack Fulton, of Frozen Food Value and Federated Breweries fleets with tyres. We once had some good times together - well, I thought so until Gordon moved to Barnsley and we drifted apart, as ships do, as they drift past in the dark. I decided at this time to buy from my old friend Alan Beumont 24 second-hand Penman Demountable van bodies, along with the Bedford Prime movers. These units had been formerly operated by United Upholstery and Bedding, who were a part of our customer the BMOC - GUS group of companies. I was to exchange my fleet of nearly new Bedford vans for these demountable vehicles. It would seem at the time that I had taken a backward step, but in fact this system proved invaluable in the future. I could now collect loads for re-delivery later, and could also on occasion store loads until I had time to deliver. The versatility and added utilisation of our fleet was now tremendous.

As I mentioned earlier, I now decided to steal my old pal Albert Massey's ideas and I proceeded to convert some old 24' Pickfords van semi trailers that I had bought from a scrapyard into draw bar trailers. Pete Rudge, my friendly auto electrician, and Jack of all trades, cut off the rear ends of some old scrap tractor units and converted these, complete with fifth wheel couplings, into trailer dollies, which were then fitted to the semi trailers, which in turn became draw bars.

The only problem was that at this time there were probably only two firms in the whole country operating anything like these vehicles. Yes, that's right Albert of Ravenscroft Removals, and my Walkers of Wakefield. Now this, was to cause a serious dilemma to the powers that be!

Our local police just could not decide whether or not we were legally towing one draw bar trailer, or with the dolly - two trailers. So they impounded one of my vehicles for two days at Dewsbury Police Station until they had consulted the Ministry of Transport. The outcome was that even they were unsure and did not know the answer. We had in fact reached a stalemate, but we decided (and the powers that be agreed) that if the dolly was locked in place and could not be removed from under the trailer by the driver, then the trailers would be treated as one complete vehicle. So they agreed that we could operate our unique draw bars legally. I therefore got a bloody great lump of chain, fastened it with a lock to the fifth wheel locking handle, and away we went! The police, in their frustration, because they couldn't prosecute me for using a vehicle towing two trailers, decided to prosecute me for running a trailer with only two wheel brakes. They lost that too! I had dug deep into my archives and discovered that these trailers had been manufactured by Adam, no less, he of the apple of knowledge and Eve fame, and they were in fact so bloody old that the existing MOT legislation did not apply to my trailers.

So they, our brothers in the police force, had to limp away once more with their tails between their legs. I then went on and bought some more Hotpoint, four in line semi trailers and converted these into draw bars too.

The next stage then was to move onto new Primrose 24' draw bar trailers, and as my fleet of vans and draw bar trailers was to increase. I decided that it was time to get rid of all my articulated vehicles, which as a comparison with draw bar outfits was no longer cost effective. Our 40' Artics were costing well over £1000 to tax at that time, as opposed to £200 a year for the draw bar outfits, and the earning potential of the draw bar units, with their 3600 cubic feet of space as opposed to the Artics 2400 cubic feet, was one third greater at much less cost. Yes, it certainly did make economic sense. And the irony was that although the driving of the draw bar units, did require more skill, because they had two pivoting points and were over 12' longer than an equivalent Articulated vehicle, the driver only needed a class 3 licence, whereas the Arctic driver needed a class one driving licence. Of course, one of those silly bloody professionals who had never even sat in the cab of a Roadtrain, let alone attempted to drive one, had thought that one out!

I also decided at this time to increase the power of my old Bedford vans, and I bought and converted Leyland 350 engines to fit my Bedfords. They were to prove a big improvement on the smaller Bedford engines, which usually lasted for about 70 - 80,000 miles if we were lucky.

I had for many years been active in our Trade Associations, the Road Haulage Association, the Association of Recovery Operators, of which we were one of the founder members, The Warehouse keepers Association and the Transport Association where we were proposed by Ackworth transport and seconded by Gills of York. Now this particular association comprised a body of the largest hauliers in the country and was designed to promote a source of help with fuel suppliers, return loads and recovery and vehicle repairs to its membership. The only problem was that the principals within the various memberships had to attend at least four meetings a year at The Grosvenor Hotel in London, and as I felt I didn't have the time to participate, I resigned my membership. But it was a brilliant association and worked well for the members. I hope you can tell that I was a bugler in the army; that's why I like blowing my own trumpet!

I did however become the Chairman of our local RHA branch and would attend meetings at Holmfield House Wakefield Park with Frank Hensbys senior and junior, the well known local hauliers and VW dealers, and some other local hauliers. We had some great nights, but unfortunately some of the good ideas that we put forward to the area committee for their approval and subsequent lobbying of the government came to naught. We suggested that road tax be abolished and substituted for an increase in fuel duty, so that the ones who used the roads the most would then use the most fuel and pay the most in road tax. We suggested that our association, the Road Haulage Association, supported by members, become a bulk buyer of fuel at large discounts for onward supply to its membership, and that it pool and use the resources within that membership for the benefit of all by offering fuel supplies, return loads, repairs and recovery, member to member. This made a lot of sense to us at that time, but it wasn't to be. It was to take National Breakdown of Bradford to set up a national recovery service to RHA members at substantial profits to themselves - and they finished up doing for us what we should have been doing for ourselves. I was to work for National Breakdown BRS and the rest with my recovery trucks. What a ludicrous situation.

It was about this time that I was elected onto the Wakefield Road Safety Committee. I represented road transport, the committee which consisted of representatives from the police, fire service, social services and Christ knows who else, was chaired by the Mayor of Wakefield, out of about 8 members there was just one, - me, from the private sector. I had by now become very disillusioned with committees, or talking shops and after just three meetings I resigned. It just wasn't worth the effort; everything was cut and dried before the meetings ever started!

I must, before closing this chapter on my involvement with these associations, just mention one really embarrassing incident that happened to me while I was chairman of the RHA. The committee had organised our annual dinner dance at the Painthorpe Country Club and it was to become the biggest attended event ever! Well, it had to be because, big time bloody Charlie - me - had invited all my customers and friends, in fact I was paying people to attend. In my capacity of Chairman (I found out later) I had to make a speech. Whose idea this was I will never know, what a bloody crazy idea. I collapsed. No way could I make that speech. I became a gibbering wimp, a bloody coward in fact, and my wife Jean, the dominant one, had to bail me out. She presented the prizes, kissed and shook hands with everybody, while I hid myself away in the gents toilets until everybody had gone home!

Never again. When I had, years later, to make speeches at my daughters' weddings, (which I was proud to do) I put it all into poetry and the poem said it all for me. There was only one other time when I found myself in a rather prominent position, but this time I didn't have to make a speech, I didn't have to kiss anyone; I only had to shake hands and present a cup to the South African winner of a Grand Prix race that Walkers had sponsored at Donnington Park race track.

We had some great times. We would organise coach trips for all the staff, we even organised a cricket team and travelled to Plysu at Woburn Sands to play our customers at cricket. They won but we beat them later at a drinking contest. Yes, happy, truly memorable times.

They were such wonderful people to know and work with - dear Karen and her sister Bridgett, who travelled on two buses from Sharlston every day to work for us and were never late. Karen (who is now incidentally the General Manager of GT Smiths Supermarket chain, bless her) could never do enough for you. There was my daughter Catherine, who had to accept so much more than anyone else. Lorraine, who came to us from school. The names are endless, but all were very special. I must not close this chapter without mentioning a really funny incident that happened about that time.

You may recall how many times I have mentioned in this book that I would do whatever I had to do to survive. Well, this particular time the country was going through a severe recession. So the government, had decided that rather than having to accept wholesale unemployment, they would introduce a system whereby people could work 2 or 3 days and draw dole money for the other two or three days that they were off work. Well this worked fine, because I put everybody on the dole for three days each week, but at the same they were all working full time, and I was making their wage up with the dole money to a full week's wages, so that no one lost out.

All the drivers were in the yard, painting their vans, the garage the warehouse and anything that moved. The girls in the office were doing their jobs. Everything was fine until one day, a strange car came into the yard and someone shouted "Eh up who's this - it must be someone from the dole office." At that there was one mad rush, a bloody stampede in fact, as all the office staff rushed out of the accounts office, through into my office, where I just sat with my mouth open. They opened my office window, hitched up their skirts, and then fought each other to climb up and out of my bloody office window. Talk about that Lord Cardigan and his Charge of the Light Brigade. It had nowt on my girls, fleeing through that window.

But all's well that ends well. It was a false alarm; the mystery man wasn't from the dole office - he was just looking for a job!

My final business venture during this period, was into the realms of Self Drive Hire. I had been making too many profits and needed (or so I thought at the time) to invest in capital items to reduce my tax liabilities. At that time a business could write down its capital assets in the first year, and obtain 100% in taxable allowances. So I decided to start a self drive hire business, and thus Walkers of Wakefield (Self Drive Hire) was born. I was to buy about fourteen new vehicles - Bedford chassis cabs with demountable motor caravan bodies for summer hire and spare van bodies for winter hire. I bought some vans and converted them into luxury motorcaravans; once I had removed the portable sink unit and fridge from the rear end, and introduced replacement seats, they became 12-14 seater minibuses. The whole operation just took 10 minutes.

I thought this idea was brilliant.

Just think of the vast savings that could be made if Self Drive van hire companies had a range of demountable van, pickup, caravan and bus bodies, eh! This all happened nearly twenty years ago and still the self drive hire firms haven't cottoned-on to the savings that could be made by using demountable bodies.

The fire brigade, with the benefit of all their highly paid professional staff, have only just decided to introduce specialist, demountable pods into their operations. My word, what a wonderful idea eh! Using these demountable bodies had to make sense and be very cost effective, not just because of their versatility, but for no other reason than that a good body will usually outlast two vehicles chassis. That's why we find farmers, market gardeners and the rest still using perfectly good bodies as sheds or fitted to trailers. Common sense, I call it!

Unfortunately, I soon became bored with the Self Drive Hire business. It was mostly weekend work, I was once again dealing with the public and that meant problems which I could well do without. So I cut my losses and ran. I couldn't do it all on my own. I had no manager as such and I didn't need the aggro - I had made a serious mistake and lost a lot of money by allowing the tax tail to wag the dog. I still believe that with the right commitment and management, this venture could have been a real success, but it wasn't to be. I was fast becoming a spent force and, I began to realise that I didn't need the aggro any more. I now felt secure, and I wasn't hungry any more.

I had simply had enough and nothing seemed to matter in the same way. I had no more fighting to do, so I decided to retire from the battle and let my daughter Catherine take over.

In 1984 my General Manager, with the help of a decent redundancy package and a pension provided by the company, had decided to move on to pastures new. He had been employed by Walkers for a period of ten years and the business was slowly going downhill, in the sense that our customer base was slowly being eroded and we were relying more and more on our two main customers, Plysu at Woburn Sands and Hotpoint, the domestic appliance manufacturer at Peterborough.

I had at this time once again elicited the help of my old friend and business consultant, Paul Bernard, in an attempt to stop the rot. Paul had suggested that we needed to inject some young blood into the establishment, with some new ideas and a fresh approach to our problems. He therefore had a long heart-to-heart with my manager and he discovered to my dismay, that the manager did not want to carry out courtesy calls and visits to our customers and that he also found it very difficult to attempt to go out and find new business. In fact, it seemed that he found it very difficult to look after the customers we had! After all, to be fair, he was now sixty years of age and he was perhaps just a little too old to manage a young, thrusting, go-getting business. Paul therefore gave me an ultimatum; if the business was to survive, then it needed new blood injecting into its veins. In fact my manager agreed with Paul. So I had a decision to make, which was one of the hardest decisions that I have ever made in my life. My general manager and I had worked together for ten years and we had enjoyed some good times together. We had been to our Albert's BAR dinner dances in Manchester, we had spent weekends at Blackpool with Arthur Owen, the manager at Eastham Burco, which was one of our customers at the time. We had spent happy hours together on a Friday after work with all our drivers in the Eagle pub on Flanshaw Lane. Yes, there were many good times as well as bad. But I had to do what I had to do! In fact Paul offered to do it for me, but I felt that I owed my manager something and it was only right that I tell him he had to leave. I am ashamed to have to admit as a grown man that I was in tears. I felt that somehow I had destroyed his life. It was one of the worst moments of my life and I will never forget that episode as long as I live. I think that my manager, for his part, was actually quite relieved. I had gone through hell trying to work with him and I had got results only by sidestepping him. I was too soft by nature to get results through him. He was an older man and at the time I was too inexperienced to deal with a man who was a master in the art of applied psychology. It was to take me five years of questioning myself before I began to realise that it maybe wasn't me expecting too much, it was my manager who perhaps couldn't give enough! I should have had the courage of my convictions and never allowed such an intolerable situation to develop but I was weak.

I couldn't give the leadership he needed. I was inexperienced and I didn't have the guts to do what had to be done and so I suffered in abject misery and frustration for ten years. But for all that, I know that deep down I loved the man - and I was sorry to see him leave.

It is said that power without responsibility corrupts, but believe me, dear reader, I found, that power with the right degree of responsibility can destroy the user. Think about that.

So my manager moved on to pastures new. He bought a little shop in Huddersfield with his redundancy money and became as happy as a little sand boy. He had never worked harder in his life and lost two stone in weight. I believe his lovely wife, who also became a close friend of my wife Jean and me, left her job as a doctor's receptionist to help him in his little shop. After a few years they decided to sell up and moved to live in a villa in Spain. We kept in touch for years and used to see each other at regular intervals. My old manager came home from Spain seriously ill with cancer and I visited him regularly just before he died, bless him. He was one of a fast disappearing band, a true gentleman. He used to play the drums in a dance band and before he died he gave me all his old eight track tapes. I cried when he left me and I cried when he died. Why? I will never know. I suppose that time and reality must indeed be important, after all! Well at least to some of us... My old manager's son finished up with a brilliant job and a new life in America, so all's well that ends well, bless him.

So we move on. Catherine, my youngest daughter who on leaving school had worked for me in the general accounts office, was hankering to get her teeth into a new challenge, like kicking me out of my office and taking over my job! So I decided on a little reorganisation. We had at this time some absolutely brilliant girls working in the office; they could do anything and did. There was, as I mentioned earlier, dear Karen Cheney and her sister Bridgett who had been with me for years; then there was Lorraine and others who came to us on leaving school.

I decided as a first priority to open my office up, dispense with the trappings of luxury and get rid of my executive suite, so I converted my office into a traffic office. Now at last we had got rid of our last vestiges of up-market nonsense and were about to return to our roots.

At last we had got rid of those bloody professionals, our company secretaries, our general managers and their offices; the receptionist had disappeared along with her reception area: The cleaner, Mrs Court, had become the night watchwoman instead and the girls took it in turns to clean their own office spaces and once a week they took it in turns to clean the toilets - only right really, I suppose - social welfare really! They mucked 'em up, they cleaned 'em out - and that is how it should be in the very nature of things. Also, everyone took turns to make the tea, including me.

Ernest, my yard foreman, had become an owner-driver and even the office cat was hired out as a professional mouse catcher. I brought two more desks into my office; I knocked a hole through me office wall into the garage area and fitted a hatch in the aperture; I put the customer vehicle service and maintenance planning charts above, along with an MOTs due chart and spares and vehicle defect summary, in fact all the visual aids necessary to operate a successful commercial garage.

I then brought Bridgett into my office and promoted her to garage service manager.

Then it was Karen's turn. She became office manager. Next it was my daughter Catherine's turn - she became the traffic manager. I placed a large scale map of England above the desk which was to become hers and then I got some   coloured pins and placed the red pins into the areas where all my customers were and some blue pins representing my subcontractors' vehicles in the areas where they would become empty. It was so simple. Well, I thought it was. All Catherine had to do was play at jigsaws and just put the pieces together.

I then drew areas onto the map and proceeded to highlight North Scotland, North East, North West, East Lancs, West Yorks etc, so that at the very least, she would have some small indication where our customers and vehicles were situated in relation to each other.

We then sat down, the three of us together, and had a board meeting. Which went as follows.

They sat at their desks answering the phones and I sat at mine. I just said, "Right, what are you waiting for then? Get on with it!" Well, it wasn't just as simple as that, the system was established and it was 100% and working well; the controls were all there too, along with all the guidelines and most importantly, they also had me as their own personal good fairy, their advisor par excellence, no less. The only problem was that although Catherine and Bridgett became terrific at their jobs and they were there to support and help each other.  Unfortunately they hated each other's guts. They were both very much alike in temperament, both prima donnas, both out to prove themselves and, more importantly, they were in competition! I knew this and encouraged it, but I had to be there as the referee or they would have eaten each other alive! They were both very assertive (or had big mouths, which they used a lot).

As for me, well, I was just the pig in the middle, but I loved it. Between them they were absolutely brilliant - it was just a pity they didn't get on.

In 1987 those two kids handled a turnover of well in excess of £2,500,000 and were providing one customer alone, Hotpoint with 50 vans each day.

If I had attempted to do all this work with my own vehicles (which would have been impossible) I would have needed a fleet, in excess of 100 vans and trailers. Yes, the mighty Transport Development Group of transport companies would have been proud to have achieved a similar performance at that time. How do you envisage an annual turnover in excess of £2,500,000 that had been earned by five office workers in general and just two in particular, with just four of our own vans and drivers, a staff in total of just 9 - 4 drivers, 3 in accounts and 2 running the garage and transport business? (The half was me - a part-time nearly has-been.) £2,500,000 plus divided by 5 office staff, equals an added value of each person of £500,000; or divided by 9 staff, including drivers, an added value of £277,777,77. We were earning profits of around 15% on turnover and 35% on capital employed, just a little more than Eddie Stobart's 3% on sales today. So much for statistics, but I reckon I got some value back for my investment in those wonderful girls who worked for me all those years ago - and not a bloody professional amongst them! Yes, I began to learn that one good girl is probably worth the equivalent of ten men. Give a girl a job to do and she will do what has to be done, usually without question. A computer works on the same principle. But give a man the same job to do and he starts to think! Once he starts to think he develops problems. Once he has developed problems, his attention level drops, he loses concentration and his job suffers. I was also to learn that it is far better for a manager employing people to select, recruit and train his own young people from the start before they have had the opportunity to become corrupted and develop bad habits from an earlier employment. Far better the devil one knows than the one who remains unknown, eh? Yes, dear reader, you must forgive my indulgences as I continue to wax lyrical about the wonderful people I once knew and in particular the people who worked for me and who I worked with. This story would have been impossible without them. I have shared their joys, their heartaches and their sadness. I have known their families, have attended their weddings, their children's christenings and sadly, some of their funerals too. I have attended my old general manager's and recently, that wonderful guy Bob Fawcett's. The best damn van and trailer driver the world has ever known.

I remember one instance, years ago, when Bob was delivering into a very narrow street, with cars parked on both sides of the road. He had to reverse his van and trailer between these parked cars to the bottom of the street with inches to spare. All the shopkeepers, shoppers and office staff reverse his van and trailer between these parked cars to the bottom of the street with inches to spare. All the shopkeepers, shoppers and office staff came out of the adjacent buildings to watch Bob perform his miracle. He did it, and everybody stood and gave Bob a standing ovation. What a performance, he deserved an Oscar! Bob worked for me and I was proud of that fact. Better be the best lavatory cleaner in town, eh, than the worst teacher - and these people didn't have any of those so-called qualifications. Bob didn't need to pass an HGV driving test, he passed my test instead, which was far more difficult than the government's, and he came through with flying colours. I missed Bob and I missed his Capstan full strength cigs too, which were the only ones that I could smoke, after becoming addicted to my roll ups.

God keep and bless you, Bob.

All these people were so very special, important and valuable, with or without those bloody qualifications, and I loved them all!

# I Reach The Crossroads Of My Life

I was now 55 years of age. I had led a very active, frustrating, satisfying life. I had been in business, working for myself for nearly thirty years and I was now at the crossroads in my life. The business didn't hold the same satisfactions and challenges for me any more. As I mentioned earlier, it had become a simple moneymaking machine. I had been to hell and back. I had done it all, from nowt to a multi million pound business, and I didn't feel I had anything else to prove, nor did I have any drive to go on.

I decided to think about early retirement and, with this in mind, I decided to plan for and provide myself with an index-linked pension, just like those in the public sector have. The only difference was, of course, that I provided my own! I had an added incentive because in the process, the company would save a hell of a lot of corporation tax and I would have an ever-increasing growing tax-free asset in the form of my own personal pension fund. I approached a firm of investment advisors, tax and pension consultants in Leeds called Charnley Davis, who were to set up and administer the Walkers of Wakefield Ltd Self Administered Pension Fund. The only problem was that I intended to retire within the next five years so I didn't have much time to provide for a reasonable pension. However, as the main incentive was and always has been to maximise tax benefits and lure as much money as I could from the Inland Revenue, I had at last found myself a real challenge, something worthy of my latent talents. I was going to pit my wits against the Inland Revenue, and they very rarely lose. The first move was to get the warehouse at Flanshaw out of my estate for tax purposes. Which meant that when and if this property was sold, there would be 40% capital gains tax on any gain. But it didn't end there, oh no. After the company had paid its share, then the residue which was left was passed on to the shareholders, my wife Jean and I. We in turn had to pay another 40% CGT, the government was in fact taking two bites at my cherry. Now I had worked hard all my life; my wife and family had struggled and we had been deprived of the necessities of life. We had made enormous sacrifices to build up a business and now the government was intent on trying to deprive us of the benefits of our labours (or ill-gotten gains, whichever suits) in our retirement. But not if I could help it, they weren't.

I sold the warehouse to my self-administered pension fund for £95,000, which in turn became a £5,000 gain made by the company. £5,000 x 40% gain = £2,000 in taxes.

My pension fund then rented out the warehouse on a rental purchase agreement to a chap called Charlesworth and his sister's own pension fund. Charlesworth was applying the same legal fiddle as me. Charlesworth then rented the warehouse back to one of his companies, Hammond Bindery, a printing company which is still occupying my old warehouse to this day. The advantages with these transactions, apart from the obvious savings in CGT, are that all the capital within the self-administered pension funds were growing inside the funds free from any form of taxation whatsoever. So in effect Mr Charlesworth's and my pension funds could charge our respective companies rental charges, thus reducing corporation tax liabilities, and in turn adding substantially to the value of our pension funds. So both ways we won. The substance of the agreement that I had with Charlesworth was that he agreed to purchase the warehouse for the sum of £250,000 over three years, which suited us both. He paid me £40,000 a year rent for three years, which left a balance of £130,000, to pay, being the actual purchase price.

When the warehouse was finally sold to Charlesworth (Hammond Bindery), Walkers of Wakefield Ltd then entered into an agreement to rent back from Hammond Bindery the garage area which was a separate part of the building, along with parking space for my vans, on a three year full repairing lease, rents renegotiated at the lease end. All very nicely packaged. I was still in business with a very low capital investment, I had got rid of the warehouse out of my estate in one fell swoop, and in the process my pension fund had made a profit of in excess of £200,000. All these payments that were made into our pension fund over the next five years were in turn invested in the stock market and were, over a short time, to grow and increase in value at a tremendous rate, all free of tax. We did, in effect, have a fund available that was eventually worth over £1,000,000.

We were then able to purchase a pension, which paid us, well in excess of £100,000 each year. Yes, my baby Walkers of Wakefield Ltd had certainly been good to me and my family.

But in 1985 things were not quite that simple. We had another bitter pill to swallow, some more heartache to endure. Charnley Davis, our pension and investment advisors, were to go into receivership and nearly took ours and many other people's pension funds with them.

Our pension fund at this time was worth about £650,000, quite a lot of money by anyone's standards.

A meeting of creditors in Leeds was in uproar. They were all fighting amongst themselves as to who was entitled to what. As my fund was the largest, I had the most to lose. I went over to the pensioner trustee and actuary,, who had been employed, as the law requires, by Charnley Davis, and asked him what I could do personally to help my particular situation. He replied: "Absolutely nothing," so I thanked him very much and left the meeting. I will never forget that episode because there was very little money left to share out between all the creditors and there was some question at the time of an agreement to share out the funds equally. If that had happened I, as the largest investor, would have lost a considerable amount of money. It did, however, turn out right in the end because pension fund investments were by law semi-protected and as such were given preferential treatment over other ordinary investments. The Actuary, Douglas Townley, was a resourceful Scotsman, no less, and he had agreed to act on my behalf in attempting to resolve this particular problem. He did, in fact, act for several other pension funds in the process and we all paid him a small fee for his efforts. Douglas recovered most of the money that was owed but it did take him about 18 months to complete. Douglas and his company were to look after my pension fund and personal assets and investments from there on in and still do, along with my children's and grandchildren's investments and trust funds. Douglas did a brilliant job on my behalf and we would laugh together about this whole episode years later, him saying how he couldn't ever forget how I had asked him what I should do at the time and had then walked away from £650,000 when he had told me that I couldn't do anything. He would always say he couldn't understand how anyone could have just walked away so calm and collected in such a predicament. I replied, "Well, if I couldn't change the situation there was no point staying to moan about it!" Mind you, I did say to Duggie, "If you had owed me a fiver I would have probably gone bloody crackers if I hadn't got it back!" Yes, little things, details, bothered me, but the big problems I could cope with. I always paid the most attention to detail. The only problem in my providing for a substantial pension was that by law one could only be provided with a pension of up to two thirds of one's salary, or in my case the aggregate of the last three years in employment. I was therefore compelled to pay Jean and myself tremendous salaries in order to provide for a decent pension on retirement. Jean and I at this time had a Deposit account with the Bradford and Bingley Building Society, and the balance of our pension fund was £926,898,70.

This was a part of, as well as other Unit Trusts and government securities invested in our retirement. Also there was another small matter of interest, a set of company accounts in 1987 showing my wife's and my salaries of nearly £300,000, including pension provision.

On 25th January 1988 we had a bank balance of £1,005,512 and were earning £9,000 + a month in bank interest charges. We must at that time have been TSB's best customer. By the way, at that time TSB were looking for commercial accounts and were fast moving away from their 'penny savings bank' image. They had therefore agreed to pay me money market rates of interest on all our cash balances. What a lovely arrangement! No more like the Midland Bank of old, having to ring up monthly to arrange to transfer XYZ of sums onto the London money markets: oh no, now the TSB did it all.

I beg to be forgiven again for my indulgence in highlighting my bank and company performance figures, but I have deliberately done this for two reasons. One: as a self-motivational tool for my grandchildren and anyone else who may be interested, in the hope that if they should ever fail at their own chosen obstacle in life, they might gain some encouragement from the fact that I a complete dummy, was able to overcome most of my obstacles and make a success of my life.

**And Without Any Of Those So Called Bloody Qualifications Either.**

Sorry, but I just couldn't resist!

And the other reason, of course, is to satisfy my own massive bloody ego!

You will by now, dear reader, have gathered that I was now spending more time on money management, taxation matters and investments than I was on man management, and providing my money printing machine, was being kept well oiled and working by Catherine, all I needed to do was to look after the money that was being produced. But I must repeat again over and over, it was not very satisfying. I could, or so it seemed, always make money. I never found it difficult to find new business when I really tried, but I always envied good tradesmen, people who were creative or skilful.

All I could ever do was make money and I never really needed the amounts that I made.

I still needed to live where my roots were, where the people I grew up with were. Not for me a move to our local residential area of Sandal along with all those professionals and yuppies: no, not bloody likely. I wouldn't have fitted in, what with my passion for roll-ups and pints of Stones Best Bitter.

Not for me a yacht on the Med with the jet set - too much aggro.

I have never ever had the inclination, or even had time to dress for dinner, and I would certainly never want to try and keep up with all those Joneses on the Riviera. Ah well, 'nuff said!

Suffice to say the business was doing well and I was reasonable happy in the late 1980s in the new bungalow that I had built on my bit of waste-land!

My daughter Catherine (Big Chief) had got married to the bloody fool she had been courting for about seven years, Mick Grimes, a lovely lad - but he must have been crackers choosing our Cath as his wife. So I gave him a dowry as a little compensation present (or a Booby Prize) to help soften the blow a little - I gave them my house, I did of course, give my other two daughters, the equivalent in money. I had in fact built my new bungalow onto my old garage on my bit of wasteland.

So I had gone full circle back to where I started, no less - back to the garage I'd build for £1,200 in 1970 on my bit of wasteland! Yes, we had all certainly moved on. It was a far cry in 1987 from my dad and mam's days in 1962, when Dad was struggling to build up the business with a turnover of £1500+ a year and the casual labour bill of 30/- a day that he paid to another pensioner to help him hump furniture didn't go far. But for all the seeming success that I had achieved in monetary terms, in building up that business, I was still not fit to lick my dad's boots as a man, for he was a man and a half with a lovely disposition. Nothing worried him or got him down, and as far as my mam goes, well she was in a league of her own and for enterprise; she was untouchable. It was so funny really, because in those days my ma used to try and keep the account books up to date and she had no chance with Dad: he didn't care.

She would ask him to give her his petrol bills etc, but he didn't, and at the year end when his books had to go into the accountants, the accountant, Peter Hepworth would go bloody berserk and play hell with Dad. He would say "How the bloody hell can I do your accounts, Wes, when you have no records of what you have earned and spent. So dad would trip away to his local garage for some blank petrol vouchers which he then had to fill in.

He would then ask the auctioneers, Ivor Applegarth at Saville & Kilburns, and Harry Thornton at Laidlaws to find out and give him a summary of what he had earned from them in the year.

This ritual took place every bloody year and he never learned. Mam used to go barmy with him. Mind you, all the cash removals and ex-saleroom deliveries were cash-in-hand jobs, so he didn't need to bother about those because these transactions would got straight into his petty cash box, into my dad's back pocket. Yeh, salt of the earth, the pair of them.

Back to the story. Although Jean, my wife, and I were earning very large salaries and extra bonus payments in order to justify a large pension income on retirement, we had a problem: for we were having to pay large amounts of PAYE taxes. Although the company corporation tax bill was drastically reduced due to Walkers of Wakefield Ltd's added expenditure in funding our pension requirements, our personal highest PAYE tax rate was at that time 60%. This state of affairs could not be allowed to go on. I was to discover that the government had, introduced certain incentives which included tax relief on certain new business ventures. These schemes were called Business Expansion Schemes and were very high risk ventures with no inbuilt guarantees. Shares once bought in these small businesses could not be traded on the Stock Exchange in the normal way and they had to be held for at least five years to qualify for tax relief. Jean and I, over a period of time, invested in total something like £400,000+ in those schemes, and all to save tax. We learned however, that whatever incentive may be introduced to save a tax liability, we must never allow the tax tail to wag the tax dog. We made some very serious mistakes, of course; it was important to try and save 60p in every £ in tax. In effect, when we bought a share in any of these companies at a price of, say, £1, we were actually, because of the tax relief involved, actually spending 40p, but as the high rates of tax were reduced, it would become 60p. The incentive was very good, but some of these companies were not. Most were onto some real fiddles and some companies were set up purely as a front to someone's other main business; and certain of these directors milked the companies dry.

There were wine importing businesses, property building and property letting businesses, and even a Gemstone business investing in precious stones. Now, the question is, how can anyone lose everything if investing in wine, property and precious stones? After all, in theory a total loss can be avoided because these products can always be sold and turned into cash. Well, Jean and I between us did. We probably lost about £100,000 - no less - and some of these so-called investments have now been held for nearly ten years, while the various company directors keep their snouts in the troughs. The biggest losses came from professionally-run businesses and one in particular, which was being managed by some of the best educated people (Eton, no less) who had the best connections in the world.

The biggest crooks, it would seem, do come from the higher echelons in society, but their thieving, unlike yours or mine, is usually done legally and within the law!

# Guppy The Thieving Yuppie

I will now introduce you, dear reader, to a chap called Darius Guppy and his partner in crime, a chap called Marsh, whose father was the chairman of a company called Inca Gemstones. Now these two so and so individuals were to rob me and my wife of a total of £40,000 when they stole our companies' gemstones. They organised a fake robbery in a New York hotel room and then tried to claim for the loss from Lloyds of London insurers. Now these two pair of...individuals had it all:

They were well respected, well known, had received the best of educations, came from good families and both had friends in high places - very high places! Guppy's father was a famous explorer, his best friend was Earl Spencer, the late Princess Diana's brother. They had it all, except perhaps the desire to earn money by working for it: they preferred instead, it would seem, to take the easier route - to let someone else work for it, then steal it from them. They had probably never done an honest, good day's work in their petty little lives.

The following letter tells the story:

For The Personal Attention.
Of Rebekah Wade.
The Deputy Editor.
The News of The World.
CG Walker

From
97A Potovens Lane
Lofthouse-Gate
Wakefield
WF3 3JH
Tel:/Fax 01924 211902

7th Aug 1998

Dear Madam,
May I draw your attention to an article published in the News Of The World 10/03/96, ref. Darius Guppy, the famous jewel robber and the fact that I was a major shareholder in Inca Gemstones, the company that was

287

formed by Guppy and his friend Marsh and in which I had invested £40,000. But unlike these two individuals, I worked for the money that I lost.

I was rather lucky. I came from an ordinary working class background, left school at fourteen with an ordinary elementary education. I was taught the basics and was not expected to wear an old school tie, or to choose a particular social class, nor was I expected to pretend that I was among the elite.

I did, however, learn to have pride, to trust people, and to treat others as I expected them to treat me, to stand on my own two feet and to accept responsibility for my own actions, and to not expect owt for now't. These lessons were to serve me well on leaving school.

I was over the years employed by twenty-three different employers. I was a butcher, a baker, worked in brickyards and quarries. I dug trenches and drove lorries. Like Guppy, I had a dream to increase my wealth, build a better life for my wife and family and to make something of my life.

So at his age I started in business with £25 capital, the two weeks holiday pay I'd received on leaving my last employer.

Unlike Guppy, I was again very lucky. I was fortunate in the fact that I had no free time to develop a social life, or make new friends. I was too busy working every hour that God sent.

I wasn't held back by family ties, because I never saw my kids grow up. As children, they were always in bed when I got home from work and because I was always working I just didn't have the time to get into trouble. Yes, I was very lucky.

I didn't need to buy expensive cigars or cigarettes. I was a thief too, just like Guppy. I used to steal cigarette ends out of ashtrays when no one was looking, to enable me to hand-roll my own homemade cigarettes.

Yes, I was lucky, I didn't get caught; Mr Guppy did! I don't begrudge the £40,000 that Guppy took from me and my kids; he deserved it. I am only sorry it didn't seem to do him much good!

My father always used to say to me as a boy, "If you ever does a bad turn, lad, you will always get paid back."

I never forgot that adage. What a shame, because I am convinced Guppy needed the money more than I, because he hadn't been taught how, or even had the time to earn his own!

I do not expect this letter to be published because, unlike a Lord Monson or a Duke of Roxburghe, who the Evening Standard quoted on 10/02/91 as being share holders in Inca Gemstones, or a Lord Althorpe, Princess Diana's brother, I am just a nobody and as a result unlike Guppy.

MY STORY WILL NOT BE TOLD.  But it needs to be, oh yes it needs to be, lessons need to be learnt.  So I will continue with my unheard cry in the wilderness and cry alone, in the hope that someone somewhere will one day hear my plea.

I don't expect anyone to come along and bail me out, but my story needs to be told, if only for the benefit of my grandchildren, who, as they get older, may read this.  Who knows, they may even get some satisfaction from the knowledge that the great jewel robber, Mr Guppy, who will no doubt write his book and make a film, once helped their grandad and grandma to lose £40,000.

I shall then probably, at the very least, be able to bask in the great man's glory, even if I did pay for the privilege.  I wonder why media attention concentrates on the fact that Lloyds of London lost £1-8 million, with little or no thought given to Inca Gemstone shareholders (all individuals) who lost approximately £1-25 million?

Where did all that money go?

Perhaps, when and if Mr Guppy tells his full true story and achieves his ambition to become a millionaire, we shall find out.  I truly hope so.

I have copies of accounts from Inca Gemstone year end 31/03/92.

£163851 of our money was spent on legal bills and £135023 was spent on directors' fees, consultancy travel and entertainment of which £30682 was for travel and entertaining, not withstanding the fact that the company wasn't even trading.

I received a letter from Mr Guppy (copy enclosed on 09/03/92) asking for my support at his and other directors' re-election to the board of Inca and his powerful testimony to his faith in their ability to defeat the action being brought against them to achieve substantial damages and to preserve the assets of all shareholders.  I believed and I trusted him.  What a fool I was!

What a disappointment.  Guppy was jailed for 5 years in March 1993 and fined £533,000 for conspiracy to defraud shareholders of Inca Gemstones.  In April 1994 he lost his appeal against his sentence, but fines were reduced to £227,000 and converted into a compensation order, in favour of Lloyds Insurers.  Why?

In Feb 1995 Guppy was granted legal aid after declaring himself bankrupt and he was subsequently released from prison after serving less than three years.  Guppy then had the audacity to say that he has paid his debt to society.  How dare he!

The great train robbers received sentences of thirty years for a similar crime involving similar amounts of money.  But they unfortunately did not attend the right schools, nor did they have the right friends in high places! So much for British justice.

I am in fact rather surprised that a man of Guppy's obvious standing in our society didn't get let off with just a caution and that he wasn't also granted a large junk of state aid to help him on his way!

A man with his background, social standing and with the right connections deserved nothing less.

How could the system have been so cruel to a man like Guppy?

He complained at the loss of his privacy and the difficulties that his wife had to endure on her visits to see him in his rest home at Ford Open Prison.

I know just how he must have felt, because I felt just the same when I was taken away from my home to go and serve my King and country. But unlike Guppy, I wasn't a criminal.

I really do feel sorry for Patricia, his devoted wife, who in between writing and selling her story to Hello magazine for £80,000, had to struggle into and out of a motor car to go and see Guppy in jail. How awful!

My wife in the 50s had to struggle on and off buses with two kids, one in her arms and one walking, and a push chair. And as an added bonus, she had a week's supply of bloody shopping too, bless her! I might also add that I wasn't a criminal, but unlike Guppy, we had to accept the responsibility for our own actions.

I also feel very sorry for Guppy's poor old dad, who lost his two houses in London and his place in the country - what a shame!

Mind you, I suppose I was rather lucky. I didn't have to face those kind of problems when I was Guppy's age. My place in the country was down an old back alley, where I lived in a little old terraced house with an outside toilet fitted with old Sunday newspapers on a bit of string. No, they were not for reading, but to wipe one's bum on. They had been used as fish and chip wrappers.

I also looked forward to and loved the excitement of slopping out; it gave me something useful to do at 5am on a cold frosty morning, walking to the outside toilet with the Jerry under my arm, before I set off on my walk to work!

And I wasn't serving time in prison for carrying out a £1.8 million jewel robbery either. Oh no, I was just living what I had been brought up to believe was a normal, honest-to-goodness life!

I understand that residents in HM prisons do not now enjoy the pleasures that my generation did, of slopping out. Ah well, as they say, times change!

There is, however, one thing that really puzzles me. Mr Guppy said that the reason he carried out his robbery and defrauded the shareholders in Inca Gemstones and then to claim the £1.8 million from Lloyd's insurers, was to wreak revenge because his father, who had been a Lloyds name, had been ruined by a series of claims against his syndicate.

I fail to understand his logic. What satisfaction could he have derived from attempting to make other names suffer because his father was ruined. Perhaps a better brain than mine will be able to work that one out; of course, I didn't go to Eton, did I?

I understand that Guppy did not receive any payment from the News of The World for writing his story and that the newspaper made a donation to a registered charity.

Now ain't that really wonderful, and now Guppy is so full of remorse that he plans to sell his story and make his film (which incidentally, wouldn't have been possible without me, and the other shareholders in our company Inca Gemstones!)

But who knows perhaps in a fit of remorse and as a nice little gesture, Guppy may decided one day to give something back to the shareholders he robbed, some of whom were pensioners and who were nearly ruined by Guppy's exploits and who had trusted him and Marsh to look after their interests.

After all, not a penny of the £1.25 million of their money that disappeared was ever recovered. But all's well that ends well, as they say, and the sun always shines on the righteous.

So now that Charlie (my namesake) Earl Spencer, or Lord Althorpe has managed to get Darius, his good friend, nicely settled in at Yew Tree Farm on his estate in Northamptonshire, Guppy will have the time to enjoy his privacy and to write his life story and maybe make a film or two . That will no doubt satisfy his desire to increase his wealth and become richer and more famous. I wish him well. So this is just a small part of my story, not very exciting, but nevertheless a life lived to the full. But as I come from the wrong side of the track, you will not publish this, so I shall publish it myself.

Then hopefully my lonely cry in the wilderness will at last be heard!
Yours Very Sincerely,

Charles George Walker.

# Decision Time Again

I had now reached another crossroads in my life and decisions had to be made. I had lost interest in the business; it no longer meant much to me and at 57 years of age I did not want to leave important decisions too late. I had always remembered three old philosophies of mine:

Do it now, because what is left today becomes tomorrow's problem.

Planning bridges the gap between where we are today and where we want to be tomorrow.

And without changes there can be no improvements.

My youngest daughter lacked a little confidence in herself, although she could and did run the business brilliantly. She had all the qualities: she had been on business management courses, she had sat and passed her CPC exam and become a qualified transport manager, but she must have felt like I did at her age - like a fairy at the top of a bloody Christmas tree, up there on your own, ever so lonely, divorced from reality, no-one around you to help with those little crises. You are responsible for all that you survey and do become inflicted with a strong sense of total inadequacy. It has been a struggle to get to the pinnacle and having got there, you find that the sacrifices are just not worth the effort, and it is a bloody long way to fall if you don't hang on!

Yes, I knew just how she felt. So rather than inflict on her the heartaches and constant problems I had had, and because I didn't want to have to destroy the jobs that I had created for my loyal friends, my employees, I decided to bite the bullet and to put the business on the market once again.

I advertised the business for sale in the Commercial Motor magazine. I was subsequently approached by many other large haulage companies, including the Transport Development Group, who all showed an interest in the purchase. Unfortunately, as usually is the case, at least 99% of the prospective purchasers didn't really want to buy, they were really just after something for nothing.

I did, however, receive a letter from a firm of business consultants who were supposed to be experts in company acquisitions and mergers. So I decided that this time, in my attempts to get rid of the business, I had better elicit the help of an expert, another one of those bloody professionals, in fact.

The upshot was that the Albert Fisher Group became interested. This group was founded by one of the new breed of up-and-coming young entrepreneurs who had just bought out one of the largest transport concerns, along with a Mercedes dealership in Bradford. They had also bought one of my customers out, Fogarty Fillings of Boston in Lincolnshire, and they also owned many other companies, Del Monte being one of them. They were a company to be reckoned with, a very successful public company, in fact!

They made me an offer of £1.8 million, which was subject to so many conditions and guarantees that from my point of view, it wasn't even worth considering. That contract drawn up by the Albert Fisher Group, was a classic, a work of art, in fact.

My advisor, of course, was happy; Albert Fisher was happy. But I wasn't.

There were too many strings attached and I wasn't about to lose my freedom and become a pawn in their game of chess - oh no, siree!

After I had decided against selling the business to the Albert Fisher Group I was approached by my accountant, Malcolm Dixon, who, it seemed, had a client who was interested in purchasing a business of our size. It seemed that their objective was to build up a group of companies and to eventually obtain a listing on the Stock Exchange and go public. Several meetings were arranged between them and me in an attempt to come to an agreement on the terms for the sale of the business. I wasn't too bothered about the final sales figure, as long as it was a reasonable offer.

My main concern was the details and how soon I could move on and out of the business after the completion of the sale. The final outcome was that I kept the assets (mostly cash) in the business, changed the company name to Walkers Investments Ltd and carried on trading, which the company continues to do very successfully as an investment company to this day. My children and grandchildren own all the shares in this company and have received substantial dividends every year for the last ten years, while the original capital injected into the business in 1988-9 has remained nearly intact.

So in effect I had sold Walkers of Wakefield Ltd and Walkers Garages Wakefield Ltd's trading names, the vehicles and the goodwill for arround £1,000,000.

I continued to trade as Walkers Investments and because I hadn't actually sold all of the business assets and the company still existed, I saved a considerable amount in Capital Gains Taxes. You many recall that I had already taken £250,000 out of the equation by selling the warehouse via Walkers of Wakefield pension fund to Hammond Bindery. I was to remain a non-executive director of the company for twelve months and my daughter Catherine had a service contract for three years. Everything in the garden seemed rosy, but there were, as usual, certain penalties to pay.

While negotiations for the sale of the business were proceeding, the Distribution Director of Hotpoint, one of my main customers, had decided to resign from the company for internal political reasons and he approached me to ask if he could be of any assistance to me in running my business.

He knew that I was contemplating retirement. I replied that I didn't think that he and I could ever work amicably together in a million years because we were both prima donnas, with egos to match!

I did, however, suggest that as I was negotiating to sell the business and were I to succeed, the new owners might be interested in employing him as Managing Director. I therefore decided to employ this chap on a part-time basis and informed the new owners of this man's interest.

They decided to interview the person concerned and subsequently, after the sale had gone through, appointed him to manage the business. Walkers of Wakefield was, or so they thought, to become the flagship of their group and the lever which moved them forward onto the unlisted securities market. But it wasn't to be. We held board meetings every month to formulate policies, but the main interest seemed to be in empire building and buying into other haulage businesses, which became the main preoccupation over the following months. The new owners became involved in attempting to purchase one of the subcontractors who received most of his haulage work from us; in fact he was one of Walkers of Wakefield's main subcontractors. My basic argument at these monthly talking shops (meetings) was: what was the point in taking over this company, if it was relying on us for a large percentage of it's work? It would hardly become an asset in that case. I also pointed out that they should concentrate their efforts on the company (us) that they had just bought, rather than wasting their time on an unknown quantity. But they wouldn't listen. The ex-Hotpoint man was in his element as a buyer of whatever, and he was made to feel very important. He loved it; he was back where he belonged, wielding power. He was introduced to Cyril Smith, the Rochdale MP, who gave him a couple of tea mugs from the Houses of Parliament - wonderful! Over the months that these protracted negotiations were taking place, Walkers of Wakefield was virtually forgotten. Hotpoint appointed a new distribution director, who was to become a distribution manager of the year. He had became an old friend over the years and after I had retired from business, he would invite me every year to Hotpoint's Christmas parties. Hotpoint were to stop giving Walkers work. The problem was that their new director had been a driver at Hotpoint and the old distribution director had appointed him as his assistant. I was told later that after Walkers of Wakefield's new manager had left Hotpoint, Hotpoint's distribution director was waiting for a phone call from him, but it never happened - foolish pride overcame common sense. I think the basic problem was the difference in culture: whereas I had always had to be ever so humble and go cap in hand sometimes begging for work from my customers, I was to become a seller of a service. Our new manager, in his former exalted position as a distribution director for a national manufacturer, was a buyer, and as a buyer he had something to offer; so naturally he was held in awe by most of his suppliers. He had the power, he had control - which was fine in a large multinational company but for a small business like ours, at the bottom of the pecking order, looking for a few scraps to be thrown from the rich man's table, our approach to customers had to be a little more humble!

The purchase of Rochdale Freight fell through and it was decided, after spending a fortune in travel, wining and dining and wasting an awful lot of valuable time, and our money, to abort the purchase. In the meantime, I just gave up. I became frustrated and got tired of banging my head against a brick wall, so I refused to attend any more of those silly bloody meetings and took my bat home. It had taken me thirty years to build that business and I knew exactly what made it tick, its strengths, its weaknesses, what it needed and what it was capable of. I had been instrumental in finding practically every customer we had had over the years; I knew it could be done. Even though for the previous five years I had tended to opt out and coast along, I really did want the business to be a success for the new owners, but they knew best and after only three months they knew more about my baby than me - or so they thought! I did say as time went on: why don't you prove that you can make a success of this business before moving on to something else?

Mind you, the basic difference in my style of management and the new managers was that when I was managing the business I was spending my own money; but when he was managing he was spending somebody else's. That is the difference that makes all the difference, and why the public sector will always be an expensive nonsense!

## Here Is A Memo I Wrote To The Main Board Of Directors, 1988.

It was decided many weeks ago that to protect the long term security of the business and to satisfy the short-term needs of the shareholders, we should attempt to buy into contract distribution. This was tried with Gyproc, but again we failed. I still think that this in the longer term is the safest way forward, (with this in mind I recommend we approach John Cotton and Alan Beaumont)

We should now approach Plysu if sufficient capital is available to see if we can get into contract distribution with them.

You decided (wrongly, I thought) to try and buy into another transport business. This is fine, provided that the company concerned is old, established and has a wide spread of customers. If not, you could eventually have a situation where you are ineffectually chasing sales for both businesses.

My recommendation is that, as far as this business is concerned, you buy in the right man with the right connections who is able to bring new business with him and to work on the traffic desk with Catherine, making every possible effort on telephone selling. This, I believe, would have achieved the desired results in the longer term, but you chose to ignore this advice.

We have lost major customers in the past and that is inevitable in the very nature of what we do; but by constant rubbing away we have always replaced what was lost.

Catherine, over the past two years, has consistently found new business over the phone.

The time to sell is during the busy periods and needs to be done now. There is a hell of a pressure on the front end on that traffic desk. That's where it all happens, and without sales nothing else exists. I still recommend that if money has to be spent, then that is where it is needed - desperately.

This business started with just a telephone and nothing else and in the first few years sales doubled every year and until someone is able to prove to me that there is a better way to get results in our business, then I must remain convinced that this is the way forward. I have tried all the other ways: national and local advertising write-ups in trade magazines, knocking on doors, gimmicks, mailshots, I even employed an advertising agency and had some marketing experts and consultants in to advise on policy. Yes. I have questioned myself over the years, I did employ professional people to give impartial advice and I did act on that advice with little result; it didn't work for me. I still went back to basics - the telephone - because, unlike most other businesses, we don't have a product to sell that can be placed in a nice fancy coloured package to show the customer what we are selling, how it works and the benefits he can get from using it.

No, we are in fact, gentlemen, selling an unknown quantity, a service that cannot be judged until it has been bought and used. It has never been easy to get that first foot into a new customer's door, but with constant pressure, coupled with a bombardment of daily phone calls, we usually succeeded and once we had got through that customer's door, then we committed ourselves to providing him with a total dedicated service and that, gentlemen, was the secret of our success. I offer you again advice which I feel to be essential to the success of this business and I would like you to place this on record. I repeat;

In the short term, buy in the right man to work with Catherine. Spend your money on the traffic desk (on whatever it takes).

Let your new manager concentrate his efforts on what he understands best logistics and distribution, and encourage him to move into contract hire and/or distribution. If you are hungry enough (I wasn't) you must in an every changing world be prepared to change, adapt and diversify to protect the longer-term interests of this business. Only as a last resort must you try and buy into another transport business, but it must be one that will fit in with what you do, a clearing house in fact.

Do it now. Look, think, listen and decide, but do it now, for tomorrow may be too late.

I am concerned that you do get the essentials right and that the business I started and put my life into will continue to prosper and be successful. I leave the company at the end of the year and I want to go, knowing that the business is on the right track and its destination assured. You will have to face up to the fact sooner or later that to try and buy your way out of trouble is a short term expedient to promoting and maintaining sales. We are a sales oriented business. That's what we do and without sales neither Walkers, Rochdale Freight or anyone else can exist. This fact must be accepted sooner or later.

The recommendation that was made regarding your making every effort to get into contract distribution to guarantee the longer term security of the business was a good one and the way forward, alongside our existing operations, but for some reason you got off the track and now seem hellbent on acquisitions, come what may. I could have understood the logic in this if you had first put Walkers on a stable footing before

297

moving on, but this wasn't to be and I do sincerely hope I am wrong. But the question does need to be asked: if you could not increase Walkers' customer base in the short term, what makes you think that you will be anymore successful with a Walkers Transport Group?

There just has to be a completely different approach to this problem: back to basics. I repeat, buy in the man that can provide, produce and maintain sales.

Because, gentlemen, Walkers of Wakefield are not transport operators, we are first and foremost a seller of a service. We sell transport, that's right, we find it and we sell it. We are a transport agency just like a travel agent selling holidays (which they don't arrange), or an estate agency selling houses (which they don't own). Or a bank lending someone else's money. I believe that the sooner these facts are accepted, then the sooner you will have a better understanding of the nature of this business.

We are not in a high-risk business. We exist to sell a service and make a profit, and that is how we made a lot of money over the years, by using other people's resources, and by not running the risks that are inherent within normal in-house, road haulage operations.

We are in fact a sales oriented business and that is what we do.

Your new manager can only do so much in a day and his time needs to be well spent. With this in mind, I feel Cath should keep on selling, establish the market and our sort of traffic in the right areas, then make appointments for the manager to visit to avoid the possibility of too many abortive calls.

There is a danger in the sense that it is probably only possible to make six to ten calls a week, so it needs to be right. On the phone twenty or forty calls a day can be made, if the time is available, and it does seem to work - ask Cath. I think it may be an idea if the new manager were to spend a couple of days on the phone to get a feeling for the situation, and to establish if there is any room for improvements in our methods. Ignore these points at your peril.

Which brings me on to another point. Decisions involving trivial matters like who signs cheques, who pays wages, staff meetings, what type of logo we have on letterheads or what colour bloody toilet paper we use are made as a group, but when it comes to major decisions, like should we declare our hand with Hotpoint, this decision was made in isolation. I deliberately postponed a meeting with Hotpoint to allow our group to decide; you decided and you must live with that, but at least you now have the consolation that it was your choice and not mine. It is a little difficult for me because I have always been able to do my own thing I must now accept that the new manager has to be allowed to manage and I must not be too critical. But none of us can be expected to be right all the time, and in the interests of the business I must make my points. I and you must decide if they are worthy of consideration. We are all concerned that the business prospers and I must therefore express my opinions.

**I offer the following points for consideration.**

1. I know this business, what it does, how it does it, why it does it and what it needs.

2. The people in it are not interested in who the new owners are, perhaps they don't even want to know. They are involved with local management and don't see any changes as yet. I think that we shouldn't rock the boat too much; leave well alone. They do a good job, let them get on with it. They have jobs to do and don't take kindly to interference, from people they consider to be intruders.

3. This is a very small family business, not a public company. There is a difference. People don't like changes.

3. Feed the baby with a spoon, don't cram it down its bloody throat. You are trying to do too much too soon and expect too much too soon.

4. Please don't lose sight of the basics, and keep things simple.

5. Two signatures required on cheques, when only one director available (me).

6. This does cause problems; we either trust people or we don't.

7. PAYE - you have got problems. I still think the simplest way is to let the holding company pay the manager's and Cath's salaries and invoice us. Why create a big problem out of a minor issue?

8. Quotes for new business should go out immediately they are agreed.

9. In April we negotiate with customers any rate increases. Your manager thinks April the wrong time, we should do it in September when they need us the most. I agree, but I still think that any increase that can be got now should be taken!

10. Spending more time at Plysu, consultant's report not out yet. Eddie trying to find us more work, perhaps in the South. Told Cath to find vehicles, return loads South and push Eddie for work.

11. We must look out for work North London and Home Counties as a priority, that is where most work is and where most of our contractors are situated for return loads. If possible work must be found just off major trunk roads, where contractors are available. We must find them work before they find their own.

12. Am taking the manager to see George Copeland, the MD at

Blowmocan, the plastics manufacturer on Monday. George is a personal friend. Let's hope we can get some more work from our customer Gyproc, and that this could well become another Plysu in the north. I feel every effort must be made to secure this business. Finally, I have three very important proposals to make: One, that major decisions should not be made in isolation; Two, that if there are intended visits from important people, we should be given as much notice as possible to allow us to put our affairs in order. And that requests to attend meetings should be more specific; and Three, All matters for discussion and comments relating to monthly meetings are submitted prior to the meeting in writing to Head Office to be recorded, documented and returned to each Director. So that he then has the opportunity to study, understand and comment on points at the next meeting. Which in turn would allow for a more constructive discussion to take place.

Perhaps this practice could be extended throughout the group, so that the executives concerned could then have the opportunity to join forces, pool their knowledge and then come up with ideas to benefit the group as a whole. "Let's face it, gentlemen, there are probably enormous, under-utilised, expensive resources under your control - other directors who have good track records, all achievers just raring to go: Why don't you tap these oil wells of knowledge, put them into harness and get them to work for you?

They do say two minds are better than one - what price ten?

I am a big believer in thoughts on paper. Good points can become lost in trivial conversations and rash decisions made, but in the cold light of dawn and on reflection a completely new picture appears from the one immediately to hand. Opinions and ideas must be allowed to ferment in isolation and then to be judged fairly on merit, rather than have a good thought lost in irrelevancies.

The people who were to buy my business in fact managed to delay the final pay-out for a further nine months after the deadline. They also paid me a substantial amount less than agreed and this on the pretence that I was supposed to know we would ultimately lose Hotpoint's work which of course was a complete nonsense.

The following correspondence sums up the problems I had to face.

(Bear in mind that my principal contender was a master at delaying tactics and a solicitor to boot) I thought that I had become a student of human behaviour, but I could not hold a candle to these people!

5th June 1989
Background

Dear Mr, AN, Other

I have been in business for thirty years and have always been profitable.

Several years ago, as my family were not interested in carrying on with the business (they are all daughters), I decided to sell and retire early. With this in mind, I set up a self-administered pension fund and sold my warehouse property into the fund. It was later decided that I retire at age 57. With this in mind I put the business up for sale in March 1987.

I was approached by the new owners (who shared the same accountants as me), who offered to buy my business. The agreed price was £1,000,000; the garage business, along with its assets of more than £50,000, I threw in for free. It was eventually agreed that I keep the cash within the business and sell for a sum of £600,000, £350,000 up front and a deferred payment of £250,000 to be paid 1/3/89 subject to profits earned in 1988. I agreed and the sale took place in January 1988. During negotiations in front of witnesses, I said that the business was vulnerable in the sense that 80% of our sales came from two customers, Plysu and Hotpoint. The business was not under contract to either of these customers, but we had worked for both for nearly twenty years. It is normal in road haulage to have a situation where most sales come from one or two customers. (You grow with your most successful customer.) I also said that although 1987 had been very profitable, they must not expect the same profits in 1988 because the amount of work received from Hotpoint had been exceptional that year and I did not expect the same amount in 1988. As Hotpoint increase their sales over the years they also increase their own fleet of vehicles and Walkers of Wakefield are brought in at different times during a year when their own vehicles cannot cope. Profits for 1987 were at £350,000 in real terms. It was agreed that the average profits in the previous three years - 1984 to 1986 - of £200,000 would be a more realistic assumption for 1988, and I did stress this fact.

With this in mind we later budgeted for around £200,000 profit in 1988. If I had anticipated an increase of £350,000 plus in 1988, I would have said so at the time and the business would have been worth more. The actual profits for 1988, were around £180,000.

Since leaving the business in December 1988, I understand there had been a further decline. One of the new owners came to see me early this year and asked for advice. I suggested that if things were so bad and the business was not paying its way, my family and I would go back into the business and work for nothing. He asked if I could defer the final payment for 12 months. I declined. The money belonged to the shareholders and there was a tax liability of £120,000 to pay. Later he rang me and requested a meeting, using emotional blackmail. He said he thought I had a moral responsibility to reduce the final price. The owners had until December 1988 to submit any claims. Why did they wait until the day to pay out if they thought there was something wrong?

28th November 1989

Walkers Investments Limited
97a, Potovens Ln,
Lofthouse-Gate,
Wakefield
WF3 3JH.

FOR THE PERSONAL ATTENTION OF MR AN. OTHER, XYZ SOLICITORS

Dear Sir,

Further to our conversation yesterday 27/11/89 when we expressed our disappointment at the lack of progress in the pursuit of our claim against the new owners. We now feel it right to express our concern and frustration at the possible loss of a substantial sum of money to this company and subsequently to my children's inheritance trusts.

To date, there will be a possible loss of approximately £17000.00 in interest on money due and an ever increasing loss of £70.00 per day until a settlement is reached in our favour.

You recall that several months ago we wrote asking when you anticipated that this matter would be resolved, the possible cost and the probable outcome.

You did not favour us with a reply to that letter. Several telephone conversations later we agreed to issue an ultimatum to the new owners to the effect, that if they refused to settle, we would institute court proceedings to recover the debt. Then and only then, did they start to make offers

302

of settlement, their final derisory offer of £157,000 was not acceptable to us, as the profit figures produced by their own accountant was far in excess of the offer they made.

How can one negotiate at a figure below the undisputed profits produced by them and agreed by us? They then advised you that we must agree to arbitrate before we choose to litigate. You wrote to them several weeks ago asking them to choose an arbitrator. They did not reply.

(Ball back in your court).

You then assured us several weeks ago on the Thursday before you had to go to London, the following Monday, that if you did not receive a reply by the following day, Friday, you would leave instructions for court proceedings to be commenced forthwith without further notice, this did not happen as promised.

On Monday the 20/11/89 we contacted you to establish what had been done. You told us that you had received a message to contact their solicitor, and you would let us know the outcome the following day, again this did not happen.

On Monday 27/11/89 you were again contacted by us to establish progress made. You again told me that you were returning their solicitors call that day and you would let us know the outcome. We are still awaiting the news of the outcome.

Perhaps you are able to understand our disappointment and frustration at these events. Without communication there can be no understanding.

I feel that the stigma of the prospect of having to go to court, as opposed to arbitration, would have forced the new owners to come to a decision one way or the other at least then we would have known what the future held sooner rather than later.

They will not move until pressed hard. You cannot demolish a stone wall with a feather duster, can you?

The other side have obviously received good advice on their methods of employing delaying tactics to their own advantage. Their gain on earned interest on the money owed is our loss. You may recall that we did suggest to you that, if you had pursued court proceedings against the other party when they had not acknowledged your letter asking them to appoint an arbitrator, you would have gained the initiative, and been perfectly justified in taking court action. Now that initiative has been lost to them, who now have the advantage again of introducing delaying tactics.

Without action there can be no results.
Without results there can be no progress.
Without progress there can be no conclusion.
And without fear there is little motivation.

We have made you aware that it is critical that we get the earliest settlement possible, because of the probable loss of interest on money due to us. If we do in fact decide to accept a reasonable offer without interest to avoid lengthy litigation, then we stand to lose a substantial sum of money in accrued interest.

This has now become a very unpleasant state of affairs. If your law practice had taken the trouble to insert a clause in the Sale and Purchase Agreement to the effect that, in the event of profits not being agreed before 5/3/89, all interest earned on the final agreed profit figure would accrue to Walkers Investments Limited, we would not now be faced with the doubt, of not knowing whether we are entitled to interest on money owing as from the 5/3/89 and we shall only know this when and if court proceedings are commenced.

Because of this particular situation, decisions are not easy and as a result we will perhaps have to make the wrong decision and go for what is on offer to avoid possible future losses of interest. That is why in this case speed is of the essence.

Your practice came to us highly recommended. We were very satisfied at the level of service received both from Mr Brown and Mr Smith, and later by Mr Jones in his dealing with our family trust and we were happy to pay quite substantial sums in fees.

But now our confidence is coming increasingly under pressure and we have serious doubts as to the successful outcome of this matter.

Our daily losses are becoming quite unacceptable. Therefore, if you are unable to achieve the desired satisfactory results quickly, we must reluctantly look elsewhere for the help that we so desperately need.

I am on holiday from the 2nd September 1989 for seven days. On my return I look forward to a positive response to this letter declaring your intentions one way or the other.

Yours faithfully
C G Walker
Managing Director


PS   Our other major concern is the fact that we have already paid Capital Gains Tax on unrealised gains and we are prevented from liquidating the company and exchanging shares for unit trusts until our claim is settled.

Having read the above correspondence, dear reader, of one of my minor dealings with a so-called professional, perhaps you are now in a much better position to judge my acute cynicism and my complete lack of faith and confidence in the professions.

# Conclusion

And so it is written that whatever goes around comes around, and those new owners were to eventually dispose of the business by virtually giving it away to another haulage company, who for years had worked for Walkers of Wakefield as one of their subcontractors. The garage business, which at the time of the acquisition was making annual profits of £12,000 a year (not a lot but, for a very small concern not to be sniffed at,) was closed down. The in-house fuel facility, Walkers bulk oil and diesel tanks was disposed of, as were the recovery vehicles, and the whole enterprise was moved to new premises. All the office staff were sacked; Catherine decided at the age of 25 to take early retirement. She couldn't take any more aggro. My old pal, Frank Kimbley, my ex-garage foreman, was appointed traffic manager, a job he hated and was quite unsuited to. Frank, like me, hated paperwork and the job had become too overcomplicated, with paper and bloody faxes flying here, there and everywhere.

The new management loved to be enveloped in a mass of paper and controls, but the silly thing was that Frank, who was supposed to be running the traffic office, did not have the necessary information to allow him to function effectively. He, in fact, had no idea what the charge-out rate for a job to a customer was, or the rate to pay the subcontractors. So every time a contractor would ask what the rate for a job on offer was worth before he would take it, Frank had to fax and ask.

In effect, there were two people doing the same job, whereas in the past Catherine had handled four times the business on her own, including all the claims for any shortages etc, and looked after our own vehicles and drivers too.

Frank had to vet each subcontractor before passing on a load and many times, by the time the decision had been made whether or not to give a certain contractor a load because of the time involved in security checks the load was lost anyway. A far cry from the early days when the only answer to "I have a load, have you got a van?" was "Yes." - And only after saying yes did one worry about finding a vehicle to carry the load, and about any problems arising later. In those days there was just one important principle for consideration - we always accepted the load. If we didn't, then someone else did and we lost it. When the business was passed over to the new owners, Frank didn't want to move, so he was eventually made redundant and became a driver for another Walker's subcontractor, an old friend Alan Howells of Castleford. Frank now seems to be in his element and is really enjoying his job. With no pressures or heavy responsibilities, he seems happier now than he has ever been.

We still keep in touch and Frank comes around and looks after me and my cars and motor caravan, bless him. For my part, in retirement I had to go through a new learning process and it was to take me the best part of two years to come to terms with the fact that I had suddenly become a non-person, an has-been, in fact. I attended art and calligraphy classes at our local technical college; I even applied to the local council for a van driving job. They wanted a volunteer driver to collect old furniture for resto-ration and then re-delivery to the less fortunate in our society, the social security claimants. I now thank God that when I phoned in for an inter-view, the manager in question was out and I was asked to call the follow-ing day. In this interim period I had the opportunity to reflect, which can be disastrous and cause problems. I suddenly came to realise that if ever I did succeed in becoming a volunteer van driver for WMDC, it could be the worst (or best) thing that had ever happened to our dear friends in the public sector. I had already thought about what I would probably do with my experience within the furniture removal industry. And I had already begun to think about possibly reorganising their whole operation to con-vert it into a semi profitable enterprise. Of course, the next extension to this thought was my dream of moving into our local Town Hall and sort-ing that bloody lot out in there too! Then I came down from the clouds and back into the realms of reality, and I decided that it wasn't such a good idea after all. The council manager who was responsible for the restora-tion of redundant furniture just did not know how lucky he had been in my decision not to apply for his driving job! I couldn't in a million years have worked within any local authority establishments, because I would have driven them all bloody crackers before going barmy myself, Eh"

So I decided on a new challenge. I have, over the last few years bought, restored, shown and won a few prizes with two fire engines, an armoured car and an Austin Champ and anti-tank gun, with which I appeared on Alan Hardwick's Yorkshire Television calendar programmed about three bloody times, or so I have been told. (They must have run out of ideas.) It was probably the cheapest way to produce a programme on prime time TV, because it cost me a day in lost time, six pots of tea and six bacon butties for the TV crew, but of course, it cost Yorkshire TV next to now't to produce!

This all came about because I had done a complete stranger a favour. I had taken his son to Ackworth School on his last day at school in my Champ with the gun on tow - I bet he never forgets that - and his father turned out to be a TV cameraman. So that was how I became involved in that bit of nonsense. My middle daughter, Anne, kidded me into writing this rubbish, so that it would give her something to do - practising her typing skills in Germany while lover-boy, her husband Del, was away on his worldwide travels for Siemens in Germany. She is now coming back to England to practise her skills as a district nurse, so I have lost my volunteer secretary. She has, in fact, deserted a sinking ship and left me struggling in mid-Atlantic without a bloody paddle, bless her. (I joke of course.)

I had been born into a real world, to a poor family. I had worked hard from the age of 14, for twenty-three different firms, started my own business, struggled, survived, built up six companies, sold out, become a millionaire. Yes, I had lived and enjoyed being in that exciting, vibrant world, my world, that I had been so much a part of.

So there ends my story for better or for worse, up to 1987. I hope you have enjoyed living for a while with me, in my world - the real one.

It has taken me 18 months and periods where I have spent up to 38 hours practically non stop without sleep sat at this, my bloody computer. (Well, doesn't everyone swear at them?)

It did become a total commitment (like old times) for me to leave something of my life to my grandkids, so that they could perhaps learn from my mistakes. It has been one of the hardest things that I have ever done in my life. I have, as in the past, had to start from scratch as a complete dummy. I have had to learn to operate a computer and to spell and to type a bit. I have produced dozens and dozens of unfinished copies, I have made thousands of mistakes and gone back again and again to the drawing board, and I know that I still haven't got it quite right.

So have I succeeded. Is my story worth reading? Was it all worthwhile?

That I can never know. Only you have the answer to that. But I must once again beg of you: please do not judge me too harshly, for I have opened my heart and I have bared my soul in public, a very rare occurrence.

So the judgment is now yours and only yours to make.
Please judge me fairly!

## SO THIS HAS BEEN MY STORY

So this has been my life story and I have nothing left to give.
Except I hope you enjoyed it and the way I used to live.
Now that you have read my story, I have nothing left to do.
Except to hope you understood me and the people that I once knew!

But before you make your judgment
(and I know that's what you'll do),
Remember hypocrisy isn't a virtue,
And you must search your conscience too.
I have sinned with the best and I hope that I have atoned
So he without sin can now cast the first stone!

But before you decide to throw it, choose your target well.
For if your aim is faulty, then you too may have a soul to sell
So if you choose to judge another and you choose to question why
Remember that old proverb: There but for the grace of God go I!

# My Favourite Poems

# My Bargain With Life

If you bargain with life for a penny, then life will pay you no more.
You may regret you bargained for a penny and reject your scanty score.
For life is but an employer and it will give you what you ask.
But once you have set the wages, then you must bear the task.

You may work for a menial hire, only to learn, dismayed,
That any wage you had asked of life, life would have willingly paid.
You must be bold enough to ask of life more than you may.
Because as surely as the world is round, life will surely pay.

So work at life your employer and do the best that you ought.
Because life can be a good employer and will never sell you short.
So never bargain with life for a penny, your life is worth more than that.
And whatever you're prepared to put into life, life will pay you back.

> Life is but a futile sham.
> A 'what am I?' or a 'who I am'.
> A moving on, a forgotten name.
> A charade, a nothing but a game.

# For My Grandchildren.
## In Hope That They May Learn From My Mistakes

Be the master of your fate and become the captain of your soul.
Do not be satisfied with a part of life, when you are entitled to the whole!
Stand up proud to be counted, never underestimate your worth
You are the most important living person, living person on earth.

Success is achieved and maintained by those who are prepared to try.
You are but a mind with a body and must persist in questioning why.
Your thoughts are evaluated by whether your attitude is positive or negative.
You are but what you think you are, and what you are prepared to give.

You are only as good as you think you are, your life is but a brain cell.
Everything in life stems from a single thought, so think it and use it well.
The mind is the seat of habit, memory, emotion, and it is who you really are.
It allows you to do anything you want to and as a true believer can take you far.


**The Science of Success**

If you have a problem, good, treat it as a challenge
But make sure you have first really established the *real* problem.
Once established, analyse and apply a logical solution.
The trick is to concentrate on the *solution* and not on the problem.
Don't waste time dwelling on your problems, *sort* them.  And ***Do It Now!***
Sow an action and you reap a habit,
Sow a habit and you reap a character,
Sow a character and you reap a destiny.
The secret is to apply only positive thoughts
And then apply *The Secret of Getting Things Done*
And that is to ***Do It Now,***
But don't ever say "I will do it now", unless you are prepared to follow through with the desirable action!
***Do It*** and ***Do It Now.***  *What you don't do today becomes tomorrow's problem. . .*

311

*Be self motivated.* Motivation is that which induces action or determines choice.

It is the force which starts the action, that produces a specific result.

Think the right thoughts and your world will be right.

Emotions are not always subject to reason. But they are subject to action.

## The way to attract the things you want and to achieve your goals

A. Set your goals down on paper, out of your mind, where they can be seen and dealt with

B. Set yourself a deadline and stick to it

C. Set your standards high - logic will make it mandatory that you aim at an immediate objective

D. Set your sights high - no more effort is required to demand prosperity and happiness than is required to accept misery and poverty!

## You Will Require

A positive mental attitude

To go that extra mile

To apply self discipline.

Applied faith,

Personal initiative,

Controlled attention.

To learn from defeat,

To budget time and money

Maintain good health.

A definite purpose

Accurate logical thinking.

To be the master of your mind.

A pleasing personality.

Enthusiasm.

Team work.

A Creative vision.

A sound mental outlook.

## The Ten Basic Motives are:

1. Self preservation
2. The strongest fear
3. Life after death
4. Anger
5. A recognition of self expression
6. Love
7. Sex
8. Freedom of body and mind
9. Hate
10. Material gain

## The Nine Virtues of Benjamin Franklin

**Silence -** Speak not, but what may benefit others or yourself, avoid trifling conversation.

**Order -** Let all things have their place, let each part of your life have its time.

**Resolution -** Resolve to perform what you ought, perform without fail, what you resolve.

**Frugality** - Make no expense but that it does good to yourself or others, waste nothing.

**Industry** - Lose no time, be always employed in something useful.

Justice - Wrong no one, by doing injuries, or omitting the benefits that are your duty.

**Moderation** - Avoid extremes, forbear resenting injuries, so much as you think they deserve.

**Tranquility** - Be not disturbed at trifles, or at accidents, common or unavoidable.

We are only what we think we are and all negative emotions, feelings, passions, prejudices, beliefs and bad habits are only there because of the wrong attitude of mind.

We are a mind with a body. Reason and emotion must be kept in proper balance.

A wrong word can cause an argument, develop misunderstanding, so we must first start with ourselves.

A right word brings love, happiness, understanding, peace.

The right or the wrong words come from a subconscious positive or negative thought!

We are advised by our peers that we must all have qualifications . . .

Yes, certain qualifications are desirable, but they can never be a substitute, or an alternative, for common sense.

Now, what are these so-called qualifications, and what do they prove?

That one can absorb knowledge, yes. That one can pass an exam, yes.

But they do not prove that one is intelligent, or that one is able to apply the knowledge that the brain has absorbed . . .

What makes for real success in life is not the acquisition of knowledge for its own sake.

But the application of common sense and the applying of the science of reasoning to everyday problems. To be able to automatically assess all the options available and then be capable of choosing the right one. That, dear reader, I was to learn from the great university of life.

In simple terms it means the ability to think logically and to be able to apply basic common sense to any given situation.

What qualifications does it take to became a millionaire and to build up a successful business, other than the ability to recognise an opportunity when you see one, or if there isn't one, to make one.

Then, through total dedication and persistance, exploit it to the ultinate, to achieve the desired objective. And that can be done without any qualifications whatsoever.

## Persistence

**There is nothing that can take the place of persistence.**

| | |
|---|---|
| **Talent can't.** | Talent is often wasted and often subject to abuse. |
| **Genius can't.** | A genius who lacks persistence becomes of little use. |
| | Many unsuccessful men with talent are simply left behind. |
| | Whilst unrewarded genius is often left to flounder in the mind. |
| **Education can't.** | The world is full of educated derelicts, who hope to learn and to then succeed. |
| | It is just persistence and determination that satisfy that need! |
| | Persistence is omnipotent, yes, it is an all powerful tool. |
| | To adapt and to become persistent, is to apply **the golden rule!** |

You have to be bold enough to ask of life more, far more than you may.
Programme your life so that you know where you are now and where you want to be one day.
So now is the time to become a true believer and to listen to what I have to say.
Then if you are properly motivated, come with me and I will show the way.

I believe that everything is possible with the right attitude of mind.
That the world can be your oyester, and your pearl, you will surely find.
For the whole world is out there waiting, there are many things to do.
So step out into life and find them, this world was made just for you.

Providing you persist, apply the necessary sacrifices, effort and the time.
Then the world is there for the taking, so listen to my rhyme.
If you hang in there and rub away long enough, a new realism you're sure to meet.
As you persist with your rubbing, those walls of **Jericho** will tumble at your feet!

Now you had better believe it, for every word I speak is true.
Because I once was a disbeliever, exactly the same as you.
Think about it and try it, adopt this philosophy as your plan.
Believe in me and you cannot fail, if you think you can, you can.

Now you have my message, now I have shown you how.
Now get out there and do it, but be sure to do it now.
What is left today becames tomorrow's problem, you have no time to wait.
Time to make your mark, do it now and do it well, tomorrow is just too late.

# The Lessons That I have Learned In My Life

### Lesson One
You don't ever get anything for nothing in this world of struggles and strife.
You get out there and earn the satisfaction of working at your goals in life.

### Lesson Two
When you have done what you set out to do and your personal battle has been won,
You have then earned the satisfaction that comes from a job that was well done.

### Lesson Three
We only pass this way but once, so we must love our fellow man.
We must be a little more forgiving and a little better than we can.

### Lesson Four
As we sow, then so shall we reap a bounty and all that it brings.
As we give, then so shall we receive, that's in the very nature of things.

### Lesson Five
Be the best in all that you do.
Far better to be the best road-sweeper and be proud of what you're at.
Than to be worst teacher and to be ashamed of that!
Recognise your own level of incompetence and stay within in too.
Understand your own capabilities, in everything you do.

**Lesson Six**
Walk tall, accept responsibility for your own actions, stand on your own two feet.
Be accountable for yourself and owe no man anything and be honourable in defeat.

**Lesson Seven**
Learn to recognise an opportunity, if there isn't one, then make one to fit your bill.
Having made one, exploit it to your advantage, use it and take your fill.

**Lesson Eight**
Always encourage people to like and to trust you, be true in all you say and do.
To be trusted is to own the world, everything is possible when people believe in you.

**Lesson Nine**
*Sympathy* - People who feel sorry for you feel a need to help you too.
Let them, but don't ever forget to show your appreciation for what they're about to do.

**Lesson Ten**
*Do in now* - Do it now, for what is left today may become a lasting sorrow.
Better do it now, than leaving the same old problem for tomorrow.

**Lesson Eleven**
*Communication* - Without proper communication, there can never be understanding.
Without a parachute, there will never be a happy landing!

**Lesson Twelve**
Without changes there can never be any improvement.
And without a purpose, there will be very little movement.

**Lesson Thirteen**
Without the will you can never hope to find a way.
And without a first step forward, still you are bound to stay.

## Lesson Fourteen

*Assumption* - Never assume, you will be invariably wrong.
Choose only clear facts to base an assumption upon.

## Lesson Fifteen

*Problems* - Identify the problem, when it is established, work on the solution.
Work on the answer, not the problem, to reach the right conclusion.

## Lesson Sixteen

*Fear* - Is the greatest motivater, exploit it when you can.
It is the greatest weapon and method of control over man.

## Lesson Seventeen

*Logic* - Is the art of applying common sense and is sure to take you far.
Everyday problems are solved by knowing what your options are.
Logic is the science of reason and how reason has evolved.
To reason by applying logic is how a problem's solved!

## Lesson Eighteen

*Human Behaviour* - To understand human behaviour is to know what life is about. The secret is to substitute negative for positive thoughts and to avoid being controlled and influenced by events. These are the day-to-day happenings that we allow to distract and muddle up our thoughts. The human brain is the most complex part of our body and the most difficult to control. It cannot be controlled like a computer, for it goes off at a tangent; thoughts are allowed to fly here, there and everywhere, like feathers on the breeze out of control. The human brain seems to be incapable of learning from others' mistakes, has or so it seems, to learn from its own! The tragedy is that the most complex piece of wizardry known to man, the embodiment of life itself, has but very limited control of itself.

The system of control that I applied was to sidetrack the brain and to bypass it by putting my thoughts to paper in a simple logical order. By doing this I took my thoughts away from my brain's subconscious, where it was apt to destroy my best thoughts, and I brought them out into the open, where I had a permanent record that I could look at, study, analyse and deal with at my leisure. I could then systematically deal with each thought, each problem in turn.

The secret is to split and divide, isolate and then deal with each thought in turn, eh!

317

**Lesson Nineteen**

I once was to know six honest men and they taught me all I knew.
Their names were What and Why and When and How and Where and Who!
My six wise men were to serve me. They served me well and true.
And when I asked of them the question. I was told what I had to do!
*With apologies to Rudyard Kipling!*

**Lesson Twenty**

*Luck* - There is no such thing as luck in life, of this I am sure.
Anything worthwhile in life can be yours, if you truly are a doer.
*Without an action there can be no result*
*Without a result there can be no progress*
*Without progress there can be no conclusion*
*Without fear there is no motivation*
*Without motivation comes stagnation!*

*Planning* - If I know where I am going, the road that I travel matters not!
Planning bridges the gap between where I am today.
And where I want to be tomorrow!

*Learn these lessons well. And your life will take on a new meaning!*

318